CAREERS

An Organisational Perspective

FOURTH EDITION

A M G Schreuder • M Coetzee

Careers: An Organisational Perspective

First published in 1997
Reprinted 1997
Third edition 2006
Fourth edition 2011

Juta and Company Ltd
First Floor, Sunclare Building
21 Dreyer Street Claremont, 7708

ISBN 978-0-70217-806-1

Project Manager: Corina Pelser
Editor: Ulla Schüller
Proofreader: Karoline Hanks
Index: Jennifer Stern
Design and typesetting: ANdtp Services
Cover design: Joan Baker & Alexander Kononov
Printed and bound in South Africa by Impressum Print Solutions

Table of contents

Table and figures acknowledgements

Table 2.1, p 28, *Differences between the traditional and modern workplace*
Adapted from Baruch, Y (2004) Transforming careers: From linear to multidirectional career paths: Organisational and individual perspectives, *Career Development International,* 9(1), 58–73; Thite, M (2001) Help us but help yourself: The paradox of contemporary career management, *Career Development International,* 6(6), 312–317.

Figure 3.2, p 74, *A career management model*
In Greenhaus, JH, Callanan, GA and Godshalk, VM, (1997, 2000) *Exhibit from Career Management.* 3ed. Harcourt College Publishers. Reproduced with permission of the publisher.

Figure 3.3, p 81, *21st century career planning model*
In Otte, FL and Kahnweiler, WM (1995) Long-range career planning during turbulent times. *Business Horizons,* Jan/Feb, 2–7. Redrawn from *Business Horizons* (Jan/Feb). Copyright 1997 of the Foundation for the School of Business at Indiana University. Used with permission.

Figure 3.4, p 87, *Career invention model*
Adapted from Coetzee, M (2007) *Career planning in the 21st century: Strategies for inventing a career in a dejobbed world of work.* Cape Town: Juta.

Figure 3.5, p 88, *Characteristics underlying a successful career*
Adapted from Coetzee, M (2007) *Career planning in the 21st century: Strategies for inventing a career in a dejobbed world of work.* Cape Town: Juta.

Table 4.2, p 104, *Holland's six modal-personal-orientations and occupational environments*
Based on Schreuder, AMG & Coetzee, M (2006) *Careers: An organisational perspective.* 3ed. Cape Town: Juta.

Figure 4.2, p 106, *Holland's hexagonal model of the interaction between personality types and occupational environments*
In Holland, JL (1973) *Making Vocational Choices: A Theory of Careers.* Englewood Cliffs, NJ:Prentice Hall, p 29. Reproduced with special permission of the publisher, Psychological

Assessment Resources Inc., from Making Vocational Choices. Copyright 1997, 2001 by Psychological Assessment Resources, Inc. All rights reserved.

Table 4.3, p 113, *Brief description of the sixteen MBTI personality types and typical occupational trends*
Adapted from Myers, IB, McCaulley, MH, Quenk, NL and Hammer, AL (2003) *MBTI Manual:A Guide to the Development and Use of the Myers-Briggs Type Indicator.* 3ed. Palo Alto, CA: Consulting Psychologists Press.

Figure 4.3, p 116, *The Life-Career Rainbow: Nine life roles in schematic life space*
In Super, DE (1988) *Career development: Who can contribute?* Unpublished handouts for seminar on Career Development. Pretoria: Human Sciences Research Council; Super, DE (1990) A life-span, life-space approach to career development. In D Brown, L Brooks and Associates (eds) *Career Choice and Development: Applying Contemporary Theories to Practice.* 2ed. San Francisco: Jossey-Bass; and Super, DE (1992) Toward a comprehensive theory of career development. In DH Montross and CJ Shink-man (eds) *Career Development: Theory and Practice,* Illinois: Charles C Thomas, 35–64.

Figure 4.4, p 118, *A segmental model of career development*
Super, DE, in Brown, D, Brooks, L and Associates (1996) *Career Choice and Development.* 3ed. San Francisco: Jossey-Bass, p 200. Reprinted with permission from DE Super. All rights reserved.

Table 4.4, p 141, *The Diagnostic Framework of Career Services*
In Coetzee, M (2005) *Career counseling in the 21st century: Practical techniques for facilitating career competency and resilience,* Unpublished manuscript, Department Industrial and Organizational Psychology, UNISA, Pretoria

Table 5.1, p 165, *Adult career development competencies*
Adapted from Zunker, VG (2006) *Career counseling: a holistic approach.* 7ed. Belmont, CA:Thomson Higher Education, p 440.

Figure 6.1, p 196, *Integrated theoretical model of the construct career anchors*
In Coetzee, M and Schreuder, AMG (2008) A multi-cultural investigation of students' career anchors at a South African higher education institution. *SA Journal of Labour Relations,* 32(2): 1–21.

Table 6.1, p 205, *Characteristics of the four career patterns*
In Baruch, Y (2004) Transforming careers: From linear to multidirectional career paths: Organisational and individual perspectives. *Career Development International,* 9(1), 58–73; Woodd, M (2000) The move towards a different career pattern: Are women better prepared than men for a modern career? *Career Development International,* 5(2), 99–105.

Table 6.2, p 209, *Consequences of work-home interference*
In Demerouti, E and Geurts, SAE (2004) Towards a typology of work-home interaction. *Community, Work and Family,* 7, 285–309.

Table 6.3, p 212 *Factors that influence how partners combine occupational and family roles*
In Gilbert, LA (1994) Current perspectives on dual-career families. *Current Directions in Psychological Science,* 3(4), 101–103.

Table 6.4, p 218, *Organisational strategies and initiatives to reduce work-life conflict*
Based on Robbins, PR and Judge, TA (2011) *Organizational behaviour.* 14 ed. Upper Saddle River, NJ: Pearson, 607.

Figure 6.2, p 220, *Four kinds of plateaued performer employee actions*
In Leibowitz, ZB, Kaye, BL and Farren, C (1990) Career gridlock. *Training and Development Journal,* Apr, 28–36.

Figure 6.5, p 228, *Factors affecting the outcome of losing a job*
In Kates, N, Greiff, BS and Hagen, DQ (1990) *The Psychosocial Impact of Job Loss.* Washington: American Psychiatric Press.

Figure 7.2, p 242, *The authentic happiness formula*
In Seligman, MEP (2002) *Authentic Happiness: Using the New Positive Psychology to Realize your Potential for Lasting Fulfilment.* London: Nicholas Brealey.

Figure 7.3, p 244, *Dimensions of state engagement*
In May, DR, Gilson, RL and Harter, LM (2004) The psychological conditions of meaningfulness, safety and availability and the engagement of the human spirit at work. *Journal of Occupational and Organizational Psychology,* 77, 11–37.

Table 7.1, p 245, *Engagement in different occupations in South Africa*
In Rothmann, S (2005, September) *Work-related well-being in South African organisations: What do we know?* Paper presented at the 7th Annual Conference of the Employee Assistance Professionals Association of South Africa, Durban.

Table 7.2, p 247, *Classification of strengths*
In Peterson, C and Seligman, MEP (2004) *Character strengths and virtues: A handbook and classification.* Oxford: Oxford University Press.

Table 7.3, p 252, *Burnout in different occupations in South Africa*
In Rothmann, S (2005, September) *Work-related well-being in South African organisations: What do we know?* Paper presented at the 7th Annual Conference of the Employee Assistance Professionals Association of South Africa, Durban.

Table 7.4, p 254, *Job-specific factors and burnout*
In Schaufeli, WB (2003) Past performance and future perspectives of burnout research. *South African Journal of Industrial Psychology,* 29(4), 1–15.

Table 7.5, p 256, *Occupational stressors in South African organisations*
In Rothmann, S (2005, September) *Work-related well-being in South African organisations: What do we know?* Paper presented at the 7th Annual Conference of the Employee Assistance Professionals Association of South Africa, Durban.

Table 7.6, p 257, *Intensity and frequency of stressors in South African organisations*
In Rothmann, S (2005, September) *Work-related well-being in South African organisations: What do we know?* Paper presented at the 7th Annual Conference of the Employee Assistance Professionals Association of South Africa, Durban.

Table 7.8, p 262, *Perceptions of helping and restraining factors of employees with strong and weak sense of coherence*
In Muller, Y, and Rothmann, S (2009) Sense of coherence and employees experiences of helping and restraining factors in the work environment. *South African Journal of Industrial Psychology,* 35, 89–98.

Table 7.10, p 269, *Outcomes of occupational stress in South African organisations*
In Rothmann, S (2005, September) *Work-related well-being in South African organisations: What do we know?* Paper presented at the 7th Annual Conference of the Employee Assistance Professionals Association of South Africa, Durban.

Figure 7.5, p 273, *Estimated contribution of different aspects to happiness*
In Lyubomirsky, S (2008) *The how of happiness: A scientific approach to getting the life you want.* New York: Penguin Press.

Figure 7.6, p 273, *Summary of individual happiness activities*
In Lyubomirsky, S (2008) *The how of happiness: A scientific approach to getting the life you want.* New York: Penguin Press.

Table 8.2, pp 290 – 292, *Career development support practices in the 2000s*
Based on Arnold, J and Randall, R (2010) *Work psychology: Understanding human behaviour in the workplace* 5ed. Harlow, Essex: Pearson Education; Baruch, Y (1999) Integrated systems for the 2000s, *International Journal of Manpower,* 20(7), 432–457; Baruch, Y (2002) Career systems in transition: A normative model for organizational career practices, *Personnel Review,* 32(2), 232–251; Byars, LL and Rue, LW (2004) *Human Resource Management.* New York: McGraw-Hill; Conger, S (2002) Fostering a career development culture: Reflections on the roles of managers, employees and supervisors, *Career Development International,* 7(6), 371–375; and Nabi, GR (2003) Situational characteristics and subjective career success: The mediating role of career-enhancing strategies, *International Journal of Manpower,* 24(6), 653–671.

Table 8.3, pp 298, *Conducting a career development discussion*
Adapted from Coetzee, M and Stone, K (2004) *Learner Support: Toward Learning and Development,* Randburg: Knowres.

Table 8.4, p 303, *Roles of mentors and mentees*
In Coetzee, M and Stone, K (2004) *Learner Support: Toward Learning and Development,* Randburg: Knowres.

Table 8.5, pp 303 – 304, *Conducting review discussions: Roles of mentor and mentee*
In Coetzee, M and Stone, K (2004) *Learner Support: Toward Learning and Development,* Randburg: Knowres.

Figure 8.2, p 306, *The four dimensions of Mass Career Customisation*
In Benko, C and Weisberg, A (2009) Mass career customization: building the corporate lattice. *Deloitte Review.* Available at: http://www.deloitee.com/view/en_US/us/Insights/Browse-by-Content-Type/deloittereview/article/35912eefad33210VgnVCM100000ba42f00aRCRD.htm [Accessed on 6 March 2009].

Table 8.7, p 314 *Career management skills workshop feedback*
In Hutcheson and Otte, (1997) *Helping Employees Manage Careers.* Reprinted by permission of Prentice-Hall, Upper Saddle River, New Jersey

Figure 8.3, p 316, *Process and outcome variables of socialisation*
Based on Feldman, DC (1976) A contingency theory of socialization. *Administrative Science Quarterly,* 21, 433–452.

Table 8.8, pp 318 – 319 *Stages in the socialisation process*
In Wanous, JP (1992) (Table 7.3, page 209) *Organizational Entry: Recruitment, Selection, Orientation and Socialization of Newcomers.* Reading, MA: Addison-Wesley. Reprinted with permission of Addison-Wesley Longman Publishing Company, Inc.

Table 8.9, p 323, *Ten critical components of a talent development programme*
In Knowledge Resources (2010) *HR Survey 2010,* Randburg: Knowres.

Preface

This is the fourth edition of *Careers: An Organisational Perspective*. The shift continues away from the traditional organisational career, which was confined to predictable upward movement, to a career that is more unpredictable and that consists of more than one role, frequent changes and varied experiences. This emerging career is often described as the protean career, a concept developed by DT Hall, which refers to a career that is not managed by the organisation but by the individual.

The modern work environment is characterised by less job security, fewer work opportunities, changes in organisational and work structure, and changes in employee/organisation relationships. All these factors have an impact on individual career experiences, decisions and career development in organisations. The following issues are relevant in the present work environment:

◆ Individuals experience career changes and transitions more frequently;
◆ Individuals are required to take control of their careers despite limited skills in this regard;
◆ Individuals are forced to enter into a different psychological and transactional relationship with organisations;
◆ The workforce is becoming more diverse and the number of working couples and the individual's concern about work-life balance are increasing;
◆ The career well-being of individuals has become important as they find the requirements and demands of the knowledge economy affecting their sense of psychological career success, security and stability;
◆ Organisations are challenged to play a supportive role in the career development of their employees to empower their employees with the career self-management skills in sustaining their employability;
◆ The nature of the psychological contract characterises a shift in loyalties and commitment;
◆ Career plateauing, obsolescence and job loss and unemployment are more prevalent; and
◆ Career adaptation in the 21st century requires, *inter alia*, an employability orientation, career adaptability, commitment to continuous learning and skills development which might be the only guarantee for sustainable employment.

The aim of this book is to provide an introduction to the psychology of careers that could assist both the individual and organisation in planning and managing the career development of individuals in the contemporary world of work. Specifically we intend that this book should be useful for undergraduate students in psychology, taking one or more modules relating to work and organisational psychology, occupational or vocational psychology, and industrial and organisational psychology. Undergraduate students in business and management taking one or more modules relating to organisational behaviour, managing people or human resource management will also benefit from this book.

The fourth edition has been updated and revised to reflect the most recent research and trends in career psychology and behaviour today. The chapters are self-contained units and the text remains flexible enough for lecturers to teach the material in the order they find most appropriate. Each of the eight chapters begins with a set of *learning outcomes* that previews content and guides the student. The end-of-chapter materials include these features:

◆ *Review and discussion questions* provide an opportunity to review chapter content and learning outcomes through questions developed to test students' memory of key issues and concepts within the chapter. The questions also give students an opportunity to apply critical thinking skills to in-depth questions.

◆ *The reflection activities* and *case studies* act as mini-cases students can use to analyse and dissect chapter concepts and applications via real-life South African-specific scenarios.

The fourth edition is arranged to introduce in the first three chapters work values that influence the meaning of work, the implications of the characteristics of the contemporary organisation for careers, and major concepts and contemporary models in studying careers. In chapter 4, we discuss career choice theories and their practical application. Chapter 5 contextualises career development in lifespan development, while chapter 6 presents issues that are relevant at any stage of the individual's working life. Finally, chapter 7 discusses the topic of career well-being and chapter 8 the factors that influence individuals' choice of organisations and contemporary organisational career development support practices.

Readers familiar with the third edition of this text, published in 2006, may find it helpful if we describe the changes we have made in this edition. All the chapters have been updated to reflect the most recent research in the field. New real-life South African-specific case studies and reflection activities have been added to chapters 1 to 7.

Chapter 1 on the meaning of work has been revised and re-focused. The emphasis is now on the work values that influence the meaning of work in people's lives.

Chapter 2 and chapter 3 retain the material of previous editions with extensive updates that reflect contemporary research regarding the nature of careers. An additional career planning model (the contextual action model) has been added to chapter 3 to reflect new trends in the career counselling field.

Chapter 4 has been restructured to reflect classical and contemporary career choice theories. Some new theories relevant to career choice counselling in the contemporary world of work have been added: Mitchell, Levin and Krumboltz's happenstance theory; Cook, Heppner and O'Brien's race/gender ecological model; and Savickas's career construction theory.

Chapter 5 has been revised and updated. The section on human development in the early childhood phase has been changed to reflect career development during childhood. A section on the career development of men and women has also been added.

Chapter 6 of the third edition has been deleted. Themes relating to organisational choice and the organisational career development support practices of orientation and socialisation have been integrated with chapter 8 (previously chapter 9 of the third edition).

Chapter 7 (career issues) of the third edition has now become chapter 6 of this edition. This chapter has been updated extensively to reflect the most recent research trends. Chapter 7 of this edition (previously chapter 8) has been substantially revised and re-focused. The emphasis is now on career well-being.

Chapter 8 (previously chapter 9) has been updated to reflect the latest research trends. As noted earlier, the sections on organisational choice and orientation and socialisation of the third edition have been added to this chapter.

Dries Schreuder and Melinde Coetzee
July 2010

Acknowledgements

Our understanding of careers in the organisational context has been shaped by many friends, colleagues, clients and students, past and present, in the South African and international multicultural workplace contexts. We are truly grateful for these wonderful people who have shared their practices, wisdom and insights with us in person and through the professional literature. We would also like to thank the contributing author, Prof Ian Rothmann, for his quality contribution, hard work and his forbearance.

Prof Dries Schreuder
Prof Melinde Coetzee
July 2010

The publishers would also like to thank the reviewers for their constructive and helpful comments at various stages of the drafting of the fourth edition. The feedback has been invaluable in shaping the book.

About the authors

Dries (AMG) Schreuder

Dries Schreuder (DAdmin) is a registered Industrial Psychologist with the Health Professions Council of South Africa (HPCSA) and a master human resource practitioner with the South African Board for People Practice (SABPP). He obtained his doctorate degree in Industrial Psychology in 1989. He is currently Professor in the Department of Industrial and Organisational Psychology at UNISA and lectures in Forensic Industrial Psychology and Career Psychology. He is a member of the Education Committee of the SABPP and also an appointed mentor of the Board. He has presented papers at various national and international conferences and has published extensively in accredited journals. He is also the author, co-author and editor of a number of academic books.

Melinde Coetzee

Melinde Coetzee (DLitt et Phil) is currently fulfilling the role of professor in the Department of Industrial and Organisational Psychology at the University of South Africa. She has 14 years experience in organisational development, skills development and HR management in the corporate environment and has been lecturing subjects such as Personnel, Career, Organisational and Managerial Psychology since 2000 at undergraduate, honours and masters levels. She also presents short learning programmes in skills development facilitation and organisational career guidance through Unisa's Centre for Industrial and Organisational Psychology. Melinde is a professionally registered Industrial Psychologist with the Health Professions Council of South Africa (HPCSA) and a master human resource practitioner with the South African Board for People Practice (SABPP). She is section editor of the *SA Journal of Human Resource Management* and also the author, co-author and editor of a number of academic books. She has published in numerous accredited academic journals. She has also co-authored and contributed chapters to books nationally and internationally. She has presented numerous academic papers and posters at national and international conferences.

Chapter Contributor (Chapter 7)

Ian Rothmann

Ian Rothmann is a professor in Industrial/Organisational Psychology at the North-West University (Vanderbijlpark Campus). He completed his BCom (cum laude), HED (cum laude), BCom Honours (cum laude), MCom (cum laude) and PhD (Industrial Psychology) at the Potchefstroom University for CHE. A total of 129 Masters and 40 PhD students completed their dissertations and theses under his supervision. He received life-long honorary membership of the Society of Industrial and Organisational Psychology in South Africa for distinguished and meritorious service to Industrial and Organisational Psychology during 2006. Ian has published a total of 116 articles in scientific journals. He has presented 144 papers and posters at national and international conferences.

The meaning of work

Learning outcomes

After studying this chapter you should be able to:

- describe pre- and post-industrial meanings of work;
- discuss work as a central life interest;
- describe the nature of values;
- discuss how the Protestant work ethic influenced the meaning of work for contemporary society;
- discuss how the work values of advancement and economic/material rewards influence the significance of work in people's lives;
- explain how work contributes to feelings of belonging and being useful in society;
- discuss the concept of work-family enrichment as a social work value;
- describe competencies currently important in work and how these relate to the work value of autonomy;
- discuss how spirituality affects the meaning of work; and
- explain the importance of diversity in the modern workplace.

Introduction

The *meaning of work* embraces the *significance* that work or working has in people's lives. Work constitutes a major element of human activity that transpires over much of people's lives. Work sustains life in the sense of biological survival and it can also sustain the quality of life. In general, next to family, work has been found to be of relatively high importance compared to other areas of life such as leisure, community and religion (Harpaz and Fu, 2002).

Different meanings can be derived from different values associated with work, for example work seen as a means of making a living, of being occupied, fulfilling a vocation, developing and utilising skills, fulfilling needs, contributing to an all-embracing lifestyle or fulfilling a life purpose.

The meaning of work in people's lives is determined within the individual (one's personal work values, preferences and work goals) and by the job and wider environment (the characteristics of the job or work itself and the organisational and socio-cultural context) (Wrzesniewski, Dutton and Debebe, 2003).

Individual meanings of work are derived directly or indirectly from *socio-cultural influences* in the context of family socialisation, school socialisation, group affiliations and work experience. Socio-cultural influences are embedded in *historical contexts* that give rise to changing meanings of work over time. Table 1.1 on p5 provides an overview of how the meaning of work evolved over time.

Three of the meanings that are associated with work in *pre-industrial times* are work as *drudgery*, work as *instrumental to spiritual or religious ends* and work as *intrinsically meaningful for its own sake*.

The *Greeks and Romans* of antiquity viewed work as a burden that contaminates the mind. It was regarded as contrary to the ideal of exercising the mind to think about truth concerning matters of philosophy, politics and art. Manual labour was the domain of slaves while, as Cicero proclaimed, the only forms of work worthy of free men were big business and agriculture and living the life of a retired country gentleman (Tilgher, 1962). Contrary to the value that today's contemporary society places on highly skilled labour, skilled crafts were somewhat patronisingly recognised as having broad social value while noble work was planning wars, large-scale commerce and the arts, especially architecture, literature and philosophy (Hamilton-Attwell, 1998).

The *Hebrews* also saw work as drudgery, but additionally as providing expiation of sin and regaining of spiritual dignity. The early Christians shared these views but also incorporated the meaning of work as charity, in that one had to share the fortunes of one's work with the needy. Catholic meanings included expiation, charity and purification. But it was also acceptable that the individual enriches himself or herself through work, although not as an end in itself, because work was merely a means to maintain life and the ultimate life was the life hereafter (Tilgher, 1962). St Thomas Aquinas constructed a hierarchy of occupations based on the perceptions of work of the church at the time. This hierarchy had a significant impact on economic affairs. The priesthood and other sacred callings enjoyed the highest ranking, while merchants and shopkeepers were rated lower than farmers, peasants and artisans (Hamilton-Attwell, 1998).

According to *Protestant* views, work was a duty. Luther maintained that man works to serve God and to serve God well was to work well, whatever the nature of one's work. No activity was superior to another, since all work helped to build God's kingdom on earth (Tilgher, 1962). The Prostestant Reformation in the 16th century largely coincided with a rapid expansion of commerce in the northern European countries. This expansion was mostly guided by the motivation to accumulate wealth, not to display it or to buy influence, but to save for the future and to reinvest in new ventures. Calvin, a Protestant theologian, advocated a morality that was consistent with the notion of acquiring wealth, abstaining from worldly pleasures, preserving wealth through savings and carefully using time with the view that time is money. He maintained that success is pleasing to God and that one should improve one's station in life, with regard to class or profession, if it will be of benefit to society. An ideology of work emerged that emphasised diligence, punctuality, deferment of gratification and the primacy of the work domain (Hamilton-Attwell, 1998).

In *ancient Persian society* work had an ethical connotation. It was seen as virtuous in the conquest of good over evil. Work was good in that it was instrumental in keeping the land fertile, acquiring property and providing shelter for man, woman, child, cow and dog (Tilgher, 1931).

In *Eastern views* work was seen as instrumental in spiritual and character development. According to Islamic thinking, those who earn an honest living by their own labour and not by begging, receive the grace of Allah. In Buddhist writings, physical labour and spiritual growth were seen as part of the same process and work was seen as instrumental in liberating one from the passions that prevent one from finding nirvana (MOW, 1987). The Japanese view of work is based on the Confucian model of human nature, affirming mankind's innate goodness. The Confucian ideology provided a basis for high trust employment practices and a sense of fulfilment from work to attain a common purpose (Hamilton-Attwell, 1998).

During the *Renaissance* in Europe, with its focus on the value of a person's mental powers rather than on his or her physical powers, work acquired the meaning of being intrinsically meaningful in itself. Work was seen as a means of mastering nature and of each person becoming their own master — that is, a creator in their own right (Tilgher, 1962).

After the Renaissance in Europe, views on work varied in terms of what constituted progress or decadence, success or failure. In the 19th century, a universal meaning emerged in which work became exalted to being the reason for all progress — spiritual, material and intellectual (Tilgher, 1962).

With *industrialisation* the meaning of work became a problem area, in that meaning was not self-evident. Industrialisation involved, *inter alia*, mass-production of objects in factories, with accompanying structural changes in the work process. Division of labour became more extensive, work tasks became fragmented and were reduced to mechanistic, repetitive functions that adversely affected workers' personal commitment to their jobs. The high rates of production expected by industry and long working hours led to a decline in the will to work and to a seeking of meaning outside work (Bridges, 1995; Weiss, 2001).

In *post-industrialism* the focus is on information rather than on industry. Production is associated with producing ideas in offices in addition to manufacturing objects in factories. The proliferation of new technologies in, for example, computerisation and communications and interaction of different cultures involves heterogeneity in beliefs and tasks in society. Consequently, the cultural climate of post-industrialisation, which is referred to as *post-modernism*, is characterised by recognition of differences, plurality, paradox and eclecticism which involves various possibilities and choices (Bridges, 1995; Weiss, 2001). Being mostly concerned with employees' attitudes to work, post-industrialism regards employees as being more enlightened with five characteristics (Hamilton-Attwell, 1998):

◆ *Self-actualisation* — behaving in accordance with one's values, focusing on personal intellectual and emotional development and growth;

◆ *Hedonism* — the right to enjoy life and the benefits of one's work: the job is just a means to an end;

◆ *Entitlementalism* — being entitled to certain things such as having the right to choose a dress code, to see sensitive organisational information and participate in strategic decisions;

◆ *Antiproductivism* — increasingly questioning the cost of economic growth versus the depletion of natural resources, pollution and the negative impact of the rising expectations of consumers on one's quality of life; and

◆ *Anti-authoritarianism* — having the right to question anybody who gives commands, even legitimate power and complying with a measure of reserve and suspicion.

The characteristics of the 21st century *workplace* put under focus the changing meaning of work. Shifts from national to global markets and from technological to information, service-based economies signal dramatic changes that are also reflected in the nature of work and the way work is performed (Weiss, 2001). Living in a more chaotic and unpredictable world, people view their lives as being under constant construction. In the 21st century workplace, the meaning of work is largely seen as being constituted at work, with others. As such the significance of working becomes a living social account that people make of their experience at work. Work meaning is viewed as people's *understanding* of what they do at work, the *significance* of what they do and their *beliefs* about the value or worth of the *function* work serves in their lives (Wrzesniewski et al, 2003).

According to Chen (2001), life experiences generate and enrich work meanings. People are purposeful and intentional beings who make sense of their living experiences. In living a holistic and integral life, people are in a continuous process of meaning making and meaning exploration. People engage in *continuous sensemaking* to discern what meaning their work holds for them and act upon their relational setting at work in a motivated fashion to shape their contact with others and the experiences they are likely to have. This process of interpersonal sensemaking is approached from three lenses: *job meaning* (the specific tasks and activities that an employee believes compose the job and the perceived value of these tasks and activities), *role meaning* (the perceived position in the social structure an employee holds in the organisation and the perceived value of this position in the organisation) and *self-meaning* (self-understanding and self-narratives [stories] about one's identity and qualities or characteristics when at work and the perceived value or worth of one's personal qualities in the job) (Wrzesniewski et al, 2003).

Three types of organisational transitions have received increasing attention during the past few years: globalisation, mergers and acquisitions, restructurings and downsizings, and privatisations. Some of the dramatic changes resulting from these transitions and that are affecting work and organisations include: increased global competition, the impact of information technology, the re-engineering of business processes, smaller companies that employ fewer people and that shift from making a product to providing a service and the increasing disappearance of the meaning of 'job' as a fixed collection of tasks. These changes are having a negative effect on employee loyalty, morale, motivation and job security as many more people are increasingly being affected by job losses (Baruch, 2006; Coutinho, Dam and Blustein, 2008; Kinicki and Kreitner, 2009).

Individuals are increasingly being forced to adopt the *protean career* (a career shaped by the individual) in response to the widespread redefinition and restructuring of the psychological contract (see also chapter 2). This trend has led to an increased pursuit of self-employment, small business proprietorships and entrepreneurship as alternative and even composite career paths. As individuals learn how to shape and manage their careers more autonomously, moving between jobs and organisations to increase their employment value. They are also adopting new and different attitudes, values and perceptions about the meaning of work in their lives (McCarthy and Hall, 2000; Sinclair, 2009).

The *search for meaning* and *spiritual sensemaking* in a workplace, characterised by heightened change, has become a dominant aspect of modern working life and a factor that is influencing the meaning of work in a *multicultural world* with *multiple worldviews*. In the contemporary workplace, work is still viewed as being central in individuals' lives. However, the choice of working now forms part of one's spiritual journey as a major mode of *self-expression* and discovering one's *life purpose* through exploring one's possible selves in the various *significant learnings and experiences* that identify one's professional working life in a boundaryless world (Crawford, Hubbard, Lonis-Shumate and O'Neill, 2009).

Table 1.1 *Evolution of meanings associated with work*

Pre-industrial era	<ul><li>work as drudgery</li><li>work as instrumental to spiritual or religious ends</li><li>work as intrinsically meaningful for its own sake</li></ul>
Industrial era	<ul><li>mechanistic, mass productions lead to decline in the will to work</li><li>meaning sought outside sphere of work</li></ul>
Post-industrial era	<ul><li>information technology and globalisation lead to multicultural viewpoints about the meaning of work</li></ul>
21st century	<ul><li>boundaryless, service-driven, technology-intensive work environments</li><li>work meaning is a socially constructed product that is dynamic and fluid and that expresses itself through the lenses of job meaning, role meaning and self-meaning in a particular socio-cultural context</li><li>heightened change and uncertain markets lead to a search for meaning, higher purpose and spiritual sensemaking through one's work activities and life roles</li></ul>

Work as a central life interest

A fundamental factor in the meaning of work is the *centrality of work*, which is the degree of importance that working has in the life of an individual at any given point in time (MOW, 1987). The idea of work as a central life interest was stimulated by the fact that for most adults working occupies a large part of their lives (Harpaz, Honig and Coetsier, 2002).

Research conducted by Dubin in 1992 showed that, for the majority of people, work is not a central life interest, although it has differential centrality for different occupational groups. In general, work seems to be losing its centrality for industrial workers, of whom two thirds state that it is not a central life interest; half of the managerial sector does not regard it as a central life interest, whereas professional groups do. Dubin (1992) suggested that work has more centrality for professional people. Because professional practice is creative, it involves personal responsibility for the outcomes of one's work performance and it involves a degree of risk and uncertainty, which requires personal accountability.

Work as a central life interest does not refer to the content of work, but to the *value outcomes* — that is, rewards of working — relative to the outcomes of other life roles. Therefore individuals who have high work centrality will probably see job performance as instrumental in obtaining many non-financial or psychological rewards such as self-worth, growth and personal satisfaction. Individuals with low centrality, on the other hand, may perceive performance as relating only to pay or other economic/material rewards associated with the job (Harpaz et al, 2002). A South African study conducted by Coetzee and Bergh (2009) in the service industry showed that managers who view their work as a calling and an opportunity to contribute to the greater good of others, rather than merely a job, perceive work as a valuable activity. The study also showed that whites, Indians and females attach significantly higher value to the significance of working than Africans, coloureds and males.

In an extensive study conducted by the 'Meaning of Work' (MOW) international research team in 1987 of over 15 000 persons in eight industrialised countries, it was found that the centrality of work decreases as the importance of leisure time increases, but that the majority of people attach meaning to working, in that they would continue working even if they had the means to live comfortably without working for the rest of their lives (MOW, 1987). Porter (2004) observes that this trend — which seems to be mostly influenced by the Protestant work ethic — is still continuing today.

The meaning of work is influenced by the multiple worldviews of a multicultural world and has evolved across time and culture. Consequently, the meaning of work constitutes a multi-dimensional phenomenon that is related to certain work values that vary from individual to individual.

Work values

The term *'values'* is used interchangeably to denote norms, beliefs, principles, preferences, needs, interests, intentions, codes, criteria, world-view or ideology. Such terms suggest that values can be seen as orientations or dispositions that selectively determine modes of behaviour and life forms, including work behaviour and work forms. Rounds and Armstrong (2005:309) describe values as beliefs that represent broad motivational goals or desirable end states of behaviours that apply across context and time. Values guide the selection or evaluation of behaviours and events, remain stable over time and are generally ordered in terms of relative importance by different people.

Values develop as a result of external *socio-cultural forces* and *internal psychological factors* that influence the individual. According to Weiss (2001), socio-cultural norms become personal objectives of the individual that are transformed to values. In this way, individual values are orientations that are socially sanctioned.

As discussed previously, Protestantism gave rise to work values which culminated in the Protestant work ethic, which constituted work meanings sanctioned by religion. The work ethic postulated that work has moral value, that each person has a calling to work, that people should develop their talents and that all, including the rich, must work. Idleness was taboo and personal salvation was achieved through industriousness and thrift. Material welfare was a sign of God's grace and it was a vice to waste it on self-gratification (Hamilton-Attwell, 1998).

The work ethic is associated with the development of *capitalism*. Max Weber maintains that it encouraged capitalistic activities such as the pursuit of profit and renewal of profit by commercial enterprise and rational organisation of labour (Furnham, 1990). Tawny maintains that it gave rise to individualism in the sense of self-reliance, which involved the belief that God helps people who help themselves. Individualism, saving one's resources and deferring gratification, became associated with the 'proper citizen' (Dubin, 1992:117).

Over time, much of the religious meaning of the Protestant work ethic declined. *Occupational achievement* through hard work and thrift remained work values, but were seen as of *intrinsic value* to the individual and not as service to God (Nord et al, 1990). The Protestant work ethic has been associated with the development of *achievement motivation*. Protestant values such as self-reliance and mastery are transferred to children by child-rearing practices, which lead to acquisition of achievement motivation (Argyle, 1989). Although the Protestant work ethic is associated with *Western capitalistic society*, research findings suggest that it has spread to *Asian countries. High productivity* in, for example, Japan is in part ascribed to the work ethic.

Research has also focused on work-related norms that are derived from socio-cultural norms, including the work ethic. Two norms that are seen as necessary in conceptualising the meaning of work are the individual's *obligations to society* and *entitlements of the working individual* (Harpaz and Fu, 2002).

The *obligation* norm includes beliefs about the duties of work, namely that workers should be expected to think of better ways of doing their jobs; that it is one's duty to contribute to society by working, that a large portion of income should be saved, that monotonous work is acceptable if pay is fair and that workers should value the work they are doing, even if it is boring, dirty or unskilled.

Entitlements concern beliefs about the rights of working, namely that a job should be provided to every individual who wishes to work, that the educational system should prepare every person for a good job if they exert reasonable effort, that, if workers' skills become outdated, their employer should be responsible for retraining and re-employment and that, when changes have to be made in work methods, the superior should ask workers for their opinions (Harpaz and Fu, 2002).

In a study of work relations in the former states of East and West Germany, it was found that the two groups did not differ with regard to obligation norms. Both groups share the ethic of work postulated as an individual responsibility and duty. The East German group, however, associated more entitlements with working than the West Germans. This difference is ascribed to expectations in the East German group that the state should supply all that is necessary for work and to expectations of improved living conditions after the reunification of Germany (Wilpert and Maimer, 1993).

In a study of black and white managers in South Africa, Watkins (1995) found no differences in obligation norms, but found that black managers show higher entitlement norms than white managers. Watkins ascribes this to a need for equity in black managers. Equity concerns individuals' perceived fairness of their input and reward ratios in comparison to other individuals in similar situations.

Since values can have an impact on work performance, performance values *per se* are important in research on values. Measured performance values include the work ethic, pursuit of excellence, status aspiration, authoritarianism, the need for material gain, mastery and competitiveness. In a study of black and white managers in South Africa, it was found that the work ethic is not highly valued by either group, that all the above-mentioned performance values are higher in white than in black managers and that, in black managers, none of the values are evident, with the exception of mastery as an existing value and excellence as a potential value (Watkins and Mauer, 1994).

The findings cited suggest that *cultural diversity* and the managing of cultural diversity are important in the work context. The cultural relativity of values is connected to the quality of work life, as well as to the quality of life in general. In this connection, Hofstede (1984) suggests that an ethnocentric approach, which has a one-sided cultural focus, has limitations in values research.

The relation between values and the meaning of work can be direct or indirect and imperceptible and it can be complicated by the fact that the meaning of work associated with values does not necessarily constitute the goals of work.

Work goals are the relative importance of various goals which are sought or preferred by people in their working lives. Research has shown that the two most dominant work goals across various cultures tend to be 'interesting work' and 'good pay'. Other important work goals include learning opportunities, interpersonal relations, promotion opportunities, convenient hours, job security and ability-job match (Harpaz and Fu, 2002). A South African study conducted by Coetzee, Bergh and Schreuder (2010) found that work goals relating to the nature of work constitute 80 per cent of the factors that significantly influence people's satisfaction or dissatisfaction with their work. These include the need for:

◆ stable or permanent employment;

◆ meaningful work;

◆ a variety of challenging, stimulating and demanding tasks that bring out the best in one;

◆ tasks that are relevant to one's expertise or qualification;

◆ tasks that provide one with opportunities to obtain new knowledge and skills; and

◆ tasks that provide one with opportunities to make a difference in the lives of others and interface with customers.

Figure 1.1 provides an overview of some of the prevailing work values that have an important influence on the meaning of work.

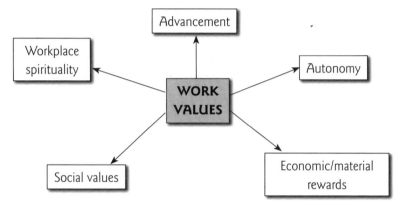

Figure 1.1 *Values influencing the meaning of work*

Advancement

People who value making *advancement* in their work and their career attach much importance to achievement (the long-term concern about doing things better, surpassing one's standard of excellence and/or wanting to do something challenging or unique), upward mobility, making progress, development, power (the concern about having control, impact or influence over others) and status (De Vos, Buyens and Schalk, 2005; Frieze, Olson, Murrell and Selvan, 2006).

Those high in power motivation often have a high interest in their image or status and how they are viewed by others. They also value having prestige possessions. Career success is also regarded as important. They will actively seek for advancement opportunities by requesting to be considered for promotion or by volunteering for important assignments. Job performance and challenging job experiences have been found to be important predictors of people's positive evaluations of their promotability (De Pater, Van Vianen, Bechtoldt and Klehe, 2009).

Organisational inducements like career development programmes and established career paths are regarded as important. Characteristics of those high in advancement and especially achievement motivation are being success-oriented and *working hard*, which is often associated with working longer hours (Frieze et al, 2006). Research also found that men tend to value power significantly more than women who seem to value achievement and the social value of benevolence significantly more than men (Lyons, Duxbury and Higgins, 2005).

Power

Power refers to a capacity that a person has to influence the behaviour of other people so that they act in accordance with one's wishes (Robbins, Judge, Millet and Waters-Marsh, 2008). Power therefore exists wherever there is a relationship between two or more people or groups. People in organisations can acquire power if they are able to provide an important resource that creates dependency on the part of other groups. Resources can be any expendable commodity such as money, time, expertise, technology, skills, knowledge or authority. Managers are often the most powerful groups in organisations because they possess money in the form of budgets and the authority to determine how these budgets should be allocated. From a post-structuralist perspective, discourse or knowledge is seen as the primary agent of power that regulates how people understand the world, each other and themselves. Discourse is produced through relations of power that exist in society. These relations are seen as temporary, unstable and challengeable. It is the inherent instability of these relations that give rise to multiple discourses targeted at regulating the behaviour of individuals in any given domain (Dick and Ellis, 2006).

Dominant groups in society and organisations transmit values and goals to the workplace by virtue of their positions of power and control over economic activity. As *power groups* subscribe to different values, different meanings of work come into practice. In democratic power structures, for example, the meaning of work revolves around human dignity, liberty, equality and solidarity, which are values that have little meaning in autocratic power structures. Power groups also determine the ways in which decisions are made in organisations, for example, whether decisions with regard to change are made unilaterally by management or by participation of workers, whether or not and how organisational values are communicated to workers and whether or not workers are assisted to understand how values incorporated in the design of jobs can be executed (Kinicki and Kreitner, 2009).

Power structures in society are constantly changing. Formerly power was mainly concentrated in large, centralised organisations such as government, the civil service and bureaucratic organisations in the public and private sectors, which were seen as equipped to plan on behalf of society. Power paths were available through experience within the organisation, which was essential for climbing the organisational hierarchy to senior positions (Peiperl and Arthur, 2000).

Currently, power is spread over less hierarchical, decentralised organisations, such as smaller, specialised business units and coordinated work teams, comprising individuals with specialist knowledge who work together on a particular project or toward a common goal beyond the boundaries of one organisation. A particular organisation is no longer host to individuals' careers because it provides a structure upon which individuals can build their careers. Individuals now have self-ownership of their careers, which can be defined in terms of individual actions that structure their careers. This involves Arthur and Rousseau's (1996) concept of the boundaryless career, which refers to a sequence of job enactments which goes beyond the single employment scenario.

In the context of a career that has no organisational boundaries, the individual can become *self-empowered* by means of continuous learning. London and Mone (1999) see continuous learning as a strong and ongoing awareness of the need for and value of learning.

Status

Advancement and power are also closely related to the need for status. *Status* arises largely from the tendency to categorise people according to work-related factors. Work therefore determines the individual's place in the *status hierarchy of the community*. Status is ascribed to individuals by society, family, friends and co-workers. Generally it is ascribed to individuals according to material achievement (that is, the financial income which work generates) and to social achievement (that is, the prestige associated with a type of job).

Besides the job, social achievement can include non-work activities and social roles, for example, membership of exclusive clubs, societies or other social groups. Such groups can have social norms that influence and reinforce the individual to comply with 'correct' behaviours and in this way social norms associated with status can become personal meanings.

Status can involve *mobility* and *directionality*. Since both society and organisations are hierarchically structured, a value judgement is attached to vertical mobility; that is, climbing the social or organisational hierarchy. Therefore status aspirations can influence achievement aspirations. The meaning of work can, for example, be derived from a job that includes increasingly more specialised responsibility, such as moving from a technical to a managerial function or becoming a specialist in a professional field.

Status aspirations can differ in different societal or occupational groups. Some regard the social status or class structure as a hierarchy, which anyone can enter provided that they have the necessary abilities and ambitions, while others regard it as a fixed aspect of life. Research shows that labourers see their situation in life as relatively fixed — they do not evaluate their careers in terms of status aspirations or in terms of developing abilities that could lead to free choice and being independent of 'bosses'. Their value system accentuates conforming to external authority, whereas non-labourers base their values on self-direction (Speakman, 1976).

Occupational or societal groups are primarily distinguished in terms of social class, for example the aristocracy versus the proletariat or the capitalistic class versus the working class, which are respectively associated with higher and lower status. Jencks (1989:44) maintains that these polarities have become irrelevant in post-modern information society. A 'cognitariat', referring to those who create and pass on information, has emerged. The cognitariat includes members of occupational groups, which are varied with regard to status, such as clerks, secretaries, technicians, teachers, programmers, managers, lawyers, writers, bankers and accountants. According to Jencks, they could be seen as constituting a new class, but are in effect beyond class. Seen this way, status becomes diffused in a meaning of work determined by socio-cultural change and organisation.

Autonomy

People who value autonomy consider a certain degree of freedom to organise their life and work as they want as important. They tend to seek for work situations in which they can be maximally free of organisational constraints to pursue their professional or technical competence. As a result, they often have compromised themselves less towards the organisation because they generally expect less of the organisation than others would do (De Vos et al, 2005). The value of autonomy corresponds to the notion of self-directedness as manifested in people's need for self-actualisation, competency and leisure.

Self-actualisation

Self-actualisation is a process of inner-directedness through which the individuals give expression to their intrinsic nature. It involves the tendency to enrich oneself by psychological growth and by seeing meaning in being (Frankl, 1969; Rogers, 1978). Characteristics associated with self-actualised people include autonomy in the sense of relative independence of the physical and social environment, democratic orientation, feeling of connectedness with others, freshness of appreciation, feeling at ease with complexity and ambiguity (Maslow, 1970). These characteristics can be condensed into a single quality, namely openness to experience (Mittelman, 1991).

'Openness' can also be associated with work that can facilitate self-actualisation — that is, intrinsic satisfaction in, for example, the form of a flexible organisational climate that provides challenge, autonomy, personal growth and complexity. As already indicated in the 1987 Meaning of Work (MOW) study, intrinsic aspects of work and self-actualisation in work are becoming increasingly important and are more important than physical conditions and working hours.

Self-actualisation contributes to one's sense of *identity*. Identity centres around questions such as 'What do I want to make of myself?' and 'What do I have to work with?' (Erikson, 1966:148). It therefore involves one's *self-concepts* and these self-concepts can find expression through self-actualisation in work. Through work, people identify themselves to themselves and to others and also see themselves as distinct or different from others. Manual workers, for example, may have a positive self-concept with regard to their superior physical strength that distinguishes them from other people.

Over time, self-concepts can change as work structures change. Women's work aspirations and expectations, for example, have evolved from a process of traditional female roles to a broad scope including management, professions and entrepreneurship and women participate increasingly in the labour market.

Self-concepts can be expressed or repressed in varying degrees by various work factors. If a self-concept is not congruent with the requirements of a job, work loses its meaning and an authentic part of the self is repressed. Crites (1969) cites as an example Fromm's view of individuals whose work demands a marketing orientation in which they have to meet the demands of the labour market by adapting themselves to the expectations and specifications of clients. In this process their abilities can be mere functional commodities which have to sell a product, but which are not integrated with their intrinsic self. If self-concepts are in harmony with job activities, individuals find intrinsic meaning in their work and feel a sense of being whole (Gibson, 2003).

Competency

Finding intrinsic meaning and a sense of identity in work amounts to a *career competency* that characterises the individual. De Fillippi and Arthur (1994) refer to it as a *knowing-why competency*, which together with *knowing-whom competencies* (which involve developing interpersonal and interorganisational communication networks) and *knowing-how competencies* (which involve acquiring skills and knowledge), contribute to the individual's cumulative competencies. These aspects of career competency are discussed in more detail in chapter 3.

The cumulation of competencies has become important in the contemporary milieu of job organisational and career structures. It serves a dual purpose by equipping the individual to adapt to change and contributing to satisfying organisational requirements.

The increasing practice of downsizing the workforce by termination and lay-offs in favour of hiring contingent workers, that is part-time, contract and seasonal workers, means that workers are hired by virtue of their existing capabilities, are not offered training by the organisation and do not become committed to a particular organisation. Thus individuals have to take responsibility for and find meaning in their performance *per se*. The organisation sees contingent workers as supplementing the skills of the core employees. Core employees are expected to be committed to the organisation. Yet, some core employees who have the required skills and abilities, for some or other reason, are not committed to using them in the organisation. Consequently, effective performance in their main job fluctuates (Coetzee and De Villiers, 2010).

Fluctuations in utilising competencies may be understood in terms of *three modes of career growth and development* which are, according to Boyatzis and Kolb (2000), recurrent and episodic throughout the individual's entire career life. These are the *performance mode*, which involves a quest for success and mastery of a job or skills and finding a standard of excellence in a particular work context to prove oneself worthy; the *learning mode*, which involves a quest for novelty and variety for self-improvement by acquiring new competencies beyond mere mastery of a job; and the *development mode*, which is a quest for meaning by seeking work/life events that will be conducive to finding a calling or purpose. The latter involves a holistic sense of self, in that integration of intellectual, emotional, spiritual and physical aspects is important. Individuals seek understanding of themselves in the context of values and future paths.

These three modes of career development are applicable when a career is seen as *lifelong development*. At a particular point in their careers, individuals will be functioning mainly in one of the modes, but since they are recurrent they may revert back to a former mode. Thus an individual who changes jobs may once again experience the excitement of mastering skills in the performance mode or be revitalised by novelty in the learning mode or discover a new meaning of work in the development mode.

Leisure

Leisure involves activities that fall outside the context of work and which are not necessarily instrumental in sustaining income, but can constitute ways in which work is connected to non-work. The relation between work and leisure is not clear-cut. Work may have a spillover effect on leisure as, if work has positive meanings for individuals, they will possibly have positive attitudes to leisure activities, whereas, if work is not meaningful to individuals, they will probably engage in non-work activities that are likewise meaningless. The reverse can also occur because satisfaction or dissatisfaction with leisure can have spillover effects on work (Brief and Nord, 1990).

Leisure can also compensate for lack of meaning in work activities. Various leisure roles can contribute to self-enrichment and to expressing parts of the personality that cannot find expression in work (Hage, 1995). The pursuit of leisure can create values distinct from work values. Consumerism, for example, which involves acquiring things, services and luxuries and using them up, can become a way of life in which consumption is a value in itself. Although consumption is necessary to sustain life, it can be devoid of meaning if it is merely a substitute for dissatisfaction of work. Applebaum (1992) sees consumption as a passive, transitory process in which things pass out of existence at different rates, while work is an active, creative process which, besides sustaining life, has value in itself for the fulfilment of human beings.

Ways of organising work influence the work/leisure relationship. Flexible working hours, a shorter working week or working year, more holidays and early retirement foster changing concepts of time. Time becomes meaningfully allocated to activities such as sport, hobbies, crafts, amusements, tourism and social relations. More leisure time means more time for interactions between members of families and, as the interactions occupy more time, communication between family members changes. Time together can mean that family members can 'play' together (Hage, 1995).

Leisure can involve activities that are work activities. Making things, selling things, providing services and running small-scale enterprises can provide meaning in terms of the value of the products and services themselves. Such activities can also acquire meaning in the context in which they are done. Pahl (1988) cites the example of a woman ironing — the activity may signify full-time work, part-time work, contractual work, entrepreneurship, play or consumption. Learning how to utilise free time effectively and realising that in utilising self-determined time individuals can create their own meaning, is also a means of coping with non-work in terms of unemployment (Ibarra, 2003; Wilpert, 1993).

Research conducted by Twenge (2010) showed that *Generation X* (those born between 1965 and 1976) and especially *Generation Y* (born after 1982 and also called *Millennials* or *GenMe*) rate work as less central to their lives, value leisure more and express a weaker work ethic than *Boomers* (those born between 1946 and 1964) and *Silents* (those born between 1922 and 1945).

Economic/material rewards

Economic/material rewards are generally associated with the need for job security, a good salary and good working conditions. Economic rewards are material or instrumental because their external nature is concrete and of practical use. People who value economic rewards strongly base their self-concept on material outcomes, in particular the amount of money they earn. They will search for work situations in which they perceive opportunities for financial rewards and will strive for money by requesting pay rises or by changing jobs for a higher paying position (De Vos et al, 2005). Studies have shown that extrinsic work values (eg salary) are higher in Generation Y and especially Generation X (Twenge, 2010).

As a work value, economic/material rewards have its origins in the Protestant work ethic of wealth accumulation and working hard. Even today, in spite of productivity gains, efforts by organised labour and technological advancement, contemporary society seems to regard paid work as important. In spite of having so many more comforts than the ancient societies, most westerners cannot seem to take the time to enjoy what they have achieved (Porter, 2004).

Some of the reasons why people keep on working hard despite living in more affluent times are the following (Porter, 2004):

◆ *Working to have things*: Increasingly work is both fed by and contributes to growing consumerism. Endless innovation and increasing standards have led people into an ever accelerating work-spend cycle. The role of work has become that of seeing the individual as only a pass-through for the money that facilitates more production of things on which to spend more money. As spending options and opportunities increase, the only way to keep the system balanced is for the individual to generate more earnings.

◆ *Working to not be left behind*: In an economic market that is characterised by uncertainty and increased competition, people lack confidence that the earnings they have today will be there for them tomorrow. Without the assurance of a steady income, people feel the need to get as much as possible now, just in case. In the knowledge-based economy, jobs seem more tentative today as compared to the past when one might have enjoyed security based on rank and seniority. Because knowledge-based jobs are currently where the most earnings are, many people opt for higher pay with the accompanying insecurities.

◆ *Working to confirm self-worth*: While work outcomes supply a scorecard to compare with others, it also serves as a basis for self-judgement. Because the economic/material rewards associated with work have become such an integral part of personal identity, the loss of work becomes loss of personhood. In an economic system that not only recognises value in those things that are easily marketed, placing high importance on economic/material rewards has led corporate decision-makers to put increasing profits before a concern for people. Individuals work more hours because the economic/material rewards associated with organisational success supply a sense of worth which offset the sacrifice of personal time. This results in organisations pushing for higher productivity by rewarding those willing to spend more time at work.

◆ *Working to use technology:* The availability of new technology has shifted into a belief that anything less than full utilisation is wasteful. Technology also seems to be governing how and when people work. Wireless technology enables broader access to people and keeping people connected electronically while away from the workplace. Along with personal computers at home, laptop computers and handheld devices increase the expectation for constant contact through e-mail. Although technology brings the potential to increase economic/material rewards along with improving people's lives it also carries ill effects in further linking people to their work. People feel compelled to take work home over the weekend, carry a computer on vacation and be available by cell phone, fax or e-mail, 24 hours a day, seven days a week.

Social values

Social values are centred around relations with people and are affective rather than material. It relates to the value of benevolence (having a concern for the welfare of others and preserving and enhancing the welfare of people). Having a sense that one belongs in society and work-family enrichment are two of the important needs associated with social values.

A sense of belonging in society

Despite the alienating negative effects of industrial development and advancement in technology, work can provide a basis for integrating people into society by providing connections between people. Sigmund Freud maintained that two important life functions are to work well and to love well (Hale, 1980). He regarded work as an essential aspect of life because it ties the individual to reality; that is, the reality of human society. Work involves membership of social groups, which is a means of satisfying the needs for affiliation and interpersonal contact and of providing social identity (Baruch, 2004; Hale, 1980).

Allied to belonging in society is the feeling of *being useful in society*. Workers may feel useful in terms of the content of their work — that is, the physical, mental or social tasks that they perform or in terms of the context of their work — that is, supplying ideas, services or products that are useful to society. Workers on any level can feel useful in society if the activity that they perform is accompanied by a sense of involvement in society. Research cited by Woollacott (1976) shows that mineworkers accept the fact that their work content is physically dirty, but they regard their work as a central productive activity. The personal meaning of work is thereby aligned to the context of a societal meaning of work. The interrelatedness of individuals' tasks or services with the tasks or services of others also extends the personal meaning of work to a broader collective meaning — individuals see their personal activities as *being part of the whole* (Harpaz and Fu, 2002).

Work-family enrichment

The notion that work and family roles can benefit one another has been referred to as enrichment. *Work-family enrichment* refers to the extent to which experiences in one role improve the quality of life in the other role, where quality of life includes high performance and positive affect (Greenhaus and Powell, 2006). The relationship between work and family is viewed as bi-directional: work can enrich family life (work-to-family enrichment) and family can enrich work life (family-to-work enrichment). Resources that promote work-family enrichment include: skills and perspectives, psychological and physical resources (self-esteem and hardiness), social-capital resources (information and influence), flexibility and material resources (money).

The availability of resources within a role enables that role to enrich another role, whereas the presence of stressors in a role causes that role to interfere with another role, which may lead to work-family conflict. Work-family conflict is produced by simultaneous pressures from work and family roles that are mutually incompatible (see also chapter 6). As a result of these incompatible role pressures, participation in one role is more difficult by virtue of participation in the other role.

While work-family enrichment expands people's capacity to achieve effectiveness and derive satisfaction from multiple life roles, work-family conflict limits this capacity (Greenhaus and Foley, 2007). The tendency of individuals to experience a higher level of enrichment than conflict is a positive sign that reflects a more optimistic view of the work-family interface (Greenhaus and Powell, 2006).

Work-family enrichment is increasingly becoming part of a work ethic that promotes a healthy work-life balance. This work ethic emphasises the importance of working smarter rather than harder and embracing apart from one's work, also one's other life obligations (Porter, 2004). Research conducted by McNall, Masuda and Nicklin (2010) found that the availability of flexible work arrangements, such as flexitime and compressed workweek schedules, have a significantly positive influence on work-to-family enrichment and people's job satisfaction.

Studies have shown that achieving a balance between home life and work life is becoming a higher priority for many people (Greenhaus and Foley, 2007). This conclusion is supported by Schein's (1996) and Coetzee and Schreuder's (2008) research findings which show that a growing number of people are endorsing a 'lifestyle' career anchor, where the individual's career is seen as an integral part of his or her total lifestyle (see also chapter 6). Studies conducted by Twenge (2010) indicate that Generation Y especially value work-life balance and flexible schedules.

Workplace spirituality

Workplace spirituality is the recognition that employees have an inner life that nourishes and is nourished by meaningful work that takes place in the context of community (Ashmos and

Duchon, 2000). Spirituality is the feeling individuals have about the fundamental meaning of who they are, what they are doing and the contributions they are making (Lips-Wiersma, 2002).

Spirituality represents the quest to unite one's inner life and outer world (ie, the community environment which provides constant connection to one's co-workers). The community environment is viewed as a place in which people can experience personal growth by being involved in meaningful work that gives a purpose to their life, where they feel valued for themselves as individuals and have a sense of working together with others for a common purpose (Crawford et al, 2009). The search for meaning and purpose and consequent realisation, provide an individual with a sense of alignment and order — a spiritual cohesiveness, which instills a sense of tightness and well-being (King and Nicol, 1999). Spiritual cohesiveness is a sense of wholeness, a oneness with who we are and an awareness of how we fit with our external environment (Csikszentmihalyi, 1990).

Because work is a central part of peoples' existence, much of this search for spiritual wholeness occurs within the context of the workplace. In the modern workplace many people are increasingly embarking upon a spiritual journey, seeking to discover their true selves through the search for a *higher purpose* that provides meaning to their lives (Conger, 1994; King and Nicol, 1999).

The spiritual journey is a process of *focusing within*. Gaining an awareness of one's higher self assists individuals to become truly actualised and find meaning and purpose in their work and their lives. This is the *individuation process* which produces both an interconnection with the higher self and a connection with others. The individuation process fosters a sense of order and balance in an otherwise chaotic life (DeLa Garca, 2004; King and Nicol, 1999).

Spirituality also represents the emerging values, priorities and skills related to the meaning that work represents in peoples' lives in the modern workplace. It is closely related to the emphasis on the *protean career* and the *internal (subjective) career* experiences of individuals. Spirituality refers to a set of whole-system, time-honoured, life-affirming and unifying *values* which enable the human spirit to grow and flourish. It includes *truth and trust* (which liberate the soul), *freedom and justice* (which liberate creative and co-creative genius), *creativity* (innovation), *collective harmony and intelligence* (wholeness and synergy), *deeper meaning and higher purpose* (Butts, 1999). Clear goals, total immersion in the activity, *transcendence of ego boundaries* and merging with the environment and high levels of motivation, self-confidence, ethics, competence, enjoyment and other *intrinsic rewards* characterise the work and life experiences of individuals who value spirituality as the core to their choice and reason for working (Csikszentinihalyi, 1990).

As the spiritual meaning of work is associated with seeking and living one's life purpose, work and one's career path are viewed as an *opportunity for self-expression, optimal development* and *contributing to the higher good of the group*, the *organisation, society* and the *planet. Authentic living* and mastering the art of ego-transcendence through peak experiences of joy, meaning, purpose, flow, inner harmony and wholeness in one's working life result in the experience of psychological career success (see also chapter 7).

Spirituality or higher purpose is a growing movement in the modern workplace and a rising priority for employees and should not be confused with organised religion. (Gibbons, 2000; Hankin, 2005). Spirituality in the workplace means creating an *environment of trust, respect and ethics* where diverse groups of individuals can do their best work.

The enlightened company lives these values and ethics every day. The modern workforce will increasingly demand something 'that is both greater than us and yet within us' (Hankin, 2005:90). According to Hankin (2005:90), spirituality at work will require the following from employees themselves, their co-workers and managers:

- acting with integrity and authenticity;
- treating people with respect;
- encouraging a work-life balance;
- connecting one's work to a larger sense of meaning and purpose;
- creating a culture which embodies core values/ethical principles;
- establishing decision-making processes that include reflection on the complex values at stake and consideration of justice for those affected; and
- doing business in a socially responsible manner.

When organisational leaders act in these ways, they honour the human spirit and create conditions where people can do their best work and contribute creatively to the human enterprise.

Conclusion

Work in the 21st century does not have a single meaning but can constitute *various meanings or a lack of meanings*. Changes in society, the workplace, work content and technology have changed perceptions of work, work values, work goals and work meanings. Living in a more chaotic and unpredictable world, people view their lives as being under constant construction. Meaning is especially found in relational settings, such as the workplace, where people engage in continuous sensemaking to discern what meaning their work holds for them.

Interpenetration of *different life roles* provides different meanings of work and non-work. Individuals have to adapt to and find meaning in several roles at the same time, including cultural roles, work roles, leisure roles and emotional roles revolving around family, friends, gender and age (Ibarra, 2003). Prevailing work values such as autonomy, economic/material rewards, social values and workplace spirituality have an important influence on the meaning of work.

The emerging importance attached to *spirituality* and authentic living (being true to one's higher self), is increasingly affecting the intrinsic meaning that work characterises in peoples' lives (see also chapter 7). Spirituality moves beyond self-actualisation — it is about transcending the ego-self to experience the soul-liberating sacred Oneness of Being. It is about embracing wider aspects of humankind, life, psyche and cosmos (Butts, 1999).

The modern work population is increasingly growing more diverse and more blended in terms of generation, race, ethnicity, nationality, religion, gender and sexual orientation. The mixing of different generations, races, ethnic groups and nationalities in the workplace requires greater awareness of differences, such as differences with regard to work goals and work values. Difference *per se* can provide meaning to work and, although it generates conflict, it can also foster sensitivity to different identities. Diversity implies variety and richness and appreciation of diversity carries with it the potential of mutual cross-fertilisation (Hankin, 2005; Twenge, 2010).

Diversity in the 21st century workplace will be evolutionary rather than revolutionary. Although employment equity and affirmative action are currently serving an important purpose by correcting historical inequalities, the successful companies of the future will increasingly embrace and embody a diverse workforce as a way to have a productive structure. Companies that pay attention to diversity and structure their organisations around it will find that they have far greater access to the best talent pool, higher profit margins and productivity levels (Hankin, 2005).

Review and discussion questions

1. What is the significance of work in people's lives? What is the significance of work in your life?
2. Briefly explain work as a central life interest.
3. Name and briefly describe the various work values that influence the meaning of work. Which of these values apply to the significance that work has in your life?
4. How do diversity and socio-cultural norms influence the significance of working?
5. Why is it important to understand the significance of work in people's lives?
6. Are power structures and status still relevant in today's rapidly changing environment? Discuss and explain.
7. Do the pre-industrial meanings of work still influence the significance of working in the 21st century? Discuss and explain.
8. Discuss how the work values that influence the meaning of working for individuals drive their needs for performance recognition, rewards, personal growth and development and choice of career; and need for work-life balance.
9. Excess working is still a matter of concern in contemporary society. How did the Protestant work ethic and advancement in technology influence the work ethic of working excessively?
10. How can the notion of work-family enrichment help people to create a healthy work-life balance? Do you think work-life balance is important? Give reasons for your answer.

11. What advice would you offer today's employees regarding the frustrations they may experience in the organisation due to unfulfilled needs relating to work being a central life interest for them?

Reflection activity

Read the following case studies of the careers of three different people. A table is provided at the end in which you can indicate the work values that influence the meaning of work that you think apply to the individuals in each of the case studies.

Corrie

As a paramedic in a large private organisation, I decided several years ago to forsake the wealth and luxuries afforded by a corporate 'suit-wearing' job for the subjective benefits attained through the provision of emergency care to those in need. Appalling salaries, difficult and dangerous working conditions and the rise in medico-legal litigation plague the industry. As paramedics, we provide care to the sick and injured 24 hours a day, seven days a week. However, we provide this care amidst scandalous articles that berate our profession and families of patients who verbally or physically abuse us out of sheer frustration. We are equally frustrated by the actions of the government and the sheer lack of resources and qualified people. We are also upset when we read about the wanton spending sprees and sheer wastefulness that government continues to approve.

For many people, the work we do seems strange. We work bizarre shifts (often through the night), climb into overturned cars or burning buildings, all without thought to the personal consequences for ourselves or the effects our work has on our families.

My career success has come from being the best that I can be. No matter what the time of the day or night, when we go to a call, we provide the very best care we can with the limited resources that are often available. I have continued my education both in the medical arena and with respect to human capital management so as to become a better paramedic. The more I know about emergency medicine, the more care I will be able to provide to my patients. The greater my level of human resource education, the better able I will be to provide for my family when I can no longer work in the pre-hospital environment.

I would describe myself as successful in my career because I feel great pride in the work that I do. The salary may not be wonderful and the working hours are strange, but ultimately I can go to bed every night knowing that I did something to help. Many people sit on their couches and complain about the state of our country — the crime, the poor healthcare, the disrepair of our schools and the inadequacy of the teachers. However, very few people get up off their couches and go and become a police reservist, a paramedic or a fire fighter. Their argument is that this work is too dangerous. This may be true, but how many people get involved in community projects that are rebuilding and repairing our country's schools or how many are willing to help teach our country's learners so that the future prosperity of the nation can be guaranteed?

I know that in my own little way I am making a difference to my country and its people every day. Career success is not about how much money you make or how many people you manage. Career success is about being true to yourself and following your dreams. Set your dreams high and know that as long as you persevere you will ultimately achieve your goal. There is no age limit on learning and you will always be able to hold your head high when you achieve the things you set out to do. That is true success...

Xolise

At the age of 48 I suddenly became weighed down with the woes of the world and personal dissatisfaction, which left me listless and at times anxious. I am a tenured professor who achieved some success but my spirit, which animated my career and home life, was flickering out. My energy was low and my attitude was negative with a 'why bother?' disposition. I spent more time learning computer programmes for online teaching and less time with students. I frequently spoke of the students as undisciplined and bothersome; another generation that expected a lot and gave too little. Co-workers heard me say that I felt tired, dull and emotionally empty.

My free time was spent watching videos while alone. I was divorced, my children were now grown and I spoke of myself as just another pebble in the universe. I was struggling to find new meaning in my work after having achieved, in my opinion, moderate success as an academic. I had set aside any aspiration of becoming a renowned scholar and after having failed to receive support from the university administration, I stopped applying for university-wide administrative roles. I questioned my life and work as a university professor and I saw retirement and an empty house looming on the horizon.

I decided to speak to a trusted career counsellor about my emotional experiences. Knowing that I had unconsciously accepted a deflated sense of the meaning in my life, the counsellor began to help me in my search for meaning. In our conversations, I confirmed that I had acquired extensive computer skills. The counsellor asked me a subsequent question: 'How might you use these computer skills to serve yourself and others?' In addition, the counsellor helped me to adopt a different outlook on and attitude towards my current circumstances. We both looked at the opportunities of the present and identified alternatives to boredom.

The counsellor prompted me with questions such as: 'Have you considered the needs of less computer literate people, the importance of supporting students who need to become excited by their education or the ways you can help your own family because of your love for them?' Since I had considered the students a serious burden at the beginning of my meetings with the counsellor, a request to teach one less class relieved some frustration and provided a space for the productive development of computer-aided teaching tools, something the department needed and which came to be a new source of meaning in my work.

I also decided to join a fitness club to feel better and to walk in the neighbourhood on a regular basis to meet new people. In addition, I also decided to design an online course, join the university in raising up and celebrating old and new courses and publications, work with students via distance learning, mentor new faculty members and to share my talents with any grown children or grandchildren. Although I suffered career and personal setbacks in my life, the counsellor helped me to recognise that the right attitude could help me find meaning in my life. Workplace fulfilment is not dependent on the work I do. The meaning I attach to the work and the value the work has for me, determine my sense of inner fulfilment.

I now understand that in the past I used adversity as leverage for success — I didn't measure success by how much I had achieved but by the obstacles I had overcome to get where I was. I now view life as a task. Life challenges us, but with a mission, a clear life purpose, life becomes fulfilling. By clarifying the purpose of my life and the meaning of my circumstances, I found new meaning and energy to live a fulfilling life. I now teach with greater motivation and peacefulness and the students respond positively to my efforts. I often return from my lectures with more energy than before I started with the lecture. Life is great!

(Adapted from King and Nicol, 1999)

William

I started out teaching medieval history at a private school in the US before switching jobs at age 38 to become an IT analyst. I took a leap, that's the best you can say. I took a leap and I found I landed in a very happy place.

Now, at the age of 50, I work for an international IT consultancy firm and in September 2008 visited South Africa for a symposium on new trends in the industry. I gave a presentation on the implications of the 2010 World Cup for telecoms in South Africa at the symposium.

Although I loved teaching I had to find better-paying work when I got married. We wanted to have children right away so my career search kind of disintegrated from 'let's find another teaching job' to 'let's just find a job'. I wrote this e-mail to all of my friends just begging them to find me anything.

A friend from university told me about an entry-level job as an IT analyst at a small market research company. So, at the age of 38 I applied for a position that a 22-year-old might have taken. I was interviewed and I'm pleased to think I did rather well — the manager offered me a position. He gave me a low offer but I'm very ashamed to say that after 13 years of teaching, with a master's degree in my subject, the offer he gave me was just about a lateral move.

But I never looked back. It's been extremely fortunate for me. I've just been very, very lucky. Analysing IT trends turned out to be a different world to discussing politics of ancient Rome.

The learning curve just keeps going up and up and up. I'm 12 years in and still feel like the roller coaster is on its first hill and not yet turned to come down yet.

I used to walk into the classroom and speak for 15 minutes at a time and I'd look at my students' faces and realise they had no idea what I was talking about.

And for the first month on the job at the market research shop, the phone would ring. I'd pick it up and say 'Good morning. William H' and they would talk for 10 minutes and I'd have no idea what they were talking about.

So it was the same process, this process of teaching about something complicated and trying to make it simple, but I was now closer to the barrel instead of the trigger of the gun.

Shortly after joining the firm, my daughter — who was three years old at the time — contracted cancer. We were looking at huge stretches in the hospital, lying next to her 24/7. In teaching, it would have been over, immediately. I'd have to resign or kill myself or something.

But with the job I had, I'd sneak off to the next room and unplug the phone and get a narrow band connection. I'd still deliver reports and everyone was extremely supportive. I worked from my daughter's bedside for 52 days in a row.

It's very strange how life works out. It turns out I needed a job that allowed me to be flexible, to work from home and working flexible work hours and that's what I stumbled into.

My daughter, now 11 years old, has gone six years without chemotherapy. The type of education I received prepared me well for my career change. The liberal arts training is supposed to be that we don't so much teach you 'what' but we teach you 'how'. And then you come out and you have this ability to pick it up on the fly.

(Adapted from Ferreira, 2008).

Work values	Corrie	Xolise	William
Advancement			
Power			
Status			
Autonomy			
Self-actualisation			
Competency			
Leisure			
Economic/material rewards			
Social values			
Sense of belonging in society			
Work-family enrichment			
Spirituality at work			

2

Changes in organisations: implications for careers

Learning outcomes

After studying this chapter you should be able to:

◆ explain the changes in organisations with regard to structure and workforce; and

◆ explain the various implications of the changing organisation for careers.

Introduction

Organisations all over the world are *changing rapidly*. These changes are in terms of structure, workforce composition, reward systems, service contracts, technology and information and are the results of technological, economic and political developments. Competition is increasing and the global knowledge economy brings new international competition. In South Africa small organisations are being established due to the entrepreneurial explosion. Large organisations are downsizing and contracting services out. Because of stiffer competition and a less stable business environment organisations are increasingly under pressure to do more with less and to be more flexible.

The following features seem to characterise today's modern organisations: they are without boundaries, knowledge-based, virtual, flexible in terms of functions and numbers, composed largely of specialists, flatter in structure, equipped with a shrinking workforce, active in learning, comprise less command-and-control, offer less defined jobs, outsource components, retain strong core competencies, employ a diverse workforce, committed to the development of their people, show a stronger attachment to a profession or project team and offer jobs and careers that are based on flexible work assignments (Baruch, 2006; Valcour, Bailyn and Quijada, 2007). Some characteristics of the traditional and modern workplace are illustrated in table 2.1 on p 28.

The Henley Centre — a dedicated forecasting centre — made the following *prediction about the changing nature of work* in 1998 (Furnham, 2000):

◆   A shorter working day amounting to about 25 working hours per week. Business will be open 24 hours per day and people will work three to four days per week. The remaining time will be spent on leisure and community work.

◆   As they become more advanced, personal computers will enable people to communicate audio-visually across the globe.

◆   About 25 per cent of all people will work from home and 10 per cent of the top companies will be virtual organisations.

◆   Careers will offer little job tenure and people will have to make provision for periods of unemployment.

Based on intensive research studies, Hankin (2005) reports the following *five future trends* that will have a major influence on the 21st century world of work:

◆   *An increasingly ageing yet active population:* Lifestyle changes and medical advances are keeping people alive and fit into their 90s; financial pressures and personal desire are keeping them working as well.

◆   *More varied household types:* The 21st century workforce will increasingly consist of female heads of households, same-sex partners, stay-at-home fathers, dual-income and dual-career families, unmarried couples and other arrangements. Company benefits programmes required to support and retain them are quickly evolving to make flexibility a key component.

◆   *Multi-generations working side by side:* Five generations — the Silent Generation (born between 1922 and 1945), the Baby Boomers (born between 1946 and 1964), Generation X (born between 1965 and 1976), the Baby Boom Echo (born between 1977 and 2000) and the Millennium Generation (born since 2000) will work side by side in the 21st century workplace. Each generation has competing needs, values, expectations and working styles. Successful companies will tap into the wisdom and experience of their older employees with the energy and stamina of the younger ones to create a powerful multi-generational workforce.

◆   *Growing diversity in the workplace:* The workforce is growing more diverse in terms of race, ethnicity, nationality, gender, religion and sexual orientation. Truly successful companies will have a corporate culture that embraces and embodies a diverse workforce as a way to have a productive structure.

◆   *Spirituality at work:* The workers of the 21st century are seeking a new focus on higher purpose in all phases of their lives — including the workplace. Employees will increasingly seek a spiritual component in the workplace, which includes personal growth, balance and meaningful purpose. Organisations that champion trust, individual respect and ethical conduct will build committed workforces and creative thinkers.

Table 2.1 *Differences between the traditional and modern workplace*

Traditional workplace	Modern workplace
◆ Stable environment, protected markets	◆ Dynamic, competitive environment, global unpredictable markets
◆ Production-driven	◆ Service-driven, technology-intensive
◆ Mechanistic, product, functional divisional structures	◆ Flat, network, cellular structures
◆ Hierarchical, multiple management levels	◆ Knowledge and information-technology-driven learning organisations
◆ Seniority-based, time-based promotions	◆ Strategic, collaboration with competitors
◆ Command and central management style	◆ Multi-cultural organisations
◆ Uni-dimensional career movements (linear)	◆ Small component of core employees, big component part-time, casual, contract staff
◆ Organisation responsible for individual career planning and development	◆ Empowerment of people
	◆ Competency-based outsourcing
	◆ Self-directed teams
◆ Individual loyalty to organisation for lifelong and steady growing employment	◆ Multi-directional career movements
	◆ Diminishing loyalty for organisation
	◆ Individual investment in employability
◆ Job security, job-for-life	◆ Increasing emphasis on work-life integration
◆ One or two career choices at early career age	◆ Career self-management
	◆ Life-long learning
	◆ Knowledge workers
	◆ Composite and customised careers
	◆ Repeated career choices at different age stages
	◆ Careers as learning cycles (several organisations)
	◆ Spirituality at work

Source: Adapted from Baruch (2004) and Thite (2001)

The Work Design Collaborative — an applied research consortium focused on defining and sharing knowledge and expertise related to the future of work — made *twelve predictions* regarding the changing nature of work in 2003 (Grantham and Ware, 2004).

These are listed in table 2.2.

◆ *Social bonds between worker and company will decrease:* Historically, workers have been subservient to corporations because companies owned the means of production, such as raw materials and factories. Individuals' livelihoods depended on companies for work; thus they formed close connections with their employers, often for life. These dependencies will increasingly decrease because large organisations are not as critical as they used to be for the creation of value in a knowledge-driven economy.

◆ *People (atoms) will combine teams (molecules):* People will become highly networked over the duration of individual projects. They will form up into 'molecules' composed of several people, stay together for a project, break apart and then recombine into new 'molecular' forms. In effect, this is like the Hollywood model in which actors, directors and producers come together for one project and then re-group for others. The average business project will last one year or less, with a multiple-year project being a rarity.

◆ *Back to guild structures:* Guilds and 'confederations' will return as the primary social organisational model for these smaller groups of people — indeed for most professional talent. Guilds will be responsible for recruitment of talent, some training (more like mentoring) and enforcing process-professional-quality standards. Guilds will be based on a common interest in a particular topic area or on common expertise, such as what we see in today's Screen Actors Guild.

◆ *Work will take place in a greater range of locations:* About 60 per cent of the workforce will work in multiple locations depending on the task at hand, the tools available and the requirements of the customer. The industrial model of everyone at the same place, same time (that was built on an 'economy of scale' principle) will begin to disappear. Work activities will be distributed across central offices (30 per cent of the time on average), remote locations (40 per cent of the time) and a variety of other community-based locations (30 per cent of the time).

◆ *Work will be spread out in time (not the eight-hour workday):* The 'normal' eight-hour workday will be spread across a fourteen-hour window to accommodate collaboration across continents, quality of life preferences and to enable workers and their families to be in sync with local community and educational activities.

◆ *Work will be more collaborative; less individualistic:* People will focus their work activities on their core competencies (what they do best) for approximately 80 per cent of their time. Everything else will be handed off to someone with complementary competencies. Individuals themselves will become less 'vertically integrated' and will grow loosely-coupled, collaborative networks to meet their needs that fall outside those core competencies. The remaining work time will be devoted to learning new skills and competencies.

◆ *Corporations will morph into confederations with shared liability:* Modern corporations are an artificial legal structure created within the past 100 years to minimise the risks associated with controlling large asset bases. The assumptions that have driven the development of corporate structures are no longer valid. Primary among these was the belief that large organisations were required in order to capitalise the large investments needed to acquire the means of production, such as factories and equipment. With the shift to knowledge work that kind of scale is not required for a large portion of the working population. Confederations of business clusters will instead move to the forefront. They will be held together by strategy and relationships, not by legal ownership of assets.

◆ *Developing and delivering work support structures will become a business in itself:* As the move towards individualism (ie free agency, microbusinesses) approaches 35 per cent of the workforce, the need for new and different workforce support structures will emerge as a new business opportunity. Companies, also referred to as 'agencies' in the contemporary business economy, will grow up to provide services such as marketing, administrative services, retirement-plan membership and group-health insurance to this growing population of workers. This business-support sector will evolve out of existing outsourced human resource operations in the 2006-7 timeframe.

◆ *The stars will be 'producers', not CEOs:* The 'cult of the CEO', which characterised the late 1990s, is waning. A small unit leader (a person whose major competency is the ability to build teams) will replace the CEO. Those front-line leaders will be the bridge between ideas and bringing products to market. These new executives will eschew the traditional trappings of corporate power, focusing instead on status and recognition among their team members as a prime motivator.

◆ *Success means mastering ambiguity:* The shift to knowledge and creativity as the source of value, coupled with the increasing velocity of nearly all-human activity, will make change and uncertainty a permanent condition. Work projects will begin with general goals and vision, but will continuously morph as the projects rolls on, responding to external influences. This ongoing evolution means that project budgets will be moving targets, deadlines will be somewhat arbitrary and final design will be impossible to predict. Managers of certainty will evolve into leaders of ambiguity — or be left behind.

◆ *Value will be embedded in social capital:* The key value added by individuals in a work effort (their brand equity) will be the amount of social capital they bring to bear on the tasks at hand. Their social capital will be the extent and strength of social bonds that exist within their social networks. These networks are now evolving from older village – or office-based models, beyond even the 'work unit' to that of a completely networked individual. Status will be individually defined; social control will be more internalised. Organisations must recognise that the value in individuals will come through their relationships and social capital; and employers will need to develop powerful but co-equal relationships with employees as well.

◆ *Live to work to work to live:* The social context of the relationship between workers and employers will shift from one based on earning a livelihood to one that focuses on enhancing the quality of life for the individual. This trend will lead to a redefinition of the implied social contract between individuals and companies that has been a source of stability for both parties for many years.

Furnham (2000:253) summarises the characteristics of work in the 21st century as follows:

Changes in the workforce, the hours of work, but more particularly technology, mean that fortunate workers of the future may have more choice, flexibility and certain benefits than those of today. They will not, however, enjoy job security, stability or much face-to-face contact with peers. They will, more than ever, be responsible for their own futures and have to develop, update and market their own skills portfolio. The able, educated and ambitious are likely to thrive in this environment; however, the less able and educated could easily fall into an employment underclass.

Table 2.2 *Twelve predictions regarding the changing nature of work*

1.	Social bonds between worker and company decrease
2.	People combine into teams
3.	Back to guild structures
4.	Work will take place in a greater range of locations
5.	Work is spread out in time
6.	Work is more collaborative, less individualistic
7.	Corporations morph into confederations with shared liability
8.	Developing and delivering work support structures are a business in itself
9.	The stars are 'producers', not CEOs
10.	Success means mastering ambiguity
11.	Value embedded in social capital
12.	A shift from live to work to work to live and to enhance the quality of life

The 21st century workforce

In the 21st century, companies will face many generations active in the workforce simultaneously, mainly due to increased longevity and people looking to remain on the job years past what used to be considered retirement age. According to Hankin (2005), by 2050 four to five generations will be working together in full force. These generations of workers will provide unprecedented opportunities for development and profitability. Finding and keeping the best and the brightest from all the generations will be the challenge of the 21st century. Human resource management strategies and policies will also be affected by the *multigenerational workforce*. Hankin (2005:48) describes the *five workforce generations* as follows:

The Silent Generation: Born 1922 to 1945

The Silent Generation is the most traditional: working fathers, nuclear families and traditional work ethics. They tend to be highly disciplined, hardworking and loyal employees who play by the rules. They are the wisdom keepers and natural workplace leaders and mentors (even if they do not hold managerial positions).

The Baby Boomers: Born 1946 to 1964

The Baby Boom Generation took the steadily increasing affluence that their parents were enjoying after World War II and ran with it. Education became a top priority. Many of the Boomers were raised in homes enjoying economic prosperity and a strong nuclear family. Most of their mothers were homemakers; most of their fathers were the family breadwinners. Boomers are surrounded by issues from elder parents on one end and adult children on the other. At the same time, more and more Boomers are being put in the position of needing to parent their parents, who are elderly and in declining health. This is quite relevant to employers whose Boomer employees face stresses, time demands and money constraints, all of which require company support and understanding.

Generation X: Born 1965 to 1976

Generation X is considered a generation raised with even more of a silver spoon and a sense of entitlement and much less political interest than the Baby Boomers. As a result, they are often viewed as slackers with less involvement in and more pessimistic views about politics and other issues. On the other hand, some Generation Xers are hard-core traditionalists — optimistic, hardworking, with a narrow-minded belief in gender roles and stereotypes.

The high rate of divorce and increased number of working mothers impacting on the Generation Xers led to them being often characterised by traits of independence, resilience and adaptability. Other traits of this group include working well in multicultural settings.

Baby Boom Echo (Generation Y): Born 1977 to 2000

The Baby Boom Echo, also referred to as Generation Y, is entering the workforce now and will be in force through the first quarter of the 21st century. The Baby Boom Echo is seen as a largely self-confident group. They like to set goals and go for them. They are multi-taskers and team players. High-tech is second nature to them. They desire structure and direction in the workplace. A natural affinity is developing between the Silent Generation and this generation. The indication for employers is that a mentor relationship between a Senior and an Echo would be a good match.

Millennium Generation: Born since 2000

The Millennium Generation or Millennials, refers to the babies being born since the turn of the 21st century. Historical, political and entertainment events will influence them in major ways. According to Hankin (2005), the Millennials who will enter the workplace will be comfortable with diversity. They will expect equal pay as an everyday occurrence and will be flexible and interested in carving out their own niche both at home and at work.

Successful companies will proactively seek *generational diversity* in their employee base for a number of reasons. These include an appreciation of the corporate and life wisdom of the older workers, valuing of the fresh ideas, independence and fearlessness of younger workers and a realisation of the importance of opening up opportunities across the generations to tap into the individual wisdom and unique skills the different generations have to offer. The five generations will be the vital and active marketplace from which the customers of companies will come. An employee base that mirrors the marketplace is largely accepted and expected to be more effective.

Workforce distribution/composition

One result of South Africa's first democratic election in April 1994 was a major change in the composition of the labour force. Today, South Africa's workforce comprises more women, is more representative of all races and the number of working couples is increasing. Females are becoming a substantial part of the labour force. At Unisa, 59 per cent of the students in 2009 were female (mostly black), where they had previously always been in the minority. This means more qualified females will be entering the labour force in due course. The general trend, nationally and internationally, is that new entrants to the job market are mostly female and that the majority of families are dual-career families. In South Africa, employment equity and the resultant affirmative action of historically disadvantaged groups is a reality. People from these groups are increasingly becoming part of the labour force.

Implementation of the Employment Equity Act has changed the face of the South African workforce significantly. The distribution between employees employed by the formal sector and those employed by the informal sector is changing rapidly. The composition and distribution of the South African labour force are affected by a number of variables, the most important one probably being the impact of HIV/Aids. It is impossible to predict accurately the future impact of the Aids pandemic. Best and worst scenarios were put forward by Van Aardt (1999). He predicted that by 2020, should a best scenario be applied (HIV/Aids occurrence low, fertility high), 29.7 million people would be economically active, of which only 14.4 million would be employed in the formal sector. This means that by 2020 only 48 per cent of the economically active population will have formal job opportunities, while more than 60 per cent of all formal job opportunities will not be permanent positions but will be casual, contract or franchise employment opportunities. Should a worst scenario be applied (HIV/Aids occurrence high, fertility very low) 19.4 million people will be economically active, of which 9.3 million (48 per cent) will have formal job opportunities. The latter is probably the most realistic scenario. Van Aardt (1999) posited that there is little hope in South Africa of a significant increase in labour demand for permanent formal-sector employees during the next two decades, while it can be expected that the number of informal sector contracts and casual opportunities will grow significantly.

Van Aardt's trend predictions seem to corroborate those in the Department of Labour's 2009 labour market survey report. South Africa's human development index declined between 1992 and 2005 and is the lowest when compared with other developing countries (such as Botswana, Brazil, Mexico, Malaysia and Thailand). The human development index (HDI), developed in 1990, is used extensively in the debates on the level of human development of a country. The downward trend in South Africa's HDI is largely as a result of the fall in the life expectancy index which is highly sensitive to the impact of HIV/Aids.

According to the Bureau of Economic Research report (2006, cited in merSETA, 2008), the HIV/Aids prevalence in the metal products, machinery and equipment manufacturing sector (merSETA) is among those on the high levels with about a 16.1 per cent prevalence rate in 2005. It is projected that by 2010 the sector will have about 2.4 per cent of its workforce sick with HIV/Aids-related illnesses and with mortality rates of about 1.2 per cent. About 48 per cent of companies in the sector complain that HIV has affected output levels; 42 per cent contend that they have lost highly skilled personnel due to HIV/Aids-related illnesses and deaths, while 58 per cent hold that HIV/Aids has contributed to lower productivity through sick leave and frequent visits to the hospital.

Due to the apartheid legacy of unequal educational opportunities and unequal employment opportunities, the racial profile of employment in South Africa remains skewed. African workers remain under-represented in certain high skill occupations. There is a much greater representation of Africans in the informal sector of the economy and a very low percentage of whites and Indians in elementary non-skilled occupations. The proportion of African workers with relatively low educational levels (up to and including Grade 12 or matric) remains large and should form a focal point in attempts to link skills development and equity. Whites and to some degree Indians are still over-represented in high skills and high salaried jobs.

However, current trends indicate that whites are not as prevalent among young professionals, implying that one can expect that over time there will be a move towards an overall profile that is more representative of the country's population. An analysis of Labour Force Survey data for 2001 to 2007 also shows an upward trend of around 20 000 per annum in the numbers of African people holding a qualification in the manufacturing, engineering and technology areas (Department of Labour, 2009).

Unemployment remains the key challenge for transformation of the South African labour market. Providing training, especially to the historically disadvantaged unemployed youth, could enhance their prospects of accessing the labour market. Such an intervention can also promote social cohesion and build the skills base from which accelerated growth and development can be launched. Further, a significantly higher burden of unemployment is borne by women and youth (particularly the 20–24 year age group) in the labour market (Department of Labour, 2009).

The National Skills Development Strategy and Employment Equity Act are legislative mechanisms, put in place by the South African Government, to correct these gender and race inequalities in the workplace.

Implications of the changing organisation for careers

The following advert already appeared in the mid-nineties on the notice-board of a company that experienced lay-offs. This illustrates the reality of the new work environment and should inspire individuals to take control of their careers (Hall and Mirvis, 1995:326):

We can't promise you how long we'll be in business

We can't promise you that we won't be bought by another company

We can't promise you that there will be room for promotions

We can't promise that your job will exist until you reach retirement age

We can't promise that the money will be available for your pension

We can't expect your undying loyalty and we aren't sure we want it

The above realities would necessarily influence the traditional working relationship in which the employee offered loyalty, trust, conformity and commitment to the organisation in return for job security, promotional prospects and training opportunities. A different working relationship, which emphasises *individual responsibility* and a *broader range of skills*, is becoming increasingly evident. The characteristics of the contemporary working relationship are (Baruch, 2004; Millward and Brewerton, 2001; Thite, 2001):

◆ less security;

◆ individuals managing their own careers;

◆ performance-related pay;

◆ a flexible employment scenario;

◆ little trust between employee and employer; and

◆ performance being substantially rewarded.

The implications of the present changing work environment for careers and career management are examined in table 2.3.

Table 2.3 *Implications of the changing organisation for careers in the 21ˢᵗ century*

Protean careers	A career shaped and managed by the individual. It consists of all the person's varied experiences in education, training, work in several organisations and changes in occupational field and is characterised by a high degree of mobility, self-reliance and internal career thinking.
Boundaryless careers	A career characterised by flexibility, mobility and movement between different global-organisational contexts.
Composite careers	Having more than one working role or holding more than one form of employment.

Entrepreneurial careers	Choosing self-employment as a career option which could include establishing and managing one's own business.
Career progress and success redefined	Career progress refers to individuals' experiences of career growth which may include moving upward, increasing competence and expertise and gaining broader experience across multidirectional career movements. Career success refers to the objective and subjective (psychological) sense of achievement and well-being individuals experience regarding their careers.
Lifelong learning	The process by which one acquires knowledge, skills and abilities throughout one's life and career in reaction to and in anticipation of changing performance criteria.
Career resilience and career adaptability	The ability to adapt to changing circumstances by welcoming job and organisational changes, looking forward to working with new and different people, having self-confidence and being willing to take risks.
New knowledge and skills required	The knowledge economy and a more complex and differentiated organisation result in the employment of more specialists and knowledge workers.
New employment relationships	Changes in the workplace are characterised by a change in employment relationships. These relationships include long-term insiders, short-term insiders, long-term outsiders and short-term outsiders.
Employability	A person's value in terms of future employment opportunities, which is determined by the accumulation of knowledge, skills, experience and reputation, which can be invested in new employment opportunities as they arise.
Individualism more valued than organisational loyalty	Individuals become proactive career agents who take responsibility for their career development. Their loyalty is now redefined in terms of their employability and professionalism.
Diverse needs of employees	Socio-demographic and generational diversity in the workplace require from workplaces to offer career development support programmes that address the needs of an increasingly diverse workforce.
Traditional male and female roles are being challenged	The shift to non-traditional family structures is challenging gender stereotypes in the workplace.

The new psychological contract	The mutual expectations and satisfaction of needs arising from the relationship between individual employees and their organisations. The contemporary psychological contract is a partnership relationship characterised by conditional attachment arrangements.

Protean careers

It is suggested that careers will have to become more protean. The term protean is taken from the name of the Greek god Proteus, who could change shape at will (Hall, 1976). The protean career is defined as follows:

The protean career is one that emphasises a self-directed approach to the career and a career that is driven by one's own values (Briscoe and Hall, 2006). The protean career is therefore a process which the person, not the organisation, is managing. It consists of all the person's varied experiences in education, training, work in several organisations, changes in occupational field and so forth. The protean career is not what happens to the person in any one organisation ... In short, the protean career is shaped more by the individual than by the organisation and may be redirected from time to time to meet the needs of the person (Hall and Mirvis, 1995b:333).

The protean career is a mindset about the career that is characterised by the following (Briscoe and Hall, 2006; Hall, 1996b):

◆ psychological success;
◆ self-direction;
◆ freedom and autonomy;
◆ choices are based on personal values;
◆ being managed by the individual;
◆ a series of identity changes;
◆ continuous learning;
◆ chronological age being unimportant;
◆ employability and work challenges provided by the organisation;
◆ a high level of self-awareness;
◆ personal responsibility;
◆ freedom and growth being valued;
◆ a high degree of mobility; and
◆ internal career thinking being emphasised.

This means that the present *contract is with the self,* whereas in the past, the contract was with the organisation (Hall, 1996a). In its extreme form, the person's attitude toward his or her career reflects a sense of calling in his or her work — that is an awareness of a purpose that gives deep meaning to the career (Hall and Chandler, 2005).

The positive potential of the protean career is described as follows:

> *The relationship is still win-win, but is more equal. The employee does not blindly trust the organisation with his or her career. The organisation does not assume an unassumable burden. The tremendous energy once required to maintain relationships can be turned to doing good work. The common ground, the meeting point, is not the relationship, but the explicit task. This task-focused relationship is not only healthier for the individual and the organisation, it also facilitates the diversity necessary for future survival, since the emphasis is on the task, not on the gender, race or traits of the person performing the task (Hall, 1996b: 11).*

The protean career offers *three forms of flexibility*. Firstly, it provides new ways of career thinking. Instead of considering traditional concepts of the career as a linear progression, the protean concept suggests a *flexible career course* characterised by moves between different lines of work. Secondly, it provides flexibility in terms of career space. The *career space is enlarged*, allowing workers to *integrate work and family issues* as the two are not treated as separate domains. Thirdly, the protean career allows workers to *work from home*, either informally or as part of a formal home work programme (Hall,1996a).

In essence, the protean career concept encourages workers to think differently about the relationship between employer and employee. In the past, the organisation was the figural element with the individual as background, but in the protean career the person is the figure and the organisation the background. The organisation should provide the environment or context in which individuals can pursue their careers (Hall,1996a).

Not everybody adapts to the protean career. The lack of external control and the increased individual responsibility often frightens people. Some individuals suffer when they operate independently in such an environment. For mid-career employees this career option can be frightening after spending many years in one career tied to a single organisation and then suddenly finding themselves on their own, expecting to adapt to new requirements (Baruch, 2004; Hall,1996b). New career management competencies are often required and the organisation's supportive role in this regard is essential.

Obviously, elements of the traditional career will remain as the present environment still complements their sentiments and values. A mixed approach will probably emerge as more and more careerists become 'proteans'. It is anticipated that the protean group will become larger as more people adapt to the demands of the environment (Baruch, 2004).

Boundaryless careers

Akin to the protean career concept is the view of a *boundaryless career* (Briscoe and Hall, 2006). It is contrasted with the traditional or organisational view of a career in which the organisation plays host to individuals' careers. According to Tams and Arthur (2006), the boundaryless career involves a physical or psychological movement away from the current employer. In the boundaryless career, individuals have self-ownership of their careers. They manage their careers in a relatively autonomous fashion between jobs, companies and professions and, in the process, their employment value is increased (Inkson, 2008).

Sullivan and Arthur (2006) note that the mobility inherent in boundaryless careers may take place between jobs, companies, occupations and countries. The boundaryless view of careers mirrors aspects of globalisation, which erases the boundaries between nations and to flourish in this new environment the individual has to become self-reliant (Gunz et al, 2000).

In the contemporary career environment, employability is determined by performance and flexibility, the individual works for multiple firms, multiple networks of associates and peer-learning relationships are developed, on-the-job training is provided, success is measured by meaningful work and milestones in the career are learning-related (Cascio, 2003).

An important feature of this career environment is that careers cannot be constrained by organisational boundaries. Individuals can move between different organisations if they have transferable knowledge, skills and abilities, for example, an electronic engineer can move between several computer firms (Cascio, 2003; Gunz et al, 2000).

In practice the dichotomy between traditional careers and boundaryless careers may not be as clear as in theory. As a so-called boundaryless career merges with various organisational contexts without boundaries, new structures in the career emerge that again present boundaries. 'Boundarylessness' cannot necessarily be applied to all occupations and work settings — it may be applicable to technical occupations, knowledge and professional occupations, but not necessarily to the boundaries that affect middle-managers in medium-sized organisations. Although boundaries in organisations and in individual careers have declined, individuals will inevitably encounter external, unobvious or subjective boundaries within themselves that define career context, choices and development (Inkson, 2008).

Composite careers

In the 21st century world of careers, individuals are likely to experience themselves as having more than one working role and holding more than one job — implying that they will have to manage their time between these different roles, companies, locations, clients, teams and schedules.

Work in a boundaryless, de-jobbed organisation is repackaged into projects and assignments and individuals are likely to be doing several at once. This composite work life forces individuals to manage their own time and efforts in the way a self-employed person with several different clients does (Bridges, 1995).

The composite career is a way to express those parts of one's multiple possible selves that are excluded from the narrow world of one-job-for-life. For example, Jackie is a professionally registered dietician with her own practice. She is also a successful painter and photographer. In her case, her trained profession is a sideline and her creativity is the vocation. She leaves her studio two mornings a week to drive in to an office she shares with a medical health clinic to see her patients. As a professionally registered dietician, she kept her practice going while she made the transition to her artwork. Now that her art sells well, she keeps the practice going to give her the opportunity to express all of her talents and skills (Coetzee, 2007).

Not all ventures ever develop significant financial value or even become standalone businesses. This may be almost invisible to the people at the organisation where the person has a regular job. For example, an executive accountant in a large company is a tax consultant on the side, although few of his colleagues know it.

Whatever the motivation and the circumstances, the composite career is a significant part of today's work world. Even after the job became a dominant work paradigm in the industrial era (as explained in chapter I), upper- and lower-income people kept their composite careers — the latter because they needed them to survive and the former because their mix of leisure, social responsibility and wide experience gave them multiple points of concern and influence. Only the middle-income people gave up the composite career and today even they are returning to it (Bridges, 1995).

In the 21st century, people create careers across a wide range of possibilities. They can no longer afford to limit themselves to only taking or passing up jobs. People are much better off composing their careers according to the myriad possible selves that they could be by expressing and using the unique skills and talents that they have in various creative ways. For this reason, workers in the 21st century will stop thinking of themselves as 'having' a job. They will increasingly think of themselves as 'experimenting' with work opportunities which allow them to discover more about themselves and live meaningful lives — lives that are in line with their unique life purposes (Coetzee, 2007).

Entrepreneurial careers

Self-employment requires a great willingness to take action, experiment and constantly innovate. Decisive and innovative actions are required to respond to changing market conditions on a continuous basis. The self-employed person can be regarded as an entrepreneur. For this reason, self-employment is often referred to as the entrepreneurial career.

Entrepreneurship (or following an entrepreneurial career) means managing a business of one's own that requires personal sacrifice, innovation and the taking to create something of value to society.

Successful entrepreneurs have the following *skills and aptitudes* (Greenhaus, Callanan and Godshalk, 2010):

- they have developed good persuasive powers;
- they are good problem-solvers and generally good decision-makers;
- they know how to manage their time as they have developed the habit to be organised and systematic;
- they know how to handle information effectively and can resolve conflict;
- they are also willing to take calculated and intelligent risks; and
- they have developed effective business management skills.

Successful entrepreneurs generally display the following *qualities and personality traits:*

◆ a need for autonomy and independence;
◆ a need for achievement, for being successful;
◆ high initiative and self-leadership;
◆ flexibility;
◆ creativity;
◆ abilities to cope with adversity and change;
◆ self-confidence;
◆ commitment to their goals and life purpose;
◆ optimistic mindsets;
◆ high levels of motivation; and
◆ positive outlook on life.

The typical *attitudes and values* of successful entrepreneurs are the following:

◆ an internal locus of control (a belief that they can create their own destiny);
◆ a high level of responsibility; and
◆ a high value on money and status, creativity and honesty.

It is a myth that entrepreneurs are born. People can become entrepreneurs. Entrepreneurial qualities and skills can be learned and improved upon.

As entrepreneurs, people should also assess how self-employment and owning a business affect their families and their family responsibilities. If important needs are not met, then changes may become necessary, which could even be leaving the world of entrepreneurship.

Becoming an entrepreneur means experiencing a career that is different from the traditional job-in-an-organisation notion. The entrepreneurial career is marked by extensive personal commitment to the success of the business, acceptance of the unpredictability of the business venture outcomes, an orientation towards action and decisiveness, the simultaneous performance of multiple-work roles (for example owner, worker, salesperson, accountant) and a willingness to accept risk. Because of these distinctive characteristics, entrepreneurs generally find substantial challenge and stimulation in their work, realising that they must deal with the unpredictability and instability that go hand in hand with the entrepreneurial career (Feldman and Bolino, 1996).

Increases in downsizing have led more laid-off workers to consider self-employment as a career option. According to a study conducted by Feldman and Bolino (2000), unemployed workers in the United States of America are, for example, about twice as likely to start new businesses as employed workers. Men currently constitute the majority of owners of small businesses, but the percentage of women entering these independent employment career paths is rising steadily. The number of women-owned sole proprietorships, partnerships and small businesses has increased from 4.1 million to 5.9 million over a five-year period, an increase of 43 per cent. As females become a greater percentage of the workforce, self-employment becomes more attractive to them as a means of balancing work and family demands. Also, some women may enter self-employment to avoid discrimination in the workplace.

The key reasons people pursue self-employment are to achieve greater autonomy, to increase flexibility in their lives, to generate wealth and to escape organisational bureaucracies. However, not all self-employed people experience success or derive satisfaction from the career path. Some of the challenges that self-employed people have to face are balancing the desired job autonomy with the loss of social interaction, which often accompanies it and dealing with the number of responsibilities of being self-employed (Feldman and Bolino, 2000).

Most entrepreneurs cope with these challenges by starting a small business with a spouse or former colleague or a 'paired business' to avoid partnership problems. They also increase their networking activity in professional associations and local business groups like the Chamber of Commerce and operate the business from a work office rather than from home. Other challenges that entrepreneurs have to deal with are having less time off and vacation time and even spending time with their own families.

Although the entrepreneurial career offers opportunities for greater wealth, it also has the potential for financial losses. Many entrepreneurs therefore often start out their self-employment part-time to grow the business before entering self-employment full-time. Some entrepreneurs have the security of a spouse who works full-time in a job with a steady income and fringe benefits. A major challenge is often uncertain and uneven cash flow that goes hand in hand with a business. Significant capital at particularly the beginning of a business venture or a steady cash flow in its early months is critical to business survival. This just reminds us that proper career planning is critical in contemplating the entrepreneurial career and achieving the success that one aspires to. Effective career planning must take into account the challenges that one will have to face when pursuing the entrepreneurial career (Greenhaus et al, 2010).

Career progress and success redefined

Career success (see also chapter 3) is not only characterised by vertical progress and by mastering a job. Psychological success, the feeling of achieving personal goals and having a general sense of well-being about one's career, is becoming the criteria for career success. The career is more cyclical, 'reskilling' is required and lateral rather than upward career moves are becoming the order of the day (Baruch, 2004). In order to survive in this environment, employees need to base their feeling of security on processes rather than on structures, on skills instead of job titles and on the satisfaction experienced from fulfilling a certain role rather than advancing up the career ladder. This approach can lead to career growth and to the individual becoming indispensable to the organisation. The traditional view of the career path (moving upward) is being replaced by the notion of moving easily across functional boundaries, thus emphasising the importance of multiple skills (Baruch, 2004). The value of the projects on which individuals work becomes more important than their level in the organisation and growth in their profession is perhaps more relevant than becoming managers (Woodd, 2000; Thite, 2001).

Career success is further assessed by the amount of learning that has taken place over a period, outputs instead of inputs and by the marketable skills of the individual. Technical specialisation, cross-functional and international experience, collaborative leadership, self-managing skills and flexibility are critical factors to future career success (Holbeche, 2000; Khapova, Arthur and Wilderom, 2007).

Career success can be increased if individuals do something they feel passionate about and if new career goals are achieved. Continuous self-examination results in new career aspirations and the effective management of time ensures the attainment of career goals (Coetzee, 2007).

As stated earlier, the above are sometimes strange concepts for employees and not always accepted, but as more and more individuals become 'proteans' and achieve success, others will also be encouraged to redefine their career progress and success (King, 2001). Organisations can help employees to regard activities such as job rotation and lateral moves — characteristics of the protean career — not as failures but as signs of career success (Baruch, 2004).

Lifelong learning

Lifelong or continuous learning — an important feature of the protean career — is a crucial requirement for employees at all levels, as changes are occurring in virtually all jobs and new skills and knowledge are required. 'Continuous learning is the process by which one acquires knowledge, skills and abilities throughout one's career in reaction to and in anticipation of, changing performance criteria' (London and Mone, 1999:199). In order to live up to new expectations, stay current in the labour market, be able to change careers and organisations more often, adapt to new situations easily and work in new relationships with the organisations, employees must become perpetual learners (Baruch, 2004). Employees who cannot adapt to this kind of change will probably find themselves sidelined by the organisation at an early age.

Individual learning is important for obtaining individual goals and an important source of competitive advantage for organisations. Self-development can help individuals realise their career aspirations and increase their life satisfaction (Sinclair, 2009). Lifelong learning is closely related to the protean career and Sternberg's notion of successful intelligence. Sternberg (2003:138) regards *successful intelligence* as the ability to attain one's goals in life, within one's socio-cultural context:

◆ by adapting to, shaping and selecting environments;
◆ through the recognition of and capitalisation on strengths;
◆ through the recognition of and compensation for or correction of weaknesses; and
◆ via the interaction of analytical, creative and practical abilities.

The notion of successful intelligence suggests that people can attempt to select life goals and achieve these goals in accordance with their own strengths and weaknesses. They can also develop their strengths and make up for their weaknesses in ways that allow them to succeed in attaining their chosen life goals.

The organisation can foster continuous learning in the following ways (London and Mone, 1999; Robbins and Judge, 2010):

◆ by creating a *culture of continuous learning* in the organisation, for example by encouraging ongoing innovation and experimentation through networking via the computer as well as through person-to-person contact and by team building across different hierarchies in the organisation with the focus on projects rather than functions;

◆ by establishing a *transfer of training climate* in which knowledge or skills are acquired at training courses and reinforced when they are applied in the organisation;

◆ by giving *constructive feedback* which addresses the causes of the individual's performance correctly and which is fair, helpful and considerate to the person and not merely aimed at getting the job done by the employee;

◆ by *managing performance*, by establishing directions for future development and by future job analyses that assist the employee in identifying dimensions of leadership and management, qualities which become increasingly important as work structures change;

◆ by focusing on *professionalism* to enhance excellence in the employee's own area of expertise; preparing employees for future jobs so that they can be re-employed by other organisations in the event of downsizing; and

◆ by *retraining displaced workers* through equipping them with coping skills as well as new skills and knowledge.

Career resilience and career adaptability

In order to survive in the present working environment individuals must develop resilience. *Resilience* can be defined

> as a pattern of psychological activity which consists of a motive to be strong in the face of inordinate demands, the goal-directed behaviour of coping and rebounding (or resiliency) and of accompanying emotions and cognitions. It is dynamically influenced by both internal characteristics of the individual and various external life contexts, circumstances and opportunities (Strümpfer, 2003:9).

Career resilience is described as the *ability* to adapt to changing circumstances. The development of career resilience as a career competency has become crucial and could become a much sought-after competency for careerists (Fourie and Van Vuuren, 1998).

Taking charge of one's own career requires career resilience. Individuals who are career resilient contribute skills aligned with business needs, are dedicated to continuous learning and committed to personal excellence, have an attitude that is focused but flexible and deliver solid performance in support of organisational goals for as long as they are part of the organisation (Collard, Epperheimer and Saign, 1996:17).

Career adaptability is closely related to career resilience and refers to individuals' *readiness* to cope with changing work and working conditions. Savickas (2005) conceptualises adaptive individuals as those who become *concerned* about their future as a worker and then take *action* to increase their *personal control* over their vocational future. Adaptive individuals are *proactive* by displaying *curiosity* and exploring possible selves and future scenarios. They also seek to strengthen their *confidence* (or self-efficacy) to pursue their aspirations.

To facilitate growth towards career resilience and adaptability, the following are suggested by Zheng and Kleiner (2001):

◆ take charge of one's career. realise that taking responsibility for a career is an ongoing process, not an event;

◆ develop people skills to improve interactions with others;

◆ sharpen communication skills;

◆ discover and adapt to changes;

◆ be flexible;

◆ embrace new technologies;

◆ keep learning;

◆ clear up misconceptions about the requirements of the company or industry when considering a new job or industry;

◆ research the options; and

◆ develop new capacities — specialised knowledge and flexible and general skills.

In light of the above, the measurement of career resilience has become important. The *Career Resilience Questionnaire,* developed by Fourie and Van Vuuren (1998), can be successfully applied within the South African context. Four characteristics, which seem to be relatively independent of one another, namely belief in oneself, disregard for traditional sources of career success, self-reliance and receptivity to change, are identified as indicators of career resilience.

New knowledge and skills required for more technical and complex work

The shift from an industry-based to a *knowledge-based economy* has resulted in a more complex and differentiated organisation of jobs requiring the employment of more specialists and knowledge workers (Lewis and Dyer, 2002). Increased complexity demands specialised knowledge and general and flexible skills. For example, particle physics is a specialised area of knowledge, but research, communication and embracing new technology are general and flexible skills. Individuals who are able to do a variety of things, as society moves forward; by staying generalised as well as specialised will have more opportunities available. Those who can only work in a specialty risk losing everything if demand for that specialty disappears for some reason (Zheng and Kleiner, 2001).

Powell and Snellman (2004:201) define the *knowledge economy* as 'production and services based on knowledge-intensive activities that contribute to an accelerated pace of technological and scientific advance as well as rapid obsolescence'. This implies that the economy relies heavily on intellectual capabalities rather than on physical inputs or natural resources. Jobs are increasingly requiring mental rather than manual skills and higher education and/or professional certification. The creation of new and more technologically advanced jobs combined with the elimination of old, 'lower tech' jobs has been referred to as the *churning of jobs.* As a technology-driven process, the churning of jobs produces new (but unpredictable) career path options (Greenhaus et al, 2010). The high pace of technological and scientific advancement therefore requires organisations and individuals to continuously adjust to this advancement as both jobs and skills can become obsolete as technology changes (Khapova, Arthur and Wilderom, 2007).

Knowledge workers are highly skilled and talented workers that organisations seek to retain. According to Kerr-Phillips and Thomas (2009), South Africa is experiencing a general skills crisis, especially pertaining to the retention of its knowledge workers. This 'brain drain' leads to the depletion or loss of intellectual and technical personnel, with a negative outcome that impacts the economic and social growth of the country. Internationally, Arnold and Randall (2010) also report on the critical labour and skills shortages in virtually all industries.

To develop competitive advantage, companies seek to optimise their workforce through comprehensive development programmes which include investments in human capital development (HCD). HCD is described as the process of helping employees become better at their tasks, their knowledge, their expriences and their lives. One of the main methods is through workplace learning, training and development and opportunities for further education (Wan, 2007).

To address the requirements of the knowledge economy and current skills shortages the South African government has introduced new legislative mechanisms such as the National Qualifications Framework Act, the National Human Development Strategy and Skills Development Amendment Act to guide the skills development of people in workplaces. The National Skills Development Strategy phase III emphasises the establishment of learning programmes in workplaces that prepare people for full occupational competence, especially **P**rofessional, **VO**cational, **T**echnical and **A**cademic (also referred to as PIVOTAL) occupational **L**earning programmes that meet the critical needs of each occupational sector for economic growth and social development (Department of Higher Education and Training, 2010).

The retention of knowledge workers with scarce and critical skills (see also chapter 8) requires organisations to (Kerr-Phillips and Thomas, 2009):

◆ develop employees according to merit and not only for equity reasons;
◆ offer a competitive remuneration package;
◆ develop a high performance work culture in which mediocrity and poor performance are not tolerated;
◆ invest in employees' personal growth and career development by allowing them to participate in leadership development programmes, continuous learning opportunities and challenging assignments;
◆ expose talented staff to all aspects of the business;
◆ demonstrate to employees that they are valued for their skills and ability;
◆ recognise staff for their contributions; and
◆ ensure that the company's employer brand is respected.

New employment relationships

Changes in the workplace are often characterised by a change in employment relationships. The way in which organisations deal with the conflicting demands of controlling the behaviour of their employees and granting them flexibility is reflected in their relationship with their employees (Gallagher, 2002).

More and more people will be working on a permanent basis for organisations although they are not actually employed by these organisations. It is predicted that work that does not follow the career ladder up to senior management will be contracted out — mainly for reasons of quality. More and more individuals are becoming freelance providers of skills and services. The outsourcing of services is increasing and will be managed more effectively in future. Through outsourcing, the work of the organisation is performed not by its members, but by others who work elsewhere, with no history or future with that organisation.

The following *types of employment relationships* are emerging (Lawler and Finegold, 2000; Rousseau and Wade-Benzoni, 1995):

Long-term insiders: core employees

An organisation is built around core employees. Their critical skills and expertise help to focus the activities of the organisation and give it a competitive advantage. By keeping these employees, the stability of the organisation is promoted. These employees know the priorities of the organisation, are expected to be loyal and are committed to the organisation and its goals.

Short-term insiders: careerists and jugglers

A careerist is someone to whom making a career within a certain industry takes precedence over a career within a certain company. Jugglers, on the other hand, are individuals to whom a career is not the most important part of their lives. Both these types are known as short-term insiders. They are characterised by the fact that, although they are employees of a company, they are not very much part of the prevailing organisational culture, despite the fact that they show behavioural conformity to some extent. As far as the company is concerned, employing short-term insiders has the advantage that the company need not invest very much in them in terms of either money or commitment, thus making the company more flexible.

Long-term outsiders: pooled workers

Employees may be called upon to work for a company for a long period in the capacity of a substitute for another employee. One type of long-term outsider is the pooled worker, who prefers to work shorter hours because of personal commitments. An example of such a work relationship would be a pool of part-time lecturers employed by a university. There is an increasing tendency to make use of workers on such a basis.

Short-term outsiders: temporaries and independent contractors

A temporary work relationship between a company and a temporary employee or independent contractor (consultant) has advantages for both sides. It gives the company more flexibility, particularly in the case of companies that have seasonal work or specific projects, while allowing the employee or contractor more flexibility in terms of lifestyle options.

The employment relationships of short-term insiders, long-term outsiders and short-term outsiders are characterised by alternative work arrangements or contingent work contracts (Marin, 2000). The term contingent work refers to those situations where workers do not have explicit or implicit contracts for long-term employment as in the case of long-term insiders. The minimum hours of contingent employment contracts can vary in a non-systematic manner. For example, an individual worker could have an agreement with a local school district or school board that they will work as a substitute teacher and be called in to work on an as-needed basis. There may be a long-standing or ongoing relationship between the teacher and the school, but there is no guarantee of work hours or a reasonably predictable schedule. The level and regularity of work is entirely contingent on the variable needs of the employer (Gallagher, 2002).

In environments where technology is rapidly changing, finding a match between new functions and the skills of the core employees may be difficult. For many organisations, contingent work arrangements represent an efficient way to address the need to secure the necessary skills which are absent or in short supply within a company's internal workforce. Research conducted by Nishikawa (2000) suggests that organisations are most likely to turn to contingent short-term outsiders (temporaries and independent contractors) when they need workers with specified technical skills.

Valcour, Bailyn and Quijada (2007) refer to these contingent work arrangements as the *customisation of careers*. Knowledge workers that possess valuable skills that are relatively rare in the labour market may find that their employers will be more willing to provide them with the work arrangements they desire. The most common pattern in customising work hours is for employees to start in traditional work arrangements, prove their worth to their employer and then negotiate customised work arrangements. These situations are often referred to as the retention of jobs because they reflect employers' desire to retain the employees.

Increasing numbers of professionals are pursuing what have come to be known as 'portfolio careers' (Valcour et al, 2007), performing a variety of assignments for different clients rather than working exclusively for a single employer.

Employability

Research suggests that the notion of lifetime employment is being replaced by the notion of *lifetime employability* (Gandolfi, 2007). Job or employment security therefore lies in employability rather than in employment. *Employability* refers to an individual's capacity and willingness to become and remain attractive in the labour market (ie, firm internal and firm external employability). It also refers to the individual's capability to be successful in a wide range of jobs (job match employability) (Carbery and Garavan, 2005). Employability is about being capable of getting or creating and keeping fulfilling work and having the knowledge, understanding, skills, experience and personal attributes to move self-sufficiently within the labour market and to realise one's potential through sustainable and fulfilling employment experiences throughout the course of one's life.

Employees' sense of security and stability is threatened to a large extent by the modern organisation. The flattening of organisational structures, downsizing and new employment relations have resulted in fewer formal career opportunities. Large organisations no longer offer stability and security as in the past and people are now confronted with risk and unpredictability. Already in 1997, Hammer (p 28) stated: 'Like it or not, security, stability are out because there simply isn't anyone on the scene who can provide them'.

Security has thus shifted from the organisation to the individual and is no longer in employment but in employability. *Employability security* comes from the chance to accumulate human and social capital that can be invested in new opportunities as they arise. *Human capital* refers to the cumulative educational, personal and professional experiences that might enhance an employee's value to an employer. *Social capital* refers to an individual's 'knowing whom' assets (attachments, relationships, reputation, sources of information) which are manifested in networking and the creation of personal contacts which can be improved through graduate studies and professional networks (Cocchiara, Kwesiga, Bell and Baruch, 2010).

While *employment* means a guaranteed job, *employability* can be viewed as the person's value in terms of future opportunities. As multiple careers become more common, individuals should have the *competitive skills* required to obtain work when necessary. The focus is on *reputation building* by which employability will be increased. Employability skills include qualification subject knowledge, understanding and skills and the following *generic skills* (Pool and Sewell, 2007):

◆ interpersonal communication skills;
◆ team work or citizenship skills;
◆ problem-solving and decision-making skills;
◆ initiative and enterprise;
◆ workplace awareness and experience;
◆ planning and organising skills;
◆ self-management skills;
◆ emotional literacy;
◆ adaptability and flexibility;
◆ career development literacy (including career self-management skills);
◆ self-efficacy and self-confidence;
◆ positive self-esteem;
◆ a lifelong learning attitude; and

◆ technological literacy.

A study in the United Kingdom indicates that people are taking up the challenge of employability, as 98 per cent of the respondents in a survey indicated that, should they lose their jobs, it would be relatively easy to find alternative employment (Holbeche, 2000). It appears that as companies start to realise that it is not their responsibility to provide long-term employment, but rather to provide opportunities for personal growth, the contract has changed from a guarantee of employment to a commitment to employability (Baruch, 2004). Bill Gates, head of one of the largest 21ˢᵗ century organisations, said that the only security his employees had was their skills and that he supported their education to maintain and improve those skills (Barker, 1997).

To remain employable demands from the individual a commitment to the ongoing development of skills and abilities to such an extent that the individual is able to offer what is required in future. If organisations do not want to lose their employees, they should provide such opportunities and play a supportive role.

Individualism is valued more than organisational loyalty

In the traditional organisation, loyalty concerns being loyal to the person next in the hierarchy; in the modern organisation, loyalty is now redefined in terms of professional standards. Kanter (1997) offers five reasons for this:

◆ people work under different leaders and a 'chair' of command will not be so easily identified;
◆ people are encouraged to challenge traditions and to move in new directions;
◆ decision-making is more decentralised and more people at lower levels are expected to make their own decisions;
◆ the increasing professionalism sets its own criteria for performance — which often outclass those of management; and
◆ people have to be more loyal to their profession than to the company, as their future depends more on their own abilities and reputation.

Professional standards and personal ethics are the criteria that are beginning to replace corporate loyalty (Kanter, 1997; McCarthy and Hall, 2000). As organisations can no longer feel betrayed when talented people leave them, employees also cannot feel betrayed if the organisation no longer needs their skills (McCarthy and Hall, 2000).

As the trends toward multiple employment will continue, individuals need to learn new knowledge and skills as part of a continuing growth pattern. A person will work perhaps three days a week at one job, one or two other days at a second job and perhaps be writing a book or doing some freelance work on the side (Zheng and Kleiner, 2001). A person's *embeddedness* in his or her job and career will determine the loyalty they feel toward the organisation.

Job and career embeddedness refers to the collection of forces that keep people in their current employment situations (eg, the links within the organisation, fit with the job, occupation or career and the perceived sacrifices associated with leaving the job, occupation or career). *Fit* refers to the extent to which people's jobs, occupations or careers are similar to (or complement) other aspects of their lives. *Links* refers to the extent to which individuals have ties to other people and activities in the job, career or occupation. *Sacrifice* is the ease with which links can be broken — what people would have to give up if they changed jobs, occupations or careers (Feldman and Ng, 2007).

The needs of employees are becoming more diverse

The South African workforce is becoming more diverse across several *primary* and *secondary* categories. Diversity includes not only cultural or ethnic diversity but also age, gender, sexual orientation and physical abilities as *primary* categories of diversity. *Secondary* categories of diversity include education, work experience, income, marital status, religious beliefs, geographic location, parental status, physical and mental disabilities and behavioural styles.

Organisations need to establish special support programmes to accommodate the career development needs of an increasingly diverse workforce (see also chapter 8). Such career support programmes should focus on bringing in the best talent, establishing mentoring programmes among employees of same and different races, holding managers accountable for meeting diversity goals, developing career plans for employees as part of performance reviews, promoting designated groups to decision-making positions, not just to staff jobs and diversifying the company's board of directors (Cascio, 2003).

The different generations that make up the workforce often have conflicting values and attitudes and diverse career needs. For example, the so-called Generation X tends to be independent and does not expect the security of long-term employment. On the other hand, the Baby Boom Echo or Generation Y, has grown up amid more sophisticated technologies and has been exposed to them earlier than members of Generation Y ever were. Generation Y desires a constant need for stimulation or entertainment and flexible work arrangements which allow them to integrate their work and family life (Cascio, 2003; Hankin, 2005).

Career success means different things to different people. More value is being placed on a balanced life and success is increasingly defined in terms not only of one's contributions to work but also in terms of one's contributions to family, community and self (Hankin, 2005; Schein, 1993). A 1995 survey indicated that 60 per cent of Americans consider personal and family life as very important in making employee decisions. Family supportive policies are regarded as a key consideration by 50 per cent of the same group in their career choice (Hall and Mirvis, 1995). Employees strive towards attaining a balance between work and leisure and more flexibility in where, when and how they work (Cascio, 2003). Research in South Africa has also indicated a strong association with lifestyle as a career anchor (Coetzee, Schreuder and Tladinyane, 2007; Coetzee and Schreuder, 2008).

Traditional male and female roles are being challenged

As is the case in the USA, it is also noticeable in South Africa that *gender stereotypes* in work and family are disappearing. A more definite trend towards equal employment opportunities has become apparent. More females are moving into management positions and family responsibilities are more equally shared between partners.

The 21st century workplace is increasingly characterised by *diverse household arrangements* which require flexibility from employers. Although *heterosexual married* couples are still predominant, couples today are much more likely to live together without marrying. *Unmarried partners* also tend to be young and have fewer children than the Baby Boom Generation. There is a particular emphasis on career and individuality. Young people want time to develop themselves as individuals before they commit to a partner or to having a child. Financial independence is also important for many, who see it as a prerequisite for marriage or children (Hankin, 2005).

A growing number of *same-sex couples* are choosing to include children in their families. Adoption and foster parenting, traditionally available only to married couples, are becoming more open to same-sex couples as well as singles (Hankin, 2005). Although *single mothers* will continue to be part of the workforce, *single-father* households are also on the increase. Many employers have already taken steps to allow special work schedules, time off when needed and other considerations such as day care and relocation packages to address the needs of the various household types.

The new psychological contract

Psychological contracts are defined as an employee's beliefs and attitudes about the mutual obligations between the employee and the organisation (Tallman and Bruning, 2008:688). The psychological contract is the unwritten agreement between an employee and the organisation that holds the organisation together and binds the individual to the organisation.

Both the individual and the organisation have their own views of their own and each other's interests. These interests usually range from gaining satisfaction, self-fulfilment and rewards from one's work on the part of the individual to achieving organisational objectives on the part of the organisation. The integration of these interests and needs emphasises the perpetual negotiation of the psychological contract. A South African study conducted by Botha (2007) found that the psychological contract consists of employees' perceptions of *entitlements* or expectations (what they think the company owes them) and *obligations* (what employees think they owe to the employer). As discussed in chapter 1, these perceptions form part of the socio-cultural norms and work ethic that influence the meaning of work in people's lives and influence their organisational commitment, job satisfaction, career satisfaction and life satisfaction.

Table 2.4 provides an overview of these entitlements/expectations and obligations.

Table 2.4 *The psychological contract: perceived employee entitlements/expectations and obligations towards the organisation*

Perceived employee entitlements/ expectations	Perceived obligations towards the organisation
◆ Transactional	◆ Producing work of adequate quality and quantity
◆ Competitive salary	
◆ Benefits	◆ Self-motivation
◆ Sufficient resources to perform the job	◆ Maintaining good interpersonal relationships with colleagues to achieve a good working environment
◆ Relational	
◆ Job-related training	
◆ Career development	◆ Self-presentation
◆ Support with personal or family problems	◆ Respect for authority
	◆ Being present and available during office hours
◆ Fairness and justice in personnel procedures, such as allocation of incentive pay	◆ Punctuality
	◆ Loyalty towards the organisation
◆ Consultation and communication with employees on matters that affect them	◆ Not abusing organisational resources
	◆ Honesty
◆ Recognition of employees' contributions and value to the organisation	◆ Setting an example to others
	◆ Keeping promises
	◆ Not committing misconduct
◆ Good relationships with supervisors and managers	◆ Serving customers with the respect and efficiency to which they are entitled
◆ Respect	◆ Not acting outside their delegated authority
◆ Job security	
◆ Promotional opportunities	◆ Adapting to changes in the work and work environment

The present work environment requires that the psychological contract is rewritten more often, as organisations are not in a position to make future promises. The demands of today's business environment should be included in the psychological contract. A positive psychological contract enhances employee commitment, intention to remain with the organisation and organisational citizenship behaviours that go beyond the formal job description (De Vos et al, 2005). Botha (2007) found that employees who perceive a breach in the psychological contract reported a violation of personal values such as social recognition, a world of peace, a sense of accomplishment, happiness, work-life balance and development and growth opportunities.

To integrate the demands of the organisation and the career needs of its employees, continuous negotiations between employer and employee are necessary. An important career management challenge is to balance organisational and individual needs. As a career is a two-way relationship, it is obvious that a balance between the interest of the individual and the interest of the employer should be found.

The employment relationship in the 21st century is a shift toward *partnership* and *self-reliance* for employees, where employees assume significant responsibility for their careers and jobs. This partnership relationship is characterised by *conditional attachment arrangements*. The 21st century organisation offers career empowerment to the employee by investing in the education and development of its people, developing a variety of multidirectional career paths based on flexibility and offering alternative work arrangements and work-family policies. Instead of formal practices based on command and control, the employee in turn needs an *organisational support system* (see chapter 8) that will take into account the wider context of careers and their multi-directionality (Baruch, 2004).

Conclusion

Changes in organisations are the result of external pressures. The first democratic election in South Africa had a tremendous impact on every sector. The political, economic and business scene changed dramatically and is set to change further. These expected changes must ultimately affect the careers of workers and career development in organisations.

The challenge is to remain adaptable and employable and individuals should regard themselves as entrepreneurs, despite being permanently employed. The career of this century is about experience, skill, flexibility and personal development. It does not involve predefined career paths and employment security (Baruch, 2006).

Furnham (2000) and McCarthy and Hall (2000) warn against the psychological impact of the new work environment on people. Organisations should guard against being insensitive to the fact that people have social needs to satisfy and that work is regarded by many as a source of creativity, identity, mastery and fulfilling a higher purpose (Hankin, 2005). The psychological impact of the nature of future jobs should also be investigated, as many jobs appear to involve electronic rather than face-to-face control.

Review and discussion questions

1. Describe the characteristics of the 21st century world of work.
2. How does the changing nature of the world of work influence individuals' careers?
3. Distinguish between the protean career, boundaryless career, composite career and entrepreneurial career. Which common characteristics do these forms of career share?
4. Why have career resilience and adaptability and lifelong learning become important qualities in the 21st century workplace?
5. Explain the nature of employment relationships and the customisation of careers in the contemporary workplace.
6. Why is it important for individuals to stay employable? How can individuals enhance their employability?

7. Do you think that individuals with successful intelligence will have higher employability? Give reasons for your answer.
8. How does diversity influence work and family values?
9. How does the traditional psychological contract differ from the new form of psychological contract between employees and their employers?
10. What are multi-directional career paths? How do they relate to the boundaryless career?
11. To which workforce 'Generation' do you belong? How do you experience the changes in the world of work?
12. What are your specific strategies toward achieving career success in the 21st century workplace?
13. Explain the concepts of knowledge economy, knowledge workers and the retention of staff.
14. Is the concept 'career progress and success' realistic in today's rapidly changing and uncertain workplace environment?
15. What can organisations do to address the career needs of members of the various 'Generations'?
16. Why is it important for organisations to take cognisance of their employees' job or career embeddedness? How would you explain your job or career embeddedness? How does it influence your sense of loyalty toward the organisation?
17. What does a career mean to you? Identify some characteristics of what a satisfying, exciting career would be for you. Review also the case studies in the reflection activity and compare them with your view of a career.
18. Can organisations expect loyalty from employees, given the changing nature of employment relationships?
19. What can organisations do to retain their knowledge workers?

Reflection activity

Read Nkele's and Bella's accounts of their careers and explain how the concepts of protean career, career progress and success, lifelong learning, career resilience and adaptability, employability and successful intelligence apply to their careers.

Nkele (26 years)

I would like to share with you the past eight and a half years of my life as an employee of an internationally successful company.

I started as an accounting clerk GR IV. Lots of ambition had me envisioning myself reaching Accountant GR IV within three years. Most people take over five years to reach that level. I kept my line manager informed about my ambitious goals. The company had a strict hierarchy with advancement based on performance. Within two years I advanced three levels and was one level away from reaching my goal. I felt like I was achieving success and enrolled for my BCom degree to show my potential to the company. Then the company started flattening its structures and I was forced to take a transfer to another department as the financial department was centralised in head office.

My dreams were shattered and I felt like a failure. However, I picked myself up and attacked my new designation with just as much drive and ambition. I had a mentor in my new position where I learnt a great deal with regard to processes to follow. This also helped me to advance in the field of my interpersonal communication skills.

Over the next three years I transferred laterally within the logistical department, handling product dispatches, local sales and eventually production and export sales. I built a network of contacts to assist with information and to support my function. This exposed me to a knowledge diversity ranging across all the dimensions of the department and it was great for my employability.

I felt I had reached the point where I had nothing more to learn in that department and applied for a transfer to the contact centre of another business unit in the organisation. There I had personal contact with clients of the organisation, addressing their concerns and learning more about the corporate affairs department as well as the procurement and supply department. I was then seconded to the PSM department as I showed promise in that direction. Again I was placed under mentorship and by using interpersonal career-enhancing strategies I learnt a lot about their processes.

By taking ownership of my career and enhancing my career development continuously over the past eight and a half years I managed to get my dream job as a consultant on Behavioural Safety — a mere year after completing my degree and just in time to assist my future studies. It may have taken longer, but nothing can take away the broad knowledge I have of my organisation and I feel confident it will serve me well.

I got detoured in my journey to career success, but as to my subjective career success now I have never felt more successful and I owe this to the knowledge I gained during my detour.

Bella (36 years)

There are four dimensions to life: love, labour, leisure and learning. I have taken the decision and made a promise to myself that my career is just one aspect of my life pie. I indulge in all the areas and have found an overall balance that leads to fulfilment.

There is power in fulfilling one's purpose in life, not achievement for the sake of becoming someone.

Having the right attitude about career change is imperative to one's ability to bounce back from setbacks, sudden changes and twists and turns along one's career path. I have made peace with the fact that I may (and probably will) experience a few career changes and transitions and I may as well get comfortable with uncertainty.

I have increased my sense of control over my career by using influencing strategies (eg self-promotion, ingratiation and upward influence) and positioning strategies (active network development, strategic choice of job move, strategic investment in human capital and job content innovation) to maximise my chances of achieving my desired career outcomes.

I have taken a proactive approach to my career development. I am constantly on the lookout for new ways to apply my gifts and talents in the new knowledge economy. This approach requires thinking creatively, actively promoting myself and being actively involved in my career progress. Staying involved in professional associations and continuously networking are excellent ways to connect with other like-minded professionals.

I keep my résumé current. You never know when you are going to want to share it with someone or pass it along. I have also considered using the power of technology to develop an interactive website.

To keep earning, I keep on learning. I do not wait until I lose my job to gain new skills or training. I have recognised the need to be open to learning and I make a point of keeping my skills sharp to make myself marketable. Top skills needed for career success include: communication, computer knowledge, creativity and customer care.

As my personal circumstances have changed and I have matured, my needs and career preferences have changed. To attain emotional satisfaction from my career, I have been able to influence the direction of my working life and have relied less on my employer to provide it.

I have built relationships with co-workers, managers and service providers and these relationships have meant a great deal to me during tough times in the organisation and in my private life. On the other hand, I participate in the life journey of individuals in need of help. First of all, an individual facing me has shown me respect by thinking I may be able to assist them. I learn from them all, whatever their age, circumstances or personality.

My work gives me a sense of accomplishment and self-worth when people seek my input and recommendations on important management decisions. My organisation values my input because I have made an effort to update my skills from time to time and have acquired new skills during the years with the organisation.

Enjoyable times in my life are not reserved for weekends and vacations. Time with my family and friends, trips to my favourite locations and self-improvement workshops are scheduled into my work pattern, not set aside to a specific period for each year. The present concerns me more than the future. My career is a fulfilling expression of who I really am. The pressures, time demands and fluctuating financial circumstances form part of this joy. None is pleasurable in isolation, but as part of the whole scheme of things is an integral part of this experience and my life purpose. Success for me is to be the best I can be.

	Nkele	Bella
Protean career		
Career progress and success		
Lifelong learning		
Career resilience and adaptability		
Employability		
Successful intelligence		

3

Career concepts and career models

Introduction

The term 'career' derives from the French word *'carrière'*, meaning a race course and for many years, careers were studied in terms of the criteria of *speed, direction* and *advancement* (Feldman, 2002). In 1976, Hall indicated four distinct meanings assigned to the concept of a career, namely:

◆ career as advancement;

◆ career as profession;

◆ career as a lifelong sequence of work experiences; and

◆ career as a lifelong sequence of role-related experiences.

Over the years, the most popular definition has been career advancement. This views a career as a course of professional life or employment, which affords opportunity for progress or advancement in the world (Moore, Gunz and Hall, 2007). Such a career is evaluated by the number of *upward moves (promotions)* during an individual's career life. A *linear career pattern* is characterised by quick upward movements in the hierarchy of the organisation (Baruch, 2004; Brousseau, 1990; Driver, 1979). This meaning includes aspects of the *external (objective) career*, which identifies the route (steps) that an individual has to follow in an organisation or profession to make progress. These are usually the aspects that appear on a curriculum vitae. In the case of a profession such as psychology, an individual has to complete a master's degree, do an internship and, in South Africa, register with the Health Professions Council of South Africa. In an organisation, human resource specialists have to follow a specific career path before they can be appointed as human resource practitioners. Today, however career experts agree that a career is not restricted to upward and/or predictable movement within one kind of work.

The 21st century world of work has moved away from an era of the one-life-one-career perspective, where one series of career stages (entrance into the world of work, establishing oneself in one's job, mastering and maintaining one's job, retiring from the workplace) covered the whole of a person's work life. In its place is a new form of career, which consists of *a series of learning cycles across multi-directional career pathways* (Baruch, 2004; Coetzee, 2007).

Careers have become *multi-directional* due to the emergence of *boundaryless* organisations and the ever-changing processes of restructuring, often accompanied by redundancies that have shattered traditional bureaucracies. In the contemporary workplace, careers are seen as a life journey where individuals' careers will consist of a greater number of transitions as a result of the changing nature of work organisations (Baruch, 2004; King, 2001).

Contemporary definitions therefore look at a career as a long-term *process of development* of the employee along a path of experiences and jobs in one or more organisations (Baruch, 2006) or as significant learnings and experiences that identify an individual's professional life, direction, competencies and accomplishments through positions, jobs, roles and assignments. Ideally, careers are selected and individuals fit careers to their aims, desires and competencies (Weiss, 2001). A career is thus not just a job, but evolves around a process, an attitude, intentional and goal-directed behaviour and a situation in a person's work life to achieve set career goals (Puah and Ananthram, 2006).

For the purposes of this book, career has been defined in terms of the contemporary perspective of a career, namely that a career is *an evolving sequence of employment-related experiences over time.* As organisations are changing, becoming virtual, more flexible, introducing fewer structures, contracting out services and using more freelance workers, careers are rather to be viewed in terms of lifelong learning than in terms of upward movements. In view of this, a definition of 'career' more suited to these new developments and changing organisations should apply.

Briscoe and Hall (2006) argue that with regard to all these organisational changes, the primary implication for employees is that careers have to become more *protean* — a shift away from the traditional organisational career. As discussed in chapter 2, in the protean career performance is defined by the person's own criteria of good performance (that is, *psychological success),* whereas in the traditional career the organisation defines success in the form of a salary and position.

Aspects of the *internal (subjective) career* are included in the protean career. Schein (1990b: 257) describes the internal career as those 'themes and concepts one develops that make sense out of one's own occupational pursuits'. This includes the attitudes, needs, values and perceptions that an individual has about a career. According to Cascio (2003), the *subjective* career is held together by a self-concept that consists of (1) perceived talents and abilities, (2) basic values and (3) career motives and needs. Whereas the subjective career consists of a sense of where one is going in one's work life, the *objective* career refers to the sequence of employment-related experiences during the course of an individual's lifetime.

In the protean career, the contract is with individuals themselves and with their work (Briscoe and Hall, 2006). Research indicates a shift in emphasis from the organisation to the work of the individual and a decrease in company satisfaction but an increase in job involvement and satisfaction. The 21st century career is no longer shaped by the organisation as individuals manage their careers more autonomously, moving between jobs and organisations to increase their employment value (Cadin et al, 2000). As externally defined careers lose their value, *internal career definitions* become psychologically more important (Schein, 1996). As a result, *self-reliance* becomes an important key to career management this century (Briscoe and Hall, 2006; Sinclair, 2009).

Both the subjective and objective careers assume that people have some degree of control over their destinies and that they can manipulate opportunities in order to maximise the success and satisfaction derived from their careers. They assume further that human resource activities should recognise *career stages* and assist employees with the *development tasks* they face at each stage. This is the topic of chapter 5.

Career concepts

Table 3.1 shows the key career concepts that are generally incorporated as distinct or relatively interchangeable explanatory constructs. These explain the objective and subjective careers of individuals. At the end of this section, Fig 3.1 provides an overview of the interrelationship between these key career concepts.

Table 3.1 *Key career concepts*

Career concept	Description
Career planning	An initiative where an individual exerts personal control and agency (initiative) over their career and engages in informed choices as to his or her occupation organisation, job assignment and self-development by conducting self-assessment, formulating goals and developing plans for reaching those goals.

Career management	The ongoing process whereby the employee takes action to obtain (1) self-knowledge, (2) knowledge of employment opportunities, (3) develop career goals, (4) develop a strategy, (5) implement and experiment and (6) obtain feedback on the effectiveness of the strategy and the relevance of the goals.
Career development	The ongoing process by which individuals progress through a series of stages, each of which is characterised by a relatively unique set of issues, themes or tasks.
Career paths	Objective descriptions of sequential work experiences, as opposed to subjective, personal feelings about career progress, personal development or satisfaction.
Career self-management	The ability to keep pace with the speed at which change occurs within the organisation and the industry and the ability to sustain one's employability through continuous learning and career planning and management efforts.
Career competency	Individuals' 'knowing why' (values, attitudes, internal needs, identity and lifestyle), 'knowing how' (expertise, capabilities, tacit and explicit knowledge), 'knowing whom' (networking relationships, how to find the right people), 'knowing what' (opportunities, threats and job requirements), 'knowing where' (entering a workplace, training and advancing) and 'knowing when' (timing of choices and activities) competencies and qualities which enable them to pursue meaningful careers.
Career success	The objective and subjective (psychological) sense of achievement individuals experience regarding their careers.
Career motivation	The persistence and enthusiasm with which individuals pursue their careers, even in the face of adversity, based on their career identity, career insight and career resilience.
Career commitment	The passion individuals have for their chosen work roles or personal career goals, including the strength of their motivation to work in a chosen career role.
Career maturity	The ability to make career decisions that reflect decisiveness, self-reliance, independence and a willingness to compromise between one's personal needs and the requirements of one's career situation.
Career self-efficacy	The degree of difficulty of career tasks which individuals believe they are to attempt and the degree to which their beliefs will persist, despite obstacles.

Career planning

Career planning can be described as an initiative where an individual exerts personal control and agency (initiative) over his or her career and engages in informed choices as to his or her occupation, organisation, job assignment and self-development by conducting self-assessment, formulating goals and developing plans for reaching those goals (Puah and Ananthram, 2006).

Career planning is important because the consequences of career success or failure are linked closely to each individual's self-concept, identity and satisfaction with career and life. The responsibility for career planning rests primarily with the individual (Baruch, 2004). In today's unpredictable and rapidly changing environment, it is even more important for employees to take control of their own careers. It cannot be left solely in the hands of the employer. However, organisations can assist by providing career planning tools or workshops through career counselling or by using workbooks or career resource centres to guide employees to conduct self-assessment, analyse and evaluate their career options and preferences, write down their development objectives and prepare a career management plan or strategy (Puah and Ananthram, 2006). The organisation's supportive role in the career development process is discussed in more detail in chapter 8.

Self-knowledge is a prerequisite for successful career planning. This involves knowledge of one's interests, skills, values, strengths and weaknesses. People who know themselves well can make more rational decisions. The career models (discussed later in this chapter) include more detail regarding the career planning process.

Career management

Once individuals have planned their career goals, they require skills, competencies and values to execute their career goals with appropriate career management practices (Puah and Ananthram, 2006). Career management can be described as an ongoing process whereby the individual takes action to: (1) obtain *self-knowledge* (interests, values, abilities, personality, career patterns, career anchors); (2) obtain a *knowledge of employment opportunities* (jobs, work roles, skills demand, skills acquisition opportunities, venture creation possibilities, work places); (3) develop career goals; (4) develop a *strategy*, (5) *implement* the strategy and *experiment* with various employment possibilities; and (6) obtain *feedback* on the effectiveness of the strategy and the relevance of the goals (Coetzee, 2007; Greenhaus, et al, 2010).

Career management is a continuous process of work life that involves making realistic choices which includes greater attention to one's own skills and the demand for those skills in the labour market. This implies moving away from an exclusive focus on interests to examine realistic choices within a zone of preferred and possible choices (Armstrong and Crombie, 2000). Career management support should therefore include guidance and counselling regarding not only interest assessment but also facilitating decision-making, enhancing the fit between the individual's ability and the demand for those skills and how the individual could acquire the required skills. *Skills acquisition* plays a critical role in occupational goal attainment (Ostroff, Shin and Feinberg, 2002).

Performance experiences continually provide opportunities for revising one's perceived talents, abilities, interests and altering one's career goals. Ostroff et al (2002) emphasise career management training for particularly new entrants to the world of work. Such training should include self-knowledge, occupational knowledge, technical skills and general employability skills due to the growing awareness that individuals need to prepare for several different types of jobs rather than a single job. Work experience through structured learnerships or internships has been shown to help young adults crystallise their vocational interests, gain a better understanding of their abilities, acquire both general employability and job-related skills and obtain better employment.

Career management is the *shared responsibility* of the employer and employee. Individuals are primarily responsible for taking control of their careers, while, on the other hand, the employer has a supportive role to play. The employer plays a career planning training role and provides facilities such as career workshops, career workbooks, career centres, counselling and other arrangements to assist employees in making better career decisions. The supportive role of the organisation is discussed in more detail in chapter 8.

Career development

From an *individual perspective*, career development can be defined as an ongoing process by which individuals progress through a series of stages, each of which is characterised by a relatively unique set of issues, themes or tasks (Greenhaus et al, 2010). Career development consists of *four phases* (Strauser, Lustig and Çiftçi, 2008):

◆ *developing appropriate work-related behaviours* — known as a work personality — that allow people to meet the interpersonal demands of the work environment (eg appropriate social interactions with others, timeliness and appropriate on-task behaviour);

◆ *developing a vocational identity* through which individuals become aware of their career interests, goals, skills and talents;

◆ *engaging in effective career decision-making* by identifying appropriate work environments that allow individuals to express their vocational identity; and

◆ *developing their ability to effectively find a job*, resulting in employment and sustaining one's employability.

A career consists of different stages and the individual is confronted with different issues during each of these stages (see chapter 5). Effective career development requires knowledge of the distinctive physical and psychological needs of the individual. The career needs of the learner, those of the employee in mid-career and those of an employee approaching retirement are not the same.

From an *organisational perspective*, career development is viewed as an ongoing, formalised effort by the organisation that focuses on developing and enriching the organisation's human resources in light of both the employees' and the organisation's needs (Byars and Rue, 2004). Career development is thus a formal approach taken by an organisation to ensure that people with the proper qualifications and experience are available when needed. In view of this, career development helps organisations avoid the dangers of an obsolescent, unacceptable workforce (Zheng and Kleiner, 2001).

Career development is seen as a *joint effort* between the employee and the organisation and the outcome of the interaction between individual career planning and the organisational career management process. In career development and transition, the employee is responsible for career planning and the organisation is responsible for career development support in the career management process. As employees grow and change, the types of work they may want to do may change as well.

Employers should assist their employees in making decisions about future work and help prepare them to be effective when they take on new positions. The individual is driven by his or her skills, knowledge, abilities, attitudes, values and life situation. Employers provide the job and the information about the jobs as well as the opportunities and constraints within which employees may pursue others jobs in the future. Organisations are also responsible for tracking career paths and career ladders (Zheng and Kleiner, 2001). The career development support that organisations can offer employees is discussed in more detail in chapter 8.

Career paths

Employees move from one job to another. These moves very often indicate a sequential pattern of jobs, which can be referred to as a career path. Career paths are objective descriptions of sequential work experiences, as opposed to subjective, personal feelings about career progress, personal development or satisfaction (Cascio, 2003).

Career paths exist on an informal basis in almost all organisations. However, career paths are much more useful when formally defined and documented. Career pathing is a technique used by organisations to specify the sequence of developmental activities involving informal and formal education, training and job experiences that help make an individual capable of holding more advanced jobs in the future (Byars and Rue, 2004). *Career pathing* is most useful when used as part of the overall career-planning process.

The perception of promotion as the only purposeful career route is now outdated. According to Cascio (2003:390), career paths should:

◆ represent real progression possibilities, whether lateral or upward, without implied 'normal' rates of progress or forced specialisation in a technical area;

◆ be tentative and responsive to changes in job content, work priorities organisational patterns and management needs;

◆ be flexible, taking into consideration the compensating qualities of a particular employee, manager, subordinate or people who influence the way that work is performed; and

◆ specify the skills, knowledge and other attributes required to perform effectively at each position along the paths and specify how they can be acquired. If specifications are limited to educational credentials, age and experience, some capable performers may be excluded from career opportunities.

Traditionally, a career path has been seen as a constant upward movement. However, a career path may also be multi-directional. It may lead sideways (transfer), downwards (demotion) and even change completely (dismissal or retrenchment). In other words, a career path should not only be regarded as a constant upward movement but also as a set of educational or behavioural requirements necessary for a particular employee to become eligible for a possible promotion. There is no guarantee, however, that the promotion will indeed take place (Baruch, 2004).

Career self-management

Career self-management is the ability to keep pace with the speed at which change occurs within the organisation and the industry and the ability to sustain one's employability through continuous learning and career planning and management efforts. Career self-management requires a general attitude of planfulness an ability to plan, optimism and initiative in and directing one's future. *Career agency* is an individual's capacity to act for themselves and speak on their own behalf (McMahon, 2007). It is characterised by the personal initiative to take control of one's career with a sense of self-efficacy and self-confidence and proactively seeking and exploring new information about a career that will enhance the fit between self, the environment, one's work values and life interests.

Research has shown that individuals practise a range of *career self-management behaviours* in the implementation of their strategies to achieve their career goals. These include (Sturges, 2008):

◆ *networking* behaviour (ie, getting to know influential people);
◆ *visibility* behaviour (ie, drawing attention to work achievements, getting credit for work done and maintaining a high profile within the organisation);
◆ *positioning* behaviour (eg, pursuing valuable job opportunities and making sure that roles and jobs enhance their career);
◆ behaviour relating to *building human capital* (eg, through training and education and informal on-the-job learning);
◆ *validating* behaviour (proving oneself or one's competence and capability to perform a job); and
◆ behaviour relating to the *management of the work/non-work boundary* (ie, preventing work activities from permeating the home environment; maximising control over one's work-life balance and protecting one's life or out-of-work interests).

Career self-management emphasises the individual's need to keep learning because jobs that are held today may evolve into something different tomorrow or may simply disappear entirely. Career self-management also involves identifying and obtaining new skills and competencies that allow the individual to move to a new position. The payoff of career self-management is more highly skilled and flexible employees and the retention of these employees. Career self-management requires commitment to the idea of employee self-development on the part of the organisation and the individual and the provision of self-development programmes and experiences for employees (Byars and Rue, 2004).

Career competency

Careers have become more open, more diverse and less structured and controlled by employers. The management of such careers requires individual qualities that differ considerably from those that were sufficient in the past. Arthur, Claman and DeFillippi (1995) suggested the phrase *'intelligent careers'* to describe the elements of pro-active career self-management in the context of the knowledge economy. Intelligent careers require career competency from individuals.

As discussed in chapter 1, *career competency* refers to abilities (or intelligence) regarding the *'knowing why'* (ie, understanding one's personal values, attitudes, internal needs, identity and lifestyle needs), the *'knowing how'* skills (ie, what one has to offer in terms of one's job-related skills and expertise and employability-related skills) and *'knowing whom'* (ie, one's social capital, networking relationships and knowing how to find the right people). In addition, career competency also includes abilities such as *'knowing what'* (opportunities, threats and job requirements), *'knowing where'* (entering a workplace, training and advancing) and *'knowing when'* (timing of choices and activities) (Parker, 2008).

Research has provided strong empirical evidence that each of these 'knowing' qualities of the intelligent career (Arthur et al, 1995) is linked to career success (Eby, Butts and Lockwood, 2003). Career success is more likely among individuals who have career insight, including realistic career expectations based on knowledge of personal strengths and weaknesses (knowing why). Career insight arouses career motivation, leads to greater role clarity and cultivates a future orientation (Eby et al, 2003). Cocchiara et al (2009) found that women are positively affected by *inner-value capital* attributes which people gain through increased self-awareness, self-esteem, self-efficacy and confidence. *Inner-value capital* attributes relate to people's knowing why competencies which provide people with a sense of overall purpose and meaning as they navigate through their careers. Having a strong sense of purpose often results in increased career motivation (Inkson and Arthur, 2001).

In the context of the 21st century, people are regarded as *competency traders* and their employability depends on their career competency and their continuous ability to fulfil, acquire or create work through the optimal use of both occupation-related and career meta-competencies (Coetzee, 2007; Hall and Chandler, 2005; Parker, 2008). Career meta-competencies include those skills and attributes that go beyond technical or occupation-specific skills. They are regarded as the psychological career resources people use to plan and manage their careers proactively (Coetzee, 2008). A person's repertoire of *psychological career resources* includes skills such as career planning and management skills and self-management and interpersonal skills. It also includes inner-value capital attributes such as behavioural adaptability, self-esteem, sense of purpose, emotional and social literacy. People's psychological career resources enable them to be self-directed learners and proactive agents in the management of their careers (Coetzee, 2008).

Psychological career resources have been found to be linked to people's experiences of life satisfaction and job/career satisfaction, perceptions of general employability and their ability to deal resourcefully with life and career challenges (Coetzee and Bergh, 2008; Fugate, Kinicki and Ashforth, 2004; Parker, 2008). People who possess a wide range of psychological career resources are generally more able to adapt to changing career circumstances and tend to demonstrate higher levels of employability (Fugate et al, 2004; Griffin and Hesketh, 2005; McArdle, Waters, Briscoe and Hall, 2007).

Career success

Career success can be defined as the real or perceived achievements individuals have accumulated as a result of their work experiences (Judge and Kammeyer-Muller, 2007:60). As discussed in chapter 1, the concept of career success has different meanings for different people. The way in which individuals define career success strongly influences their career decisions. To some, success means promotion. To others it means becoming an expert in their occupational field. Some think of a successful career as one in which a person has developed many different skills and abilities and is now using those abilities to help other people grow and develop — perhaps a life of social contribution. It could also mean moving frequently from one challenge to another. Success can also mean the extent to which there is a match between individuals' career anchors (self-perceived talents and abilities, motives and needs, attitudes and values) and the perception of their jobs (Schein, 1993).

Peiperl and Jonsen (2007) distinguish between *objective or extrinsic success* (how well the person has done in terms of rewards, promotions, recognition and other such visible indicators) and psychological, intrinsic or *subjective success* (subjective evaluations and feelings of job, career and life satisfaction, sense of accomplishment and sense of self-worth). Research indicates that women tend to use more personal criteria for career success, such as employability and career satisfaction rather than the 'male' criteria for promotions, organisational level attained and salary (Ackah and Heaton, 2003).

People's sense of *job satisfaction* (their immediate emotional reactions to their current job and the satisfaction they have with the challenge and meaning ascribed to their current jobs) and *career satisfaction* (their satisfaction with both their past and future work history taken as a whole, especially their rates of progress toward achieving their career goals based on their accumulated work experiences), have been found to be significantly related to their sense of career well-being (Erdogan, Kraimer and Liden, 2004; Kidd, 2008). People's career *well-being* (see chapter 7) is affected by their career experiences which lead to positive and/or negative evaluations (thoughts) and feelings about their jobs or careers.

Kidd (2008) found that the most frequently cited *positive experiences* were reported as career transitions (moving into a conducive new role or career path, with or without a promotion), interpersonal relations (receiving recognition and positive feedback from others), having autonomy and power, work performance, sense of purpose, learning and development opportunities and work-life balance. *Negative career experiences* related to interpersonal relations (interpersonal conflict and lack of support), lack of feedback or recognition of others, organisational change, inequitable treatment, dislike of ethics or morals displayed by the company, career transitions (redundancy, redeployment), work adjustment, lack of promotional opportunities, lack of learning and development opportunities and having no sense of purpose (not seeing any future progression within the company).

Career success is also linked to individuals' *goal orientation* which is centred in a particular *cultural value system*. According to Smit and Cronje (2002:258), Africans relate to an Afrocentric value system, while whites relate more to a Eurocentric value system. In terms of the *Afrocentric* value system, psychological feelings of career success are based on a preference for *quality of life* and *rewarding common vision for communal effort*. The Afrocentric culture is related to the values of a *'feminine' culture* that emphasises nurturance, the commonality of all people, vision, values and efforts, as well as a concern for relationships and the living environment. On the other hand, career success according to the *Eurocentric* value system is related to achieving *material success, position* and *rewarding individual merit*. The Eurocentric culture is also related to the values of a *'masculine' culture* that is characterised by assertiveness, being ambitious and competitive.

As discussed in chapter 2, in the light of current business trends (downsizing and restructuring), it is essential that the meaning of success should no longer be dependent on the traditional Eurocentric characteristics of success — namely promotion, salary increases and perks (objective success) — but should rather be reflected by individuals' perception of their internal career (psychological success). To encourage this, the employer should allow employees to succeed more on their own terms within the framework of the organisation's needs.

Career motivation and career commitment

Career motivation is 'a multi-dimensional construct internal to the individual, influenced by the situation and reflected in the individual's decisions and behaviours' (London, 1983: 620). It consists of three major domains, namely *career identity, career insight* and *career resilience*.

Career identity is defined as:

> *a structure or network of meanings in which the individual consciously links his own motivation, interests and competencies with acceptable career roles (Meijers, 1998:201).*

It is the degree to which people define themselves by their work and by their organisation (London, 1983). It is also how central individuals' careers are to their identity (Ibarra, 2003; London, 1983).

Career insight can be defined as 'the extent to which the person has realistic perceptions of him or herself and the organisation and relates these perceptions to career goals' (London, 1983:621). It includes self-knowledge, that is, individuals being aware of their strengths and weaknesses and can be tied to individuals' work commitment, organisational commitment and the feeling of being citizens in the organisation (Feldman, 2002).

Career resilience is the ability to adapt to changing circumstances. 'It encompasses welcoming job and organisational changes, looking forward to working with new and different people, having self-confidence and being willing to take risks' (London, 1993:55). Career resilience derives from the concepts hardiness, self-efficacy and achievement motivation (London, 1993). The opposite of career resilience appears to be career vulnerability. This is defined as 'the extent of psychological fragility (eg, becoming upset and finding it difficult to function) when confronted by less than optimal career conditions (eg, barriers to career goals, uncertainty, poor relationships with co-workers)' (London, 1993:621).

The concept career commitment is closely related to career motivation and is defined as the *strength of one's motivation* to work in a chosen career role (Ballout, 2009). It is also seen as the passion individuals have for their chosen work roles and the willingness they have to commit to the efforts needed to attain their personal career goals. Day and Allen (2004) found career commitment to be positively related to career satisfaction, salary level and performance effectiveness. Poon (2004) provided evidence that career commitment predicted both objective and subjective career success.

Career maturity and career self-efficacy

Career maturity is a concept that is linked to career resilience. Individuals who make career decisions that reflect decisiveness, involvement, independence, task orientation and willingness to compromise between needs and reality have usually achieved a high degree of career maturity (London, 1993).

The concept of career maturity is also closely related to *career self-efficacy*. Career self-efficacy refers to the degree of difficulty of career tasks, which individuals believe they are to attempt and how well they believe they can execute the courses of actions required to deal with those tasks and the degree to which their beliefs will persist, despite obstacles. Furthermore, career self-efficacy refers to the degree to which individual's beliefs can be transferred to other tasks necessary for making career decisions. While low career decision-making self-efficacy facilitates avoidance of career decision tasks and prolongs career indecision, high career decision-making self-efficacy leads to a higher level of participation in career decision-making behaviours and tasks (Watson, Foxcroft and Eaton, 2001). Day and Allen (2004) found career self-efficacy to be related to indicators of career success and performance effectiveness.

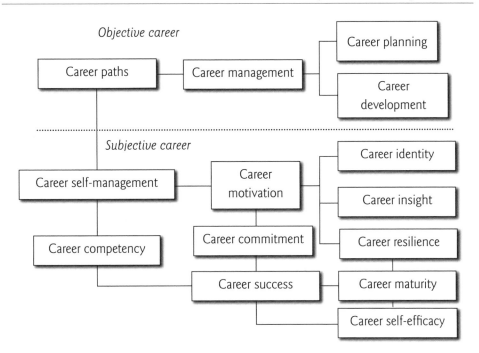

Figure 3.1 *Interrelationship between the key career concepts*

Career models

One major consequence of boundaryless careers and multi-directional career paths is the emergence of the so-called test-and-learn career planning and development models. The traditional career management models emphasised the plan-and-implement aspects related to career management (Ibarra, 2003).

The traditional plan-and-implement career models view career management as a linear process in which dissatisfaction with the status quo leads to setting a goal, from which flows an implementation plan. The end goal is fixed, with the ideal of identifying the end goal as clearly as possible at the outset. The process of career management is deductive, with career progress in stages, each building on the preceding step. Individuals require explicit knowledge of themselves and the working environment as an input to the career-management process (for example what jobs exist, what skills they prefer to use, what occupation areas interest them, what their personality is).

The plan-and-implement career models also view the individual's career self (the individual's subjective or psychological sense of their careers, their vocational identity and self-concept) as being based on one true self which has been fully formed by adulthood. Individuals use introspection to find an inner truth linked to their one true self to help them identify the desired end goal. Career management then consists of devising and implementing an action plan to get to that goal.

In contrast, the *modern test-and-learn career models* view career management as a *developmental process* that is *circular* in nature. Career planning and management is a process in which iterative rounds of *action and reflection* lead to updating personal career goals and possibilities. The emphasis is on change that accompanies frequent *career transitions* with the ideal of improving individuals' ability to formulate and test hypotheses about *future possibilities* and *multiple work roles or identities* they could explore along their life journey. This process is inductive in nature, with progress by iteration with leaps of insight or 'ahas'. Individuals require implicit knowledge which is continuously created throughout the career planning and management process (for example, exploring and testing what is feasible and what is appealing to them).

The modern test-and-learn career models view the individual as having many possible career selves which are always changing, with some selves more developed or appealing than others. These possible selves reside in both people's minds and their actions. They exist as images of the future, which are linked to a core life purpose or mission to be fulfilled. The career self is shaped and revealed through testing and experimenting with the multiple possibilities available in a boundaryless workplace. Individuals learn from *direct experience* to recombine old and new skills, interests and ways of thinking about themselves and to create new opportunities that correspond to the evolving self. The modern test-and-learn career models are developmental in nature and the emphasis is on continuous reinvention and renewal. The individual and his or her environment shape each other in ways that can produce possibilities that did not reside in either at the start of the planning process.

Both the traditional plan-and-implement career models and the modern test-and-learn career models will be useful for individuals in managing their careers in the 21st century workplace. Young adults in the early career stage who do not have a clearly developed career self or self-concept will still require the basic steps and principles underlying the traditional plan-and-implement career models to kickstart their careers. The modern test-and-learn career models may be more appropriate for employed adults who are experiencing the turbulence and uncertainty of the contemporary workplace and who have to deal with frequent career transitions. The modern test-and-learn career models represent a proactive and creative approach toward career planning and development in the 21st century workplace (Baruch, 2004; Betz, 2003; Coetzee, 2007; Ibarra, 2003; Pringle and Dixon, 2003).

Table 3.2 *Characteristics of the traditional plan-and-implement career models and the modern test-and-learn career models*

Plan-and-implement career models	Test-and-learn career models
Use a *linear process* in setting career goals, from which flows an implementation plan.	Use a *circular process* in which iterative rounds of action and reflection lead to updating goals and possibilities.

The end goal is usually *fixed* with the ideal of identifying the end goal as clearly as possible at the outset.	Career goals are continuously *changing* with the ideal of improving one's ability to formulate and test hypotheses about future possibilities along the way.
Career planning and management process is *deductive*, with progress in stages, each building on the preceding step. The starting point is *analysis and reflection:* Individuals use *introspection* to find an inner truth that can help identify the desired end goal. An action plan is devised and implemented to get to that goal.	Career planning and management process is *inductive*, with progress by iteration with leaps of insight. The emphasis is on *taking action* and *experimenting* with various future *possibilities*. Individuals learn from *direct experience* to recombine old and new skills, interests and ways of thinking about themselves and to create opportunities that correspond to the evolving self-concept.
Individuals require *explicit knowledge* which is used as an input to the career management process, eg, what jobs exist, what skills they like to use, what areas interest them, what their personality is, etc.	Individuals require *implicit knowledge* which is continuously created through the career management process, eg, what is feasible, what is appealing.
Useful in facilitating *career competency*, *career self-efficacy* and *career maturity* in particular young adults or *new entrants* to the world of work.	Useful in facilitating *career adjustment* and *career resilience* in adults dealing with *career transitions*.

A plan-and-implement career model

To illustrate how individuals manage their careers according to the traditional plan-and-implement career model, the model of Greenhaus et al (2010) is used (figure 3.2). The extent to which organisations are willing to share information with employees and support them in their efforts will to a great extent determine the success of this model. Individuals can use this model to make informed decisions about their careers. It illustrates how people should manage their careers, not necessarily how they do manage them. The various steps of the career management model will now be discussed.

Career exploration

Career exploration is the collection and analysis of information regarding career-related issues. Career exploration can help people become more aware of themselves and the world of work, formulate career goals and decisions and develop strategies necessary to accomplish significant goals (Greenhaus et al, 2010).

Career exploration can be divided into *self-exploration* (one's own qualities) and *environmental exploration* (occupations, jobs, organisations and families).

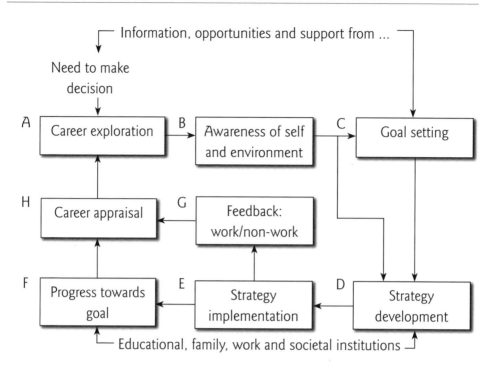

Figure 3.2 *A career management model*

In Greenhaus, JH, Callan, GA and Godshalk, VM (1997, 2000, 2010)

Self-exploration

During the *self-exploration* process individuals seek information about themselves (personal qualities) that can be valuable in career decision-making. *Self-knowledge* is the cornerstone of successful career planning. Personal qualities include interests, values and proficiency. *Interest* can be described as an individual's preference for specific activities and objects. Interest can be measured by instruments, such as the Strong Vocational Interest Blank (SVIB), Kuder Preference Record, 19 Field Interest Questionnaire and the Self-directed Search. A *value* is a disposition by which a person's preferences and behaviour are directed (Plug et al, 1997). The *Value Scale* of the Human Sciences Research Council gives a measurement on twenty-two values that can be used.

According to the same source, *proficiency* is the manifested efficiency to perform a specific task. It is determined through the inherited aptitude of the individual and the forming influence of the environment. Accomplishments at school, past work histories and other achievements can be indicators of proficiency.

Activities and programmes that can be followed to assist the employee with self-assessment are discussed in chapter 8.

Environmental exploration

Environmental exploration enables the individual to gather information about the environment. Environmental exploration should consist of at least an investigation of occupations organisations and family needs. The objective of environmental exploration is to obtain enough information about these aspects and others to make a career decision. Information about possible occupations might include task activities, financial rewards, security, physical setting, information on task variety and training requirements. Information on organisations could include financial health, strategies, career management structures, etc. Information on families would be the spouse's career aspirations, the spouse's emotional needs, the children's emotional needs, the family's financial needs and the family's desired lifestyle (Greenhaus et al, 2010).

Awareness

Awareness is a relatively complete and accurate perception of one's own qualities and the characteristics of one's relevant environment (Greenhaus et al, 2010). A proper self– and environmental exploration will result in a deep awareness of self and of the environment, which will help the employee to set realistic career goals. As indicated in the previous section, this is the cornerstone of successful career management.

Career goals

'A *career goal* is a desired career-related outcome that a person intends to attain' (Greenhaus et al, 2010:53). When formulating career goals, individuals decide what they want to accomplish and then formulate their strategies accordingly.

Elements of career goals

Career goals can be seen from the following angles (Greenhaus et al, 2010):

Types of goal

Career goals can be distinguished by their *conceptual* and *operational* nature. The *conceptual* career goal sums up the career ambitions of a person, his or her values, interests, aptitudes and preferences. A conceptual career goal captures the type of work a person wants to do, the type of contact with other people that he or she wishes to have and the physical environment. An *operational* career goal is the job that the person concerned is aiming for. It is the way in which the person wants to achieve his or her conceptual career goal.

The functions of a career goal

A career goal has an *expressive function* — that is, the pleasure gained when goals are achieved and when the related work is gratifying for the individuals who do it because they can make use of their experience. It may also have an *instrumental function* — that is, achieving one goal will enable the person concerned to aim for the following one.

The period covered by a career goal

A long-term goal may be anything from *seven to ten years*, while a short-term goal may vary between *one and three years*. The present, more unpredictable environment requires that career goals should be revised more frequently.

Characteristics of career goals

In addition to Greenhaus's explanation, career goals can be extended to the *characteristics* of goal setting for managerial purposes, namely specificity, flexibility, measurability, attainability, congruence and acceptability (Smit and Cronjé, 2002).

Specificity

'Good goals should be specific and should indicate what they are related to, the time frame for accomplishing them and the desired results' (Smit and Cronjé, 2002:142). A career goal could be to become a human resource director within five years in the motor industry at an annual package of R750 000. This is more specific than to say 'to move into human resources'.

Flexibility

A changing world requires organisations to be flexible in their goal setting. The environment is not static; occupations disappear while new ones arise. Effective career management also requires *flexible* career goals. The information explosion, intensified competition, changes in organisations, changes in the composition of the labour force and changes in the nature of managerial work sometimes make the setting of long-term career goals inadvisable. As we grow older, our needs and preferences change. This unpredictability requires flexible career goals.

Measurability

Goals must be specified in such terms that they can be evaluated. Career appraisal, which gives feedback on career-related issues, can serve as an aid to evaluating career goals.

Attainability

Career goals should be realistic and *attainable*. Realistic and attainable career goals should take into account the qualities, needs and values of the individual whose lifestyle, career anchors and career motives should be considered when formulating career goals. No real experience of success can be obtained from setting goals that are too easy to attain, while career goals that are too difficult to achieve will cause a feeling of failure. The feedback that is obtained by career appraisal can be used to determine the attainability of a career goal. Career exploration, which includes self-exploration and environmental exploration, is therefore an essential prerequisite for formulating attainable career goals.

Congruency goals

Career goals should be *congruent,* which means that the attainment of one goal should not preclude the attainment of another. Career goals should be formulated in terms of long– and short-term goals. The short-term goals should be congruent with the long-term goals in the sense that they should identify the education, training and experience needed to attain the long-term goals.

Acceptability

Individuals are most likely to follow career goals that are in line with their perceptions and preferences. Through the process of self-exploration (identifying personal qualities, values and needs) goal *acceptability* can be achieved, which will promote career commitment.

Importance of setting career goals

Well-set career goals are one of the prerequisites for career satisfaction and growth. The absence of a career goal relates to career indecision. *Career indecision* (and its mirror image career decidedness) refers to the absence (or presence) of a career goal, as well as the degree of certainty attached to the goal. Employees are career undecided if they have either: (1) not established a career goal; or (2) established a goal with which they experience substantial uncertainty and discomfort. Employees are *career decided* if they have established a career goal with which they experience relative certainty and comfort (Greenhaus et al, 2010).

Greenhaus et al (2010) identified the following types of career indecision/career decidedness:

◆ Indecision includes people who lack information about themselves and the work environment and are usually between twenty and thirty years old; and people who are prone to chronic indecision are above thirty years of age and have a persistent inability to set career goals.
◆ Decidedness includes people who decide on a career goal without prior career exploration, thereby making a decision without sufficient knowledge of themselves and the work environment, as well as people who decide on a career goal after executing a thorough career exploration.

Career strategy

'A *career strategy* is a sequence of activities designed to help an individual attain a career goal' (Greenhaus et al, 2010:54). The aim of career strategies is to assist people in attaining their career goals. People who are actively involved make decisions about the steps that they will take to achieve a desired result.

Research has determined that career strategies can be divided into *seven categories* (Greenhaus et al, 2010):

◆ *Displaying one's current proficiency*: Although this may seem obvious, it is true that employees are evaluated on their everyday performance when promotion decisions are taken. In addition, performance in any other job may depend partially or wholly on present accomplishments.

◆ *Working long hours*: This is a very common career strategy that is often used to show loyalty to the company and a sense of responsibility, without employees actually increasing their output. Long working hours may also have a negative effect on the private lives of employees.

◆ *Acquiring new skills*: This may be done to improve employees' present performance or to prepare them for a new job. New skills may be acquired by formal means such as university degrees or training courses or by informal means such as taking on more responsibility or doing another job outside working hours.

◆ *Taking advantage of opportunities*: This career strategy involves increasing one's visibility within the organisation by making others (particularly those higher up in the organisational hierarchy) aware of one's skills and potential. The employee may also actively pursue a relationship with like-minded colleagues ('networking') or take on temporary duties.

◆ *Developing an association with a colleague*: An inexperienced person may develop a close relationship with another employee (usually a senior colleague) who will serve as a role model and 'mentor'. Such a relationship also enhances the self-image of the senior partner.

◆ *Strengthening one's image*: The aim of this strategy is to gain positive feedback by being perceived as 'fitting in'. This involves observing unspoken dress codes and other customs. This particular career strategy may be perceived as being more important than it really is.

◆ *Taking part in company politics*: Employees may publicly support their company's policies and regulations to demonstrate loyalty, although this may not be in keeping with their personal principles.

The effectiveness of the above-mentioned career strategies remains a debatable question. Although it was found that the enhancement of skills and experience was positively correlated with career success in most companies, an examination of state organisations in particular showed that increasing the awareness of superiors, networking and a display of competence all served to increase an employee's career chances. The choice of a career strategy may also depend on the type of job and the industry, as well as on company-specific procedures. A career strategy that works in one job may have a negative effect in another (Greenhaus et al, 2010).

It appears, then, that the following conclusions can be drawn from the literature (Greenhaus et al, 2010):

◆ There is no single strategy that works every time.
◆ The career goal of the individual employee will determine the strategy to be applied.
◆ The procedures and practices within an organisation will influence the degree of effectiveness of any particular career strategy.
◆ A combination of various strategies may be better than choosing a single career strategy.

◆ A career strategy should be used as a means of self-examination by employees to review their goals and interests.

◆ Employees should be aware that choosing the wrong strategy may have a negative effect on their career.

Although the finer details of career strategies cannot be planned in advance, people usually acquire new insight into a particular career strategy once they have begun to follow it. When compiling a career strategy or combination of career strategies, individuals should begin by reviewing their long-term goals. This involves setting an operational goal (the means). An operational goal is the way in which a certain job can be used to achieve the conceptual goal or reward (the end). They should then list the actions or conduct necessary to achieve this long-term goal.

Each of these actions or modes of behaviour should be evaluated on the basis of its potential contribution towards achieving the goal and of its acceptability in an ethical sense. The potential contribution of an action or mode of conduct can be gauged by discussing it with more experienced employees and by paying attention to the way in which other people behave. In addition, the feedback received from performance evaluations and conversations with superiors is useful for identifying career strategies. It may also happen that the implementation of one part of a specific career strategy can turn out to be an obstacle to another part. Rigid adherence to dress codes may, for example, result in reduced visibility.

A career strategy must thus be regarded as a whole. In addition, the career strategy chosen should not be in conflict with the person's ethical values. The final list of items on the long-term career strategy list should be fairly brief. It should also include reasons for including each item and an estimated period of implementation. Once the long-term goal has been established, a short-term goal can be set and possible actions and modes of conduct for achieving this short-term goal can be listed. The short-term goal should constitute a step in the attainment of the long-term goal. It is then time to look at the overlap between the strategy lists for the short– and long-term goals. Activities that feature in both lists should be given priority and set out in chronological order (Greenhaus et al, 2010).

Although the above-mentioned process may appear to be perfectly rational, it must be remembered that the various steps may overlap to a certain extent and that some steps cannot be decided on until others have been taken. It is vital that employees should remain open to new information and be willing to update their strategy as the need may arise.

Career appraisal

Career appraisal is the process by which people acquire and use career-related feedback (Greenhaus et al, 2010). As performance appraisals are used to give employees feedback on their job performance, career appraisal also gives individuals feedback on how they are progressing in their career and on the extent to which they are attaining their career goals.

The aim of career appraisal is to allow people to assimilate new information about themselves and their environment. To do this, they require feedback to test whether a particular career strategy will bring them closer to their goal and whether they are pursuing an achievable goal. Career appraisal thus helps to make career management a more flexible process.

It is most important, however, that individuals should obtain early feedback from their environment so that steps can be taken in good time to avoid potential failure. By constantly monitoring their actions and the effect they have on the environment, individuals will establish a system of continuous career appraisal.

Greenhaus et al (2010) suggest that the following questions be asked about the type of information to be attained:

◆ What do individuals wish to achieve? Is the information gained relevant to their goal and what has it taught them about values, interests and aptitudes?
◆ Will the practical steps they devised to attain this goal take them there? Is the goal an appropriate one and can the present job be used to achieve it?
◆ Are individuals using the correct strategy to progress towards the goal? Are they obtaining the additional skills required to reach the goal?

According to Greenhaus et al (2010), the feedback related to goals and strategies may be derived from various sources:

◆ through social interaction with people who either know the people concerned or who have experience that can be of assistance to them, for example, supervisors, mentors, friends and relatives;
◆ through observing either the work environment, for example, quotas and production rates or the private environment, for example, the family life of individuals; and
◆ through individuals' own evaluation of their performance.

To turn this feedback into an ongoing career appraisal Greenhaus et al (2010) suggest the following guidelines:

◆ Individuals must be prepared to revise their goals and strategies when necessary. When, for example, it becomes apparent that a certain strategy will not work, pursuing it further would be counterproductive. Such a revision requires that individuals should be honest with themselves and willing to make changes, even if this shows an apparent inconsistency of action.
◆ The career strategy should include minimum intermediate goals and milestones to be achieved.
◆ Both the conceptual and the operational goals must be revised from time to time to accommodate the new information obtained.
◆ Information exchange is vital. Much information about current performance, strong and weak points can be obtained from individuals' supervisors. Similarly, supervisors should be informed about aspirations to enable them to provide more focused feedback.
◆ Conversations with colleagues can be useful. A new perspective will be gained and individuals' own goals, ambitions and strategies will be placed into context.

◆ Conversations with family members can serve to establish their feelings about the career strategy and about the sacrifices that must be made to achieve career goals, for example, long working hours.

Test-and-learn career models

The models of Otte and Kahnweiler (1995), Coetzee (2007) and Young, Valach and Domene (2005) are examples of the modern test-and-learn career models. These three career models will each be discussed in turn.

The 21ˢᵗ century career planning model

Because jobs and organisations change, long-term career planning is seen as concerning the individual's being; that is, finding a purpose in life and finding personal meaning in work. Success is seen as embracing not only traditional terms of economic gain, but also the individual's spiritual and emotional development.

The model of Otte and Kahnweiler (1995) is based on the quest for personal development and is facilitated by interaction with factors that are relevant to career planning for the 21ˢᵗ century.

The various steps of the model (figure 3.3) will now be discussed.

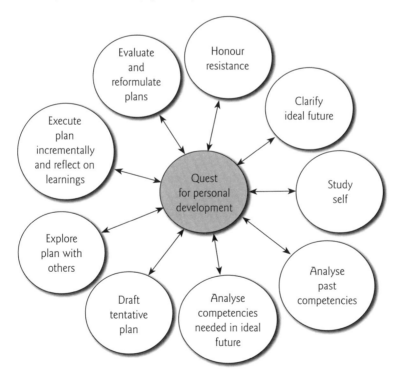

Figure 3.3 *21ˢᵗ century career planning model*

In Otte, FL and Kahnweiller, WM (1995:6)

Quest for personal development

In planning a career, the focus should be on becoming aware of one's inner depth; that is, the spiritual and emotional aspects that let us know who we really are and how to seek vitality and joy in life. Individuals are often not aware of their personal depths because, in the process of learning to adapt to the adult world as society expects, some childlike spontaneity is lost. Being out of touch with one's deepest feelings may give rise to a sense in mid-life that 'something is missing'. Finding one's inner depths may be facilitated by therapy, meditation or dream analysis or expressing oneself in art, music, craft or other activities. This contributes to career planning as an evolutionary process in which one finds answers in oneself rather than in the outside world. In this process, career plans can change. Change does not necessarily mean changing one's job, but can mean seeing one's present job in a new way and finding new ways of personal development.

Honour resistance

At times individuals tend to get 'stuck' rather than focus on the quest for personal development. They may ascribe this to their lacking willpower or being lazy. Instead of such a self-judgmental approach, a more healthy approach would be to attempt to understand the reasons for getting 'stuck'; that is, discovering why one is resistant to personal growth. It could be due to incompatibility between one's needs and desires or to not 'listening' to certain parts of oneself that want to be expressed or to the fact that one's plans have become inappropriate to external circumstances.

Means of gaining understanding of the reasons for not growing include talking to a friend or counsellor, revising one's career plan or accepting the fact that one can become confused and doubt one's self-worth.

Clarify ideal future

In dreaming of what one wants to be in the future, one should not think in terms of a job title, but rather in terms of an ideal role one would like to be in, in two to three years' time. This involves fantasising about the details of what an ideal work day, work week or month would constitute. This provides deeper knowledge of oneself, knowing one's aspirations, desires, fears and doubts. It can also lead to the actual creation of a job that at present does not yet exist, for example, a new way of solving problems for uses of new technology.

Study self

Deeper self-understanding may be sought by not seeing oneself merely objectively as a configuration of traits, but as a being capable of creating meaning. Some of the following techniques may be used:

◆ Assessment by a psychologist or counsellor for recommendations on career issues, taking into account personality traits, personal situation and the willingness to take risks.

◆ Analysing both one's positive and negative past experiences by thinking of the most rewarding or most dreaded activities or by drawing up a list of the things one enjoys doing, looking for common factors such as enjoying solitary activities, social activities, outdoor, physical or mental activities. Friends and colleagues may be asked for feedback on one's analysis of oneself.

◆ Trying to remember one's early childhood to find some basis for career dreams and sources of pleasure in work.

◆ Working through a set of symbolic exercises to discover one's more profound unconscious motivations.

◆ Dream analysis and imagination to reveal emotions.

Analyse past competencies

All capabilities involved in each previous phase of the individual's life should be examined. Such soul-searching may result in some surprises, as people often find that they have developed more skills than they had realised, for example, leadership skills.

Analyse competencies needed in ideal future

It is also necessary to analyse the skills that would be required in one's ideal career, because some of them will have to be acquired. This will determine one's learning goals, for example goals concerning practical skills in human resource management.

Draft tentative plan

Plan learning by writing down a goal, compiling a list of the steps necessary to reach that goal and deciding what resources and how much time are required.

Explore plan with others

Share the results of the above steps with trusted others who are committed to helping, who can provide some feedback on one's goals and who will understand one's fears and aspirations.

Execute plan incrementally and reflect on learning

As individuals realise that their future vision will change with experience, the next step to be taken in their careers involves three guidelines:

◆ working on the skills required to achieve goals, choosing either the most urgent or those that are most fun to undertake;

◆ making career choices that are on the whole consistent with the future vision; and

◆ taking time to become aware of feelings towards the activities the individual wants to undertake.

Evaluate and reformulate plans

All the factors in the plan should be revised at least annually by writing down reflections and discussing the results with trusted friends. This will keep individuals flexible — aware of their feelings and of what they have learned. This will counteract merely drifting and facilitate personal planning, growth and change.

This career-planning model is developmental in nature and presents a long-term view, but also makes provision for short-term survival in changing and uncertain times.

The career invention model

The career invention model suggested by Coetzee (2007) is based on the principle that the 21st century career is circular and that individuals have the power to change the nature of their career paths. Individuals are not dependent on the environment or organisation to make jobs available to them — individuals are the ones co-creating new alternative forms of work or employment through their creativity and talents. The times when individuals find themselves unemployed are periods for deep self-reflection on past experiences. It is also a time in which individuals review their development and the competencies they have gained. This process of deep self-reflection helps individuals to remember the dreams and desires they have not yet explored. Individuals also need to use the 'in-between' jobs period to figure out what they truly want and how their needs, desires and dreams are linked to their overall life purpose (Ibarra, 2003).

As individuals get more skilled in inventing or co-creating their lives and careers, changing career paths proactively may become the norm — individuals will start to be the ones deciding on how long they want to stay with a company before exploring new and better career possibilities. Individuals will become competency traders — they negotiate the conditions for their careers based on their convictions about their skills, expertise, knowledge and personal attributes they believe they will add or contribute to the organisation.

The career invention model is depicted in figure 3.4. The *cycle of career invention* constitutes three steps, namely (1) *self-exploration*, (2) *exploration of career possibilities and* (3) *experimentation with various career possibilities.*

The following brief example introduces these three steps:

Nomfusi is a 17-year-old High School student. She is pondering her future and the type of life she would one day like to lead. Nomfusi has high expectations for herself. She wants to live a quality life, maybe marry sometime in the future and, most importantly, she wants the type of job that will bring her a steadfast high income! Nomfusi decides to take an active role in the planning of her career. She has some important decisions to make.

The *first step* in the career invention model indicates that Nomfusi should engage in *self-exploration*, that is, she should explore her possible future selves (possible future working roles). Nomfusi can start doing this by asking questions such as: 'Whom might I become?' 'What are the possibilities?'

Nomfusi might start to test possible working selves by gathering information about herself such as:

- Who would she like to be one day?
- What does she enjoy doing?
- What would she like to contribute? Could she make a contribution to society and the planet?
- Where do her talents lie?
- What are her unique aptitudes and skills?
- What special career interests does she have?
- What is her preferred career orientation or pattern?
- What are her career values or motives?
- What are her personality preferences?
- What types of jobs are available in the market that match her interests, talents, aptitudes and skills, career orientation, career values and personality?
- What are the salaries related to these jobs?
- What alternative forms of employment or work are available (temporary projects, assignments, additional sources of income)?
- What are the requirements of these jobs and alternative forms of employment (does she need a university degree, specific training and experience)?
- Are there learnerships available as a starting point in her chosen career field to help her gain the experience she needs?

Proper self-exploration will enable Nomfusi to become more fully aware of her possible future selves, her talents, needs, desires, skills and aptitudes and career interests. Furthermore, *(step two)* she ought to gain insight into her career values and career orientation and *explore possibilities* and the options available in the marketplace. She should also start contemplating the possibility that she could create a career for herself by exploring various possibilities, including starting her own business. Finally, she needs to recognise the requirements of the career options and what she still needs in terms of skills, knowledge, education and experience to meet those requirements.

A greater awareness of herself and the possibilities that the work environment offers, can help Nomfusi to prioritise the options, set specific career goals in terms of what she would like to pursue in the short and long term. The information can also help Nomfusi to draw up a plan of action in terms of exploring and *experimenting* with her short-term options *(step three)*.

The short-term plan may include actions such as applying for a vacation or volunteer job at a company to be able to get a feel for the preferred position or to approach a company for some mentoring on the position. Nomfusi could, for example, do interviews with people or specific role models that she has identified. In terms of starting her own business, Nomfusi could do some volunteer work with someone who runs his or her own business in her chosen area of interest to get a good feel for what would be required of her.

Once Nomfusi has gathered first-hand experience of her short-term career options, she can step back and reflect on her experiences, her abilities and needs and the requirements of possible future working roles. She will then be able to develop a more realistic written career plan and will have a clearer idea of where she wants to go and what she would and could achieve in her life.

If one doesn't feel like experimenting first with one's identified career possibilities, one could still follow the long and hard way of drawing up a tentative short-term career plan. This would mean taking the actual step of finding employment, learning from the experience and going through the process of discovering what one really wants and what one doesn't like. This can often be very painful and demotivating (or damaging to one's self-esteem) when the job that one got appointed into is actually a living nightmare! Experimentation helps individuals explore, without committing themselves. They become creative and with some risk taking they build their self-confidence.

The effectiveness of the career-planning process depends also on the support received from various people and organisations. For example, learnership programmes, vacation or temporary job options, career-counselling services, career-assessment services, mentoring by role models and advice, love and support from families can all contribute to the success of the career invention effort. However, the key for individuals is to follow their heart, to listen to that inner calling and not to attempt to please others by living their dreams and aspirations for them. Individuals need to learn to live their own dreams.

Overview of the career invention model

The three steps of the career invention model constitute the following activities:

Step 1: Self-exploration

- identifying one's possible selves or working roles;
- assessing one's career interests, career orientation, career values, skills, knowledge, talents and abilities, career personality preferences, career assessment; and
- figuring out what one really wants, one's dreams, desires and life purpose.

Step 2: Exploration of possibilities

- researching career possibilities and alternatives that match one's career-assessment and general self-exploration, activity outcomes;
- prioritising the identified career possibilities;
- writing a short– and long-term career plan; and
- writing a plan of action to explore and experiment with the identified career options.

Step 3: Experimentation

◆ take action — finding the job or form of work/employment;

◆ achieving small successes;

◆ reflecting on achievements and failures and learning from them;

◆ updating goals, possibilities and self-conceptions about one's skills, abilities and possible selves;

◆ allowing 'in-between' periods of unemployment; and

◆ seizing new opportunities by taking action *(repeat steps 1 to 3 continuously).*

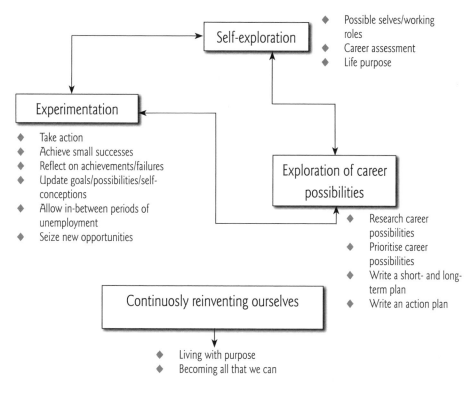

Figure 3.4 *Career invention model*

Adapted from Coetzee, M 2007

The career-invention model is also developmental in nature and emphasises career self-management and the notion of subjective career success. In order for individuals to be successful in the pursuit of their careers within the context of the 21st century world of work, they must develop a set of key characteristics. Figure 3.5 gives an overview of these characteristics.

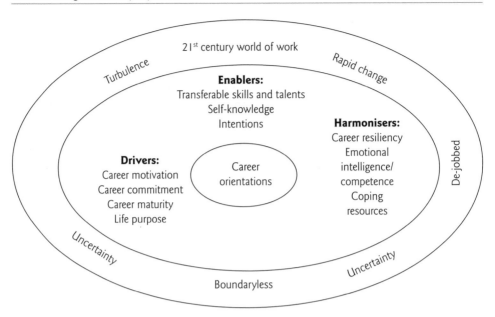

Figure 3.5 *Characteristics underlying a successful career*

Adapted from Coetzee, M 2007

The 21st century *world of work* is characterised by turbulence, uncertainty and rapid change. Flatter organisational structures and the emergence of the boundaryless career have led to the disappearance of traditional jobs. Employment opportunities, rather than jobs, are the new perspective of the 21st careerist. Individuals' *career orientations* (unique views about the paths their careers should follow) and values guide their career decisions.

The *drivers* (individuals' career motivation, career commitment, career maturity and life purposes) energise individuals and drive them towards experimenting with career possibilities that are based on their viewpoints of the possible selves they could become or the possible working roles they could experience.

The *enablers* (individuals' transferable skills and talents, self-knowledge and intentions) are those characteristics that help them to succeed in their careers.

The *harmonisers* (individuals' career resiliency, emotional intelligence/competence and coping resources) on the other hand, act as controls and keep the drivers in balance so that they don't overdo it (or burn themselves out) in the process of pursuing and reinventing their careers.

The contextual action model

The contextual action model (Young et al, 2005) is based on the classical *action theory* (Von Cranach and Valach, 1983) which addresses the goal-directed, intentional (or purpose-driven) behaviour of people from an *action system* perspective. Although developed as a post-modern counselling model, the principles of action theory can be used to guide individuals' career planning and development in the contemporary world of work (Young et al, 2005). Within the context of career development, the contextual action model asserts that career-related action is constructed socially through individuals, groups, communal and societal processes that are intentional and goal-directed.

The theory underlines the fact that people are required to take action in their daily lives that is both practical and symbolic. Individuals make sense of their lives and construct their careers through goal-directed actions. The notion of *career construction* recognises that work represents one of many domains within the human life structure wherein people enact multiple social or life roles (Hartung and Taber, 2008). It also addresses the contemporary notion of a career being an evolving sequence of employment-related experiences and significant learnings over time that lead to new choices and actions. *Significant learnings and experiences* identify the individual's professional life (career), direction, competencies and accomplishments through positions, jobs, roles and assignments (activities) (Weiss, 2001). As stated by a client:

Looking back in my life, my career has been determined by my life experiences and my work experiences. For me, therefore, a career is a whole set of various happenings in life, in my schooling, family, environment, society and different work situations that I have so far gone through. In every step of these occurrences and events I have learnt something that helped me to control my career and take responsibility for my career development.

Because *career action* occurs in a particular socio-cultural context and setting (ie, workplace) and significant others are involved in the career development process, career development is seen as an action system that derives meaning through the social interaction between individuals and others in their social environment (Kidd, 2007). As discussed in chapter 1, life experiences generate and enrich work (and career) meanings. People live holistic lives and are in a continuous process of meaning making and meaning exploration. The process of *interpersonal sensemaking* is approached from the lenses of job meaning, role meaning and self-meaning (see chapter 1). Contextual action theory adds to these three lenses a fourth, namely that of *social meaning*.

The contextual action model emphasises the role of individuals as *active career agents* in the career development process which is regarded as a *career action project* managed by the individual. *Career development support* from significant others (eg, family, career counsellors, mentors, peers, supervisors) in the career development process is seen as a *project* where the individuals and supportive others are involved in *joint action* (Kidd, 2007). *Social meaning* is particularly important in the career development support relationship, where language and narratives (career life stories) help people make sense of live events and provide meaning to the working life.

People's ability to act depends on having the relevant knowledge, skills and experience to do so. Their actions are also influenced by their personal and others' values and attitudes and are generally constrained by the conventions, rules and norms of the particular socio-cultural context and setting within which the career is pursued.

As shown in figure 3.6, a *three-dimensional conceptual framework* is used to analyse the actions people use in their daily behaviour: the *perspectives* that one can take on action, the *levels* at which action is organised and the *systems* of action.

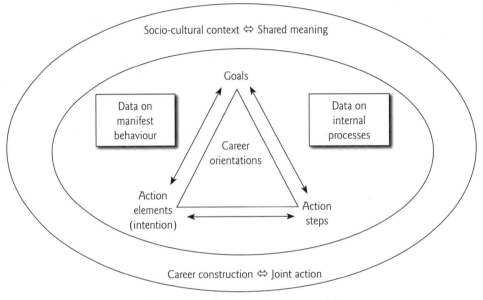

Figure 3.6 *Contextual action model*

Perspectives on action

In action theory, action is considered from three perspectives:

- ◆ *its actual manifestation*, that is, the external, observable range of verbal and non-verbal behaviours;
- ◆ *internal processes*, that is, the conscious cognitions (attitudes and core self-evaluations) and emotions that direct, guide and accompany the actions. The cognitive steering and subconscious self-regulation of actions are energised by individuals' emotional processes in the case of individual action and communication in the case of joint action; and
- ◆ *its social meaning*, that is, actions are understood by oneself and others in a socially shared way as having goals and representing intentionality.

Levels and dimensions of action

Action is also organised at *three levels*: (1) action *elements* (intentions or desires), (2) functional action *steps* and (3) as *goals*. Intentions or desires (action elements) inspire functional action steps which serve to reach a goal. The functional steps foster movement toward some type of goal, either as a process or as a desired end-state. Goals can refer to short-term action, project or career.

Goals are part of the action project itself and are therefore seen as the action-accompanying processes — the execution of an action depends on goals that emerge *within the action* and not just on prior goals. *Talking* about a goal is not the same as *having* a goal — when someone performs an action, the goal becomes operational. Goals are influenced by the social conventions of the particular socio-cultural context (eg, the organisation) and represent the meaning of action processes as agreed between the career agent (individual) and the observer of the action (eg, supervisor, mentor, counsellor).

Action is cognitively and socially regulated and steered. It is organised as a system that has *three dimensions*: (1) hierarchical, (2) sequential and (3) parallel. *Hierarchy* pertains to the super– and subordination of actions towards goals; for example, quitting this job and finding another may be part of a superordinate action of working in a field that is consistent with one's values. *Sequence* refers to the temporal ordering of actions; for example, applying for a job may involve reading the advertisement, preparing a résumé and being interviewed. Actions can also be *parallel;* that is, different actions for different goals can coexist (Valach and Young, 2004).

Systems of action

Four action systems are differentiated: (1) *individual action* and (2) *joint action* (both are *short-term* actions anchored cognitively, socially and environmentally in individuals' *everyday lives*), (3) *project* (mid-term actions that constitute a series of actions constructed as having common goals, eg, further education project, family health promotion project) and (4) *career* (long-term projects or projects that have a highly significant place in individuals' lives, (eg, motherhood) (Young, Valach and Collin, 2002). Joint action refers to the action that people take together with others (eg, spouse, parent, supervisor, mentor, peers, counsellor).

Career refers to those connections and actions that contribute to a long-term goal and broad life meaning, as is frequently the case in one's occupations (eg, the human resource practitioner career, the industrial psychologist career), parenting (eg, the motherhood career) or life partnerships (eg, the spouse career) or intensively in domains such as illness or a life of crime (eg, the patient career, the criminal career). By examining actions individuals begin to see career in the process of *continuous construction.*

Similar to the career invention model (Coetzee, 2007), career is invented as people engage in new individual or joint-action projects as part of their willingness to experiment with new possibilities. The notion of *project* offers a *heuristic system* (ie, an experience-based system) that helps in problem-solving, learning and discovery, enabling individuals to study and describe their careers and proceed toward their goals by exploring possibilities through continuous testing-and-learning rather than following strict guidelines (Valach and Young, 2004).

As individuals have their own intentions and goals, a dyad or group also develops joint goals and joint actions. In the joint action of counselling for example, career identity, values, interests and behaviours are not shaped from the outside in; rather, they are constructed through social discourse and personal narratives. For example, a couple may discuss career issues as the initial project. As their project develops, other concerns and tasks may arise for the couple, for example, responding to an employment lay-off or the equal sharing of the care of their children or elderly parent. Initially only intentions may be expressed as broad, undefined goals. The project goals are defined and redefined as the couple actually engages in actions and activities and is confronted by life circumstances.

Like project, career allows people to construct connections among actions, to account for effort, plans, goals and consequences; to frame internal cognitions and emotions; and to use feedback and feed forward processes. Joint action brings to the fore the contextual and social nature of the career development process. The critical component of making career meaningful is the realisation that meaning is not just in our minds as a representation, but in our actions and careers as an ongoing process of construction (Young and Valach, 2004).

People develop a sense of *identity* through their actions and the construction of narratives (career life stories). Goals and intentions, constructed through social discourse (discussions and interactions), serve to establish coherence in people's lives. The importance of shared *understandings* and emotional states and of joint goals and actions in the projects and careers that individuals and for example families and/or organisations construct together, is emphasised. Shared constructions and goals are associated with mutual feelings of satisfaction, stemming from positive appraisals of self and the other. The cognitive and emotional processes function commonly between the parties involved in career-focused exploration to promote joint goals and constructions of career, resulting in more emotionally supportive relationships (Valach and Young, 2004).

In the career counselling process (ie, the joint action project between the individual and the career counsellor or supervisor or mentor) *data* is also collected on *social meaning*, *internal processes* and *manifest behaviour* through interviews, logs of activities and follow-up discussions or regular telephone calls that monitor the project across time. Narrative feedback is used to summarise one's analysis of common activities based on the data collected. *Self-confrontation* is used to help individuals recall their feelings and thoughts during social discourse events (discussions) to facilitate insight and generate new actions and projects (Valach and Young, 2004).

Conclusion

The career models presented in this chapter illustrate that career management is an ongoing planning and developmental process. Self-knowledge as the basis for career planning, the ability of the individuals to direct their own careers and organisational career support are becoming increasingly important in the turbulent and changing economics of the world today. The traditional plan-and-implement and the modern test-and-learn career models can be used by both the individual and the organisation to plan and manage multi-directional career paths that provide meaning to people's working lives.

Review and discussion questions

1. Distinguish between the traditional and contemporary definitions of a career.
2. Differentiate between the concepts objective career success and subjective career success.
3. Differentiate between job satisfaction and career satisfaction.
4. How will individuals go about planning and managing their careers in the 21st century?
5. Why has career competency become important? Explain the various competencies, psychological career resources and inner value capital associated with career competency.
6. Explain the phrases 'intelligent careers' and 'career competency'.
7. How does career self-management relate to career maturity and career motivation?
8. How will career self-efficacy enhance an individual's career maturity?
9. Distinguish between the traditional plan-and-implement and the modern test-and-learn career models. How do these models complement one another?
10. Explain the steps you followed in planning and managing your career. Review the career planning models — which of the steps did you follow?
11. Discuss the advantages of career self-management.
12. Discuss the skills, attitudes, attributes and behaviour that helped you to achieve success in your career.
13. Why is self-knowledge critical in career planning?
14. Review the contextual action model and work through the case study in *reflection activity 3.3* on page 96. Then, reflect on your own career. Which individual action projects and joint action projects did you get involved in to help you construct a meaningful career?
15. What advice would you offer today's employees regarding career planning and management?

Reflection activities

Reflection activity 3.1

Read the case study of Mehboob and identify the characteristics of the **protean career** and aspects of **career self-management, career paths** and **career success** that apply to his career. Also, identify the various steps of the **career invention model** in his career. How does the contemporary definition of a career compare to Mehboob's definition of a career?

Managing your own success

Mehboob (30 years)

Mehboob Alie 'Mebs' Loghdey's ideal career path reads something like this: spend three years at a job, take a three-month sabbatical to 'consolidate' the lessons learnt and then start another job.

Loghdey, who is Director: Tailored Programmes at the University of Cape Town's Graduate School of Business, believes this is not impossible to achieve. 'If your career management is an active and considered progress, you are able to do this.'

Loghdey found his job in the *Sunday Times* while finishing his MBA at UCT's Graduate School of Business.

'When I applied for the job, I wrote a page on why the position excites me, reflecting that the job and I were a cultural and intellectual fit.'

Arguing his viewpoint was an aspect he had enjoyed in his MBA programme. 'One had to defend one's position, values and principles in an argument.'

Loghdey chose this particular business school because he liked its approach. 'I identified with its beliefs about management as a developmental process and its views on business education.'

His belief that management is transdisciplinary influenced his thesis, which looked at 'the management of organisational politics and emotions in the workplace'.

He believes that a new employee has 100 days to make an impression. 'When I was interviewed for the position at the business school, I articulated what I thought the job entailed and what I planned to do. I spoke as if I was already part of the business.'

Loghdey studied his MBA in order to 'accelerate' his career and get more general management skills.

He had earlier worked at *Dimension Data* for a spell of two years. Before that, he was Western Cape regional business development manager for *Global Access Telecoms*.

Before joining *Didata*, Loghdey, who comes from a family of doctors, studied sociology, economics and English literature at the University of Natal. 'It provided me with a good base from which to understand how societies and the economy worked.'

At university, Loghdey was already running his second business, a movie home delivery service. In high school he had launched a branded T-shirt business. His energy and enthusiasm continued during his MBA, when he made sure he 'kept in touch with the marketplace'.

'It was important to show the market I was grooming myself to take on bigger and more complex roles. An MBA graduate has no more than an entry ticket to the world of senior business leadership: an MBA alone is not the key to a good job. I made sure I kept up to date with what was happening in various business sectors.'

He is enjoying the challenge that comes with the position of director of customised programmes. Customised management programmes are typically used by organisations to train up those whom they regard as their next crop of managers and business leaders.

The management-training environment is highly competitive and when Loghdey and his team tender for contracts, they have to have an approach that will make them unique.

Loghdey and his team create tailored programmes that have theoretical and practical components. 'When we design the programme, we include a project issue or challenge that the organisation wants to develop a solution for, like designing a new product or entering a new market. We make that the focus of the programme to ensure that our intervention achieves personal and organisational learning as well as a tangible business impact. A contract can take between 18 months and two years.'

Loghdey would one day like to work overseas. 'I want to internationalise my career.' If that happened, he would return to share his new skills and experience in South Africa, preferably in a job that uses academic and commercial skills.

I see a career as a series of transitions, where one moves from managing oneself to managing others in organisational settings of increasing role, financial and people management complexity. — Vaida (2003).

The different steps of the career invention model	Mehboob's application
Self-exploration	
Exploration of career possibilities	
Experimentation	
Contemporary definition of a career	**Mehboob's definition of a career**

Reflection activity 3.2

Plan your own career by considering the steps of either the 21st century model (Otte and Kahnweiler, 1995) or Career invention model (Coetzee, 2007).

Assume that you are responsible for career guidance at your company and help an employee to plan his or her career by referring either to the 21st century model (Otte and Kahnweiler, 1995) or Career invention model (Coetzee, 2007).

Having implemented the model, consider your findings about the following:

◆ Did you gain new insight into yourself, your dreams and goals?
◆ What factor(s) did you find the most interesting and/or beneficial?
◆ What are your major strengths and development areas?

◆ Could you assist another person in his or her career planning by using the model you have chosen?

Reflection activity 3.3

Read the case study of Sarah and identify the characteristics of employability (discussed in chapter 2), career competency, career commitment, career self-management behaviours, career agency and objective and subjective career success.

Also review the **contextual action model** of career planning and answer the questions that follow.

Sarah (26 years)

Career success in my opinion is any advancement or progression that you have made towards fulfilling your ultimate dreams and goals in your career. It is a process that a person goes through; it does not just happen overnight. There are certain choices that you can make that will either make or break your career success.

I chose to take productive steps in my studies through my three undergraduate years, to make every bit of success that I could out of it. In studying I chose to always try and apply my knowledge that I had gained from the textbooks as well as in the classroom and attempt to visualise how it would transpire in the workplace. Although I don't have the knowledge of the experience of putting theory into practice in the workplace, I feel that I have taken all necessary steps in order to be productive in applying my knowledge. From gaining success out of my studies I was awarded the Golden key award for the top 15 per cent at the University. This will indeed open many doors with the aim for me to achieve success in my career, in striving to become a very competent industrial psychologist one day.

I feel very privileged and honoured that my hard work and perseverance were recognised. I can use this as a tool for me to advance in my career. I attended a networking breakfast that brought to light the networking techniques that people can use to their advantage to obtain the path of choice in their career. We were given the opportunity to meet CEOs of companies who joined us at the breakfast, to practise our networking skills. I feel that from all the advice and techniques that we learnt, I will be able to use them to my advantage to gain as much career success as possible.

I have job-shadowed an industrial psychologist to really get a feel of what transpires in the workplace. She has led me to certain competencies that I may need to accomplish one day to be successful at what I do. I have already achieved success in my studies and advanced on to Honours level, which are a few steps closer to a Master's degree and then practising as an industrial psychologist.

I will use what knowledge I have gained in the past as well as all the advice received from individuals I have met along the way to achieve success. I feel to assess whether I have in actual fact achieved my goals of success, I will need to be satisfied in my job and have a healthy and pleasant environment, be content with the work that I am undertaking and maintain high quality human relations with clients, colleagues and managers. I also feel that I will need to be able to work under pressure and deal with any obstacles that I may encounter. This all encompasses being emotionally intelligent and maintaining a healthy balance with work, family and social life.

All these aspects will stand me in good stead to climb the corporate ladder (so to speak) and realise success in my future career as I have achieved in my studies.

Questions

1. In terms of her career desire, what intentions and goals did Sarah set for herself?
2. What short-term and mid-term functional action steps did she take toward attaining her long-term career goal?
3. What is her *career* (long-term project)? What is her *individual* career action project (mid-term actions) to achieve her career goal?
4. What *joint* action project was she involved in as part of her mid-term actions?
5. Would you agree that she is aware of how her midterm actions all contribute toward the construction of her career as an Industrial Psychologist?
6. How would you describe the *social meaning* that Sarah attaches to becoming an industrial psychologist? What meaning do you attach to the career of an industrial psychologist?
7. What internal processes (cognitions and emotions) helped her to stay motivated and committed? Can you identify the psychological career resources and career competencies she applied in the process?
8. Describe *the action system dimensions* that apply to Sarah's career project goals: *hierarchy* of actions (super- and subordination); *sequence* of actions; and *parallel* actions.
9. Are the principles of action theory useful in understanding Sarah's views of what career success means to her? Give reasons for your answer.
10. Would you agree that the *actual actions* Sarah took toward her career as industrial psychologist helped to make her career meaningful? (If she had only kept on dreaming about becoming an industrial psychologist in her mind and had never actually taken action steps (in the form of individual action projects or joint action projects) toward it, would her career be less or more meaningful? Review chapter 1 (meaning of work) to formulate your answer.

4

Career choice and counselling

Learning outcomes

After studying this chapter you should be able to:

- discuss the trait-and-factor/person-environment-fit approaches;
- describe the categories of types and relationships between types in Holland's theory;
- describe the psychological processes that constitute types in Jung's theory and indicate their relevance to occupational choice;
- explain Dawis and Lofquist's view of how the fit between the individual and work contributes to work adjustment;
- explain Super's views on self-concepts, career maturity, career adjustment and life stages;
- discuss the cognitive-behavioural approaches to career decision-making;
- describe the determinants and outcomes of the decision-making process in Krumboltz's theory;
- explain how self-efficacy expectations are involved in differential career development of men and women in Hackett and Betz's model;
- discuss the life-career theory of Tiedman, O'Hara and Miller-Tiedeman;
- explain the influence of childhood experiences on career choice and decision-making as discussed in Bordin's theory;
- explain the role of needs and parent-child relations in Roe's theory;
- discuss the person-in-environment perspective of Cook, Heppner and O'Brien;
- describe Brown's view of values in career choice;
- describe the contribution of Savickas's career construction theory and logotherapy to career development counselling in the modern workplace;
- discuss the application of the various career theories in practice; and
- discuss ethical considerations in career counselling.

Introduction

The term *career choice* refers to the decisions people need to make or remake about their careers and work (Miller and Brown, 2005). Because all individuals at some stage in their lives experience difficulties with making career choices, they often turn to career counsellors to guide them in the decision-making process. Career counsellors work with clients of any age and at any stage in their careers, helping individuals with a wide range of career-related concerns. In the context of more flexible and diverse career patterns, career counselling is seen as a process that helps individuals not only make career-related decisions but also effectively manage their careers over the life course and develop the psychological career resources and competencies they need to deal emotionally intelligent with the challenges that arise as their working lives progress.

Kidd (2006:1) defines career counselling as:

a one-to-one interaction between practitioner (or counsellor) and client, usually ongoing, involving the application of psychological theory and a recognised set of communication skills. The primary focus is on helping the client making career-related decisions and deal with career-related issues.

Career development theories offer a framework for career counsellors within which individuals' career behaviour can be examined and explained. Each theory offers a *specific map* to career development and choice. Some theories are better at addressing specific choice points in the career process, others are better at explaining the development of career interests or the adjustment process to the world of work. Others are better at explaining the external factors that impact choice and persistence in the realm of careers (Shoffner, 2006). Career counsellors must understand well-established and emerging career theories, their strengths and weaknesses and how to apply them to client career development and choice to be able to effectively and efficiently provide career services appropriate to the 21st century world of work context.

As summarised in table 4.1, the various career theories that guide career counselling practice can be classified as:

◆ trait-and-factor/person-environment-fit theories;
◆ life-span development theories;
◆ cognitive/learning theories and approaches;
◆ psychodynamic approaches;
◆ relational approaches to career development;
◆ person-in-environment perspectives; and
◆ post-modern perspectives.

Table 4.1 *Overview of major career theories*

Career theories	Examples
Trait-and-factor/person-environment-fit theories	Parson's trait-and-factor theory
	Holland's theory of personality and occupational types
	Dawis and Lofquist's theory of person-environment correspondence
	Jung's theory of personality types

Career theories	Examples
Life-span development theories	Super's career development theory
Cognitive-behavioural theories and approaches	Krumboltz's career decision-making theory
	Mitchel, Levin and Krumboltz's happenstance approach theory
	Hackett and Betz's theory of self-efficacy
Psychodynamic approaches	Bordin's theory of personality development
	Tiedeman, O'Hara and Miller-Tiedeman's lifecareer decision-making theory
Relational approaches to career development	Roe's theory of parent-child relations
Person-in-environment perspectives	Cook, Heppner and O'Brien's race/gender ecological theory
	Brown's theory of values
Post-modern perspectives	Savickas's career construction theory
	Existential career counselling based on Frankl's Logotherapy

Trait-and-factor/person-environment-fit theories

The trait-oriented theories evolved from the measurement movement in the early part of the 20th century that focused on the assessment of characteristics of the person and the job. The theories are embedded in Parson's (1909) vocational counselling paradigm of matching individual traits with requirements of occupations (Zunker, 2006). The term *trait* refers to a characteristic of an individual that can be measured through testing. *Factor* refers to a characteristic that is required for successful job performance (Sharf, 2010). The key characteristic of this theory is the assumption that individuals have unique patterns of ability and/or traits that can be objectively measured and correlated with the requirements of various types of jobs (Zunker, 2006).

Parson's trait-and-factor theory

Parson (1909) developed a three-pronged approach (see figure 4.1) to help young people to make wise decisions and become successfully employed. The approach consists of helping people to develop (Sharf, 2010; Shoffner, 2006):

◆ a clear understanding of themselves (*individual knowledge*), including their aptitudes, interests, abilities, skills, attitudes, values, personality, ambitions, achievements and resource limitations;

◆ *knowledge of the job or occupation*, including the requirements and conditions of success, advantages and disadvantages, compensation, opportunities and prospects in different lines of work; and

◆ *logical or reasoned matching* of the individual's traits to the job that best 'fits' him or her.

Integrating information about one's self and about jobs and occupations is seen as the major goal of career counselling. Traits and factors can be reassessed as clients have new experiences that affect their assessment of their aptitudes, achievements, interests, values and personality.

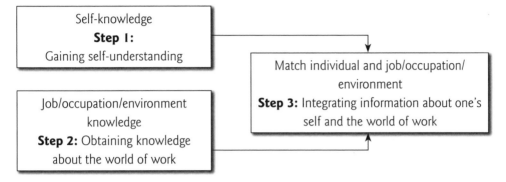

Figure 4.1 *Parson's trait-and-factor theory*

In the application of Parson's approach, the nature and requirements of the occupation determine which individual characteristics are measured. In general, those characteristics (traits and factors) that are measured for vocational guidance purposes are mental abilities, personality characteristics, interests and, to a lesser extent, values.

◆ *Mental abilities* include intelligence and aptitude. *Intelligence* consists of a combination of various factors that represent judgement, reasoning, problem-solving and learning ability, while *aptitude* refers to the potential to acquire skills through training and experience — that is, skills related to intelligence or specific aptitudes such as artistic, musical or mechanical aptitudes.

◆ *Personality characteristics* include factors such as dominance, emotional stability, shrewdness, introversion and extraversion. Such factors can be combined in a *personality profile* of the individual, which can be matched with occupational requirements.

◆ *Interests* concern likes and dislikes, for example, the individual's preferences for certain occupations or fields of study. These may involve social, practical, commercial, aesthetic, outdoor or intellectual/scientific activities. Measuring interests provides information from which needs and motives can be inferred.

◆ *Values* concern intentional behaviour and influence preferences as they involve interests, needs and motives. Values are measured in terms of *general values*, such as economic, political, social, religious, aesthetic and theoretical and in terms of *work-related values*, such as financial security, authority, altruism, autonomy, risk, variety and creativity.

The trait-and-factor approach is the general approach used in all of the career theories (eg, Holland's typological theory and Dawis and Lofquist's theory of work adjustment/

person-environment correspondence) that are based on matching individuals to work environments so that they will be successful in and satisfied with, their work. Parson's trait-and-factor approach has led to the development of assessment instruments such as achievement batteries, intelligence and academic aptitude tests, vocational inventories, interest and values inventories and personality inventories. Classification systems for occupations such as the Dictionary of Occupational Titles (DOT) and the Occupational Information Network (O*NET) — which replaced the DOT — have also been developed in the United States of America.

Information and tests that are available in South Africa for measuring individual characteristics can be obtained from the Test Catalogue of the Human Sciences Research Council. The effectiveness of the trait-and-factor approach depends on the *reliability and validity* of the tests used and on the *professional expertise and orientation* of the individuals applying the approach. Their orientation determines which tests they use and whether they regard the approach as sufficient or limited.

One of the *disadvantages* of the trait-and-factor theory is that it comes across as a deceptively simple theory. Because tests and inventories seem so authoritative to the client, they can prevent an easy interaction and rapport between the client and counsellor. The approach is limited because it is a mechanistic approach in which the machine is seen as a metaphor for man; in other words, man is seen as a passive rather than as an actively functioning being and psychological phenomena are reduced to mere *quantitative variables* in the form of measurable traits.

The theory also does not provide a guide to which tests or inventories the counsellor should include in his or her repertoire. It is also regarded as a *static* rather than a developmental theory. By focusing only on identifying traits and factors, the theory ignores how achievements, aptitudes, interests, values and personalities grow and change over time (Sharf, 2010). Career choice is likewise postulated as a static concept. Insufficient attention is paid to the fact that individuals, as well as jobs, can change — both have growth potential. Therefore, career choice cannot be likened to prediction of a final fit between the individual and the job at a given point in time. Research has shown that prediction of success in specific occupations is not absolutely reliable if it is based solely on the measurement of traits, because tests do not supply sufficient information on the individual.

Individuals choose occupations for various reasons, including reasons which are of personal significance to them, but which cannot necessarily be ascertained by measuring traits. In addition, different individuals vary in the way they perform the same work as well as non-work roles, to the extent that it can be difficult to differentiate between individuals with regard to their suitability for a particular job (Brown, 1990). Brown's (1995) criticism of trait-and-factor's reliance on psychological testing is pertinent for *South Africa's historically disadvantaged populations.* Considerable concern has been expressed about the reliability and validity of many psychometric measures that have been standardised for various South African population groups (Foxcroft, 1997). However, factors in South Africa's macro-environment, such as unemployment, organisational restructuring and resultant employee redundancies, may continue to reinforce the use of trait-and-factor procedures for career counsellors.

Notwithstanding these disadvantages, the standardised assessment and occupational analysis procedures emphasised in the trait-and-factor approaches are useful in career counselling. Growing numbers of research projects have focused on the development and refinement of assessment instruments and the optimal use of job descriptions and requirements, work environments, job satisfaction and work adjustment studies (Zunker, 2006).

Holland's theory of personality and occupational types

John Holland presented his theory of career choice in 1959. The underlying premise was that individuals choose situations and environments that satisfy their personality orientations. Holland is generally acknowledged as among the most influential people in the field of career counselling and practice. Apart from prompting a tremendous amount of empirical research in vocational and industrial and organisational psychology, the theory has provided major breakthroughs in conceptualising vocational interests and career decision-making, constructing interest inventories, organising occupational information, counselling for career development and structuring career education curricula (Shoffner, 2006:42).

According to Holland (1973), people search for environments that will let them exercise their skills and abilities and express their attitudes and values and take on agreeable challenges and roles. The key concept is that individuals are attracted to a particular role demand of an occupational environment that meets their personal needs and provides them with satisfaction (Zunker, 2006).

The theory in its simplest terms suggests that at first people can be characterised in terms of their resemblance to each of *six personality types (or modal-personal- orientations)*: **R**ealistic, **I**nvestigative, **A**rtistic, **S**ocial, **E**nterprising and **C**onventional (hence the reference to it as a **RIASEC** model). The closer people resemble a type, the more they exhibit the traits and behaviours of that type (see table 4.2). Similarly, career or occupational environments can also be characterised in terms of their resemblance and support of the six personality types (referred to as modal-occupation-orientations). The six basic modal-personal-orientations and six modal-occupation-orientations are based on the belief that people will enter and stay in work that is similar to (or congruent with) their personality type (Shoffner, 2006). A person's behaviour is determined by an *interaction* between personality and the characteristics of the environment. Choice of a career is an extension of one's personality type into the world of work. The stability of career choice depends primarily on the dominance of personal orientation. The strength or dominance of the developed modal personal orientation as compared with career environments will be critical to the individual's selection of a preferred lifestyle.

Table 4.2 *Holland's six modal-personal-orientations and occupational environments (based on Schreuder and Coetzee, 2006)*

Personal orientation	Themes	Occupational environments
This type is shy, conformist, frank, genuine, masculine, materialistic, natural, stable, persistent, uninvolved, practical, thrifty and shows lack of self-insight. ♦ *Preferences* include well-ordered, systematic handling of tools, machinery and animals and importance is attached to the concrete, such as money, power and status. ♦ *Aversions* include educational activities and social occupations and situations. ♦ *Dispositions* lead to the acquisition of hand, mechanical, agricultural, electrical and technical skills and lack of social and educational skills.	Realistic	Realistic occupations include jeweller, joiner, locksmith, miner, wall and floor tiler, bookbinder, furniture upholsterer, rigger, welder, plumber, panel beater, theatre technician, air traffic controller, computer programmer, hairdresser, butcher, machinist, dental technician, surveyor, electrical, mechanical, chemical, civil and mining engineer, forester, nature conservationist, post person, sailor, bus driver, truck driver, chef, ophthalmologist, airline pilot, ship's pilot, farmer, supervisor, tailor, train conductor, detective.
This type is analytical, cautious, critical, curious, introspective, independent, intellectual, passive, rational, methodical, reserved and unassuming. ♦ *Preferences* include observation and the systematic, symbolic and creative examination of physical, biological and cultural phenomena, with the object of understanding and controlling them and importance is attached to science. ♦ *Aversions* include persuasive, social and repetitive activities. ♦ *Dispositions* lead to the acquisition of scientific and mathematical skills and lack of persuasive abilities.	Investigative	Investigative occupations include mathematician, statistician, market researcher, economist, advocate, agriculturist, choreographer, pharmacist, botanist, zoologist, veterinarian, scientist, geologist, pathologist, physician, explosives technologist, electronics, industrial, aeronautical and telecommunications engineer, physiologist, psychologist, home economist.
This type is complex, emotional, disorderly, feminine, imaginative, idealistic, impractical, impulsive, introspective, independent, intuitive, nonconformist original. ♦ *Preferences* include ambiguous, free, un-systematic activities that involve manipulating human, physical and verbal material so as to create art forms or art products; importance is attached to the aesthetic. ♦ *Aversions* include explicit, systematic and ordered activities. ♦ *Dispositions* lead to skills in the musical, entertainment and fashion worlds, public relations, journalism, architecture, photography.	Artistic	Artistic occupations include singer, musician, actor, artist, art teacher, interior decorator, fashion designer, graphic designer, floral arranger, copywriter, editor, radio/television announcer, landscape architect, cartoonist, animator.

Personal orientation	Themes	Occupational environments
This type is friendly, generous, co-operative, persuasive, idealistic, kind, tactful, understanding, sociable, responsible, feminine, helpful and shows insight. ◆ *Preferences* include informing, developing and helping others and importance is attached to social and ethical activities and problems. ◆ *Aversions* include ordered, systematic activities that involve using materials, tools or machines. ◆ *Dispositions* lead to skills in human relations such as interpersonal and educational competencies and a lack of manual and technical skills.	Social	Social occupations include different types of social and educational work, nurse, ambulance worker, fire fighter, historian, funeral undertaker, job analyst, restaurateur, waiter, occupational therapist, speech therapist, beauty therapist, homemaker, librarian, customs official, airways ground host, police officer, traffic officer, members of the clergy and training officer.
This type is adventurous, acquisitive, ambitious, dependent, domineering, exhibitionist, impulsive, optimistic, energetic, self-confident and pleasure-seeking. ◆ *Preferences* include manipulating others in order to reach organisational or economic goals and significance is attached to political and economic gains. ◆ *Aversions* include observational, symbolical or systematic activities. ◆ *Dispositions* lead to the acquisition of leadership, interpersonal and persuasive skills and a lack of scientific skills.	Enterprising	Enterprising occupations include business people, personnel manager, marketing manager, banker, postmaster, insurance broker, travel agent, flight attendant, fashion model, auctioneer, estate agent, hotel manager, buyer, building contractor, public relations officer and attorney.
This type is conformist, defensive, conscientious, efficient, inflexible, inhibited orderly, practical, persistent, prudish and lacks imagination. ◆ *Preferences* include explicit orderly, systematic handling of data, such as keeping of records and numerical data and processing machines to achieve organisational or economic goals. ◆ *Aversions* include ambiguous, free, investigative and unsystematic activites. ◆ *Dispositions* lead to clerical, business and computer skills and a lack of artistic skills.	Conventional	Conventional occupations include office worker, clerk, bookkeeper, machine operator, receptionist, teacher of commercial subjects, secretary, typist, bank official, finance expert, work study officer, library assistant, accountant, proofreader, post person and meter-reader.

In 1969, Holland introduced the circular and hexagonal structure of his six personality orientations — shown in figure 4.2 — to provide a visual representation of the relationships among personality types and/or occupational environments. For example, adjacent categories on the hexagon (eg, realistic and investigative) are most alike, whereas opposites (eg, artistic and conventional) are most unlike. Those of intermediate distance (eg, realistic and enterprising) are somewhat unlike (Zunker, 2006).

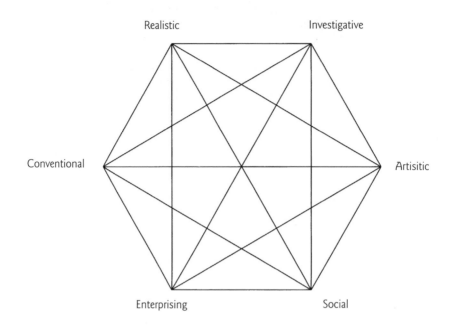

Realistic   Investigative

Conventional   Artisitic

Enterprising   Social

Figure 4.2 *Holland's hexagonal model of the interaction between personality types and occupational environments*

In Holland JL, 1973:29. Making Vocational Choices

Holland's theory posits *four basic theoretical constructs* that provide additional information when examining an individual's typology in interaction with the occupational environment: *congruence, consistency, differentiation* and *identity*.

◆ *Congruence* refers to the compatibility between a personality type and an environment. Congruence is highest when a personality type and environment match, for example, when a social type works in a social environment. Congruence is less high when a personality type works in an adjacent environment, for example, a social type in an artistic or enterprising environment. Congruence is lower when a personality type works in an environment separated by another environment, for example, a realistic person working in an enterprising or an artistic environment. If a person works in a diagonally opposite environment, for example, an artistic type in a conventional environment, the relationship is incongruent and conducive to job dissatisfaction and ineffective coping behaviour.

◆ *Consistency* refers to the similarity among types or environments. Adjacent personality types, such as investigative and artistic, have more consistency; that is, they represent a personality pattern that is relatively integrated in terms of similar personal characteristics. Types that are separated by another type, such as realistic and artistic, have less consistency because they include fewer similar characteristics. Opposite types, such as realistic and social, have low consistency because they comprise a personality pattern including diverse characteristics. Environments likewise have different degrees of consistency according to the similarity or diversity of work behaviours they involve. In general, high consistency with regard to personality and/or environment has higher predictive value for the outcomes of career choice. Inconsistent personality patterns and/or environments are less predictive because of their diversity, that is, the wider range of characteristics and behaviours they involve.

◆ *Differentiation* refers to the degree to which a person or environment is clearly defined. A person or environment that represents a single type, for example, only artistic, is differentiated. A person or environment that represents different types to the same degree — for example, one that is more or less equally artistic, enterprising and investigative — is undifferentiated. The interaction of a differentiated person and a differentiated environment has the highest predictive value for the outcomes of career choice. The interaction of an undifferentiated person and an undifferentiated environment has low predictive value because of the diverse aspects that the person seeks in the job and the diverse aspects that the job offers.

◆ *Identity* refers to the extent to which a person has a clear and stable perception of his or her characteristics and goals and to the degree of clarity and stability which an occupational environment provides. The individual's identity is related to differentiation and consistency: the higher they are, the higher the degree of identity (Gevers et al, 1992).

Extensive testing of Holland's theory suggest that his constructs are valid (Sharf, 2010; Zunker, 2006). Holland's typological system is particularly useful because it provides an easy framework for conceptualising all occupations. There are also a number of valid, reliable instruments based on the theory that can be used by career counsellors (eg, *Self-Directed-Search-R; the Career Attitudes and Strategies Inventory; the Position Classification Inventory; the Environmental Identity Scale; the RIASEC Activities List; Dictionary of Holland Occupational Codes; The Occupations Finder; and The Educational Finder*). The theory can be applied in career counselling, recruitment, personnel selection and placement.

Although Holland presents a complex theory of the relationships and interactions between individuals and work environments, the greatest weakness of Holland's theory may be the potential simplicity of its *application*, which can lead to the possible misuse of results. Less experienced or unaware counsellors may allow the test results to lead to recommendations of a limited number of career choice possibilities (Shoffner, 2006). In addition, a personality-environment-fit is not absolutely applicable to availability of jobs in the existing job market.

Dawis and Lofquist's theory of person-environment-correspondence

The *person-environment-correspondence theory* (Dawis and Lofquist, 1993) — originally referred to as the *theory of work adjustment* (Dawis, England and Lofquist, 1964) — is also developed from the trait-and-factor approach to career counselling.

The theory of work adjustment (TWA) focuses primarily on the *adjustment to work*, while *person-environment-correspondence* (PEC) focuses on the *'fit'* of a person for a particular work environment. The *PEC theory* posits that the career development process is the unfolding of the individual's abilities and requirements, in interaction with the individual's various environments (ie, home, school, play and work). Based on the premise that person and environment attempt to achieve and maintain correspondence with each other, it is assumed that *optimal correspondence* between the person and the environment will lead to success and satisfaction (Dawis, 1996:81).

Job fit involves matching the individual's traits with the requirements of the work environment. In PEC (and in TWA), an individual has many observable skills and a few inferred abilities. An individual also has a set of needs which are seen to be primary in their influence on fit. Individuals' needs can be grouped by *inferred values* (Sharf, 2010). For example, Dawis and Lofquist (1984) define status (a reinforcement value) as including the need for advancement, recognition, authority and social status (see also chapter 1). A client with a high need for advancement in his or her career (with increasing responsibility and authority) can be inferred to place a high value on status.

In addition to skills, abilities, needs and values, individuals have a personality style and various adjustment behaviours. One's personality style is composed of *celerity* (speed of initiating environmental interaction), *pace* (activity level of interaction), *rhythm* (pattern of interaction) and *endurance* (sustainability of interaction).

A person's *adjustment behaviours* include individual levels of *flexibility* (tolerance for non-correspondence with the work environment before action is taken to change the non-correspondence), *activeness* (actions to change the work environment in the event of non-correspondence), *reactiveness* (activities to change ways in which the personality structure is expressed) and *perseverance* (tolerance of non-correspondence before leaving the situation) (Dawis, 1996).

Work adjustment is indicated by an individual's overall job satisfaction, satisfaction with the various aspects of the work environment, satisfaction of needs and fulfilment of aspirations and expectations. Work adjustment is also indicated by the perceptions of the individual's productivity and efficiency as held by the supervisor and others in the work environment. *Satisfaction* drives the system and the satisfaction-dissatisfaction continuum influences the individual's behaviours on the job, as well as the work organisation's organisational behaviour. Satisfaction is related to work adjustment, which leads to job tenure and better job performance (Dawis, 1996).

The central points of the theory of *work adjustment/person-environment correspondence* are the following:

- Work involves the *interaction between the individual and the work environment* and in this interaction the environment has requirements of the individual concerning work performance and the individual has requirements of the environment concerning compensations for work performance. Compensations may include safety, comfort, congenial atmosphere, effective supervision and opportunities for achievement.

- If the requirements of both are met, the individual and the work environment are mutually responsive — that is, they achieve *correspondence*. The ongoing process of achieving and maintaining correspondence indicates work adjustment.

- There are two criteria of work adjustment, namely the *satisfaction* of the individual with the environment and the *satisfactoriness* of the environment with the individual.

- Both satisfaction and satisfactoriness are necessary if the individual is to remain in the work environment. *Tenure* is therefore the result of both factors and it is also the main indicator of work adjustment.

- Work adjustment (as well as tenure) can be predicted from the correspondence between the individual's so-called work personality and the work environment and to predict this correspondence the two variables should be described in corresponding terms.

- Corresponding terms are *structure and style*. The structure of the individual's work personality involves skills and needs, which derive from values. Work personality style involves typical ways in which the individual interacts with the environment, including celerity (speed of responding), pace (level of activity), rhythm (pattern of pace) and endurance (duration of responses). The structure of the work environment involves skill requirements and need reinforcers (stimuli that are conducive to need satisfaction). The style of the work environment involves requirements for celerity, pace, rhythm and endurance.

In the exposition of their theory, Dawis and Lofquist formulate the central points in terms of formal propositions that provide a basis for predicting work adjustment (see Dawis and Lofquist, 1984). On the whole, the propositions indicate that in predicting work adjustment, cognisance should be taken of individual skills, needs and values, work environment requirements and reinforcers as they are related to satisfaction, satisfactoriness, correspondence and tenure. The *Minnesota Importance Questionnaire* (MIQ) is used to assess values. Personality style is to be evaluated by the counsellor in an interview. The *Minnesota Occupational Classification System III* provides an index for level and patterns of abilities and reinforcers that different occupations provide.

The strength of the theory lies in a solid research foundation. Another strength is its applicability to many issues regarding work adjustment, for example, problems concerning co-workers, superiors, boredom and incapacity to meet work requirements (Sharf, 2010). Adjustment requires change in the individual or the organisation or both. The model can be used to assess resistance to change, flexibility and perseverance in both the individual and the organisation. It can also indicate how difficult an adjustment problem is and how much adjustment can be expected realistically (Dawis, 1996). Although work adjustment counselling is viewed differently in today's society, where clients are faced with constantly changing work environments, the general themes of work adjustment, work environment and job satisfaction derived from the PEC theory should continue to be recognised as viable factors in career counselling (Zunker, 2006).

Jung's theory of personality types

Carl Gustav Jung developed a theory of personality in which he posits *psychological type* as a major construct by which personality can be understood. Psychological type is akin to personality type, in that it refers to a personality pattern which involves certain psychological processes that determine the individual's orientation to life. Individuals vary according to different combinations of the processes that constitute their types (Jung, 1971). Jung's views were first published in 1921 and have become applicable to career choice by the development of two instruments which measure psychological types, namely the *Myers-Briggs Type Indicator* (Briggs Myers and McCaully, 1985) and *the Jung Personality Questionnaire* (Du Toit, 1983).

The psychological processes that Jung (1971) designated as constituting psychological type include two *attitudes* and four *psychological functions*. The attitudes are *extraversion* and *introversion* and the functions are *sensing* (sensation), *intuition, thinking* and *feeling*:

◆ *Extraversion* involves an attitude in which individuals focus their psychic energy on the external and the objective outside themselves. They think, feel and act in relation to the object in a direct and observable fashion. Their interest is in the immediate environment, in people and things and that which is objectively possible.

◆ *Introversion* is the opposite of extraversion and involves an attitude in which individuals focus their psychic energy on subjective factors within themselves. Although they are aware of objective data or external conditions, they select subjective data to think, feel and act. Their interest is motivated by the inner world of concepts and ideas, while the object and external events are of secondary importance to them.

◆ *Sensing* (sensation) refers to a perceptual mode mediated by the sense organs and body senses — that is, perception of external and internal physical stimuli. Since the senses provide perception of the present moment, it involves an orientation to experience that which is present, visible or concrete.

◆ *Intuition* is the opposite of sensing and refers to a perceptual mode mediated by the unconscious. It is not based on objective facts, but involves an instinctive kind of apprehension beyond the visible, in which something is experienced as whole or as complete — that is, one knows something without knowing the reasons why.

◆ *Thinking* refers to a mode of judging by which individuals try to understand things and link their ideas by means of a concept. It involves judging that can be intentional or unintentional.

◆ *Feeling* is the opposite of thinking and refers to a mode of judging by which the individual accepts or rejects things or ideas because of the pleasant or unpleasant feelings they evoke. It is a totally subjective process by which the individual imparts a value judgement.

Jung (1971) regarded sensing and intuition as opposite yet related functions, in that both are *irrational psychological functions*. Neither follows the rules of reason, but is beyond reason, although not contrary to reason and both processes involve perception rather than judgement when conclusions are drawn. Likewise, Jung regarded thinking and feeling as opposite yet related functions, in that both are *rational psychological functions*. Both are influenced by reflection in accordance with the laws of reason and involve judgement rather than perception when conclusions are drawn.

These functions and attitudes combine in different ways to constitute psychological types. Jung (1971) maintained that individuals mostly use one of the attitudes and one of the functions in orienting themselves. An individual may, for example, be an extraverted sensing type, an introverted intuitive type, an introverted feeling type and so forth.

The psychological processes are, however, not all equal in strength. An individual may, for example, be more or less extraverted, more or less introverted, more or less sensing or more or less thinking and so forth. Individuals can also vary at different times of their lives by, for example, being more introverted than extraverted at some stage and more extraverted than introverted at another stage, but, in general, certain processes seem to develop as the dominant, stronger processes in the individual's orientation, while the opposite processes remain undeveloped (Myers, McCaulley, Quenk, and Hammer, 2003).

The relative strengths of the psychological processes can be conceptualised in terms of *bi-polar processes;* that is, contrasting processes on a continuum. Therefore, extraversion/ introversion, sensing/intuition and thinking/feeling each form a continuum.

Both the *Myers-Briggs Type Indicator (MBTI)* and the *Jung Personality Questionnaire* include three scales that measure the relative strengths of the three continuums. Both instruments also include a fourth scale that measures judgement/perception on a continuum. This scale measures the relative strengths of judging and perceiving, thereby serving as an index of the relative strengths of an individual's stronger rational function (either thinking and feeling) in comparison to the individual's stronger irrational function (either sensing or intuition). One individual may, for example, predominantly use feeling rather than intuition to orient himself or herself, while another may predominantly use sensing rather than thinking and so forth.

The Jung Personality Questionnaire is designed to yield eight psychological types from the four scales. Each type is an indication of the predominant attitude, the predominant irrational function and the predominant rational function.

The *eight types* that can be derived are:

1. Extraversion with Thinking and Sensation;
2. Extraversion with Thinking and Intuition;
3. Extraversion with Feeling and Sensation;
4. Extraversion with Feeling and Intuition;
5. Introversion with Thinking and Sensation;
6. Introversion with Thinking and Intuition;
7. Introversion with Feeling and Sensation; and
8. Introversion with Feeling and Intuition.

In each of these eight types, variations can occur according to the relative strength of either a rational or an irrational function.

The *Myers-Briggs Type Indicator* is designed to yield *sixteen psychological types* from the four scales. Judging and perceiving are measured as distinct, rather than implicit parts of a personality pattern that can be derived from the four scales constituting the instrument. One individual's type may, for example, constitute introversion, intuition, feeling and perceiving, while another's type may constitute extraversion, sensing, feeling and judging and yet another may constitute extraversion, sensing, thinking and perceiving and so forth. In their implementation of Jung's theory, the compilers of the instrument see judging and perceiving as the individual's preferred processes for dealing with the outside world. Judging involves an orientation for making decisions, planning and organising, while perceiving involves an orientation to be attuned to incoming information and adaptability (Myers, et al, 2003).

The relation between typical occupational trends and the psychological processes constituting the MBTI types is indicated in table 4.3. In De Beer's (1997) analysis of type preferences in South Africa, she reports ESTJ and ISTJ as the most common types for black South Africans, as well as for whites.

Although not developed as a career theory, both the *Myers-Briggs Type Indicator* and the *Jung Personality Questionnaire* are useful instruments for vocational counselling and guidance. The *Myers-Briggs Type Indicator* is particularly helpful within the context of the 21st century world of work. Personality Type theory assumes a developmental component so that individuals can adapt to new situations using all parts of their personalities. Counsellors can use type to help identify the more satisfying situations and roles, as well as to help individuals adapt to those that seem to be a challenge for them (Myers, et al, 2003). The *Jung Personality Questionnaire* is especially useful for selecting a suitable occupation as the manual accompanying the test includes an extensive list of occupations suitable for each of the eight types that it measures. The occupations are divided into sections according to the educational qualifications required.

Table 4.3 *Brief description of the sixteen MBTI personality types and typical occupational trends (adapted from Myers et al, 2003)*

ISTJ	ISFJ	INFJ	INTJ
Analytical manager of facts and details, dependable, decisive, painstaking and systematic, concerned with systems and organisation, stable and conservative *Occupational trends:* management; administration; law enforcement; accounting	Sympathetic manager of facts and details, concerned with people's welfare, dependable, painstaking and systematic, stable and conservative *Occupational trends:* education; healthcare, religious settings	People-oriented innovator of ideas, serious, quietly forceful and persevering, concerned with the common good, with helping others to develop *Occupational trends:* religion, counselling, teaching, arts	Logical, critical, decisive innovator of serious intent, highly independent, concerned with organisation, determined and often stubborn *Occupational trends:* scientific or technical fields, computers, law
ISTP	**ISFP**	**INFP**	**INTP**
Practical analyser, values exactness, more interested in organising data than situations or people, reflective, a cool and curious observer of life *Occupational trends:* skilled trades, technical fields, agriculture, law enforcement, military	Observant, loyal helper, reflective, realistic, empathetic, patient with details, gentle and retiring, shuns disagreements, enjoys the moment *Occupational trends:* healthcare, business, law enforcement, service	Imaginative, independent helper, reflective, inquisitive, empathetic, loyal to ideals, more interested in possibilities than practicalities *Occupational trends:* Counselling, writing, arts	Inquisitive analyser, reflective, independent, curious, more interested in organising ideas than situations and people *Occupational trends:* scientific or technical fields
ESTP	**ESFP**	**ENFP**	**ENTP**
Realistic adapter in the world of material things, good natured, tolerant, easygoing oriented to practical, first-hand experience, highly observant of details and things *Occupational trends:* marketing, skilled trades, business, law enforcement, applied technology	Realistic adapter in human relationships, friendly and easy with people, highly observant of their feelings and needs orientated to practical, first-hand experience *Occupational trends:* healthcare, teaching, coaching, child-care worker, skilled trades	Warmly enthusiastic planner of change, imaginative, individualistic, pursues inspiration with impulsive energy, seeks to understand and inspire others *Occupational trends:* Counselling, teaching, religion, arts	Inventive, analytical planner of change, enthusiastic and independent, pursues inspiration with impulsive energy, seeks to inspire and understand others *Occupational trends:* science, management, technology, arts
ESTJ	**ESFJ**	**ENFJ**	**ENTJ**
Fact-minded, practical organiser, assertive, analytical, systematic, pushes to get things done and working smoothly and efficiently *Occupational trends:* management, administration, law enforcement	Practical harmoniser and worker-with-people, sociable orderly, opinioned, conscientious, realistic and well tuned to the here and now *Occupational trends:* education, health care, religion	Imaginative harmoniser and worker-with-people, sociable, expressive orderly, opinioned, conscientious, curious about new ideas and possibilities *Occupational trends:* religion, arts, teaching	Intuitive, innovative organiser, analytical, systematic, confident, pushes to get action on new ideas and challenges *Occupational trends:* management, leadership

Life-span development theories

The life-span development orientations to careers and career counselling take the view that choosing a career and managing one's career development involves a continuous process that carries on through life. These theories also use concepts from developmental psychology, such as developmental stages and tasks and career maturity, to describe and explain the process of career development (Kidd, 2007). The theory of Donald E Super is the most commonly associated with the developmental approach to careers.

Super's career development theory

Donald E Super developed his views on career development over a period of approximately forty years of research. A research programme at Columbia University, the *Career Pattern Study*, contributed to his formulation of a theory of career development seen as a process over *five life stages* from childhood to old age.

Fundamentally, career development is seen as comprising the formation and implementation of *self-concepts* in occupational contexts. It is a process that involves a synthesis or compromise between the individual's self-concepts and aspects of reality such as social, economic and cultural factors (Super and Bohn, 1971).

Self-concepts are individuals' own views of their personal characteristics. These develop through individuals' *interaction with the environment,* in which they develop concepts of themselves in certain roles, such as that of student, worker, friend or family member. Different self-concepts may be related, but not all of them are relevant to all life or work roles and some may be positive, while others are negative. Self-concepts may also change over time as social, economic and cultural factors, occupations and technology change. Such changes influence the *process of synthesis* between the individual and reality (Super, 1990).

Synthesis is essentially a learning process in which *role playing* plays a part. Role playing begins in childhood when roles such as those of teacher, nurse or sales person are play-acted and it continues in adulthood when individuals imagine themselves in the role of, for example, boss or manager. Role playing is functional and whether it is played in fantasy or in reality or in work or non-work situations, it may eventually contribute to career adjustment. *Adjustment* refers to the outcomes of behaviour in career development. Depending on the *outcomes,* self-concepts may be modified in the process of adjustment (Super, 1990).

Related to career adjustment is *career maturity,* which includes types of behaviour conducive to adjustment. It refers to general types of *behaviour* in specific life stages, as well as to prior aspects of behaviour manifested in the particular developmental tasks of a given stage. In this context, maturity is not a unitary trait that increases with age. *Age* is a factor in maturity only in that a person is evaluated in terms of the behaviour of other people at the same stage; that is, a person may be mature at any age, depending on her or his adjustment in a stage associated with that age. Career maturity amounts to readiness to make career decisions and to cope with the developmental tasks of particular life stages (Super, 1992).

Life stages

Super (1992) describes the following life stages:

Growth (birth to age ± 12–14)

Children develop concepts of themselves through contact with adults who become role models. Curiosity drives them to explore and experience the world around them. Pleasant experiences lead to the development of interests, which, together with the development of self-esteem, autonomy and future perspective, provide the capacity for forward planning. If these characteristics do not develop, feelings of alienation, of being helpless in a world dominated by other people may result, with the possibility that the individual may become either a conformist, a drifter or a flounderer. Fantasy influences the development of interests, but as experience makes children more aware of their capacities, their interests become more realistic.

Exploration (adolescence, age ± 14–25)

Adolescents at first make tentative career choices, which may be tried out in the exploration of part-time or holiday work. Tentative choices are usually followed by exploration of a chosen field in greater depth. Sometimes the exploration of a chosen field precludes considering alternative choices. An individual may also pursue a particular field as a result of the inspiration or expectations of parents and other adults. Such an early choice may, at a later stage, result in career crises when individuals cannot cope with change because they are accustomed to seeing a career as encompassing 'an occupation' rather than as different roles or directions.

Establishment (early adulthood, age ± 25–45)

Generally, establishment involves a period of trial in the late twenties and a period of stabilisation in the thirties and early forties. Trial includes a succession of job changes before a final choice is made or before it becomes clear that the career will consist of changes. During stabilisation, security and advancement become priorities. Frustration due to unsuccessful stabilisation may lead to either stagnation or to change. Some individuals, however, thrive on change — they do not stabilise and their careers may consist of a series of trial periods. Super contends that most people, including those who find stabilisation and those who favour change, see the years of early adulthood as the best years of their lives.

Maintenance (middle adulthood, age ± 45–65)

At this stage, there is generally continuation along established lines in one's work. Some individuals, who have not achieved what they wanted to, may stagnate in the *status quo* and avoid actively acquiring new knowledge and skills. Others may focus on reaching further goals, for example, by means of continuing education, while still others become innovators of change, akin to some individuals in the establishment stage.

Decline (old age from ± 65)

As people enter old age, they first tend to decelerate work activities by, for example, seeking less responsibility or selectively changing work roles. As they sense a decline in their physical and mental powers, they may selectively start disengaging from work roles. Disengagement varies from person to person. Some occupations and circumstances enable individuals to choose when they wish to disengage by retiring, while others are forced to retire and thus disengage. Depending on the person and the situation, retirement may result in a sense of loss or it may be stimulating in that new choices can be made.

Although Super distinguishes these life stages, he stresses the point that individuals do not develop uniformly. Life stages normally occur at the approximate ages indicated, but are not discrete and not invariable. The ages at which they begin and end are *flexible* and transition to a particular stage may include characteristics of another stage. Exploration, for example, which is generally associated with adolescence, may manifest in adult stages in the form of exploring occupational change and new opportunities or after retirement in the form of exploring new roles. The underlying principle of exploration remains the same, but manifests in different forms in different stages. A career may include not only new explorations but also new growth in different stages or re-establishment in different types of roles or jobs. This process of recurring life-stage characteristics is referred to as *recycling* (Super, 1990).

Super's view of a career as a series of life stages in the course of the total life-span is graphically portrayed in figure 4.3 as a model called the *Life-Career Rainbow* (Super, 1988, 1990, 1992).

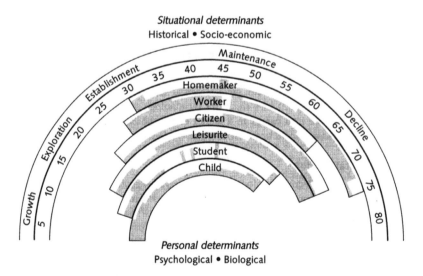

Figure 4.3 *The Life-Career Rainbow: Nine life roles in schematic life space*

Super, DE (2001:212)

The Life-Career Rainbow

The two outer bands of the Life-Career Rainbow depict the five life stages and the approximate ages at which they occur. The inner bands each represent one of *six life roles* that individuals may occupy in their life space, namely that of child, student, leisurite, citizen, worker and homemaker. The significance of any one or more roles varies from individual to individual and according to the relevant life stage of the individual. For one individual, for example, the worker role may be the most significant role in the establishment and maintenance stage, while, for another, the role of homemaker may be more significant than the worker role in the establishment stage. Yet another individual may regard the roles of homemaker and worker as equally significant in the establishment stage, with the role of citizen becoming increasingly important in the maintenance stage, when the significance of being a homemaker declines.

When the *Life-Career Rainbow* is implemented as an assessment device, the individuals concerned indicate the significance of a given role at the present or as they would like it to be in the future, by shading the band that indicates a role or roles. The intensity of the shading and the amount of space taken up indicate their choice with regard to the beginning and end of growth and the fluctuation and decline of a given role in a given life stage.

Below the rainbow figure, *personal determinants* involving psychological and biological factors, which have an influence on the significance of particular roles in the life space, are indicated. Above the figure, situational determinants involving historical and socio-economic factors which influence the career process are indicated.

The personal and situational determinants may also be referred to as individual and environmental determinants respectively. Super (1990, 1992) uses the latter terminology and synthesises their significance in a career in a model called the *Segmental Model of Career Development* or the *Arch of Career Determinants* (figure 4.4).

The Segmental Model

The Segmental Model is the portrayal of a structure analogous to the structure of the archway entrance of a Norman church near Cambridge, England. As the architectural structure consists of building blocks which in their interaction determine the form of the whole, the determinants of a career are seen as segments or building blocks which in their interaction determine the career as a whole. The biological-geographical foundations of development are presented as the step at the entrance.

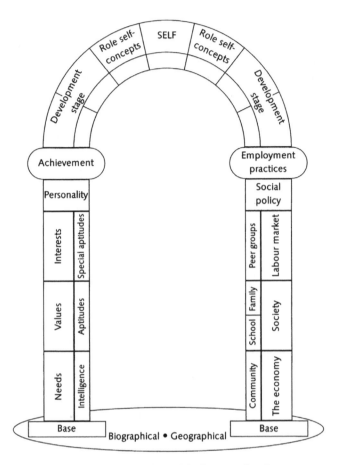

Figure 4.4 *A Segmental Model of career development*

Super, DE (1996:200)

The segments form two columns, each with a base fundamental to development. The column on the left has a *base* from which *personality variables* develop through the individual's interaction with *environmental variables* depicted in the column on the right. As a result of this interaction, foundations of personality develop into *needs* which, in turn, give rise to *values*, which lead to *interests*.

Intelligence, seen as general intelligence, also develops through interaction of the individual with the environment and forms specific *aptitudes* such as verbal, spatial and numerical aptitudes which, in turn, give rise to *special aptitudes* such as mechanical or clerical aptitudes. All these variables culminate in the capital of the column, which represents an analogy to *personality* as a whole and influence the individual's achievements. Super (1992) maintains that the top segments of the column, involving interests and special aptitudes, are influenced more by the interaction of the individual with the environment than are the variables close to the base and that they also have relatively more predictive value for career choice than the lower segments.

The column on the right has a *base,* involving *environmental variables,* which in interaction with personality variables gives rise to particular environmental determinants of a career. The community determines *schooling, family life and structure and peer group influence,* while the *economy* has effects on *society,* which has effects on the *labour market.* All these variables culminate in the capital of the column, which represents an analogy to *social policy* as a whole which, in turn, influences *employment practices* such as training requirements and fair career practices (Super, 1992).

The two columns and their reciprocal interactions culminate in the arch. The keystone of the arch represents the *self,* which is a synthesis of the individual's role and self-concepts in development in stages and also incorporates the personality and environmental determinants. The development stages on the left of the arch represent *childhood* and *adolescence,* while those on the right represent *adulthood* and *old age* (Super, 1992).

The self is thus the central segment of a career, but is nevertheless not the cement that holds the determinants together. Super (1990) sees *learning processes* as analogous to the cement that binds the components of the architectural structure. Learning takes place through interaction of the individual and the environment and therefore binds the determinants of the career.

Super's views are conceptually comprehensive and provide useful terminology for career counsellors, such as role concepts, career maturity and choices over the life-span. His ideas have stimulated a large body of research which, on the whole, supports his ideas (Brown, 1996).

One of the great strengths of Super's theory is its flexibility in incorporating cultural variables. In South Africa, all these constructs, with the exception of life themes, have also been widely examined in the different cultures (Langley, 1999). According to Baloyi (1996), Super's constructs such as self-concept, career development, career maturity, values and life roles seem generally acceptable in the African context. Career adaptability, where the individual is ready to cope with a changing world and working conditions, seems to be particularly appropriate in the context of the 21st century world of work (Langley, 1999).

Cognitive-behavioural theories and approaches

The cognitive-behavioural career theories arose out of behavioural psychology and emphasise a change-focused problem-solving approach and the cognitive processes through which people monitor their career behaviour (Kidd, 2007).

Krumboltz's career decision-making theory

John D Krumboltz posits a theory of career choice, which is an application of *social learning theory,* in that career choice is seen as a decision-making process in which learning plays a major role (Krumboltz, 1979; Krumboltz et al, 1976; Mitchell and Krumboltz, 1990). In social learning theory it is assumed that learning experiences are major determinants of personality and development. In Krumboltz's theory it is stated that learning experiences, together with genetic factors, environmental factors and abilities that are called task approach skills, are determinants of the decision-making process. The interactions of these determinants result in certain outcomes, which include actions with regard to career decisions.

Decision-making determinants

Genetic factors that influence choice are *genetic endowment* and *special abilities:*

◆ *Genetic endowment* includes gender, race and physical appearance, as well as physical handicaps, which may set limits on career choice. Gender may play a part in choice in that, for example, female and male children are exposed to different types of environmental experience that ultimately influence career choice. Physical appearance may be relevant to career choice in that bodily strength or height is relevant to particular occupations.

◆ *Special abilities* include inherited aptitudes which, through environmental influences, may become occupational skills involving intelligence, artistic ability, musical ability or muscular co-ordination. *Environmental factors* include social, cultural, political and economic factors that influence career decisions. Examples of such factors are job and training opportunities, family and community influences, education system, social organisation with regard to selecting workers, monetary and social rewards of jobs, labour laws and union rules, technological development, natural resources and natural disasters such as droughts and floods. Such factors may have an influence on individuals' career decisions that are beyond their control.

Learning experiences include two types of learning, namely instrumental learning and associative learning. In *instrumental learning,* reinforcements influence choice. Antecedents to choice may be special ability for a particular occupation and an environmental factor such as a training opportunity for the occupation, which results in choosing a job in that occupational field. If job performance results in positive reinforcement, for example, feedback and praise, the individual will continue with the desirable performance and acquire more skills in that direction, while negative reinforcement may lead to selecting an alternative job.

In *associative learning,* which involves classical conditioning, a neutral stimulus is associated with a particular stimulus and thereby acquires the same connotation or emotive meanings that the particular stimulus has. A neutral stimulus may be an occupational title such as medical doctor or electrician which, when it is associated with the connotation that medical doctors or electricians make money quickly, acquires the connotation of a preferred occupation. Such associations may become stereotyped views of certain occupations. The associations may, however, change over time. The work of a medical doctor or an electrician may, for example, be associated with long and irregular working hours and thereby acquire a negative connotation.

Instrumental and associative learning experiences influence career decisions through direct experience, but associative learning also includes indirect experience, which in social learning theory is referred to as vicarious learning experience. Vicarious learning is mediated by the observation of real life or fictitious models that set examples for occupational associations.

The varied sequences and patterns of learning experiences that affect the individual result in learning experiences that are unique to the individual. Learning experiences may have inevitable effects on the individual's decisions, yet may not be retrievable in their exact forms, because of the complex and varied nature of learning sequences and patterns. Learning experiences may, however, change as reinforcements and associations change.

The interaction of genetic factors, environmental factors and learning experiences leads to the development of *task-approach skills*. Such skills are more likely to be learned if they are conducive to positive reinforcement. Seen as determinants in the decision-making process, task-approach skills, in essence, refer to skills and standards that individuals bring to their work, for example, work habits, work values, performance standards, mental sets, cognitions and emotional responses that influence their approach to occupational tasks. Task-approach skills may be more or less effective and may become modified through new learning experiences.

Decision-making outcomes

The interaction of genetic factors, environmental factors, learning experiences and task-approach skills results in certain decision-making outcomes, namely self-observation generalisations, world-view generalisations, task-approach skills — seen as outcomes and not only as determinants — and career actions. These outcomes apply to all individuals, but their nature or content varies from individual to individual.

Self-observation generalisations refer to individuals' perceptions of themselves in terms of their self-efficacy; in other words, their estimate of their ability to perform certain tasks according to certain standards, for example, perceiving themselves as good at a subject because they passed the examination, their interests; that is, their likes, dislikes, as well as indifferent feelings about occupational concerns and their personal values. Personal values concern the desirability and importance that certain choices and their consequences have for them, for example, monetary rewards, prestige or other factors that they have come to value through instrumental and associative learning experiences.

World-view generalisations refer to individuals' observations in certain environments that they generalise as applicable to other environments, for example, the generalisation that social contacts facilitate job success or upward mobility. Both self-observation and world-view generalisations may be more correct or less correct.

Task-approach skills, besides being seen as determinants of decision-making, are also seen as outcomes in decision-making. As such, they refer to any skills or abilities that are used to cope with the environment and include information seeking, setting goals, generating alternatives, assessing the accuracy of one's self-observation and world-view generalisations, planning and predicting future events.

The interaction of self-observation and world-view generalisations and task-approach skills leads to new learning experiences and decisions, thereby generating another decision-making process. The implication is that, seen as such, career decisions involve decision-making processes over the lifetime of the individual. Each process culminates in actions concerning choosing or not choosing particular fields of study and training, applying for jobs, selecting alternative options, seeking promotion, learning new skills and changing jobs.

Krumboltz's theory may be applied to career counselling by determining in which of the decision-making outcomes an individual requires assistance, be it in self-orientation or world-view generalisations, task-approach skills or actions. Techniques that may be used include cognitive strategies in which incorrect thought processes or generalisations may be changed to become adaptive or realistic, reinforcement strategies in which performance is positively reinforced by means of, for example, feedback or role models which provide positive associative-learning stimuli.

Some empirical research findings lend support to the postulations of this theory. In particular, research supports the hypotheses concerning the nature of learning experiences that lead to the development of task-approach skills, the nature of learning experiences that influence education and occupational preferences and factors that lead to relevant actions when entering selected occupations (Mitchell and Krumboltz, 1996).

Mitchell, Levin and Krumboltz's happenstance approach theory

Mitchell, Levin and Krumboltz (1999) developed happenstance approach theory for career counselling. The primary premise is that unpredictable social factors, environmental conditions and chance events over the life-span are to be recognised as important influences in clients' lives. Chance events over one's life-span can have both positive and negative consequences. For example, an individual may lose a job as a result of outsourcing only to find a better one. The illness or death of a loved one can, for example, have negative consequences for career development. Happenstance approach suggests that counsellors are to assist clients to respond to conditions and events in a positive manner. They are to learn to deal with unplanned events, especially in the give-and-take of life in the 21st century workforce (Zunker, 2006).

Mitchel et al (1999) identified *five critical client skills*:

◆ *curiosity* (exploring learning opportunities and taking advantage of options offered by chance events);

◆ *persistence* (a way of dealing with obstacles that may be the result of chance events);

◆ *flexibility* (learning to address a variety of circumstances and events by adapting and adjusting as events unfold); and

◆ *optimism* (adopting a positive attitude when pursuing new opportunities) and *risk taking* (realising that risk taking can result in positive outcomes for career development such as finding a more secure or better paying job).

The goal of career counselling is to help clients look for solutions to their circumstances and develop strengths based on their past experiences in life and work. Clients should be guided to approach the future with a positive attitude and the curiosity and optimism that produce positive results; that is, the career counselling process should help to foster an attitude of taking advantage of unplanned events and dealing intelligently with negative consequences in the future (Zunker, 2006).

Hackett and Betz's theory of self-efficacy

Hackett and Betz (1981) present a model that applies *social learning theory* to career choice. Based on the work of Bandura (1986) and that of Krumboltz, Mitchell and Jones (1976), *self-efficacy*, an aspect of social learning theory, is seen as the key concept in career decisions. Self-efficacy refers to individuals' sense of having some control over events that affect their lives. It involves their judgement of their capacity to use their skills effectively in performance — in other words, their judgement of what they are capable of doing with their skills, but not judgement of their skills as such (Bandura, 1986).

Hackett and Betz (1981) postulate that men and women differ with regard to *expectations of self-efficacy*. In contrast to men, women have low expectations of self-efficacy because their socialisation experiences result in their having low expectations of success. This gives rise to internal barriers that prevent them from fully realising their capabilities and talents. Consequently, they limit their career choice to a narrow range of options. This is reflected in the relatively higher representation of women than men in lower-status and lower-pay jobs and the low representation of women in professional fields such as law, engineering, science and mathematics, as well as in management and administration positions and the skilled trades.

Women's career development can be understood and facilitated by taking into consideration certain mechanisms that play a part in the development of personal efficacy expectations. These are *performance accomplishments, vicarious learning, emotional arousal and verbal persuasion.*

Performance accomplishments

Successful performance in a task or role increases expectations of efficacy in that task or role. Men and women *differ* with regard to expectations of efficacy possibly because their access to successful performance and their interpretation of success differ.

Men have more access to successful performance in that stereotyped masculine roles are associated with qualities that are instrumental to successful task performance, such as assertiveness, activity, competition and dominance. Furthermore, men are exposed to a greater variety of socialisation experiences outside the home, such as sport and mechanical activities. Together, these factors may provide more access to success and they can also increase and strengthen self-efficacy expectations.

Stereotyped feminine roles are generally associated with qualities such as nurturance, passivity, sensitivity and submissiveness which, although positive in nature, do not necessarily lead to successful task performance. Women's socialisation experiences are furthermore focused more in the home than outside the home. These factors provide a narrow range of access to successful performance, which may lead to lower and weaker expectations of self-efficacy. Generally, women have a higher sense of self-efficacy with regard to domestic activities, but a lower sense of self-efficacy in most other behavioural domains.

Differences between men and women with regard to the interpretation of success could be related to differences in their evaluations of their self-esteem or to differences with regard to the causes to which they ascribe success or failure. Causes may be seen as external, for example, luck or the difficulty of a task or causes may be seen as internal, for example, ability or effort. Hackett and Betz (1981) cite research findings which suggest that women, more than men, interpret their successes and failures as being caused by external factors such as luck, rather than finding causes in themselves.

Vicarious learning

Vicarious learning refers to learning by *observing other people's behaviour*. Generally men's socialisation experiences, more than women's experiences, are conducive to acquiring career-related self-efficacy by vicarious learning. Women are less exposed to successful female role models who represent women over the full range of career options. In the media and in educational and occupational information, women are mostly portrayed in traditional homemaking and mother roles, with limited portrayal of them as successfully engaged in pursuits not traditionally associated with women. There are also fewer female role models available to women for fewer women occupy non-traditional — that is, male-dominated — occupations such as management and the skilled trades. Women therefore have higher self-efficacy with regard to traditional female roles and lower self-efficacy with regard to occupations not traditionally associated with women.

Emotional arousal

Emotional arousal can involve anxiety and susceptibility to stress, which can negatively influence self-efficacy expectations and performance. Research findings quoted by Hackett and Betz (1981) indicate that women in general show higher anxiety levels than men and that individuals who are typed as feminine sex-types report higher anxiety levels than individuals typed as masculine sex-types. The implications of such findings are that anxiety in women and in individuals of both sexes typed as feminine sex-types could be detrimental to self-efficacy expectations.

In individuals who lack self-efficacy with regard to certain tasks or roles, anxiety could be a result or effect of their lack of self-efficacy. Anxiety may, however, also become a cause that has a further limiting effect on self-efficacy and performance in specific tasks or in general.

Verbal persuasion

Verbal persuasion involves encouragement or lack of encouragement from others to engage in career pursuits. Encouragement may increase self-efficacy expectations, while lack of encouragement may decrease self-efficacy expectations with regard to career pursuits.

In general, males receive more encouragement from parents, teachers, friends, as well as counsellors, for career pursuits and achievements than do females. Females are generally not encouraged or are actively discouraged from engaging in non-traditional pursuits such as science or mathematics. The result is lower self-efficacy expectations with regard to a variety of career options.

Hackett and Betz (1981) maintain that four of the mechanisms interact in complex ways in the development of self-efficacy. These mechanisms provide a basis for integrating existing knowledge of women's career development and for interventions that can be implemented to influence women's sense of self-efficacy. By increasing their sense of self-efficacy, women's career choices may include a wider range of alternatives.

Hackett and Betz (1981) state that their views apply to the career development of both men and women, but their main aim is to focus on the career development of women.

The model cannot be seen as an independent theory of career choice, but as an emergent theory that presents self-efficacy as a construct that can be linked to career issues. It has generated a large body of research relating self-efficacy to, *inter alia*, occupational interest, aspirations, academic subjects chosen, achievement and gender differences (Lent et al, 1996).

Psychodynamic approaches

Psychodynamic theories of career development focus on issues of ego-identity, life scripts and life themes and are often extensions of the theories of Alfred Adler (life themes) and Erik Erikson (ego identity development). These approaches are based on internal structures of motivation and the constructs of identity, lifestyle, the self and family systems (Shoffner, 2006).

Bordin's theory of personality development

Edward S Bordin (1990) applies *psychodynamic theory* to career choice. In psychodynamic theory *childhood experiences* are associated with personality development. In Bordin's theory, childhood experiences are seen as basic to the relation between personality and work.

This relation is rooted in the urge to *play*. Play is an intrinsically satisfying activity that gives the individual a sense of wholeness and joy and, in work, involves the search for a self-satisfying vocation. All individuals seek this wholeness and joy in almost all aspects of life, including work. The urge to play may be unconscious and unarticulated, yet it functions as a guidance mechanism that influences personality development and its relation to career choice with regard to training, job entry and job change. The nature of play changes as the individual develops. In childhood, play is initially spontaneous, but as it becomes linked with *effort*, it becomes more complex, intense and directed.

Closely related to effort is *compulsion*. The individual's experience regarding effort and compulsion determines the degree to which play and work become fused. This fusion is influenced by external pressures exerted by parents and other caretakers. If these pressures are coupled with love, the child internalises them as concepts of conscience, duty and expectations that society has of the individual. Compulsions thereby involve the individual's coming to terms with the wishes and expectations of others.

Compulsions may, however, become extreme to the extent that effort becomes compulsion. As such, compulsion is self-alienating and the fusion between play and work is severed. Piano playing or athletics, for example, may change from being self-satisfying activities to self-alienating compulsions that amount to the drudgery of enforced practising if the individual is no longer provided with intrinsic satisfaction.

A compulsion may remain active even when parents or others no longer enforce it. Some individuals become so highly sensitised to compulsions that they seek to keep play and work apart. This occurs when, for example, individuals become over ambitious or too analytical about their efforts to master an activity. A compulsion may, however, cease when external pressures cease or the compulsion may cease when individuals realise that their talent for the activity is limited. On the other hand, the realisation of limited talent may result in sustained compulsion.

If the parent-child relationship involves mutual love and respect between parent and child, the less likely effort is to become a compulsion and the more likely effort is to retain a fusion of play and work. Since compulsion is inevitably part of social organisation, the ideal situation does not totally exclude compulsion, but rather includes compulsion in forms that can fit the intrinsic aspects of the self. If the intrinsic aspects are part of work life, work becomes a self-fulfilling vocation instead of being a mere necessity for survival.

By using the *tree as a metaphor for career choices*, Bordin (1990) sees the spontaneity of play, *effort and compulsion as roots* from which branches grow in different directions. The *branches comprise the individuals' career decisions during their lives*, which reflect reaching out to an ideal fit between the self and work.

The most useful way to determine what this fit entails is to map occupations in terms of *intrinsic motives* that determine *lifestyles* and *character styles* and incorporate developmental aspects. Lifestyles and character styles determine the forms of satisfactions that the individual seeks.

In an earlier statement of Bordin's theory (Bordin et al, 1963, quoted by Bordin, 1990), satisfactions that types of adult work activities may provide, are associated with influences in the *psychosexual stages* of childhood delineated in Freudian theory. These stages include the *oral stage*, which is associated with the sensuality of touch and sound and with activities involving nurturing and fostering, the *anal stage*, which is associated with aggression in various sublimated forms and with activities involving acquiring, hoarding or time-ordering and the *genital stage*, which is associated with forms of producing.

In the later statement of his theory, Bordin (1990), while acknowledging the validity of the earlier view, uses terms associated with *ego-development* rather than psychosexual stages to explain career choice. These terms indicate intrinsic motives that determine lifestyles and character styles that are incorporated into the individual's work life. They are curiosity, power, precision, expressiveness, concern with right and wrong and nurturance. Curiosity may be satisfactorily incorporated in certain aspects of law, psychiatry, clinical psychology, medical dentistry and general science; precision may also be incorporated in certain aspects of law, as well as in accounting, engineering, the work of a machinist, clerk or academic scholar; power may be incorporated in aspects of law, in writing, management, being an athlete, engineer or tractor operator; expressiveness may be incorporated in aspects of law, teaching, the ministry and being an actor, artist or musician; concern with right and wrong may be incorporated in law, the ministry and the work of a police officer; and nurturance may be incorporated in the work of a teacher, cook, gardener, pediatrician and other occupations that involve intimacy (that is, intimate involvement with the person who is being nurtured).

These intrinsic motives that influence career choice are part of individuals' *ego-identity* — that is, their personal identity. Everyone seeks to build a personal identity and, in this process, incorporates aspects of father and mother, but retains aspects unique to themselves. This process occurs on the unconscious level and, while parents are core influential figures, ethnic, cultural and national factors also play a part in the building of self-identity.

At different points in their careers, individuals may experience doubts and dissatisfactions concerning themselves, which will be a source of perplexity and paralysis concerning career decisions. Factors related to the educational system, the economy or technological development may, as they are related to work, play a part in doubts and satisfactions, yet these factors can be seen as presenting pressures to re-evaluate personal resolutions towards developing fuller self-realisation.

Bordin (1990) maintains that since the mechanisms of personality development involved in career decisions are largely unconscious and therefore not directly perceivable, they can be inferred from an examination of individuals' life history, their feelings, fantasies, dreams and imaginative wishes and desires concerning the past, present and future. As far as the practical application of the theory is concerned, its effectiveness in career counselling will depend on the skill of the therapist, as is the case in practice based on psychodynamic theory (Minor, 1992).

Tiedeman, O'Hara and Miller-Tiedeman's lifecareer decision-making theory

In the theory originally formulated by David V Tiedeman and Robert P O'Hara (1963) and later expanded by Anna Miller-Tiedeman and David Tiedeman (1990), career choice and development are seen as decision-making involving the development of ego-identity over the life-span. The theory is based on Erikson's view that ego-identity develops over stages in the life-span.

Tiedeman and O'Hara (1963) view ego identity as a self-organising system that develops through the mechanisms of *differentiation* and *reintegration*. Through differentiation individuals distinguish between themselves and the environment and separate different aspects of the self, such as their knowledge and ideas concerning certain occupations.

Through reintegration the different aspects of the self are structured into meaningful wholes that contribute to the wholeness of the self, such as experiencing congruence between the self and the work sphere. Together differentiation and reintegration constitute a *decision-making process* in which new knowledge and experience are constantly formed, reformed and integrated into ego-identity. In career development many differentiations and reintegrations influence decisions in the context of career choice, entry and progress.

A decision-making process can be divided into two phases, each involving different steps of decision behaviours, namely *anticipation* and *implementation*.

In the *anticipation phase four steps* may be discernible:

◆   *exploration*, which refers to becoming aware of job requirements and possibilities;
◆   *crystallisation*, in which awareness is focused on particular and alternative patterns of choice;
◆   *choice*, which involves making a tentative choice; and
◆   *clarification*, which involves organising and preparing to implement the choice.

In the *implementation stage three steps* may be discernible:

◆   *induction*, which involves entry into the job;
◆   *reformation*, which involves becoming proficient in the job and feeling good about it; and
◆   *reintegration*, which, as it involves the emergence of meaningful methods of experience, provides the individual with a perspective about himself and the work sphere.

These steps illustrate the nature of a decision-making process. Career development over the life-span, however, does not involve only one process, but multiple decision-making processes of this kind. The sequence of the steps is not necessarily the same in each process. As the individual's life direction can change, so too can the steps of a decision-making process. The steps may occur in reversed order or after reintegration a new cycle may occur. Some steps may occur simultaneously in one cycle, while some may be eliminated from the decision-making process. Each step represents a change that occurs in the individual, but the change may be so slight that the individual is unaware of it.

Miller-Tiedeman and Tiedeman (1990) expand the basic theory by incorporating two types of *realities* of which the individual becomes aware in decision-making. These realities concern individuals' perspective regarding the advancement of their careers, which can be inferred from the language they use when talking about their careers. The realities are:

◆   *personal reality*, which refers to ideas, acts or career directions that individuals feel are right for them, irrespective of what others might think; and
◆   *common reality*, which refers to what other people and society regard as good or right for the individual.

In attempting to advance their careers, individuals must become aware of differences between the two realities and must realise the importance of their personal reality in decision-making. By seeing their personal reality in perspective, they come to understand what they experience and decide how they act on common reality. By being conscious of their personal reality, individuals experience a type of consciousness, which gives them a sense of being personally empowered to form, reform and renew the resources of their lives. Individuals' lives and careers are inseparable concepts for their lives are their careers. Hence, career choice and development concern decision-making in terms of the concept *life-is-career.*

Life-career is seen as the dynamic, lived-in-the-moment process defined by each person in individual moments. Because life is your career, you can flow with it, not fight it or work against it. In essence you are doing what you want to do, not what others think is best for you (Sharf, 2010).

The theory does not aim at providing a basis for predicting occupational behaviour, but provides a model for describing inner experience in decision-making (Miller-Tiedeman and Tiedeman, 1990). Although the theory has stimulated some research, it is not frequently researched and its main contribution lies in its emphasis on the individuality, as well as on the complexity, of the person making decisions (Sharf, 2010).

Relational approaches to career development

The relational approaches to career development attend to the involvement of parents and families in the career decision-making of children, adolescents and adults. These approaches regard relationships of many types as being important to consider in understanding the career choice process (Sharf, 2010).

Roe's theory of parent-child relations

Anne Roe's theory evolved from the basic notion that career choice involves *needs.* Roe maintains that the individual's occupation, more than any other situation, can potentially provide some satisfaction on all need levels (Roe, 1956; Roe and Lunneborg, 1990).

Roe sees Maslow's (Maslow, 1954) view of a hierarchy of needs as a useful theoretical framework for understanding the relevance of needs to occupational behaviour. According to Maslow, needs acquire motivational value in a specific order. The usual order in which satisfaction is sought starts with physiological needs, followed successively by safety needs, the need for affiliation and love, the need for importance, respect, self-esteem and independence, the need for information, the need for understanding, the need for beauty and the need for self-actualisation. A need on one level does not have to be completely satisfied for the next level of need to emerge, but generally, at least partial satisfaction of a need level is necessary before the next need level acquires motivational value.

Work can satisfy needs in different ways (Roe, 1956). The need for belonging and love may, for example, be satisfied by the congeniality of being part of a work group or by being necessary for the effective functioning of the group, while the need for importance, respect, self-esteem and independence may be satisfied merely by having a job or by the status or prestige associated with a job or by the degree of freedom and responsibility a job entails. One work situation may satisfy different needs in different ways, thereby incorporating lower level and higher level needs. Individuals differ with regard to the strength that different needs have. The need for information or the need for beauty, for example, may be stronger in some individuals than in others.

The relative strength of needs, as well as the mode of satisfying them, are determined particularly by *parent-child relations*. These relations involve satisfactions and frustrations that determine which needs will become the strongest motivators. Lower level needs, referring to the first three levels of needs will, if frustrated, become dominant and prevent the development of higher level needs. The higher level needs, referring to the other five levels will, however, if frustrated, become motivationally insignificant. Some needs may also remain unconscious motivators even when satisfied because the length of time between their arousal and satisfaction was too long. Need satisfactions and frustrations lead to the development of personality variables, such as interests and attitudes, which are measures of satisfaction sought in occupations.

Roe (1957) conceptualised three types of parental behaviours in parent-child relationships resulting in basic orientations, which are either toward or not toward persons and which ultimately influence career choice. The parental behaviours are *emotional concentration* on the child, *avoidance* of the child and *acceptance* of the child. Emotional concentration on the child may be either overprotective or overdemanding, while avoidance may be rejecting or neglecting and acceptance may be casual or loving. Loving, as well as overprotecting or overdemanding, results in a basic orientation toward people and the choice of an occupation in which this orientation can be expressed and satisfied, such as service and entertainment occupations. Rejecting, neglecting and casual acceptance (the latter implying a minimum of love or indifference) result in a basic orientation away from people and the choice of an occupation involving, for example, technological, scientific or outdoor activities.

In order to systematise the wide range of occupations, Roe developed a *classification system* which consists of eight occupational groups, each including different occupations. Each group is distinguished by primary occupational activities as they involve the intensity and nature of interpersonal relations. The groups are conceptualised as if on a continuum in which adjacent groups are more similar to each other than groups that are further apart. The nature and order of the occupational groups are described as follows (Roe, 1956; Roe and Lunneborg, 1990):

- ◆ *service,* including occupations in which the primary concern is doing something for another person;
- ◆ *business contact,* including occupations in which primary concerns are selling or supplying services, with the focus on persuasion rather than on helping;
- ◆ *organisation,* including occupations in which the primary concern is management in business, industry or government and in which person-to-person relations are mainly formalised;
- ◆ *technology,* including occupations in which primary concerns are production, maintenance and transportation of commodities and utilities, with the focus on things rather than on interpersonal relations;

- *outdoors,* including occupations in which primary concerns are with cultivating, preserving and gathering natural resources and with animal husbandry and in which interpersonal relations are largely irrelevant;
- *science,* including occupations in which the primary concern is scientific theory and its application and, depending on the occupation, work in which person orientation is either largely irrelevant or only relatively relevant;
- *general culture,* including occupations in which the primary concerns are preserving and transmitting the cultural heritage, with interest in human activities rather than in individual persons; and
- *arts and entertainment,* including occupations in which the primary concern is using special skills in creative art or entertainment, with the focus on a relationship between the artist(s) and entertainer(s) and a general public. In this group, personal relations are important, but are not as direct as in service occupations which are, according to the continuum on which occupational groups are arranged, adjacent to arts and entertainment occupations.

Under each of the eight occupational groups Roe included particular occupations according to levels of difficulty and responsibility required in the occupations. The levels are as follows:

- *professional and managerial I,* which refers to independent responsibility and involves important and varied responsibilities, policy-making and education and includes top management, administration and professional jobs which, when a high level of education is required, often include individuals with doctorates, such as international bankers or industrialists in the organisation occupational group;
- *professional and managerial II,* which is similar to the first level, but which involves relatively less independence and less important decisions, policy interpretation rather than policy making and may require a bachelor's or higher degree, but not a doctorate, including, for example, business and government executives and union officials;
- *semi-professional and small business,* which involves a low level of responsibility for others, application of policy and usually requires high school or technical school education including, for example, employment managers and business owners;
- *skilled,* which includes occupations requiring apprenticeships or special training or experience, including, for example, cashiers, sales clerks and warehouse supervisors;
- *semi-skilled,* which includes occupations requiring some training or experience, but less than is required in skilled occupations, for example, filing clerks and typists; and
- *unskilled,* including occupations in which no special training or experience is required, for example, messengers in organisations.

In the presentation of eight occupational groups and six occupational levels, Roe's theory provides a two-way system for classifying occupations. This system can have valid applications in career counselling, career development, research and teaching (Roe and Lunneborg, 1990). The greatest support for Roe's theory is provided by research findings concerning the classification system. In general, however, research findings do not support the relation between parent-child relations and occupational choice posited in the theory (Brown, Brooks and Associates, 1996).

Person-in-environment perspectives

The person-in-environment perspective views career and career development as embedded in the larger context of social and environmental interchange and relationship (Shoffner, 2006). The focus is on *contextual interaction* over the life-span (see for example the contextual action model discussed in chapter 3). An individual's career development is thought to be influenced and constructed within several environmental systems such as family, church or synagogue, neighbourhood, school, neighbours, friends, workplace, community, agencies, culture and customs of the larger environment. Counsellors are to look not only for internal pathology but also for causes of client concerns that may have developed through a variety of experiences, relationships and situations. Career counselling procedures attempt to unearth both internal and external variables that contribute to career development (Zunker, 2006).

Cook, Heppner and O'Brien's race/gender ecological theory

Cook, Heppner and O'Brien (2001) use an ecological model to develop what they title a race/gender ecological approach to career development. The ecological model states that human behaviour results from the ongoing, dynamic interaction between the person and the environment. Vocational or career behaviour is understood as an 'act-in-context' where the context is essential to the explanation and meaningfulness of the individual's behaviour (Gysbers, Heppner and Johnston, 2003).

Bronfenbrenner (1979) suggested that there are four systems that make up an environment: (1) the *microsystem* or the person; (2) the *mesosystem* of family, peer group and school mates, among others; (3) the *exosystem* of friends of family, extended family, neighbours, workplaces, media and others; and (4) the *macrosystem* which is the sum of broad ideologies expressed and modelled by the larger sociocultural group. Career behaviour is thought to be determined by the *interrelationships* between the four subsystems in a larger ecosystem. Interrelationships occur simultaneously on multiple levels, so that a focus on any one level of interaction is only a limited picture of the dynamics shaping career behaviour over time. The macrosystem embodies values such as, for example, male privilege, Eurocentric or Afrocentric world views or race/gender stereotyping of occupational choices. These macrosystem values may be internalised by the individual and on the microsystem level influence how others treat a person because of their gender or race (Gysbers et al, 2003).

The race/gender ecological model of career development recognises that by their very nature humans live interactionally in a social environment. The model posits that every person has both a gender and a race and that these factors decisively shape the individual's career throughout life, as she or he encounters opportunities or obstacles because of race or gender. Although individuals of the same biological sex or race may encounter similar circumstances because of their demographics, each career path is unique because of individual circumstances and the unique interactions of their subsystems (Gysbers et al, 2003).

In the ecological approach, the counsellor goes beyond the co-construction of meaning to address specific *environmental factors* that may be influencing the client's optimal career development. The focus in career counselling is often on changing the individual's interactions with the environment which involves clarifying and affirming life options, managing multiple roles, obtaining needed resources, creating healthy work environments and linking individuals with role models and mentors (Shoffner, 2006).

Brown's theory of values

Brown (1996) presents a model of career development that stresses the importance of *values* in career decision-making (see also chapter 1). Values are seen as incorporating cognitive, affective and behavioural components and serve as standards by which individuals evaluate their own actions and the actions of others.

The model is based on *six propositions,* namely:

◆ the values included in the value system are acquired from society and each person develops a small number of values that become priorities in the value system;

◆ values with high priorities are the most important determinants of life role choices, providing that people have more than one alternative available that will satisfy their values;

◆ culture, gender, socio-economic status, opportunities and social interaction influence the development of values. Therefore considerable variation occurs in the values of the different subgroups in society;

◆ life roles that satisfy all prioritised values are essential to life satisfaction;

◆ the significance of a role is determined by the degree to which it is expected to satisfy prioritised values, which will shift as the individual shifts between different life roles; and

◆ success in any role depends on the abilities and the aptitudes required to perform the functions of that role.

The central premise of the theory is that individuals function holistically. Therefore career counselling must incorporate the interactions of various life roles in the entire life space (Brown, 1996). The model has varying degrees of research support (Brown, 1996) and can be seen as an emerging theory of career choice (Niles and Hartung, 2000).

Post-modern perspectives

The post-modern perspectives believe that individuals construct or perceive their own reality or truth and that there is no fixed truth. *Constructivism* is related to post-modernism and focuses on how individuals think and how they process what they learn. The focus is on individuals' *subjective experience* of their career development and individuals are seen as the agents who construe their careers, that is, constructivists view individuals as creating their own views of events and relationships in their lives. According to *social constructionism,* knowledge and meaning are actively constructed through *social interaction* and *relationships* within a specific sociocultural context (Palladino Schultheiss, 2005). Career counsellors attend not only to the meaning that their clients give to their own problems, but they also help clients see problems as meaningful options that are no longer helpful (Sharf, 2010). Career counselling becomes a process of meaning making and co-construction of meaning. Autobiographies or life stories are of more importance than the results of 'objective' testing. Clients' lives are interpreted as texts and careers as stories. Assessment is still deemed to be essential in defining and understanding the client's world view along with the therapeutic value of implementing storytelling and 'restorying' (McMahon, 2007).

Savickas's career construction theory

Career construction theory asserts that individuals construct their careers by imposing meaning on their vocational behaviour and occupational experiences. Career denotes a *subjective construction* that imposes personal meaning on past memories, present experiences and future aspirations by weaving them into a *life theme* that patterns the individual's work life. Thus, the *subjective career* guides, regulates and sustains vocational behaviour by the patterning of work experiences into a cohesive whole that produces a *meaningful story*. In telling career stories about their work experiences (usually by means of early recollections or childhood memories), individuals selectively highlight particular experiences to produce a narrative truth by which they live (Hartung, 2007).

Counsellors who use career construction theory listen to clients' narratives for the story lines of *life structure* issues (the assemblage of work and other roles that constitute a person's life), *vocational personality style* (personality traits such as abilities, needs, values, interests and other traits that typify a person's self-concept), *career adaptability* (the coping mechanisms used by individuals to negotiate developmental tasks and environmental changes that accumulate in the course of a lifetime) and *thematic life stories* or *life themes* (the motivations and driving forces that pattern lives) (Hartung, 2007; Savickas, 2005).

Life structure

Career construction theory reinterprets career choice and development to mean work as situated within a web of *social roles* that individuals enact and that form the basis of the human life structure (Hartung, 2007). According to career construction theory, individuals seek career counselling at times of role change and when they want to reconfigure their life structures into a different pattern of life roles (Savickas, 2005). Individual behaviour in social roles differ as a function of the range of behavioural role options that a given culture makes available to its members based on variables such as gender, age, race and social class.

Career construction theory attends to the relative importance that individuals ascribe to *roles* in family, play, leisure, school, work, community and other domains over the life-span, rather than the work role. Prevailing cultural value orientations, the changing nature of work, the growing diversity of society, a global economy and marketplace and occupational and other barriers influence individuals' levels of role salience and role viability. Personal, structural and cultural factors, such as gender expectations, social class, discrimination, personal choice and family expectations influence role commitment and role participation (Hartung, 2007).

Career adaptability

Career construction builds on Super's view of the career as a series of attempts to implement a self-concept. Developmental career stages and tasks constitute societal expectations that individuals experience as career concerns about growing self-awareness, exploring occupations and making decisions, establishing stable commitments, managing roles and disengaging from roles (Savickas, 2005).

According to Hartung (2007), career construction theory incorporates and advances Super's (1990) developmental career stages using the rubrics of growth, exploration, establishment, management (maintenance in life-span, life-space theory) and disengagement (see chapter 5). Each career stage with its concomitant developmental tasks entails a primary *adaptive goal*. Completing all tasks associated with each stage builds a foundation for success and future adaptability and reduces the likelihood of difficulties in later stages.

Career adaptability shows how an individual can deal with current developmental tasks and job crises. It entails distinct attitudes, beliefs and competencies that influence the strategies used to solve problems and behaviours employed to align one's vocational self-concept with work roles over the life course (Savickas, 2005). These include *career concern* (orienting oneself to the future and feeling optimistic about it); *career control* (increasing self-regulation through career decision-making and taking responsibility for ownership of the future); *career curiosity* (engaging in productive career exploration and approaching the future realistically); and *career confidence* (acquiring problem-solving ability and self-efficacy beliefs). Career adaptability helps individuals implement their self-concepts as they deal with current work and other demands (Sharf, 2010).

Super's (1990) concept of recycling is closely related to Savickas's (2005) notion of career adaptability in career construction theory. In dealing with career adaptability there are several developmental tasks that individuals must face during the various career stages of growth, exploration, establishment, management and disengagement. During the *growth phase* (before age 15) children's stories reflect their growth in relationship to issues that concern dealing with teachers, peers, parents and siblings. In the *exploration phase* (from about 15 to 25 years of age), young people's stories are made up with talk about their first full-time job and the type of encounters they have with superiors and co-workers. In the *establishment phase* (ages 25 to 45) stories reflect promotion and pay increases. Stories in the *management (maintenance)* phase (ages 45 to 65) include holding on to one's job, while at the same time learning more about what is required in the job and dealing with technological advancements.

In the *disengagement phase* (around the age of 65), thoughts of planning for their retirement and actually retiring are tasks that individuals may discuss with a counsellor (Sharf, 2010).

Personality style

Career construction theory attends to individual differences in values, abilities, needs and interests by considering the principles of the trait-and-factor theories in the career counselling process. Vocational personality traits (such as those described in Holland's theory) represent adaptive coping strategies. From Holland's perspective, his concepts should be measured and should be related to each other using statistical analysis. Career construction theory concentrates on using Holland's types to understand the client's narratives about how they have constructed themselves and built their careers (Sharf, 2010).

Personality traits and interests are therefore viewed as dynamic, fluid and subjectively experienced possibilities for adaptation to the social world rather than stable, static and objectively tangible entities. Empirically-derived trait categories, such as those in Holland's (1997) RIASEC model, are perceived as socially constructed by people living within a distinct and particular temporal, situational and cultural context that sustains their use and meaning. Vocational personality types and occupational interests constitute resemblances to socially-constructed clusters of attitudes and skills appropriate only to the extent that they indicate similarities among types of people. Individuals can retain or discontinue using particular adaptive coping strategies depending on situational demands (Hartung, 2007).

Life theme stories

The life theme component of career construction theory emerged from Super's (1990) view that people, in entering an occupation, seek to implement a concept of themselves; and after stabilising in an occupation, they seek to realise their potential and preserve self-esteem. As previously discussed, occupational choice is seen by Super (1990) as implementing a self-concept, work as a manifestation of selfhood and vocational development as a continuing process of improving the match between the self and situation. Work provides thus the context for human development and constitutes an important location in each individual's life (Savickas, 2005). In constructing a career, individuals engage in an ongoing process of adaptation to enhance the match between self and situation and better realise their self-concept in work (Hartung, 2007).

Career counselling gives emphasis to identifying the client's *life themes* by using Savickas's (2005) *Career Life Story Index* in the career interview. The life themes component of the theory deals with the reason or why people move in the particular direction that they do; it represents the private meaning people attach to their particular career life stories. Life themes explain an individual's life structure, vocational personality style and career adaptability strategies. Personality styles indicate *what* a person has achieved and career adaptability strategies reflect *how* the person has achieved it. Self-defining stories about vocational development tasks, career transitions, triumphs and traumas indicate life themes that play out between self and society and that give shape to the role of work in a person's life (Hartung, 2007). According to Savickas (2005), counselling for career construction encourages individuals to use work and other life roles to become who they are and live the lives they have imagined.

Savickas (2009) argues that people draw on autobiographical reasoning when they make a change in their lives. Their personal life stories (based on early recollections or childhood memories that clients recall) are used as a *carrier of meaning* (or holding space) during times of transition to facilitate continuity in a chaotic and fragmented world. The counsellor's main aim is to help clients narrate and listen to their own stories. The counsellor tries to help clients give meaning and purpose to what they do in life by guiding them to reflect on their dominant life themes or lifestyle. Early memories of events that occurred at the age of 4 or 5 years are often the most helpful, because they occurred when the lifestyle was being crystallised. The concept of *mattering* (turning the client's thoughts or preoccupations into a life interest or an occupation that they will do or participate in, within society) is an important component of an individual's life story and a core focus of the career counselling process (Sharf, 2010).

Frankl's theory of existential guidance (Logotherapy)

Existential career counselling is also an emerging post-modern approach. In this approach, counsellors include existential guidance (based on the principles of Frankl's *Logotherapy*) to help individuals recognise the role of the human spirit in finding meaning in life. The existential approach is particularly useful in today's workplace characterised by economic uncertainty which results in people feeling despondent, anxious or frustrated by their employment circumstances.

By applying *Logotherapeutic techniques,* such as the *Socratic dialogue,* career counsellors guide individuals to find *meaning* in their lives and efforts. The Socratic dialogue involves a *provocative question or challenging statement* on the part of the counsellor or therapist, eliciting from the client hidden meanings and a realisation or a grasp of their existence. The logotherapist's approach is therefore confrontational rather than prescriptive, eliciting from the client a realisation of the unique meanings of his or her life and freeing the client's *will to meaning* in searching and finding his or her own destiny in life (Shantall, Moore and Rapmund, 2002).

While an individual may experience psychological illness, physical ailments or social estrangement, the human spirit by its nature remains indomitable. The human *spirit's* resistance to assault makes it vital to helping people who have experienced or will experience disappointment, hurt or loss in the constellation of factors that combine to shape their careers (Coetzee, 2007; Frankl, 1967, 1986; Schultz and Miller, 2004).

Counsellors can raise up *a will to meaning* when individuals express frustration with their present situation or future opportunities. For instance, a counsellor may discuss a *'meaning contract'* that sketches out a career plan that focuses on the ending in one's life and which highlights the meaning in the person's present work and non-work life. Such a contract would identify the important relationships, experiences and talents of the individual. Counsellors, who assist others in their career journeys by sharing some understanding of Logotherapy, guide them in advancing their *human dignity* and discovering their *life's meaning and purpose* (Schultz and Miller, 2004).

The post-modern approach is also an emergent approach that extends the theory and research of pre-existing theories. As in the case of other emergent theories, it has been found to be applicable to diverse client groups (Niles and Hartung, 2000). Approaches such as *Narrative therapy* and *Logotherapy* offer a common language for career-development counselling in a multicultural world with multiple world views.

Career theories in practice

The career-choice theories can be applied in various ways to facilitate career interventions that will enable clients to exercise meaningful choices and to derive meaning from their career journeys in the modern workplace.

Coetzee (2005a) has constructed a *diagnostic framework* for helping career counsellors identify the core needs of clients and then, based on the identified needs, apply the principles underlying the various career-choice theories in constructing a career-development counselling process that will facilitate career competency and career adjustment.

The Diagnostic Framework for Career Services

The *Diagnostic Framework for Career Services* (see table 4.4) is based on Savickas's (1994) model for coherent career services. Each of the *career services* in the framework draws upon different *career theories* because each service addresses a distinct problem related to either the individual's *vocational self, career self* or *various life roles*.

The *vocational self* consists of individuals' attitudes and behavioural responses that are related to their *vocational tasks and situations*. The *career self* explains the *subjective sense* of the individual's career. The subjective sense of career refers to the self-awareness that individuals have of their own career behaviour, their self-concepts and identities. The career self evaluates and corrects the vocational self. The career self permits individuals to *make meaning* and to use this meaning to *direct their own behaviour* in a mature and efficacious manner. It allows individuals to develop life themes, career values, career beliefs and long-range career goals. The career self is the core of the subjective career, the vocational identity and the self-concept. The *environment* constitutes the various *life roles* and the related career/life tasks and challenges that individuals have to deal with in their career journeys (Savickas, 1994).

The *Diagnostic Framework for Career Services* depicts the coherence among the services and the various career theories. A *career intervention* would typically draw upon more than one service at a time. The career services include *career counselling, career guidance, career placement, career therapy, career education* and *career coaching*. A discussion on each follows below.

Career counselling and *career therapy* address the *career self*. When confronted by the environment with behavioural choices, people can use the career self to respond with thoughtful decision-making. Behaviour may occur at the provocation of the environment or be self-initiated (Savickas, 1994).

The career services, *career guidance* and *career education*, relate to the *vocational self*, while *career placement* and *career coaching* relate to the *environment* in which the vocational self has to act out the particular *life roles*.

Career counselling

The career counselling service facilitates *self-reflection* and *cognitive restructuring* in clients who need to develop *career competency, career maturity* and *career self-efficacy* (as discussed in chapter 3). Counselling helps clients to elaborate their self-concepts by introspection and discussion of their *subjective careers*. Career counsellors who provide the counselling service use self-reflection techniques developed by, for example, person-centred counsellors (such as Carl Rogers) and the post-modern approaches (such as *Savickas's career construction theory* and *Logotherapy*) to clarify choices through meaning-making activities and life-script analysis.

Career guidance

The career guidance service helps individuals who are undecided to articulate their behavioural repertoire and then translate it into *vocational choices*. This service emphasises *vocational guidance techniques* provided by the *Trait-and-factor theories* such as *Holland*, the use of tests and inventories such as the *MBTI (Jung's theory)* and *Schein's career anchors*. Educational and vocational information are provided, occupational exploration and matching choices are encouraged. The counsellor helps clients to crystallise a vocational identity and to envision a subjective career.

Career placement

Career placement assists individuals who have chosen an occupational field to *secure a position* in that occupation. Clients are helped to *gather information, write résumés, search for employment* and *prepare for interviews*. Counsellors use *social-learning theory* as articulated by Krumboltz and Hackett and Betz, for example, to *reduce employment search anxiety*, counter mistaken beliefs and *increase their life skills*. Placement works best with clients who are ready to *implement a choice*, that is, those who have committed themselves to a field and seek an opportunity to gain experience in it.

Clients exposed to *career counselling, guidance* and *placement* will develop, in the process, *career self-efficacy* and *career maturity* which enhance their *career self* and sense of *career competency*.

Career therapy

Career therapy assists individuals who have trouble developing a clear and stable *vocational identity* to examine what they need to feel secure. It focuses on facilitating *career adjustment* of individuals who are experiencing *career transitions*. Counsellors who provide career therapy seek to integrate personal and career counselling models such as the *psychodynamic* approaches of *Bordin, Roe* and *post-modern approaches* (eg, *career construction theory* and *existential career counselling)*.

Career education

Career education assists individuals who encounter difficulties in enacting their subjective career intentions and goals (the career self) through their objective vocational behaviour (vocational self). It helps these clients to develop *career self-management attitudes* as well as *career competencies* such as *planning and decision-making*. It also develops their *readiness to cope with the life tasks and challenges* related to their life/career stage. Counsellors who provide career education use deliberate *psychological education, cognitive-behavioural and developmental counselling* (for example, theories such as the happenstance theory of Super, Mitchell et al, race/gender ecological theory of Cook et al, lifecareer theory of Tideman et al and Savicka's career construction theory).

Career coaching

Career coaching assists individuals who encounter *problems adjusting to occupational positions* to learn better *adaptive skills* and to become more *career resilient*. It helps clients to balance work and life, as well as to cope with organisational culture, the requirements of their positions and their co-workers through mentoring and training. Counsellors who provide career coaching use *ecological systems and cognitive-behavioural theory* (eg, theory Cook et al, Krumboltz's theory, happenstance theory Mitchell et al, Hacket and Betz's theory); *organisational-development theory* and the *theory of work adjustment/Person-environment correspondence* as articulated by Dawis and Lofquist to mentor individuals.

Clients exposed to *career therapy, education and coaching* will become more *career resilient* in the process.

The case study that follows illustrates the application and utility of the *Diagnostic Framework*. The systematic application of the *Diagnostic Framework* may advance contemporary efforts to devise better means for matching clients to appropriate career interventions (Savickas, 1994).

Table 4.4 *The Diagnostic Framework of Career Services (Coetzee, 2005)*

LOCUS OF CAREER SERVICE				
Purpose	**Career self**	**Vocational self**	**Life roles (environment)**	**Outcome**
Facilitate career competency	**Career counselling** **Client need:** To learn more about subjective views of life; develop personal and vocational identity; crystallise occupational field and ability level preferences; mature/ deepen personality **Purpose:** To crystallise vocational identity and envision a subjective career by facilitating self-reflection and cognitive restructuring; elaboration of self-concept through introspection and discussion of subjective career **Model(s):** Person-centred (Rogers) Career construction theory (Savickas) Happenstance theory Contextual action model Cognitive-behavioural theories Post-modern approaches Super-life/career stages	**Career guidance** **Client need:** To articulate behavioural repertoire (interests, abilities, preferences, motives, anchors) and translate it into vocational choices and options (congruent occupational fields and levels/person-environment fit or correspondence) **Purpose:** To translate self-concepts into occupational titles for clients who possess clear and stable vocational identities but have no vocational destiny in mind **Model(s):** Trait-and-factor/ person-environment-fit theories (Parson, Holland, Jung/MBTI) Tests and inventories (MBTI/Schein's Career Orientations Inventory/ Coetzee's Psychological Career Resources Inventory)	**Career placement** **Client need:** To implement vocational choice and secure a position in a chosen occupation **Purpose:** To reduce employment seeking anxiety, increase assertiveness, counter mistaken beliefs, coax exploratory behaviour, increase social skills and refine self-presentation behaviour by assisting clients who are ready to implement a choice with information gathering, writing résumés, networking, searching for forms of employment and preparing for interviews/guidance on self-employment/ learnerships/ employability **Model(s):** Cognitive-behavioural theories Self-regulatory employability models/ inventories Career management and planning models	Career self-efficacy/ career maturity

Facilitate career adjustment	**Career therapy**	**Career education**	**Career coaching**	Career resilience/ career adaptability
	Client need: To form a personally meaningful vocational identity **Purpose:** To help clients who experience motivational problems (eg, job loss/career transitions/mid-life/ late life/quarterlife crises), excessive indecisiveness, anxiety and conflicts to develop clear and stable vocational identity by examining personal motives and recurring problems and modifying distorted motives **Model(s):** Psychodynamic models Existential guidance (logotherapy) Career construction/life design Cognitive-behavioural approaches Person-in-environment perspectives	**Client need:** To learn to better manage one's motivation and implement one's self-concept, enact one's subjective career intentions (life/career stage challenges) **Purpose:** To assist the development of self-management attitudes (foresight/ autonomy) and competencies (planning/ decision-making) and readiness to deal intelligently with vocational development tasks (life/career stages developmental tasks), fostering career adaptability behaviour, attitudes and competencies **Model(s):** Super's theory Cognitive-behavioural theories Psychodynamic approaches Career construction theory/life design (Savickas) Career invention model/contextual action model	**Client need:** To adjust to/ deal intelligently with challenges of occupational position (eg organisational culture, job requirements, co-workers, entering the world-of-work, school-to work transition, accelerated career development challenges, work-family imbalances, limited progression routes, job insecurity) **Purpose:** To teach adaptive mechanism through coaching (skills training) and mentoring **Model(s):** Organisational development Organisational career development support practices (eg, mentoring, coaching) Person-environment correspondence/theory of work adjustment (Dawis and Lofquist) Career invention model (Coetzee) Self-regulatory employability models Happenstance theory (Miller et al) Contextual action model	

Ethical considerations

In South Africa, as in many other countries, the practices of psychologists and career counsellors are controlled by legislation and controlling bodies such as the Health Professions Council of South Africa. All professional and practising career counsellors and psychologists must be registered with the Health Professions Council of South Africa which, through the Professional Board for Psychology, controls and applies the laws regarding psychological training and professional actions. The Psychological Society of South Africa (PsySSA) and its various institutes and interest groups to which psychologists can voluntarily subscribe, promote the interests of clients and psychologists through conferences, training, publications, newsletters and marketing actions. PsySSA manages a publication, *Ethical Codes for Psychologists,* which stipulates values and norms for psychologists with respect to professional actions such as testing, therapy and research, personal actions and behaviour towards colleagues and especially clients.

According to PsySSA (1992), the basic ideals and assumptions underlying psychological practice are based on the recognition of the *worth and dignity of the individual* irrespective of race, creed, sex, status, language and other personal factors. This includes the understanding that people are all alike in some respects, that some people are alike in some respects and that every individual is also unique in some respects. It is the responsibility of psychologists (and career counsellors) to use research knowledge, methods and skills *objectively and unbiasedly* to understand human behaviour better and to improve the welfare of people. Psychologists and professional career counsellors should maintain *high standards* by reflecting their qualifications and experience accurately, keeping up to date in their methods of practice and performing tasks *professionally* and in a *planned* and *responsible* way.

Moral and legal standards compel psychologists and career counsellors to be aware of and sensitive to standards and issues and not to act or use methods in a way that will offend or not be in the best interest of clients. *Psychological tests* and other processes and decisions involving people must be *fair and undiscriminating.*

Confidentiality and informed consent should be honoured by all psychologists and career counsellors. *Confidentiality* implies that any information about any client will be respected as private. Such privileged information may not be divulged, except with the client's consent. *Informed consent* refers to the client's autonomy and freedom of choice in anything that will take place and the client's right to be informed about any overt or covert procedures. The client's *privacy* may not be invaded, except if the client is aware of this.

The *welfare* of individuals and groups is always paramount. Clients must not be subjected to physical or mental discomfort which is not realistic in the situation. No action, procedure or type of relationship must harm the *integrity of the professional contract* between psychologist/counsellor and client. Psychologists and career counsellors must be open with clients about *fees and termination of services* if no progress is being made. *Professional relationships* must be upheld at all times.

Conflicts over ethical principles may arise when the psychologist or career counsellor has to make decisions that might seem contradictory. Divulging confidential information, for instance about a client's dishonesty, may represent invasion of privacy but it may be in the client's best interest if the decision is not meant to cause harm.

Case example: Application of the Diagnostic Framework for Career Services

Determining the client's profile: Applying Super's Segmental Model of career development as a framework

Biographical and geographical information

Sue is 48 years old and married with no children. Her husband is 53 years old and is a journalist and artist by profession. He is currently self-employed and writes on a full-time basis. Sue has lived and worked in Pretoria (City of Tshwane) all her life and is currently employed as an organisation development consultant in the HR department of a higher education institution.

Personality and achievement: Needs, values and interests

In terms of Maslow's hierarchy of needs, most people experience physiological needs, safety needs, affiliation and love needs, self-esteem needs and self-actualisation needs. In Sue's case, spirituality, values and autonomy are very important and her need for self-actualisation is therefore very high.

Schein's career anchors

Schein (1978) defines a career anchor as a pattern of self-perceived talents, motives and values, which serve to guide, constrain, stabilise and integrate a person's career (see chapter 6). The career anchor holds an individual's internal career together as dramatic changes are experienced in the external career due to the turbulence of the post-modern society. Sue identified her main career anchor as service/dedication to a cause, combined with the secondary career anchor of technical/functional competence.

Personality preferences

In terms of Jung's psychological types, Sue reported her type as INTP. According to the MBTI description of INTP types, these people are independent problem-solvers who excel at providing a detached, concise analysis of an idea and situation. They ask the hard questions, challenging others and themselves to find new logical approaches. INTP types highly value intelligence and competence. They love to theorise and discuss abstractions and are intensely curious about ideas and theories. They like developing underlying principles and logical structures for understanding and explaining the world. They approach almost everything with scepticism, form their own opinions and standards and apply these standards rigorously to themselves. They also tend to be detached and contemplative.

Intelligence, aptitudes, special aptitudes

In terms of her MBTI type and the OPQ, Sue's professional strengths include abstract thinking, independent-mindedness, planning and organising, specialist knowledge, problem-solving and analysis, written communication, creativity and innovation and strategic awareness.

Social policy and employment practices

Community, school/family and peer groups

Sue's community, family and peer groups include mostly Afrikaans-speaking artistic, professional, intellectual and independent-minded individuals who are very individualistic and like to question things and form their own opinions. Her career and her master's studies contribute to greater acceptance and esteem from her community and peer group.

The economy, society, labour market, social policy and employment practices

The labour market is characterised by high unemployment rates and high demand for black people in order to eradicate the injustices of the past. The legal framework that currently regulates employment practices includes the Labour Relations Act (LRA), the Employment Equity Act (EEA) and the Skills Development Act (SDA). Although, as a white woman, Sue classifies as a previously disadvantaged person, she feels that the high unemployment rate and the higher demand for black workers pose threats to her long-term job and career security.

Role self-concepts and development stage

According to Greenhaus et al (2010), Sue is currently in her mid-career stage, which roughly spans a 15-year period between the ages of 40 and 55. According to Greenhaus et al, the mid-career years pose two major career/life tasks, namely confronting the mid-life transition and remaining productive.

Diagnosing the interventions required

In terms of the *Diagnostic Framework for Career Services* (Coetzee, 2005a), Sue was diagnosed as needing *career adjustment facilitation* to help her deal with the mid-career stage of her life and integrate the knowledge and competency she is gaining through her master's studies into her career and job. The outcomes of the career adjustment facilitation should be greater career resilience, greater job satisfaction, increased performance in her current job and better utilisation of job and career opportunities.

Client needs

Sue's current career needs are mainly the following:

◆ To *implement her career intentions* of becoming a competent industrial psychologist and a more competent human being and of applying her competence in her personal life and her current job to better satisfy her safety, affiliation, self-esteem and self-actualisation needs. At the same time as satisfying these needs, Sue's career intentions should also be of benefit to her family, friends, colleagues, her employer and the industrial psychology profession.

◆ To *handle the development tasks* related to Sue's career stage effectively in order to maintain and enhance her personal motivation, well-being, life satisfaction and effectiveness.

◆ To *better cope with the challenges and demands of her current position* of organisation development consultant at her employer, especially in view of the demands placed by the merger in order to obtain more job satisfaction and add better value to her employer.

Sue believes that she will need to explore the strategies of *career education* and *career coaching* to achieve these outcomes.

Career education: Purpose

The purpose of the strategy and intervention will be to assist Sue with the following tasks so that she can maintain and enhance her *career motivation, career maturity* and her *career success* as perceived by herself and others:

◆ *Readiness to cope with vocational development tasks* related to her career stage (mid-career); and

◆ *Self-management attitudes and competencies* such as personal and professional growth, autonomy and self-efficacy.

Models

The models that can be used to guide Sue's career education process are *Super's* developmental model and *Tiedeman, O'Hara and Miller-Tiedeman's decision-making* theory, combined with *Schein's career anchors* and the *MBTI*.

Super's developmental model

According to Super's developmental model, Sue is in the fourth or maintenance stage of her life (45–65 years). According to Super's theory, there is generally continuation along established lines in one's work during this stage. Some individuals, who have not achieved what they wanted to, may stagnate and avoid actively acquiring new knowledge and skills. Others may focus on reaching further goals by means of, for example, further education, while still others may embrace change and become change agents.

One of the important purposes of Super's model is to enhance career maturity through effective career adjustment to particular life stages. Career maturity is thus not a unitary trait that increases with age, but is conceptualised in terms of the tasks of each specific life stage. According to Super, career maturity is linked to career resilience and to how well individuals cope with the developmental tasks of particular career stages. Individuals who make career decisions that reflect decisiveness, involvement, independence, task orientation and willingness to compromise between needs and reality have achieved a high degree of career maturity.

Application of Super's developmental model to Sue's career development

Sue has approached the maintenance stage in her life and career by deciding not to stagnate in the status quo but to focus on reaching further goals by means of her master's studies.

A few years back, Sue made a mid-career change from a career in linguistics to a career in industrial and organisational psychology as the latter career offered more opportunities for personal growth and contribution and also entailed better career and financial opportunities. Because of this change Sue is somewhat 'behind' in her current career, seen from a traditional perspective of linear careers. She thus has to speed up her development and growth. In order to achieve this, she has to increase her career resilience and has to assume a new career identity as an industrial psychologist. Sue also has to redefine the meaning of career success from an external perspective of having progressed along a linear career path to an internal perspective of achieving psychological success through moving into another field of expertise that she finds more meaningful, challenging and satisfying. Part of Sue's adjustment to the mid-career stage of her life and career is to ensure congruence between her career development and her career anchor and personality type.

Sue's main career anchor of service/dedication to a cause is the reason why she finds it gratifying to work at her current employer. She is dedicated to the cause that her employer stands for, namely of serving humanity and increasing well-being and prosperity through the increase of knowledge, understanding and critical thinking. This dedication to a cause, combined with her secondary career anchor of clinical/functional competence and practical issues such as career and financial opportunities, is the reason why she moved to industrial and organisational psychology. Sue feels that this profession will enable her to become a happier and more competent human being and to make a more meaningful contribution to human development.

Sue's MBTI type (INTP) is also congruent with her current job and her master's studies. As mentioned before, INTPs highly value intelligence and competence. They love to theorise and discuss abstractions and are intensely curious about ideas and theories. They like developing underlying principles and logical structures for understanding and explaining the world. They approach almost everything with scepticism, form their own opinions and standards and apply these standards rigorously to themselves. They also tend to be detached and contemplative.

The above preferences are well matched with the culture and values of an academic institution. The curiosity about ideas and theories and the preference for developing underlying principles and logical structures to understand and explain the world are in line with her studies and her work in organisation development.

Tiedeman, O'Hara and Miller-Tiedeman's life-career decision-making theory

Tiedeman, O'Hara and Miller-Tiedeman's decision-making theory postulates two major decision-making stages, namely the anticipation and adjustment phase. The anticipation phase, in turn, consists of four basic developmental phases: exploration, crystallisation, choice and clarification. The adjustment phase consists of three phases, namely induction, reformation and integration.

Application of the model to Sue's career

Sue has already gone through the anticipation phase of the decision-making process when she decided to start her master's studies in industrial and organisational psychology. She has thus taken the steps to exploration, crystallisation, choice and clarification.

Sue is now busy adjusting to her choice to become an industrial psychologist and a more competent human being. She is currently going through the induction phase by trying to qualify as an industrial psychologist. Once she qualifies, she will enter the reformation phase by becoming part of the industrial and organisational psychology fraternity. In this phase, according to Tiedeman et al, an individual often feels hesitant to join or feel part of a group but may later become an advocate of the group. Sue can thus expect to have such feelings of hesitancy once she qualifies. According to Tiedeman et al, the third phase consists of integration, where the newness wears off and the group and the individual accept each other. The excitement about the new choice may diminish and become an integral part of the individual. Sue can thus expect to eventually integrate the new career identity of industrial psychologist into her personal makeup.

Career coaching: Purpose

The purpose of the strategy and intervention is to teach adaptive mechanisms through mentoring and coaching.

Models

The models that can be used to decide on interventions are organisational career management and Dawis and Lofquist's *Theory of Work Adjustment.*

Organisational career management

Organisational career management practices such as mentoring and coaching will assist Sue to handle the adjustment to her accelerated career development as an industrial psychologist. In this sense, Sue's internship programme — which is a combination of mentoring and coaching — will assist greatly, as it will provide her with challenging assignments and learning opportunities.

Dawis and Lofquist's Theory of Work Adjustment

In terms of Dawis and Lofquists Theory of Work Adjustment, there are two major components to the prediction of work adjustment: satisfaction and satisfactoriness. Satisfaction refers to job satisfaction, whereas satisfactoriness refers to the employer's satisfaction with the individual's performance on the job. The internship programme will assist to enhance Sue's job satisfaction and her satisfactoriness as her competence and self-confidence as a prospective industrial psychologist will be enhanced.

Evaluating the effectiveness of the career intervention

Sue will be able to evaluate the effectiveness of applying the above models and interventions to improve her career adjustment in her current life stage by means of the following measures and outcomes:

- feelings of greater career satisfaction;
- feelings of general well-being;
- feelings of greater self-confidence;
- enhanced job performance;
- reduced stress levels; and
- greater sense of coherence.

These measures and outcomes can be measured through self-reporting, performance appraisal results and tests such as the Orientation to Life Questionnaire, the Organisational Commitment Questionnaire (OCQ) and the Job Involvement Questionnaire.

According to Greenhaus et al (2010), some employees may exhibit a burst of ambition to fulfil long-standing goals, whereas others may reduce their involvement in work and turn their attention and energies toward their families and themselves.

Sue sees her decision to start her master's studies as a part of a reappraisal of her accomplishments and life goals, which made her realise that she wanted to become more professional in her work so that she could make a more valuable contribution and thus also feel more pride in her accomplishments. The decision was what Greenhaus et al (2010) refer to as 'a burst of ambition to fulfil long-standing goals' as Sue realised that she did not have much time left to do this.

Sue currently has a fair amount of job security and thus financial security. She believes that if she qualifies as an industrial psychologist, this will enhance her professional value and thus also contribute to long-term career opportunities and less dependence on her current organisation for job and financial security.

Although her need for affiliation and her need for self-esteem are quite well satisfied by her current job, Sue believes that these needs will be even better satisfied by qualifying as an industrial psychologist, as she will then belong to the industrial and organisational psychology fraternity and will classify as a professional. The need for self-actualisation plays a critical role in her life. This is why Sue is drawn to work in an academic institution and environment. Sue's master's studies contribute greatly to satisfying this need, as they bring meaning to her life and help her to be a more competent worker and human being.

Conclusion

Career theories differ with regard to their predictive value and with regard to the scope and application of the constructs they entail. Some theories are substantiated by research that has validated their constructs or has provided instruments to measure them, while other theories remain more or less theoretical suppositions. The extent to which research substantiates theory can, however, be difficult to ascertain. Researchers may construe the constructs of a theory in ways that differ from the original conceptualisation of the theorist. Research may sometimes be conducted with groups that do not include a representative sample — that is, all groups of people to which the theory is supposed to apply (Sharf, 2010).

Most career counselling practice and research originate in the USA. It is important for South African career counsellors and psychologists to also develop and employ theories, models and techniques that originate in Africa (Stead and Watson, 1999).

Basically, theories are conceptualisations that order and systematise those variables which influence career choice, adjustment and development. They provide frameworks that the counsellor and, in some cases, individuals themselves can apply either empirically by testing or otherwise through intuition.

The *Diagnostic Framework for Career Services* showed the utility of the career theories in practice by demonstrating how theorists and professional career counsellors use career theory to enrich career interventions. Theories are conceptual tools that must be used in practice to be meaningful. Moreover, the meaning of a theory changes as it is used. Each time a concept is applied to a new situation, its meaning deepens. In this regard, career theories provide lenses through which selected segments of vocational behaviour can be viewed and interpreted (Savickas, 1994; Shoffner, 2006).

Review and discussion questions

1. What are the differences and commonalities between the various career theories and approaches?
2. How can the various career choice theories be applied in practice?
3. What are the ethical implications of using career tests and inventories?
4. Review the career models in chapter 2. Which of the career choice theories can be useful to apply in the career and self-exploration phases?
5. Why is Super's self-concept so important in career counselling and career development?
6. How useful are the career choice theories in helping individuals in the 21st century with their career planning and management? Identify and discuss the aspects of each theory that could be useful to assist individuals.

7. Discuss the *Diagnostic Framework for Career Services*. How could you apply the framework with regard to your own career?

Reflection activities

Reflection activity 4.1

1. Read Holland's theory and indicate the personality and occupational type(s), adjacent types and degree of congruence and consistency applicable to each job for each of the following, as described in the two advertisements below:
2. Read Jung's theory and study the MBTI types in table 4.3. Indicate the personality type(s) most applicable for each position, as described in the two advertisements below:

| XYZ Game lodge
Assistant Lodge Manageress — Hospitality
Industry — Limpopo

Professional duties:
Ensure ultimate guest relations in the lodge and ensure that the 'at home' attention is maintained.
   Maintain the highest standards of housekeeping and maintenance and ensure that the lodge functioning is kept under tight control. Efficient financial management through the administration of orders and effective stock control of all departments. Communicate efficiently and commercially with South African, German and other European guests as well as tour operators. Assist Marketing Department and Product Management, attend Indaba. Follow up on the international enquiries and bookings. Development of the lodge marketing, especially towards high potential customers and tour operators. | *Holland's personal and occupational (environmental) type (including adjacent types):* |
| **Minimum requirements:**
Minimum of 5 years' working experience in the tourism industry, including consulting and Product Management experience. Negotiation skills as well as having experiences at travel trade exhibitions (INDABA) are essential. Completed Commercial school, strong communication skills and experience in tourism industry a must. Thorough knowledge of English and German is essential. Strong organisational skills, methodical and diplomatic skills are also required. Furthermore, a certificate of Advanced English and Computer literacy on MS Office is compulsory. | *MBTI type(s):* |

Graphic designer — part-time	*Holland's personal*
The ideal candidate will:	*and occupational*
◆ Have thorough knowledge of Corel Draw 13 or higher and Adobe Photoshop.	*(environmental)* *type (including*
◆ Be fully computer literate with the ability to learn new packages quickly.	*adjacent types):*
◆ Have some previous work experience in publishing or a similar environment.	
◆ Be creative and careful in the design of display advertisements for our publications.	
◆ Have the ability to work to deadline.	
◆ Have access to own transport.	
◆ Be available to work on Mondays, Tuesdays and alternate Fridays.	
◆ In return we will offer you an exciting and dynamic working environment with plenty of room for personal growth.	*MBTI type(s):*

Reflection activity 4.2

Read the following case study about the life and career of Paulina and then answer the questions that follow.

Paulina (21 years)

Paulina's subjects at school included Maths, English, Afrikaans, Home Economics, Biology and Computyping. Her favourite subject was Biology as she found it interesting and enjoyed learning about people, animals and nature. Maths and English were her least favourite subjects. She struggled to understand maths and did not enjoy writing essays in English. Paulina is currently doing a marketing degree and enjoying it as she is learning a lot and exploring different fields. She would like to continue with social studies as she would like to help people. Interests include boyfriend, parties, hockey, movies and outdoor activities such as skiing, tennis and swimming.

Paulina's achievements include being a prefect, being in the first hockey team and getting merits and awards at school. She considers her best talents as leadership (she got a special leadership award), having good listening skills, talking to people and selling skills. Her aspirations are to excel in marketing and sales and earn enough money to be able to open and run a non-profit organisation — particularly one involving orphans. She did state that this would be much later in life. The activity that gives her the greatest satisfaction is socialising with friends and family and to relieve stress she enjoys walking, going to the movies and sleeping.

Paulina has been a sales asistant in a clothing shop for about 4 years during school holidays and now during university breaks and weekends. She thoroughly enjoyed dealing with customers, building relationships and making new friends, giving advice, receiving commision and incentives when she reached the sales goals. She found it rewarding. When she left school, she worked for a year in a small company. She started as a receptionist and did that for about seven months and then went into sales. She didn't enjoy the reception job as it was very repetitive and boring. There were not enough challenges and she didn't feel a sense of satisfaction. She was earning a very good salary, especially as she did not have previous experience and didn't have a formal qualification. She enjoyed the sales side far more but realised she wouldn't have a good future without formal qualifications so she decided to leave the job and become a student.

The skills Paulina learnt in her job were interpersonal relationship skills, communication skills, dealing with people (she used to be shy), assessing needs and giving advice and basic computer skills. At home, Paulina learnt life skills (eg, coping with setbacks), how to have a positive attitude and be resilient. She also realised that she can achieve whatever she puts her mind to and that she has the ability to learn quickly which will enable her to have many options and doing things properly once she starts them. The skills she has learnt elsewhere include team work, leading people, not to take everyone at face value and that people must earn trust and respect.

Paulina feels the qualities that have helped her in life include confidence, resilience, tolerance, ability to make decisions, ability to lisen well and communicate, persistence and determination to do what she puts her mind to. The qualities she would like to work on are patience, focus, attention and stubbornness. She feels she has a good balance between work and family life. The meaning of work is important to her as it is a means of meeting basic needs, reaching goals and achieving satisfaction of something done well, the ability to learn and grow and improve one's mind and abilities. Career success for Paulina is excelling in what one does and striving to do better and improve the way things are done. It includes earning a good salary, enjoying what one does and knowing that one has achieved one's goals. The greatest concern is not being able to get a job, especially in current times or accepting a job that one doesn't enjoy as one cannot find anything else.

Questions

1. Study Super's theory. What are the key developmental life tasks that Paulina is currently facing?
2. In terms of Savickas's *Career Life Story Index*, one's favourite school subjects indicate preferred work environments. Favourite leisure activities deal with

self-expression and reveal manifest interests. Read Holland's theory and identify the most appropriate personality and occupational environment(s) that can be associated with Paulina's favourite school subjects and leisure activities. Can you see a link with Paulina's interest in sales and marketing?

3. Study Savickas's description of career adaptability — which of the skills and qualities that Paulina has developed can be related to her career adaptability? Would you say she has well-developed career adaptability?

4. What is the meaning of work for Paulina? How does her perception of the meaning of work compare with yours? Do you share similar or different interests?

5. Study Hacket and Betz's theory on self-efficacy. What role did Paulina's accomplishments in life play in enhancing her self-efficacy?

6. Study Tiedeman, O'Hara and Miller-Tiedeman's lifecareer decision-making theory. Describe the decision-making process of Paulina by applying the principles and concepts of the lifecareer theory.

7. Study Krumboltz's career decision-making theory. Describe the decision-making outcomes of Paulina's career as illustrated in the case study.

Reflection activity 4.3

Read the following case study about Lindiwe's concerns about her current career situation. Apply the **Diagnostic Framework for Career Services** to describe how you would go about advising Lindiwe on her career concerns. Complete the table provided to help you in your planning.

Lindiwe has been accepted onto a learnership programme in a large manufacturing company. She is twenty-three years of age, has never been employed and was grateful for the opportunity to further her educational studies and to gain the practical work experience offered by the learnership. Although she has been enjoying the learnership programme, Lindiwe has been quite depressed for the past few weeks as she has received the news that her learnership agreement will be terminated. Although she has been an excellent learner, the company will not be able to absorb her into its structure due to a major restructuring that will lead to a redundancy exercise. Being young and inexperienced, Lindiwe is in a state of anxiety as she doesn't know where to turn. She is also not sure whether she is following the right career. What if she has wasted her time on the learnership programme? What if she has made the wrong choice? Where could she find the employment she so desperately need Lindiwe has decided to make an appointment with the company's career psychologist. Maybe she will find the answers that will help her to the clarity she needs.

Client profile		
Life/career stage	Self-concept development	Career service needs
Career choice theory/theories that could be useful		
Potential steps that can be followed in the career discussion (based on the career choice theory/theories)		
Benefits of the chosen approach		

5

Life and career stages

Learning outcomes

After studying this chapter you should be able to

◆ explain the concept of life/career stages;

◆ explain how development in childhood can affect adult career development behaviour;

◆ explain the career development tasks of the adolescent;

◆ explain the career development tasks of late adolescence and adulthood;

◆ differentiate between the career development of men and women;

◆ describe the characteristics and life tasks of the early life/career stage;

◆ describe the establishment and achievement phases of the early life/career stage;

◆ describe organisational and individual actions for assisting with early career issues;

◆ describe the characteristics and life tasks of the middle adulthood life/career stage;

◆ explain what individuation involves; relate generativity to the mid-life/career stage;

◆ discuss the mid-life crisis;

◆ describe organisational actions for assisting with mid-life/career issues;

◆ describe the characteristics and life tasks of the late life/career stage;

◆ discuss retirement in terms of motivation and adjustment;

◆ describe theories that explain retirement;

◆ indicate the nature of organisational pre-retirement programmes; and

◆ describe factors that can influence early retirement.

Introduction

Career development can be studied by relating career stages to stages during the lifespan. People go through relatively predictable phases or stages in their lives and careers. Each life/career stage is characterised by a somewhat distinctive set of developmental themes or tasks that need to be confronted (Super, 1990).

Traditional linear career models tie life/career stages to chronological age. In contrast, life-span theory recognises that career changes and events may take place at any point throughout the life-span (Staudinger and Bluck, 2001). The basic assumption is that individuals have the potential for change throughout their lives (Valsinger, 2000). According to Baruch (2004), change means that individual development necessarily occurs in multiple dimensions and potentially in multiple directions.

The sources of change are the contexts in which the individual exists, including biological, psychological, social, spiritual, cultural, economic and historical contexts. Just as individuals can change, their contexts are also subject to change. In the interaction between the individual and the environment, both are transformed. As much as individuals' development is influenced by their contexts, they are capable of influencing and creating contexts (Valsinger, 2000), for example, by contributing to social and economic factors through their work.

In essence, development may be seen as the emergence of novelty, in that individuals can create novelty by reorganising their perceptions, for example, by changing the perception that their job is boring, to seeing it as unique and potentially novel (Valsinger, 2000). By relating careers to life stages, it is assumed that the two are intrinsically interwoven. In industrial and post-industrial societies, people increasingly do not compartmentalise their lives into job and personal activities, instead they seek balance and integration (Boyatzis and Kolb, 2000; Hankin, 2005).

Traditionally, the chronological age (of the person) has been used to determine developmental turning points in the person's life. The course of life is generally studied in terms of age-related approximations. It is divided into childhood (up to 12 years), adolescence (up to 18 years), early adulthood (18 to 40 years), middle adulthood (40 to 60 years) and late adulthood (starting at 60 years). However, the contemporary career is not measured by chronological age and life stages, but by continuous learning and identity changes. Rather than thinking of a career as made up of a lifelong series of developmental stages, the contemporary career is a series of short learning stages. A person will go through several developmental phases, characterised as an exploration — trial (experimentation) — mastery series of learning experiences. *Career age* (the individual's professional work challenges, experiences and relationships — continuous learning — across organisations) has become most important (Weiss, 2001). Since career competency (learn-how and know-how) has become important, a person's career age is a more meaningful indicator to organisations and to a person's self-understanding (the career self) than one's chronological age development.

Life/career stages therefore must not be seen as discrete entities with clear-cut time, psychological or social boundaries. They are distinguished by *developmental factors* that are generally typical of certain stages of life. These factors include periods of relative stability, as well as periods of change (Levinson, 1986; Valsinger, 2000). In broad terms, each stage can be studied in terms of physical, cognitive and psychosocial development, the latter including needs, life tasks, as well as issues and social factors that are significant in the work life. Career development involves understanding both personal and career developmental issues. Career self-management in the forties and fifties involves dealing with life issues that are different from those of people in their twenties and thirties (Weiss, 2001).

Career development in childhood

One of the distinctive features of a developmental perspective on work and careers is its attention to the development and implementation of a self-concept, career attitudes and behaviours prior to individuals' entering the workforce itself. The developmental approach to careers assumes that important elements of career identity — skills, career and life interests and work values — begin forming at an early age (as early as four or five years) and are shaped by experiences with members of the nuclear and extended family (Feldman, 2002c).

Linda Gottfredson (1981, 2005) is one of the few theoreticians who has presented a theory — called the *theory of circumscription and compromise* — on how childhood influences the career development behaviour of adults. According to Gottfredson's (1981, 2005) theory, career development is seen as an attempt to implement the *social self* and, secondarily, the *psychological self*. Individuals establish social identities through work. *Self-concept* in vocational development is seen as a key factor to career selection because people want jobs that are compatible with their self-images.

Self-concept is a multi-faceted schema and has *three levels* of identities: *individual level identities* which define one's uniqueness and differentiation of the self from others; *relational identities* which define the self in terms of specific roles or relations and often include others in the definition of one's own self-identity; and the *collective identities* which define the self in terms of specific collectives such as groups or organisations and creating a desire to develop in oneself the qualities that are prototypical of these collectives (Densten, 2008).

Cognitive development, personality and interest play an important role in vocational choice and are influenced by genetics and environmental factors (Sharf, 2010). Gottfredson (2005) states that people are *active participants* in their relationships between their biological selves and their environment, which are constantly changing. Even the environment that people share with their siblings may look different from the environment that they are in as they become adults. Based on thorough research and study, Gottfredson (2005) points out that where one's parents live, how much schooling they have and how wealthy they are seem to have little impact on one's personality traits at any age. In addition, the impact of one's parents on one's intellectual abilities wanes as one becomes an adolescent.

People's interests, attitudes and skills are more influenced by the environments that they share with others. Vocational interests are affected by the relationship between genetics and the environment. Interests are particularly influenced by one's world, whereas temperaments and intellect are influenced less by one's environment and more by one's genetic makeup. Interests emerge as they fit with human traits that people in specific cultures develop to meet their needs. As people interact with their environments their genetically-based temperaments become stable or *traited*. As they repeat experiences, traits develop. Individuals will also gradually choose more events that help to define various traits. In this way, traits develop and the effect of genetics on individuals becomes stronger rather than weaker as people age. Regarding intelligence, adopted children become more and more like biological relatives that they have not met rather than more like their adoptive parents (Sharf, 2010).

When making choices about what to do and how to understand their role, people are influenced by an *internal genetic compass*. This compass is an internal guide as to what people generally prefer (also regarded as their core life interests). For example, children with a compass that includes drawing ability are likely to choose more artistic activities, whereas those with a proclivity towards sports will choose more sports activities (Sharf, 2010).

Apart from genetics, people are also influenced by environmental factors in their career decision-making. For example, wanting to go to medical school while raising a family does not make attending medical school impossible, but it makes it more difficult. Or having an unemployed parent may have an impact on the schools or university one may be able to afford (Sharf, 2010).

The process of self-concept development is seen as a process of *self-creation* — people are seen as *active agents* in their own creation. In the process of developing one's self-concept and interacting with one's environment, individuals are seeking *niches* throughout their lives. Niches are the life settings and roles that individuals occupy. The process of choosing careers is one type of niche seeking and each individual has a *unique pattern* of niche seeking.

Gottfredson's theory focuses on how cognitions of self and occupations develop from early childhood. Because a *cognitive map* of occupations is integrated into an individual's self-concept, a core developmental task of individuals is to determine which occupations are *compatible* with how they see themselves. Apart from being compatible, with one's view of oneself, occupations must be *accessible* or attainable. If they are not, the individual is not likely to pursue these occupations (Sharf, 2010).

The theory's premise is that career choice is a process of *circumscription* or *eliminating options*, thus narrowing one's choices. Individuals *compromise* their goals by giving up alternatives that they may not like for ones that may be more accessible to them. This is done by *eliminating the negative* (rather than selecting the most positive) as individuals try to implement their aspirations. Compromises are based primarily on generalisations formed about occupations or *'cognitive maps'* of occupations. Although each person develops a unique map, each uses common methods of evaluating similarities and differences, namely through sex-typing, level of work and field of work. In this way, individuals create boundaries or tolerable limits of acceptable jobs (Gottfredson, 1981; Zunker, 2006).

Key determinants of self-concept development are one's *social class, level of intelligence* and *experiences with gender-typing* (Gottfredson, 1981). According to Gottfredson (1981), vocational self-concept begins early in childhood and is defined through *four orientations* to work:

◆ *Orientation to size and power* (ages 3 to 5): During this stage, children's thought processes are concrete and they develop some sense through gender roles of what it means to be an adult (Zunker, 2006). Children begin to show interest in certain types of careers based on the perceived power that those in that career have. This is often in the form of physical power (eg, fireman, athlete) or social power and fame (eg, rock star, movie star) (Shoffner, 2006).

◆ *Orientation to sex roles* (ages 6 to 8): The self-concept is influenced by gender development and children further delineate their occupational 'space' based on sex roles. Girls begin to rule out careers that they see as male dominated (eg, scientist) and boys rule out careers that they see as female oriented (eg, nurse, office secretary) (Shoffner, 2006).

◆ *Orientation to social valuation* (ages 9 to 13): The development of concepts of social class contributes to the awareness of self-in-situation. Preferences for level of work develop. Children *circumscribe* their options based on the prestige and perceived social valuation of occupations. Children now talk about being doctors, lawyers or policemen for example, with the previously delineated sex roles restrictions still in place (Shoffner, 2006).

◆ *Orientation to the internal, unique self* (beginning at age 14 to early adolescence): Introspective thinking promotes greater self-awareness and perceptions of others. The individual achieves greater perception of vocational aspirations in the context of self, sex role and social class (Zunker, 2006). The focus is on the unique self, consisting of interests, abilities and other traits specific to the individual.

Occupational preferences emerge within the complexities that accompany physical and mental growth. A major determinant of occupational preferences is the *progressive circumscription* of aspirations during self-concept development, that is, from the child's rather simplistic and concrete view of life to the more comprehensive, complex, abstract thinking of the adolescent and adult (Zunker, 2006). As children proceed through the four orientations, they limit or 'circumscribe' an occupational space, which is referred to as a region or zone of acceptable alternatives. Occupations and career that fall out of this region are no longer considered as options (Gottfredson, 1981). This is often an unconscious process, in that these possibilities are often not even readily accessible to the individual as possible self schemas (Shofffner, 2006).

The matching process in vocational choice is cognitively demanding. The tasks it involves span all *six levels* of Bloom's (Moseley et al, 2005) widely used taxonomy of cognitive tasks in teaching and learning: (1) learning isolated facts (*remember* — Bloom's lowest level), (2) spotting and understanding similarities and differences (*understand*), (3) drawing inferences from and assessing the relevance of information (*apply*), (4) integrating information to assess the pros and cons of a decision or course of action (*analyse*), (5) applying one or more criteria to judge which choices are better than others (*evaluate*), and (6) developing a plan to meet a goal (*create* — Bloom's highest level).

Children's capacity for learning and reasoning (their *mental age*) increases with chronological age from birth through adolescence. Children progress from thinking intuitively in the preschool years to concretely in the elementary years to abstractly in adolescence; from being able to make only simple distinctions to multidimensional ones. They recognise more similarities and differences and increasingly abstract ones, which they use to make sense of diverse phenomena in their lives. Children thus become able to take in, understand and analyse ever larger bodies of information of increasing subtlety and complexity. They gradually notice and figure out more aspects of the many-layered world around them. Children's steady growth in mental competence affects their behaviour and lives. In the vocational realm, its two major products are the *cognitive map of occupations* and the *self-concept*. Although both are incomplete, they are organised understandings of the occupational world and of the self that children develop and elaborate with age (Gottfredson, 2005:73).

According to Super (1990), children develop a concept of themselves that includes *planfulness, career decision-making* and *time perspective*. A basic drive in children is *curiosity* which is often satisfied through *exploration* as a lifelong activity. The exploratory activity leads to the *acquisition of information*. One important source of information is the key figure, that is, a person who a child may choose to imitate. Interests are developed by using information derived from exploratory activities and impressions of role models. During the *maturational process*, children develop ways to control their own behaviour by listening to themselves and others. To make career decisions, children need to develop a *time perspective*, that is, a sense of the future. This, together with the development of a *self-concept*, will eventually lead to planful decision-making (Sharf, 2010).

Career development competencies that children need to develop are (Zunker, 2006:384):

◆ *self-knowledge*: knowledge of the importance of self-concept; skills to interact with others and awareness of the importance of growth and change;
◆ *educational and occupational exploration*: awareness of the benefits of educational achievement, the relationship between work and learning, skills to understand and use career information, the importance of personal responsibility and good work habits and how work relates to the needs and functions of society; and
◆ *career planning*: understanding of how to make decisions; awareness of the interrelationship of life roles, different occupations and changing male/female roles and the career planning process.

These career development competencies can be developed in the preschool and elementary school environments by (Zunker, 2006:394-395):

◆ establishing effective classroom guidance activities such as fostering peer relationships, understanding of self, communication skills, decision-making skills and study skills;
◆ developing effective individual and small group counselling addressing such topics as self-image, self-esteem, interpersonal concerns, family issues, personal adjustment and behaviour problems;
◆ using assessment instrument as measures of ability, interests, academic achievement and skills;
◆ fostering the developmental process through career awareness of lifelong growth of values, interests and skills that will influence future work roles; and

◆   co-ordinating programmes that will involve school and community resources, all school career-related activities and other programmes that promote children's self-knowledge and skill development.

Adolescent career development

During adolescence (ages 11 to 25), the child develops into an adult on a physical, cognitive and social level. The age demarcation may vary but usually adolescence is seen as starting at puberty. At *puberty*, sexual interest is a biological certainty and, as such, becomes an arena for different forms of culturally construed forms of regulation. Teenagers are confronted with the complex task of establishing a 'structure' for their biological maturation by incorporating the various social suggestions that are received from the outside world. Whatever structure is chosen, eventually *role relationships* in adult social roles are accepted, for example, that of marriage (Valsinger, 2000).

During the *second stage* of development, *formal operational thinking* equips the adolescent with the ability to construct theories, either about aspects of the world or the self. These theories do not necessarily comply with requirements for scientific theories, such as being empirically valid in terms of objective evidence or even being useful. Young adolescents tend to have fixed, simplistic views that they generalise. Older adolescents, however, as young adults can construct views based on considering, comparing and integrating different factors, including factors that may initially seem unrelated (Harter, 1999).

With the *meta cognitive ability* to analyse their own thinking, adolescents also conceptualise the thoughts of others during the *third stage of development,* but do not necessarily differentiate what is important to others. They therefore develop a kind *of self-absorption* and create personal fables, such as being invulnerable and immortal (Craig, 1996).

On a *moral level,* a *fourth stage* emerges as adolescents become socially conscious. The concern is not so much with individual rights but with the welfare of society or the group in terms of the roles and rules of the system. An action is considered right if it involves fulfilling the duties to which they have agreed and obeying rules that they can identify with. At *stage four and a half,* the *sense of duty* becomes arbitrary as moral thinking becomes more subjective and personal. At this stage, there is not a generalised commitment to society as adolescents see themselves as individuals capable of making their own decisions. The *fifth stage of moral thinking* concerns *rights* that are agreeable to all in a fair, democratic society. The moral and legal aspects of society are acknowledged, but the adolescent cannot always integrate the two (Kohlberg and Ryncarz, 1990). Craig (1996) points out that moral thinking also does not necessarily imply moral behaviour.

Adolescents create their own inner culture and motivation. They construe themselves in various ways and may even transgress social norms by seeking new thrills and trying out new ways of conduct beyond socially defined boundaries (Valsinger, 2000). Through introspection and their cognitive apparatus they have to organise their various attributes into role-related selves and as multiple selves proliferate they experience conflict regarding the different roles (Harter, 1999).

Adolescence has been described as a period of turmoil resulting in a transition from childhood. Continuity of development is, for some, sporadic and chaotic (Zunker, 2006).

Erikson (1963) sees adolescence as the *quest for identity* in terms of self and gender roles and roles in the broader society. The different expectations and opinions of others can cause *role confusion*, which the adolescent carries into adulthood. According to Erikson (1963:155), these new identifications are no longer characterised by the playfulness of childhood and the experimental zest of youth. Adolescence forces the young individual into choices and decisions which will, with increasing immediacy, lead to commitments for life.

The choice of career and commitment to a career has significant impact on *identity*. Many adolescents delay commitment or place a psychological moratorium on the decision until further options are explored. A young person unable to avoid role confusion might adopt what is referred to as a 'negative identity', assuming forms of behaviour that are in direct conflict with family and society. Those who develop a more appropriate sense of direction can find this experience positive, but for others the negative identity is maintained throughout adulthood (Zunker, 2006). Identity diffusion often results in lack of commitment to a set of values and, subsequently, to occupations (Erikson, 1963).

Individuals go through stages as they choose their initial careers. In the *first stage*, the exploratory period, adolescents begin to consider what their interests and values are and where their talents lie. In the *second stage*, the crystallisation period, individuals begin to think more specifically about the career options they could realistically pursue and what the advantages and disadvantages of different careers might be. In the *third stage*, the specification period, individuals make concrete decisions about the career they will enter and commit themselves to pursuing. As individuals pass through childhood and adolescence, they develop some level of career resilience, that is, self-confidence in their skills and some persistence in the face of obstacles. As they enter late adolescence and their twenties, they subsequently develop career insight (Feldman, 2002c).

Developing *career maturity* (decisiveness and independence in planning and decision-making skills) is therefore regarded as a crucial developmental task in adolescence. Defining appropriate sexual roles and achieving relationships with peers are also important developmental tasks for adolescents. Socially responsible behaviour implies that the first steps have been taken in achieving emotional independence from parents and other adults. Social relationship patterns learned during adolescence greatly affect an individual's adjustment to roles and life roles, including the work role, of the dominant society (Zunker, 2006).

Career development competencies that adolescents need to develop are (Zunker, 2006:421):

◆ becoming aware of personal characteristics, interests, aptitudes and skills;
◆ developing an awareness of and respect for the diversity of the world of work;

- understanding the relationship between school performance and future choices;
- developing a positive attitude towards work;
- clarifying the role of personal values in career choice;
- distinguishing educational and skill requirements for areas or careers of interest;
- recognising the effects of job or career choice on other areas of life;
- beginning realistic assessment of their potential in various fields;
- developing skills in prioritising needs related to career planning;
- refining future career goals through synthesis of information concerning self, use of resources and consultation with others;
- identifying specific educational requirements to achieve goals;
- clarifying own values and life interests as they relate to work and leisure;
- making final commitments to a career plan in the school-to-work transition phase;
- understanding the potential for change in own interests or values related to work;
- understanding the potential for change within the job market;
- understanding career development as a life-long process; and
- accepting responsibility for own career directions.

Late adolescent and adult career development

Career development during the late adolescent and adult life stages is seen as an *ongoing process* by which an individual progresses through a series of stages, each of which is characterised by a relatively unique set of issues, themes or tasks. The major developmental tasks during *late adolescence* (ages 18 to 25), also called the exploration phase, are: developing an occupational self-image, assessing alternative occupations, developing initial occupational choice, pursuing necessary post-school education and developing one's employability and obtaining job offers from the desired organisations (Greenhaus et al, 2010). The exploration phase is seen as a period of self-discovery and the establishment of a professional self-image. Dominant needs include peer acceptance, support and a job in which one can succeed (Miao, Lund and Evans, 2009).

Adult career development is characterised by *three life/career stages*: the early life/career (ages 25 to 40), the mid-career (ages 40 to 50) and the late life/career (ages 55 to retirement). The *early life/career stage* encompasses two periods, the establishment and achievement phases. Major developmental tasks include: learning the job, learning organisational rules and norms, fitting into chosen occupation and organisation, increasing competence, sustaining employability and pursuing one's career goals and life interests. The *mid-career* is initiated by the mid-life transition which serves as a bridge between early and middle adulthood. Major developmental tasks include: reappraising early career and early adulthood, reaffirming or modifying career goals, making choices appropriate to middle adult years, remaining productive in work and sustaining one's employability. The developmental tasks of the *late life/career* stage include: remaining productive in work, maintaining self-esteem and preparing for effective retirement (Greenhaus et al, 2010). Each of these stages is discussed below in more detail. Table 5.1 provides an overview of the career competencies that adults need to develop to sustain successful careers.

Table 5.1 *Adult career development competencies (Adapted from Zunker, 2006:440)*

Career development competency	Description
Self-knowledge	◆ Skills to maintain a positive self-concept ◆ Skills to maintain effective behaviours (emotional intelligence, managing stress, managing financial resources, identifying support and networking arrangements, working in teams) ◆ Adaptability and understanding development changes and transitions (changes in personal motivations, physical changes that occur with age, changes in work circumstances, external events that require life changes)
Educational and occupational exploration	◆ Skills to enter and participate in education and training ◆ Skills to participate in work and lifelong learning ◆ Skills to locate, evaluate and interpret information (career information, self-assessment, career planning, occupations, prospective employers' organisational structures and career pathways, employer expectations) ◆ Skills to prepare to seek, obtain, maintain and change jobs ◆ Understanding how the needs and functions of society influence the nature and structure of work
Career planning	◆ Skills to make decisions ◆ Understanding the impact of work on individual and family life ◆ Understanding the continuing changes in male/female roles ◆ Skills to make career transitions

In line with Super's (1990) concept of life stages (discussed in chapter 4), these three major adult life/career stages constitute a *maxicycle* in the sense that they are age-related. However, it is also possible for an individual to experience a series of *substages* (which are not age-related) that can occur *within each* of the three major life/career stages within the maxicycle, namely the substages of exploration, establishment, maintenance and disengagement. These substages can be referred to as a *minicycle* (Super, 1990).

The following is an example of a minicycle within the maxicycle (Sharf, 2010:259): a 42-year old dentist (mid-career) could be in the establishment stage. She may be becoming less concerned with stabilising and advancing in her practice. She may explore ways to maintain herself in her practice and gradually disengage from the establishment stage and grow into the maintenance phase. Or she could start to explore other career options and discover that she wants to become an artist and disengage from dentistry.

According to Super (1990), people reassess their career plans at various points during their lifetime and recycle through the various substages within the maxicycle. When they do this, they re-enter the exploration stage and may reassess their values, interests and capacities. When they enter a stage that they have been through before, they are said to *recycle* through it (see also chapter 4). Individuals entering the *maintenance phase* of their careers generally tend to consider whether they would like to make a career change. If they decide to change jobs, company or career, they recycle back to earlier stages, crystallise new career development objectives and move forward from there. For those who hold on, they maintain what they have, upgrade their skills and knowledge and innovate.

The concept of *recycling* through the various substages or minicycle is especially important in the context of the 21st century world of work where people will tend to experience more frequent career transitions and need to readjust to new situations throughout the life-span.

Career development of men and women

Societal changes over the past 40 or 50 years have led to work being a critically important part of women's lives and thus resulted in changing the assumption that women's careers are not as important as men's because they tend to occupy only short periods of the adult woman's life-span. Although women now constitute a significant portion of the labour force, their work continues to be focused in traditionally female occupations and to be less well paid than that of men (Betz, 2005).

There is general consensus that women's lives are fundamentally different from men's and that they construct their careers in different ways. Although research suggests that the process of career development is essentially the same for women and men, women and men face different challenges as they advance through their careers. Gould (1978) found that men and women differ regarding their career experiences. His research indicates that during their 20s, men tend to use work as the major way to differentiate themselves from their parents and become an adult. During their 30s, men seek career success. The 30s are the time of career commitment or change, with some men believing that work will somehow protect them from misfortune and maladies. In their 40s, men realise that the belief they held in their 30s that 'work success will make me happy' is a false assumption. Men become more in tune with their inner selves, are more likely to engage in mentoring, feel rejuvenated about work or, failing that, realise that they need to change careers.

Women in contrast have different career experiences. Spencer (1999) suggested that women have different developmental patterns than men do: women experience intense role confusion early in their development due to gender stereotyping; they tend to be more inhibited in their self-expression; they tend to delay their career aspirations in lieu of family responsibilities; and their developmental patterns are more individualised. Women often have multiple roles and responsibilities and tend to celebrate a greater variety of career forms and lifestyle choices (non-linear career patterns and preferences) rather than paid work and status (or linear career patterns) as the distinguishing features of their career (Cohen and El-Sawad, 2009).

Research has shown that although women tend to progress through similar periods of stability and transitions than men, they tend to have 'split dreams'. Unlike men who had 'the dream' that focuses on the career and is supported by relationships with the mentor and the 'special women', women by age 30 tend to change their focus from either career to family or vice versa (Sullivan and Crocitto, 2007:298). Many women face a delicate 'balancing act' between the pursuit of career progress and the demands of motherhood (Greenhaus et al, 2010). Childhood socialisation often results in women wishing to maintain a traditional family role. Some women may fear career success because they believe it will lead to isolation. Women who choose careers in their 20s may forego having children until later in life when they feel the pressure of their biological clock. Others without children face the quandary of being unable to fully commit to their careers because they feel they should have children. Some women in dual career situations may hire assistance with household tasks or may temporarily leave the workplace (Sullivan and Crocitto, 2007:298).

Based on an in-depth study of 60 women, O'Neil and Bilimoria (2005) suggest that women's careers could be divided into *three quite long phases:*

Phase 1: idealistic achievement	(in the 20s and early 30s) with the emphasis on personal control, career satisfaction and achievement and positive impact on others.
Phase 2: pragmatic endurance	(in the mid-30s to late 40s) with the emphasis on doing what has to be done, whilst managing multiple relationships and responsibilities. This phase is characterised by less personal control and more dissatisfaction especially with organisations and managers. Around the age of 40 women also tend to re-evaluate the career-family balance (Arnold and Randall, 2010); and
Phase 3: re-inventive contribution	(around age 50 onwards) to organisations, families and communities without losing sight of self. Careers are viewed as learning opportunities and a chance to make a difference to others.

Using the metaphor of the *kaleidoscope (or varied) career* to illustrate the varied career paths and directions of women, Maineiro and Sullivan (2006) suggest that men and women alter the patterns of their careers by rotating the varied aspects of their lives to arrange their relationships and roles in new ways. In terms of moral development, women tend to be more care-oriented and men more justice-oriented. Women tend to take a *relational approach* to their careers by basing career-related decisions on the potential consequences for other members of the family.

Research by Maineiro and Sullivan (2006) indicates that women were more likely than men to make career transitions for family reasons (ie, factoring in the needs of others such as, for example, children, spouses, ageing parents) and to achieve a more satisfying balance between work and family. Women therefore tend to have more frequent employment breaks or interruptions than men. On the other hand, men tend to focus more on justice, rules and agency (Sullivan and Crocitto, 2007). Mainiero and Sullivan (2006) found that men make career decisions from a goal orientation, focusing on independent action. Unlike women, men tend to keep their career and family issues separated.

Early life/career stage

In early adulthood (ages 25 to 45) *physical and cognitive development* is at its peak. *Physically* it is a time of energy, health and biological vigour, with instinctive drives high. *Cognitive functioning* is characterised by good memory, abstract thinking ability, problem-solving ability and learning new skills (Levinson et al, 1978).

Kohlberg's *fifth stage of moral development,* which starts in adolescence, characterises most young adults as well. In some adults, a *sixth stage* emerges in which what is right is determined by *universal ethical and moral principles,* such as justice, equality of human rights and respect for human dignity. Adults who develop this sixth stage are not merely aware of these principles by comprehending them with their abstract cognitive abilities — they are committed to these principles which determine their actions.

Tappan (1999) sees the essence of morality in post-modern society as acknowledging diversity. Amidst the plurality and paradoxes of a multi-racial, multi-ethnic, multi-cultural and multi-religious society, it involves an ongoing critical discourse as issues such as what is right, what is real and what is identity, are rethought.

Phases of early adulthood and life tasks

Life tasks of early adulthood include challenges concerning achieving independence and responsibility, establishing one's identity, finding a place in and contributing to society and becoming established in an occupation and in family life (Feldman, 2002; Scandura, 2002). A conscious commitment is made to a particular occupational field and effort is expended to stabilise oneself and establish a secure place in the working world (Miao et al, 2009).

Levinson, Darrow, Klein, Levinson and McKee (1978) distinguish *three phases* of early adulthood, namely the novice, transitional and settling down phases. The first fifteen years of early adulthood (approximately between ages 17 and 33) is described as a *novice phase* during which the individual is a novice adult, that is, a novice lover, a novice spouse and a novice worker. In all these aspects of life, new relationships have to be found, including relationships with family, mentors, bosses and seniors at work.

Primarily the task of this phase is *finding a place for oneself in the adult world.* This involves *two tasks* which can be of an opposing nature, namely *exploring the adult world* and *creating a stable adult life structure* at the same time. In *exploring the adult world* options are kept open, commitments are avoided and alternatives are maximised with a sense of adventure and wonderment in which aspirations can be coloured by fantasies. *Creating a stable adult life structure,* on the other hand, involves becoming responsible for establishing family relations and a stable work structure. Inability to find a balance between these tasks can cause confusion and stress and consequently, either a rootless, transient quality of life or a premature adult life structure that is not based on sufficient exploration.

Research indicates that approximately 95 per cent of young adults enter marriage, although men, in comparison to women, are less motivated to marry and are more concerned about their future careers, while women are concerned about both career and family considerations (Sdorow, 1995). Younger women in the early career stage try to balance family and career needs through following the 'superwoman approach', with career needs often dominating. They tend to focus on career and family only, not recognising that they also need personal time besides time for work and family. They have strong needs for advancement, which is traditionally associated with success (Gordon and Whelan, 1998).

A further phase of early adulthood is a *transitional phase* that Levinson et al (1978) call the *'age thirty transition',* which lasts for approximately three to five years. In this phase the individual experiences life as becoming more serious and has a sense of having to change before it is too late for change. This transition can be smooth or amount to a crisis, but in general it involves modification of some aspects of life, but not revolutionary changes.

The 'age thirty transition' phase may now occur between the ages of 20 and 35 due to the changing characteristics of the contemporary workplace and dynamic nature of the 21st century career. This phase is generally being referred to as the *quarter-life quandary* and can be quite overwhelming for the young adult (Jowell, 2003).

Jowell (2003) identified that individuals in their early life/career stage experiencing the *quarter-life crises* or *quandary* are confronted by *life questions* such as:

- What career should I focus on? Careers in the contemporary workplace offer numerous possibilities and young adults have multiple interests;
- Where should I live? Should I stay with my family, follow my friends or follow my heart?;
- Shouldn't I be more settled by this stage of my life? Is it okay to still be experimenting with my life's options?;
- Where do I belong?;
- Am I useless just because I can't define what my life's dream is?;
- Don't people expect bigger and better things from me at this stage?;
- What if I try something new and I fail?; and
- Why is it that everyone seems surer of themselves than me?

The quarter-life quandary is usually followed by a phase that Levinson et al (1978) call *settling down*. During this phase, the self has to become engaged in the world; in other words, individuals have to fulfil goals and aspirations set earlier and they have to find a niche in society. 'Becoming one's own man' (Levinson et al, 1978:60) and advancement in the sense of 'making it' become important.

Promotion is of primary concern at this time and the psychological success resulting from high performance during this time period is expected to add to greater work involvement. Challenges include balancing the demands of career and family and needs include achievement, esteem, autonomy and competition (Miao et al, 2009). Scandura (2002) maintains that the *need for competence* is especially strong in young adults. He defines it as the need to have an impact on one's environment. Ostroff, Shin and Feinberg (2002) indicate that the need for competence as well as the need to develop *occupational identity* are major tasks of the early career.

Related to competence is *self-reliance* or *autonomy*, a characteristic which is often regarded as typifying maturity. Self-reliance must, however, not be confused with independence. Dependence on others in the sense of needing others is not necessarily a mark of immaturity. people's involvement in social and intimate situations, such as marriage and certain types of work, necessarily brings out dependency, for example the interdependence of husband and wife or that of colleagues. Healthy dependence is instrumental to social involvement, in which a person can function as a self-reliant being as well as a being that is connected with others.

Erikson (1963) regards the developmental task of early adulthood as *developing intimacy,* which refers to *commitment and involvement.* This task is realised through relationships with a loved one, with a co-worker, with a boss or, to a certain extent, through involvement in a commitment to an organisation. Young adults' sense of ego-identity revolves around intimacy, which has developed from role testing in adolescence to more stable affiliations in early adulthood (Erikson, 1963). This is based on a readiness to develop ethical strength by binding themselves to that to which they are committed, although it may involve sacrifices and compromises.

Some young adults encounter problems because their newly found sense of ego identity is still fragile and they fear that they may lose it. Consequently, they avoid involvement in life aspects that provide intimacy and, according to Erikson, this leads to isolation, which involves exaggerated self-concern. This can harm the development of healthy task orientation which, for work adjustment, must occur in harmony with healthy ego orientation. Task orientation is reality bound and facilitates balancing subjective aims and objective responsibilities.

Subjective priorities that young adults seek in their first jobs include:

◆ opportunities for advancement;
◆ social status, prestige and recognition;
◆ responsibility;
◆ freedom from supervision;

- opportunities to use special aptitudes and educational background;
- challenge and adventure;
- opportunities to be creative and original; and
- high salary.

A survey conducted by Coetzee and Schreuder (2004) amongst a group of 167 students indicated that young adults between the age of 20 and 30 are experiencing the following *life/career challenges:*

- earning a living;
- finding a job matching one's qualifications;
- continuously furthering one's qualifications;
- gaining more experience;
- being more assertive;
- work disillusionment;
- upskilling oneself; and
- living one's dream.

Objective responsibilities, which are expectations that the organisation has of new employees, but which are not necessarily priorities or characteristics of new employees, include:

- competence to get a job done;
- ability to accept organisational realities, such as office policies;
- ability to generate and implement ideas;
- patience and perseverance in wanting acceptance for new ideas;
- ability to translate technical solutions into practical terms;
- ability to handle interpersonal relations;
- loyalty and commitment to the goals and values of the organisation;
- high personal integrity and the ability to compromise; and
- capacity to grow and learn from experiences.

Greenhaus et al (2010) see *establishment* and *achievement* as two overriding early career issues that have to be dealt with by the individual as well as the organisation. For the individual, *establishment* generally involves learning, testing competence, fitting in, seeking approval, coping with dependence and insecurity. *Achievement* generally involves contributing, increasing competence, moving up, seeking authority, finding independence and self-confidence.

Career establishment

Generally speaking, the early career is the period of career establishment or stabilisation. The organisation must assist new employees in fitting into their jobs and provide the necessary training, while employees should be willing to learn about the job and themselves in order to evaluate their job match.

Socialisation in the organisation (see chapter 8) forms an integral part of establishment. To become socialised to the organisation involves learning more about it and becoming adjusted to its expectations, policies, procedures and culture. Furthermore, a well-negotiated *psychological contract* can increase mutual acceptance and minimise uncertainties in both employer and employee.

To make this period less traumatic and more productive, Greenhaus et al (2010) suggest some actions to be taken by the organisation, namely actions related to *recruitment orientation, challenge* and *feedback.*

The successful *adjustment* of a new employee to an organisation may vary due to differences between the individual's expectations of the job and the reality of the job. Therefore, a *realistic recruitment programme* is a precondition for facilitating adjustment.

The most difficult period for newcomers is the first few days or weeks in the company. Therefore, an effective *orientation programme* should initiate them into the company's policies, benefits and services.

Most new employees enter an organisation expecting a high level of challenge and personal responsibility. However, very few companies are prepared to meet newcomers' expectations before they have gained experience and trust and therefore exercise strict supervision and control over new employees. *Early job challenge* can have positive long-term results. Research has shown that management trainees who are given early job challenges perform better than those who are not. Early job challenge also has the advantage of faster promotion to higher management positions and it also tends to motivate employees to further their education.

The mere allocation of challenging tasks is, however, not enough. New employees should be given *frequent feedback* on their performance to enable them to feel accepted, develop competence and adjust their behaviour, thereby accelerating the learning process. Positive feedback — that is, not being punished for mistakes — reinforces the learning experience and performance feedback on the whole is a way of specifying the details of the psychological contract.

Feedback can, however, involve varied *strategies.* A supervisor may, for example, implement a 'sink or swim' approach, which involves substantial responsibility with little support. Whether or not this approach succeeds, depends on how the organisation deals with success or failure. It can succeed if the person is not punished for failure, is given clear feedback on the degree of success or failure and is shown how to rectify mistakes. Another strategy is to give individuals a task in which they are virtually sure to fail, in that it is difficult to execute. This may have a tempering effect and make the new employee susceptible to feedback from a supervisor (Schein, 1976).

Satisfaction of needs for competence and acceptance enables new employees to develop feelings of success. In this, the new employee's direct supervisor plays an important role by being role model, provider of feedback, protector, coach, trainer and mentor. A prerequisite for enacting these roles is that the supervisor should feel secure in his or her own position, without feeling threatened by the newcomer. The supervisor thus plays a major part in developing the subordinate's career and the organisation should encourage employee–mentor relationships. Studies of executives show that those who had mentors earn more money at a younger age, are better educated, are more likely to follow a career plan and also mentor others (Clutterbuck, 2001).

Mentoring is particularly related to early career promotions and to work and career satisfaction (Whitely and Coetsier, 1993; Ostroff et al, 2002). Although mentoring facilitates career development, new employees themselves are ultimately responsible for his or her effective career management.

Tenure plays a role in establishment with regard to performance. Research indicates a strong, positive relationship between the *length of job experience* and the *performance* of early-career managers. Those with longer tenure achieve, for example, higher sales and larger profits (McEnrue, 1988). Despite the importance of organisational actions in establishment, the role of non-work factors should be considered in research on the early career and job change (Dougherty et al, 1993).

Flexible work hours can facilitate retaining individuals who have major roles beyond working for the organisation. Younger women, for example, require flexibility to handle the demands of childcare and to devote time to spouses. In France, reducing the work week to 35 hours has resulted in decreased unemployment and has benefited working mothers (Sunday Times, 07/01/2001). Computer technology has also made it possible for employees to be attached to an organisation but to work from home.

With regard to actions that the individual can take in the early career, Greenhaus et al (2010) suggest that new employees must learn about their own *developmental needs* and find out whether they are matched to the organisation. They must *obtain information* about themselves and the organisation by carrying out the tasks allocated to them, *studying performance reviews, making observations* and *forming informal relationships.* This can provide them with the understanding that is necessary for them to adjust their career goals to the reality of the organisation. Despite the fact that the new employee must adjust to the new environment, he or she can take an active role in ensuring that the socialisation process is successful. The newcomer should attempt not only to understand the culture of the organisation but also to influence the organisational environment.

Job transitions are becoming more frequent during the establishment years since many organisations can no longer promise long-term employment. Movement across organisational boundaries is thus becoming more common. According to Waterman, Waterman and Collard (1994) dependency issues play a role in how resilient an individual is in coping with numerous job transitions during the establishment years. Those who are passive may experience more difficulty coping with job changes compared with those who are independent (Scandura, 2002).

Organisations are responsible for creating new learning mechanisms, such as greater information sharing, career management support practices and exposure to new skills through training to ensure the future employability of the new entrant. Such practices will also enhance the ability of the individual to respond to job and life changes.

Career achievement

Once a certain degree of security and acceptance has been established in the organisation, the individual strives for achievement. *'Achievement'* has been related to an *'advancement phase'* because it involves a period during which the individual displays a desire for promotion and advancement within the organisation.

Greenhaus et al (2010) also outline some *actions* that can be taken by the organisation to increase effective achievement. *Early job challenge* makes it possible for new employees to test their abilities and contribute towards the success of the organisation they have joined. After the early years of their careers, new employees become ready to take on *more responsibility* and seek achievement by expanding their sphere of responsibility and becoming more independent.

Promotion automatically entails more responsibility, but newcomers can be given the chance to grow in their job. It is the direct supervisor's responsibility to provide challenges and to transfer responsibility without overburdening the new employee. Goals must be set together and the new employee should be permitted to take part, for example, in determining schedules, controlling the budget and participating in special assignments. However, employees generally require *feedback* on their performance as far as their career goals are concerned.

A career path consists of a series of positions within a company through which employees pass during their career (see chapter 3). The organisation is responsible for constructing realistic and flexible *career paths*. Growth and development in a career should not be neglected by the organisation as traditional career paths are no longer readily available.

An organisation can also promote the *self-assessment* of its employees by providing workshops, seminars, discussion groups and guidance and performance feedback. The organisation should also provide its employees with *information* on job opportunities, specifying the duties, knowledge and skills required, as well as the demands that will be made on employees and the rewards that they can hope to obtain. This information will be useful to employees planning their career paths only if it is sufficiently detailed. The organisation may even have a 'job-posting programme' or hold a career day to assist its employees with career path planning.

The organisation can help employees to develop a career development plan consisting of the following:

◆ a statement describing the employee's ideal work environment;
◆ a specified target job linked to a timetable (up to three years);
◆ a list of the individual's strong points and special talents;
◆ a list of skills and experience that the individual must acquire to obtain the specified target job; and
◆ an idea of the strategy or plan of action required to obtain the target job, including a time schedule and the purpose of each action.

A career development plan can only be drawn up with the aid of a supervisor who provides *performance appraisal and feedback*. In addition to actions by the organisation, employees also have a responsibility towards their achievement. Employees who fail to establish their own goals may find that the organisation sets the goals on their behalf. It is thus in the employees' interest to adapt their career goals on an ongoing basis and to ensure that the organisation is informed about them. In time, employees should nominate themselves for promotion when they are ready for it. It is thus necessary for employees to remain informed about which particular career path will result in the achievement of their career goals (Greenhaus et al, 2010).

Middle adulthood life/career stage

The *mid-life transition* and *middle adulthood* is dominated by conscious *ageing*, an acknowledgement of mortality and, with that, a potential for increased illness and diseases (Pringle and Dixon, 2003). Middle adulthood involves *physical changes*, such as bone loss and a decline in muscle activity, lung capacity, visual acuity, reaction time and the strength or endurance required for strenuous tasks. Concerns with the body remain of primary importance and may become issues when, in Freudian terms, the body ego is threatened when it is perceived as disintegrating (Kets de Vries, 1999). The likelihood of cardiovascular and respiratory diseases increases stress, while stress in itself can give rise to these diseases. The way stress is experienced, however, depends on the personality style of the individual and the meaning that stress has for the individual — for some people it is debilitating while for others it is challenging (Craig, 1996).

At age 50 and older, women experience the physical changes of menopause that is regarded as being symbolic of death (Bardwick, 1986; Pringle and Dixon, 2003). The time that follows menopause is labelled as post-menopausal zest (Sheehy, 1995). Menopause is a time of physical changes that create the need for emotional and psychological accommodations (Pringle and Dixon, 2003).

Psychological benefits in mid-life are more wisdom, more autonomy, being less driven by instinctual drives, coming to terms with limitations, having social concerns and a broader life perspective (Levinson et al, 1978). *Cognitive functioning* is characterised by being able to look at matters more objectively, being able to see several points of view regarding a matter and finding a synthesis that integrates opposing points of view (Louw and Edwards, 1997). Some aspects of intelligence show continuity and others change. Crystallised intelligence, which involves knowledge that has been acquired through experience, education and training, shows continuity and can improve up to beyond the age of seventy. Fluid intelligence, which involves inborn abilities such as the speed of memorising, perception of relationship and inductive reasoning ability, may decline (Craig, 1996).

At mid-life many individuals are at the height of their powers and feel that they are in the prime of their lives. For some, however, responsibilities are experienced as draining their time and energy. It is typically a time of self-questioning and inner seeking, referred to by Jung as greater interiority (Kets de Vries, 1999).

Life tasks and challenges in middle adulthood

Life tasks include redefining one's identity, clarifying one's values and philosophy of life, adjusting to changes in family life, utilising more leisure time and finding new occupational satisfactions as training and experience become consolidated (Gerdes et al, 1988).

A survey conducted by Coetzee and Schreuder (2004) amongst a group of 167 students indicated that adults in the 31 to 50 age group are facing the following life/career challenges:

- earning a living;
- upskilling oneself/further development;
- living one's dream;
- achieving one's goals;
- recognition;
- plateauing; and
- downsizing/redundancy.

Adults in the middle life/career stage struggle to find a balance between *agency* and *communion*. *Agency* expresses itself through control over the environment and is manifested in self-protection, self-assertion and self-expansion. In contrast, *communion* manifests itself in the sense of being one with other individuals and the environment. Communion is part of a wider context of openness and flexibility to the environment (Pringle and Dixon, 2003).

Women often seek the freedom to investigate other activities and interests in a more agentic way. New levels of autonomy (after a life of accommodating the spouse and children) can give rise to increased energy and exploration of activities that may have been adolescent interests. Some women enter paid work, some retire and others move into self-employment (Still and Timms, 1998).

Levinson et al (1978) maintain that the individual acquires a *stronger sense of identity* in the middle years through greater *individuation*. Individuation clarifies the boundaries between individuals and the outside world, as well as individuals understanding who they are and what they want to be and do. In order to achieve individuation, certain *psychological polarities* must be resolved, namely young/old, destruction/creation, masculine/feminine and attachment/separateness. If individuals can integrate these contradictory feelings they attain greater individuation, which provides the necessary self-confidence and independence to modify the structure of their lives.

- *Young/old* involves feeling young by having a sense of initiation, possibility, energy and potential, yet feeling old by having a sense of termination, stability and completion that can become associated with fear of losing youth.
- *Destruction/creation* involves destruction in the sense of one's mortality, one's guilt and grievances, harm one has done to others and that others have done to oneself and realising that one is not a hero and it involves creation in the sense of wanting immortality, being creative and wanting to provide products or things for oneself, for others or for human welfare.

◆ *Masculine/feminine* is not easily distinguishable because of changing gender distinctions over time and culture, but traditionally, masculine has been associated with achievement, ambition, thinking, power, bodily strength and stamina, while feminine has been associated more with unassertiveness, submissiveness, feeling and weakness.

◆ *Attachment/separateness* involves the need to belong and to participate in the external world on the one hand and, on the other hand, besides attachment to the external world, to be primarily involved in one's inner world, exploring one's real or imagined self, which fosters personal growth and creative adaptation.

According to Erikson (1963), the adult's greatest need is for generativity. *Generativity* refers specifically to the care and guidance of the next generation and Erikson contends that productivity and creativity in other spheres of life cannot compensate for it. It involves the need to be needed. The antithesis of generativity is a psychological state *of stagnation,* in which individuals can become excessively self-indulgent, to the extent of loving themselves as if they were their own only child.

Researchers generally use the term generativity in a broader sense of adult development, involving giving and growing. Clark and Arnold (2008) view generativity as accomplishments and activities which reflect concern for the next and future generations, as expressed in (1) productivity; (2) nurturance of family; (3) care for society and its values and institutions; and (4) leadership. In a study of 41 men aged 45–55 in England, they found that generativity was more on men's minds than personal growth in terms of skills/knowledge and achievement. Most generativity occurred outside work, especially in the family setting. The results of Clark and Arnold's study indicate that generativity outside one's immediate family and friends (so-called mature radius generativity) was associated with psychological well-being and with personal growth.

Hall (1976) maintains that a sense of generativity can be achieved through the development of theories, discoveries or products, through guiding younger colleagues and in developing organisations. Kets de Vries (1999) indicates that everyone has a generativity script; that is, leaving a legacy for the next generation and attaining a kind of immortality by creating something that will outlive the self. It involves an expression of oneself that others will share, be it through parenting, teaching, leading or doing something for the community.

The mid-life crisis

During the late thirties or early forties, a so-called *mid-life crisis* can occur. In the mid-life crisis, some individuals once again have to contend with identity questions like 'What have I achieved?' or 'Where am I going?' The person stands on the delicate threshold between the outcomes of exploration, establishment and maintenance and the threat of decline. Researchers agree that the transition to the middle years can be just as critical and, in some respects, more agonising than adolescence (Sheehy, 1976).

Mental torment about disappointments, thwarted hopes, anxiety about health problems, such as heart disease, obesity and cancer and a sense of 'now or never' can cause various kinds of crisis behaviour, such as:

- anxiety;
- depression;
- hypochondria;
- alcoholism;
- change of work, home and/or spouse;
- obsession with denigrating one's life at present;
- attempts to regain youth through dieting and youthful clothing; and
- workaholism, recklessness and ruthlessness (Pitt, 1984).

Jacques, quoted by Pitt (1984), feels that crisis behaviour arises when the individual denies the unavoidable realities of the middle years and still clings to the 'mania' and idealism of early adulthood when 'everything' seemed possible.

Jacques coined the term 'mid-life crisis' on the basis of his observation of trends among artists. After the age of 35 they are inclined either to stop being creative (Rossini) or to begin creative work (Gauguin) or to change their direction (Goethe, Shakespeare).

A mid-life crisis may manifest in what Kets de Vries (1999) refers to as organisational sleepwalking. Some individuals become *alexlthymic*, which in Greek means no word for emotion. Such individuals are unable to understand or *struggle with their emotions* and negate that they exist. They appear to be unruffled, become robot-like mechanics with no self-awareness and are preoccupied with the concrete and objective. The origin of this type of behaviour is traced back to childhood by some psychologists. According to them it stems from an unhealthy symbiotic relationship with an overprotective mother who frustrated her children's individuality and play, not allowing them to feel for themselves.

Organisations can also contribute to denial of emotions by a division of 'emotional labour' in which blue-collar workers are allowed emotional expression but white-collar workers are meant to be models of emotional control (Kets de Vries, 1999).

A critical issue in mid-life can be the *spiritual search for authenticity* (see chapter 1 and chapter 7). Sheehy (1976) maintains that authenticity can be accomplished by disassembling the self to renew it. The self that is disassembled was constructed by the individual to satisfy society or other people. It forms part of individuals' identities that they relied on before. These identities are used to stabilise individuals before they have the personal reserves to rely on their own inner authority. Examples of such identities are the ambitious executive, the fearless politician, the super mother and the submissive wife. Such a self is narrow and should be expanded to incorporate positive as well as negative aspects of the real or total person.

In the work context, mid-life is generally a time of *reappraisal of the past* and appraisal of long-term career plans — an assessment of real progress measured in terms of ambitions. The 'dream' is compared to the 'reality' of progress. If a disparity exists, individuals may resolve the problem by re-evaluating long-term goals and aspirations or by trying to modify the nature of their work as well as their view of work. Practical solutions may be found by viewing this as a period for growth and enrichment, rather than one of stagnation or decline. By setting new goals and acquiring new knowledge and skills individuals can optimally re-engage exploratory needs and by acquiring emotional intelligence they can gain self-knowledge concerning their motivation (Kets de Vries, 1999).

Elliot (1994) suggests that the *protean career* concept gives the individual the responsibility to meet specific mid-career needs, that is, realistic self-assessment, opportunity to learn new skills and sharing of skills and expertise. With the shift from the traditional organisation career to the protean career, Hall and Mirvis (1995a,b) suggest that the organisation can assist older workers with a *new career contract*, which is based on continuous learning rather than retraining.

Continuous learning is required for continued success and the keys to mid-career success are the ability to self-reflect about one's identity and to develop adaptability. These are known as meta skills in that they are skills with which one learns to learn. Individuals become responsible for their own success, whereas in retraining, the employer is seen as the source of individuals' career direction as well as their career wisdom.

Retraining by experts is costly and timely, skills and tasks are usually theoretical or simulated, whereas continuous learning occurs in the real work situation. It is facilitated by organisations that are designed for adaptability and are characterised by decentralisation (that is, employing core full-time as well as contract contingent personnel), diversity (that is, age, gender, ethnic and lifestyle diversity) and delegation of authority (that is, empowerment). Adaptability in organisations fosters adaptability and the possibility to remain productive in older workers.

Remaining productive can be hampered by *career issues* such as job loss, obsolescence and discrimination. Discrimination is more prevalent among women than men and mid-career women report less income, career satisfaction and boss appreciation than men (Schneer and Reitman, 1994).

Gordon and Whelan (1998) find that women who have reached mid-career and have achieved accomplishment, list being prepared for changes over the next ten years as a major priority. As the nuclear family changes and older children require less time and attention, mid-career women have and desire more personal time besides time for spouse, children and work. They see success in terms of personal meaning and choice rather than in terms of social definitions of success. They express the need to be perceived as valuable to the organisation and can therefore be retained by the organisation if the latter fosters satisfaction by encouraging mid-career women to engage in entrepreneurial activities, by moving them to top management and by allocating equitable rewards with regard to pay as well as positive feedback on performance.

The flexibility needed by employees has translated into insecurity, financial pressures, overwork and increased risk of income and quality of work life especially for older workers. The contemporary workplace demands *proactivity* and creativity on the part of the mid-career individual. One aspect of this proactivity is anticipating how one's work, one's industry and/or one's organisation will change during the next three to five years. Organisations also need to discuss with mid-career employees the different ways in which they can prove themselves useful to employers (Betz, 2003).

Organisational career development support

Essentially, employees should be helped to decide among *four developmental directions:* task development, specialist development, vertical development and niche development. These developmental directions involve *three levels of mid-career development:* job oriented, work maintenance (task development in multiple employer contexts) and work growth mid-career development (the employee seeks growth and change although he or she must still select a developmental direction) (Betz, 2003). Organisations also need to recognise and differentiate between the diverse needs of women and men (Pringle and Dixon, 2003).

Greenhaus et al (2010) suggest the following actions that the organisation can take to help employees manage their careers during the mid-career stage:

◆ help employees understand mid-career experiences;
◆ provide expanded and flexible mobility opportunities;
◆ let them utilise the current job;
◆ encourage and teach mentoring skills;
◆ provide training and continuing education;
◆ broaden the reward system; and
◆ allow for creativity and provide challenge and variety in the workplace.

Late life/career stage

Although a late life/career stage is distinguished, in that the life activities of some individuals in late adulthood include work-related tasks, generalisations about the relation between late adulthood and work should rather make place for an individualist approach. Significant individual differences characterise individuals between 60 and 70 and 70 and 80 years of age. Late life workers or pensioners should thus rather be studied as *individuals* than as a group that is associated with stereotypes such as unproductive, unmotivated or intellectually too rigid to adapt to change (Craig, 1996).

Physical decline in late life is inevitable as, for example, motor co-ordination and speed declines, blood vessels become less elastic and chronic conditions such as arthritis, high blood pressure or dementia become possibilities.

Decline in all areas of cognition is not inevitable. Research based on psychometric measurement is generally inconclusive about cognitive decline, but upholds the following hypotheses (Salthouse, 1989):

◆ speed of information processing declines with ageing;
◆ cognitive abilities decline with disuse; and
◆ aspects of the environment, such as decreased sensory and intellectual stimulation and lack of social support, result in cognitive change, irrespective of the individual's abilities.

Although not generally seen as such, work issues can comprise a significant part of the late career life cycle. Higher life expectancy, for example, influences people's availability for work. At the beginning of the 19th century, life expectancy averaged 47 years, while it has since increased to approximately 75 years (Raubenheimer, 1991).

In late adulthood individuals still make valuable contributions to the organisation. Some individuals only then move into senior positions, with more responsibilities and decision-making requirements. Research findings with regard to the performance of employees in the late career are varied. Some, for example, report that older managers are unwilling to take risks, while others indicate that age has little effect on the performance of manual and clerical workers (Vroom and Pahl, 1971). Studies on older workers also indicate lower turnover rates and no differences in attendance records in comparison to younger employees (Sonnenfeld, 1989).

Life tasks and challenges in late life

In late adulthood, individuals are confronted with not only bodily and possible cognitive decline, but also with *socio-emotional losses,* such as losing recognition and authority as they retire from work. As a result, individuals become less interested in the rewards of society and more interested in utilising their inner resources, thereby finding a new balance of involvement with society and with self (Levinson et al, 1978).

Life tasks include establishing an explicit affiliation with one's age group, establishing satisfactory physical living arrangements and adjusting to changes concerning one's spouse (Gerdes et al, 1988).

Individuals also have to accept their life cycle, which Erikson (1963) relates to the life task of ego integrity versus despair. *Ego-integrity* refers to emotional integration which provides ego-identity. If the ego is strong enough to integrate the life experiences of previous life stages, individuals have a spiritual sense of order and meaning in their lives.

Lack of ego-integrity is characterised by *despair,* involving concern with regrets or a fear of death. Integrity amounts to identity maintenance in the face of changing life circumstances when the individual accepts that this is 'what/who I am'. Peck (1968), as cited in Craig (1996), sees identity as the resolution of conflict between ego pre-occupation and ego transcendence. Related to this could be Kohlberg and Ryncarz's (1990) view of a seventh stage of moral reasoning that develops over adulthood. This stage of reasoning goes beyond previous stages that develop from egoistic thinking to social consciousness which is based on development from concrete to abstract thinking in Piagetian terms. It relies on reflective thinking provided by some type of transcendental experience in which an intimate bond between the self and the cosmos is experienced. It offers the individual solutions to fundamental ethical questions, such as why be moral and just in an unjust society.

Older workers' attitudes toward career development activities and mobility relate to such factors as employment (experience or fear of lay-offs), tenure or stage in their careers and need for achievement and growth. In addition, fear of stagnation, marketability perceptions, self-esteem and job market contribution play a role in career decision-making. A decision to engage in training or retraining can lead to identity growth and enhanced self-esteem which, in turn, may result in greater commitment to future development goals (Wrobel, 2003). Research suggests that older workers are more likely to consult, seek self employment, perform community service and are more likely to work part-time (DBM, 2001).

Preparing for retirement

Generally, late adulthood is associated with *retirement*. For most people retirement is associated with a modification of identity rather than an identity crisis (Liber, 1982). Factors influencing it include the self-concept, the extent to which goals have been attained, attitudes and expectations of other people, financial status and health.

Although old age is associated with progressive physical deterioration and social loss, it is not necessarily a frustrating period psychologically. Depending on the individual, retirement from a career can be enriching or impoverishing. It may be welcome if it means freedom from unsatisfying work and/or freedom to do what one wants to do.

Generally a distinction is drawn between *retirement* and *retirement from a particular occupation*. Retirement from a particular occupation can be associated simply with a change of existing or traditional work roles, for example, changing to pensioner work, while retirement — that is, disengagement from work — can be perceived by the individual who stops working as a downward change, involving a loss of status with consequent feelings of lowered self-esteem. Men who have been mainly career- oriented may feel the loss of achievement through climbing the organisational hierarchy, while according to Craig (1996), women may adapt more easily to retirement because they are used to fulfilling different life roles.

Adjustment to retirement is also influenced by *motivational factors* in the late career. Raynor, quoted by Liber (1982), contends that *neutrally motivated individuals* will have few problems, because they have already 'retired' and that *success-oriented individuals* could die soon after retirement if they do not do other work, while *someone who fears failure* will flourish after retirement.

Lowenthal et al found that retirement has the most *detrimental effect* if it occurs shortly before the traditional retirement age of 60 to 65 (Back and Bourque, 1977). However, some people retire earlier than this from meaningful career activities or from a particular organisation. The retirement age varies from 55 to 60 or 65. Individual reasons vary, but if such individuals remain engaged in some constructive task, they may still feel socially acceptable because they would still, to some extent, be functioning within the framework of the majority, that is, the working population. The task should, however, be such that the sense of self-esteem it inspires is equal to that engendered by the individual's previous job.

Adjustment to retirement is also influenced by the *degree of self-actualisation* reached throughout the course of life. If individuals have attained self-actualisation, they will probably be able to adapt to enforced retirement or retirement from a particular occupation and be able to function as a psychically growing person, for example, through part-time work or hobbies, according to their abilities and interests.

If work, however, merely means 'keeping busy', in other words, if individuals function only on the basis of a lower level need such as the search for activity, this need may become even stronger when directed job activity is lost and these people can become a burden to themselves and others or become incapacitated by their ineffectual passivity. Some workers regard 'keeping busy' as synonymous with 'keeping alive' and fear that lack of activity lead to death (Hall, 1976). The activities that retirees choose to engage in have important implications for life after retirement. In particular, participating in bridge employment (paid employment after one's career job ends and before permanent full-time retirement begins) and leisure activities have positive effects on retirement satisfaction (Kim and Feldman, 2000).

The *quality of the career process* therefore contributes to the quality of retirement. Effective adjustment to retirement is explained by various *theories*, which include the following:

◆ *Continuity theory*, which postulates that activities and roles during retirement should be similar to those undertaken before retirement. This approach is applicable to people who derived satisfaction from their work.

◆ *Activity theory*, which accepts that work has different meanings for different people and that substitutes have to be found for work roles. This approach is applicable to success-oriented people who have potential for the future with regard to work-related activities.

◆ *Disengagement theory*, which contends that effective adjustment to retirement involves withdrawal from work-related activities. Liber (1982) maintains that this approach applies to people who felt threatened in their work by conflict or failure or success-oriented people who suffered so many losses in the past that they have stopped growing psychologically or people who are no longer work-oriented.

◆ *Differential disengagement*, whereby people retire only from certain aspects of work and continue with other activities. Adjustment can be successful if the latter are available. The effectiveness of various ways of adjusting depends on the interaction between career factors, the meaning of work, environmental factors and the individual's self-perception. Events which are regarded as negative by outsiders or researchers are not always negative for the person concerned. Erikson, quoted by Ridley (1982), found that a group of elderly people he studied were dynamic and diverse; they had a strong will to live, enjoyed living and regarded old age as a time of fulfilment.

Organisational career development support

Organisations can assist employees in preparing for the *transition to retirement* by encouraging them to accept themselves and to broaden their interests and develop new skills, by providing a phasing-out programme allowing them to do part-time consulting work and by providing pre-retirement programmes a few years before retirement (Schein, 1990b).

Individuals who attend *pre-retirement programmes* experience more satisfaction and fewer psychological and financial problems than individuals who do not (Noe et al, 1994). These programmes usually address the following topics (Noe et al, 1994; Schein, 1990b):

◆ psychological aspects of retirement, such as developing personal interests and activities;
◆ housing;
◆ healthcare during retirement;
◆ financial planning and investments; and
◆ estate planning.

Preparing for retirement also requires learning how to use leisure time. This can be facilitated by scheduling working hours and vocational leisure time in ways that help individuals to learn how to use leisure time effectively. Leisure activities can provide alternative sources of self-esteem and a continued source of identity, particularly if they are regarded as useful by society. Such activities can include voluntary services or activities that generate income.

Changing structures of work result in organisations offering early retirement packages. These packages consist mainly of offering employees financial benefits as inducements to leave the organisation. Older people may perceive such offers as discriminatory (Noe et al, 1994). Therefore, offers of early retirement must include an employee benefit plan, justify age-related distinctions for eligibility for early retirement and allow employees to choose early retirement voluntarily.

Whether retirement is voluntary or enforced, it influences the individual's perception of retirement and, whichever it is, requires that the individual be *psychologically prepared.*

Voluntary retirement before the age of 65 is steadily increasing. Feldman (2002c) speculates that the following factors lead to early retirement:

◆ staying in the same occupation for a long, uninterrupted period of time;
◆ being married to a working spouse;
◆ major physical illness;
◆ certainty about future plans;
◆ working for large firms in declining manufacturing industries;
◆ higher current wages and pension benefits;
◆ extensive pre-retirement counselling;
◆ negative impact of age on performance;
◆ self-identity tied to work;
◆ perceived discrimination against older workers; and
◆ organisational flexibility in handling older workers, for example, allowing leave for trial retirements, shorter work weeks and transitions to less demanding job assignments.

Feldman (2002b) maintains that individuals whose identities are tied to work will have difficulty adjusting to full-time retirement and are likely to accept *bridge employment* (that is, part-time, temporary or self-employment) similar to their current work. Individuals who retire early because of perceived discrimination against older workers are likely to accept bridge employment that differs from their current occupation.

Research by Ingram (2010) indicates that the happiest retirees were those who usually:

◆ specialised in some set of transferable skills;
◆ generated income for their organisations or themselves, ie, people who had a greater degree of control over their income generation;
◆ leveraged their time to their advantage, leaving some room for interests outside of work and career;
◆ enjoyed the line of work that they made a career in;
◆ aimed to achieve broader objectives or goals, ie, their sole focus was not on pure money-making but a bigger contribution to society; and
◆ persevered in their careers through both the good and bad times.

Table 5.2 *Life tasks and challenges of the early, middle and late life/career stages*

Life/career stage	Key life tasks/challenges
Early life/career stage	◆ Achieving independence and responsibility ◆ Developing self-reliance or autonomy ◆ Establishing one's identity ◆ Finding a place in and contributing to society ◆ Making an impact on one's environment ◆ Becoming established in an occupation and in family life ◆ Developing intimacy, becoming committed and involved ◆ Developing stable affiliations ◆ Becoming employable and career resilient (dealing with job transitions and sustaining employability) ◆ Dealing constructively with quarter-life crisis
Middle life/career stage	◆ Refining one's identity ◆ Clarifying one's values and philosophy of life ◆ Adjusting to changes in family life ◆ Utilising more leisure time ◆ Finding new occupational satisfactions ◆ Sustaining employability ◆ Dealing with career transitions ◆ Finding a balance between agency and communion ◆ Resolving psychological polarities to achieve greater individuation: young/old; destruction/creation; masculine/feminine; attachment/separateness; generativity/stagnation ◆ Dealing constructively with mid-life crisis ◆ Maintaining health and emotional well-being
Late life/career stage	◆ Dealing with socio-emotional losses ◆ Establishing satisfactory physical living arrangements ◆ Adjusting to changes concerning one's spouse ◆ Maintaining health and emotional well-being ◆ Preparing for retirement ◆ Sustaining ego integrity ◆ Remaining a productive citizen

Conclusion

Career development consists of different life/career stages. Although childhood and adolescence are not part of individuals' careers, influences in these early stages have implications for their work lives. Life stages and career stages are intrinsically related, yet different substages, including both life and career aspects, can be distinguished in terms of general characteristics, life tasks, needs and problematic issues. Changes in life and career aspects can be conducive to personal growth, psychological renewal and vitality, which generate further development. Life/career stages involve the contexts of personal, societal and organisational structures. Organisations and career counsellors need to consider the varied needs and career development orientations of men and women in the career development process.

Review and discussion questions

1. How does one's life/career stage influence one's career development?
2. Compare the life/career tasks and challenges of the early, middle and late life/career stage.
3. What can organisations do to assist individuals in dealing with the life/career tasks and challenges related to the early, middle and late life/career stages? At which life/career stage are you? What are your major life/career challenges currently and how do you deal with them?
4. What are some of the unique challenges that women have to face in their career development?
5. How does the changing nature of organisations and careers impact on the career planning and management activities of individuals in the early, middle and late life/career stages respectively?
6. What advice would you offer individuals facing the quarter-life quandary?
7. What practical steps can you suggest to minimise mid-career crisis?
8. Is the notion of life/career stages still relevant in terms of careers in the 21st century? Discuss your answer.
9. Write a paragraph describing the advice that you would offer a manager who has appointed an employee in his or her early life/career stage. Offer also some advice on the impact that a first job has on employees.

Reflection activities

Reflection activity 5.1

Read the following two case studies that apply to the early adulthood life/career stage and answer the questions that follow.

Caroline (35 years)

Career success to me has so many different meanings. I have always felt that I have achieved career success although I have had my ups and downs. I started working at the age of thirteen as a waitress; this was the first step to my journey of success. I then moved onto 'greater' things such as a restaurant hostess, hotel receptionist, restaurant manageress, personal assistant, tupperware consultant, accounting article clerk, wage clerk, personnel consultant, branch manager of agency, HR assistant, HR process co-ordinator and junior HR consultant. I have been fortunate enough to have a variety of positions which all added value to my choice of career.

While working as a waitress I found that as I built a name for myself in the industry as hard working and dedicated, people would offer me positions and tell me of job opportunities. In every position I had worked towards having the right attitude, keeping my values and at times sacrificing if necessary, but I never gave up even though at times life was hard. At one stage in my life I had three jobs working as a Restaurant Hostess, selling Tupperware and working as an Article Clerk. Up until the age of 23 I worked two jobs at a time — my day job and then my position as either a Restaurant Hostess or waitress in the evenings.

I was exposed to powerful networks in my position as an Article Clerk, Personnel Consultant and Branch Manageress and eventually worked my way into the company I wanted to build on my final career choice.

In my career I have had many mentors and have often watched how they dealt with situations, people and their work ethic and have learnt from this and tried to ensure that I follow the right route.

Although I do not enjoy criticism I have often asked for positive criticism, from which I can learn and grow. At times it was harder to take the criticism. I have done many assessments on myself to test that my self-knowledge is correct and to ensure that what I think of myself is close to how others perceive me and how I perceive myself. I have found that I am quite in touch with who I am and where I am going and am confident in being 'me'. I have set certain goals for myself which I have worked hard towards achieving and have made sure that I achieve them although at times it took me longer than planned.

I know that in this day and age spending the next twenty years at a company is not always recommended, but I believe in continuous learning; building on one's own strengths and weaknesses rather than only changing companies in order to grow. In my current position I still network with other consultants and agencies, finding out where I still need to develop and what is happening in other markets.

I used positioning strategies in that I work towards optimising my skills and experience and also have widened my list of contacts in order to work towards my pinnacle position. I recently moved from the HR Process Co-ordinator position (this is a position where I dealt with all HR projects for the area) to a Junior HR Consultant by influencing the Head of Human Resources. I worked hard towards proving myself in the position; I worked long hours and sacrificed time with my children to prove that I could add value. In doing this the Head of the area saw my dedication and worth and offered me the opportunity. I am aware of where I can add value and what I need to work on (my strengths and my limitations) — for example, by nature I am not very results-driven but I have worked towards becoming results-driven and have found that this is one of the aspects that people respect me for.

I believe that one needs to experience a balance between work life and family life and therefore have tried my best to keep my life balanced. I have taken ownership of my career and have ensured that I was developed in the areas I needed to be for my promotions to take place. I set time lines for myself to achieve certain goals and managed my expectations. Mostly I have met my time lines — the only time I was out was the extra year I spent in 2006 on only two modules of my post-graduate studies as my mother was ill and I needed to look after her. It therefore took me four years to complete my degree and not three as I had planned.

Nomfundo (28 years)

My personal career anchor is embedded in lifestyle, which elaborates on why a flexible work environment is attractive to me. It shows that I am highly motivated towards a meaningful career, as long as it is integrated with a complete lifestyle. This means that there has to be assimilation between my family, my career and myself. Today's companies require their workers to be flexible and give preference to achieving company objectives, largely due to the ratio of available employment to seeking workers. But for me, the needs of my lifestyle and family will always take preference, albeit at the expense of assignments which require geographical relocation. I therefore seek out organisations that embrace an attitude of flexibility and genuine respect for my personal concerns, where there is a positive psychological contract between the employer and employee.

This has been observed in my recent relocation to Johannesburg after accepting a management trainee position in one of the country's growing retail companies. It was an important career move and would launch my career with a big impact nationally. Initially I realised it would be hard being far away from home, but knowing I would grow stronger and wiser by being independent was a deciding factor. Four months into a 12-month contract I had drafted my resignation letter ready to go back to Cape Town even though I knew I had no pending employment prospects to go back to.

Being back at home was all that mattered. Despite the bi-monthly visits, my performance dropped and I grew increasingly depressed with time. Nothing about the job or the city comforted me. Only being in the company of loved ones mattered!

This illustrates that the core career anchor type will influence your functionality in business and when it is not met, it can be to the detriment of both the organisation and the individual (resources and emotional unhappiness).

As a young black female entrant to the world of work in South Africa there are many challenges. The business world is slowly opening up to black males as companies strive to balance their cultural numbers in line with the Black Economic Empowerment (BEE) policy. Admittedly there are more opportunities for black females than ever before and renewed motivation of the prospects of women leadership as the country embraced a female deputy president recently. As part of my proactive approach to business I am determined to exploit all the skills I gain from any organisation that I am part of in order to broaden my knowledge base and give myself a competitive advantage.

Women generally have a varied value system compared to males and this influences our decisions. But because the business world is still very much a male-dominated area, male values prevail. My motivation comes from intrinsic values, which include autonomy, quality feedback, development opportunities and occupational challenges. Recent business environments encouraged and allowed me to be a better organisational investment than my male counterparts whose extrinsic values lead them towards seeking job security and fringe benefits.

Personal success for me means achieving the economic sustenance of my career either within an already established organisation or by finding and maintaining a new one. Intellectual recognition and monetary rewards are as important as autonomy in my work and flexibility in my work schedule.

Questions

1. Review the life tasks and challenges of the early life/career stage. List the key factors of the early life/career stage that apply to Caroline and Nomfundo.

2. Review the varied needs of women and men regarding their career development. Identify the unique challenges both Caroline and Nomfundo have to face because of their gender.

3. Study the various phases of Caroline's career by referring to the various minicycles of the career development stages. List the career competencies and characteristics that enabled her to deal successfully with the challenges and tasks of the early life/career stage.

4. Do you agree that life/career stages cannot be delineated in absolute terms and that certain aspects can overlap? From Caroline's case we can see that a person does not necessarily have only one career. What are your personal experiences regarding your career?

5. Reflect on Nomfundo's career. Do you think her struggle to relocate to a new area (apart from her lifestyle need) is related to the challenges and tasks that the young adult has to deal with? Describe the life tasks and challenges that she faced in her career.
6. Review the career theories in chapter 4. Which theory would you recommend for guiding Nomfundo in her career development? Give reasons for your answer.

Reflection activity 5.2

Read through the article below and answer the questions that follow.

Survey Results

Generation Y choosing 'cool, creative careers'

02-JUN-09 (www.skillsportal.co.za)

Medicine, Law and the Arts — previously the careers of choice for the prospective professional — are now decidedly 'uncool', according to a comprehensive career study conducted in Australia.

The study, which polled school-going students across the continent, sought to gauge perceptions of different industries within the 16–18 age category, in a bid to discover the decision-making process used to define their eventual career path.

And the results, recently unveiled to the public, showcased Generation Y's affinity for both practical education and to pursue cool, 'sexy' careers, mostly within the creative industry.

Of the students polled, careers in television (25 per cent), the music industry (24 per cent), film (23 per cent) and digital media (22 per cent) featured most frequently, with over 65 per cent of respondents rating 'acting' as a job which 'attracts the sexiest people'.

The survey also showed a marked shift towards practical education, with an astounding 83 per cent of those considering future education specifying that they would rather pursue studies that will give them practical skills which are 'useful in the real world'.

Respondents also felt strongly about aligning their personal proficiencies with their chosen career path, with 67 per cent actively searching for careers that 'fit their interests and talents', allowing them creativity and the opportunity to be innovative in the workplace.

'We weren't actually surprised at the results,' comments Marco Bettelli, Managing Director of the Asia Pacific, Middle East and Africa regions for SAE Institute, the global college which commissioned the study.

'We've seen a considerable increase in interest from students wishing to pursue non-traditional areas of study, as students choose to take advantage of the opportunities available in the new creative industries.'

SAE Institute, the world's largest provider of creative media education, recently opened a Cape Town campus in a bid to offer creative certificates to South African students.

The Institute, which offers both short courses and full-time courses in Film, Audio, Animation and Interactive Media Design, provides the hands-on experience and creative technology which local students need to compete in the global marketplace.

'Cape Town is a hub for creative activity and we are seeing many local school-going students interested in the various creative fields. Whether it's computer animation, audio engineering or studying to become the country's next big film director — local creative students are definitely poised to increase SA's 'cool quotient' on a global scale,' commented Eva Grotzinger, Cape Town Institute Manager.

Questions

1. Study Gottfredson's theory on how the self-concept and environment influence the career development behaviour of adolescents and adults. Do you think that the knowledge economy and technological advancement affect the career development aspirations and career choices of the Generation Y young adult?

2. Explain how the concepts of circumscription and compromise will apply to the career decision-making of the Generation Y young adult when considering the skills development needs of South Africa and the demand for knowledge workers and employability. Review chapters 2 and 3 to help you formulate your answer.

3. Review the concept of 'quest for identity' as an important life task for the adolescent. Do you think that the demands of the contemporary world of work (explained in chapters 2 and 3) will add to the role confusion of the young adolescent (ie, creating a larger gap between the individuals' needs, values, interests and the requirements of the knowledge economy which may influence the availability of matching jobs)? Give reasons for your answer.

4. Review the career theories in chapter 4. Which theory would you recommend for guiding the Generation Y young adult in making career decisions in the contemporary world of work? Give reasons for your answer.

6

Career issues

Learning outcomes

After studying this chapter you should be able to:

- define career anchors;
- describe the different career anchors;
- describe the different career patterns;
- define the notion of working couples and describe the different family patterns;
- define work-family conflict and describe the different types of work-family conflict;
- explain the concept of work-family balance and the demands it makes on working couples.
- describe actions to be taken by organisations to accommodate employees in balancing family and work needs;
- define career plateauing;
- describe the different sources of career plateauing;
- describe the different types of career plateauing;
- discuss organisational actions to be taken to address plateauing;
- define obsolescence;
- illustrate and discuss different models of obsolescence;
- name organisational actions to be taken to reduce obsolescence;
- explain job loss and unemployment;
- describe the effects of job loss on the individual;
- describe ways in which individuals are affected by losing their jobs;
- describe the stages of job loss; and
- discuss organisational actions to be taken to assist laid-off people.

Introduction

In chapter 5 the different life and career stages were examined. Usually, each of these stages is characterised by its own unique issues. Establishment and achievement are issues of the early career while remaining productive and obsolescence and job loss are generally issues of the middle career. The late career involves issues such as disengaging from work and retirement.

Current changes in the nature of work and the business environment, such as restructuring, downsizing, specialised jobs and subcontracting, mean that career issues can occur more often and to a greater extent in any one particular career stage. Obsolescence, job loss and unemployment, for example, may occur in the early, middle and late career.

Establishment, achievement and retirement were discussed as issues of the early and late career in chapter 5. In this chapter additional career issues are examined. Such issues concern individuals' career anchors and career patterns, working couples, 'plateauing', obsolescence and job loss and unemployment. These issues are not related to a specific career stage or to a chronological age.

Career anchors

An issue which comes to the fore during the early years of a career is the development of a *career anchor*. Although some people become aware of their career anchor for the first time during the mid-career stage, it actually starts to develop in early adulthood during the *establishment* and *achievement stage*.

Definition of career anchor

The concept of a career anchor refers to a pattern of self-perceived talents and abilities, basic values and the evolved sense of motives and needs (as they pertain to the career) that influences a person's career–related decisions (Schein, 1974, 1975, 1978, 1996, 2006). The conceptual model associated with Schein's (1978) career anchor theory is best understood in terms of a person's career self-concept, which develops as a person gains life experience. As individuals are required to make choices related to their self-development, family or career, they may become more aware of the values and motives that frame the choices they make. In other words, an individual's career self-concept acts as a stabilising force; when an important life (or career) choice needs to be made, there are certain concerns, needs or values that the individual will not give up (Schein, 1978). A career anchor can therefore be defined as 'a cluster of self-perceived talents, motives and values that forms the nucleus of a person's occupational self-concept' (Greenhaus et al, 2010:68). Schein (2006:65) describes a career anchor as 'the pattern of self-perceived areas of competence, motives and values that guide and constrain career choices'.

Career anchors are an important element of the individual's internal career and signify the non-monetary or psychological factors in the career decision-making process (Custodio, 2004). Employees generally discover their career anchors after they have worked for a number of years (generally by the age of 30 or older) by using both self-observation and external feedback on their behaviour in actual job situations (Erdogmus, 2003; Schein, 2006). People with insufficient work experience will, by definition, have no career anchor as they will not have obtained enough feedback to know what their competences, motives and values really are (Schein, 2006).

The career anchor concept is not a theory of occupational type. In a specific occupation different career anchor types will be found pursuing that particular career (Schein, 2006). Schein (2006:64) summarises this phenomenon as follows: 'People with different career anchors desire different kinds of work settings, are motivated by different kinds of incentives and rewards and are vulnerable to different kinds of mismanagement'.

Although Schein (1978) argued that, by definition, an individual can maintain only one dominant career anchor, his own empirical evidence suggested that individuals may nonetheless have more than one strong career anchor. However, Schein emphasises that most people will find that if they reflect carefully on the decisions they have made, they will find that they fit into one of the eight anchor categories. Should this not be the case and more than one anchor seems to fit, the person should examine possible situations that might require a choice and think about what he or she would do if forced to make a choice. Should individuals be exposed to new experiences, anchors can change, but for most people once they have formed a clear self-image, the tendency is to hold on to that image (Schein, 2006). Arnold and Randall (2010) state that the individual must have a close look at which anchor would win if he has to choose and based on Schein's argument, this winner is the real career anchor. Other researchers argued, given that the career anchor includes needs, values and talents that surface to the top of a persons' self-concept, one to three anchors tend to cluster together to form an individual's career and work preferences (Coetzee and Schreuder, 2009; De Long, 1982; Feldman and Bolino, 1996; Rodrigues, 2010) and that to date, no empirical data has eliminated the possibility that multiple career anchors may stabilise over time, thus resulting in multiple stable dominant career anchors (Feldman and Bolino, 1996; Kniveton, 2004; Ramakrishna and Potosky, 2002).

Origin of the concept career anchor

The concept career anchor has its origin in a longitudinal study started by Schein in 1961, which involved 44 graduates at the Sloan School of Management. In 1973, approximately 10 to 12 years after graduation, Schein once more conducted interviews with the subjects to analyse the specific career pattern which each of them had followed. The interview focused on the real employment history of each subject, as well as on the reasons for choices made and decisions taken by each of these persons — decisions such as whether to leave an organisation or whether to seek additional education. Little consistency was found in the actual employment history, but there was a great deal of parity in the reasons for making decisions.

As employment experience increases, these reasons become more apparent. At first, people tend to be interested only in a career which holds a challenge and which offers more money and more responsibilities. After a few years of job experience, these same persons tend to select a specific type of career or responsibility with which they feel an affinity. The concept career anchor was coined to describe and explain the manner and the pattern of reasons given by the subjects. Individuals often become aware of their career anchor when their self-image is boosted or damaged by compulsory career moves, such as promotion or discharge (Schein, 1996). The career anchor has the function of organising individuals' experiences, identifying individuals' long-term contributions and establishing criteria for success by which individuals can measure themselves.

Types of career anchors

Schein (1978, 1990, 1996, 2006) suggests that most people's career self-concepts (motives and values) are grounded in eight categories or anchors. Feldman and Bolino (1996) reconceptualised Schein's eight career anchors into three distinct groupings along with their inherent motivations, these motivations being talent-based, need-based and value-based anchors. The *talent-based* anchors consist of managerial competence (willingness to solve complex, whole-of-organisation problems and undertake subsequent decision-making), technical/functional competence (the achievement of expert status among peers) and entrepreneurial creativity (opportunity for creativity and identification of new businesses, products or services). The *need-based* anchors consist of security and stability (long-term employment for health benefits and retirement options), autonomy and independence (personal freedom in job content and settings) and lifestyle motivations (obtaining a balance between personal and the family's welfare with work commitments). The *value-based* anchors consist of pure challenge (testing personal endurance through risky projects or physically challenging work) and service and dedication to a cause (working for the greater good of organisations or communities). Figure 6.1 on p 196 gives an integrated overview of the concept of career anchors. Following is a description of the characteristics of the eight career anchors.

Technical/functional competencies

If employees should regard *technical/functional competence* as a career anchor, they will always be prepared to find a way to use their skills to improve this competence. These employees require a fair amount of *challenge* in their work, which allows them to develop self-confidence. This group of individuals may do very well managing others in the area of their competence, but they are not suitable for general management positions.

Brousseau (1990) refers to such career paths as the *'expert career pattern'* because people who pursue this career path often develop a strong identity with a particular occupation or profession. Individuals with this dominant anchor desire a type of work which is challenging. The intrinsic content of a job concerns these people. These individuals start to see themselves as lawyers, doctors, psychologists or engineers. As far as rewards are concerned, they want to be paid for their level of skill and they prefer the 'cafeteria' benefit system, where the kind of benefits they need can be chosen. With regard to promotion, these individuals prefer a professional promotional ladder parallel to the managerial ladder. What is important is not to be promoted in terms of rank, but rather to increase the scope of the job. With regard to *recognition*, the opportunity for self-development in their particular field is highly valued and the resources allocated to ensure this are of great importance.

This group is confronted with the reality of knowledge and skills becoming rapidly obsolete, as continued training and education are not guaranteed by organisations. However, the world will always need experts and the need is on the increase. Continuous training and updating of skills should be emphasised in an effort to prevent obsolescence. The individual and the organisation should take responsibility in this regard, clarifying each role.

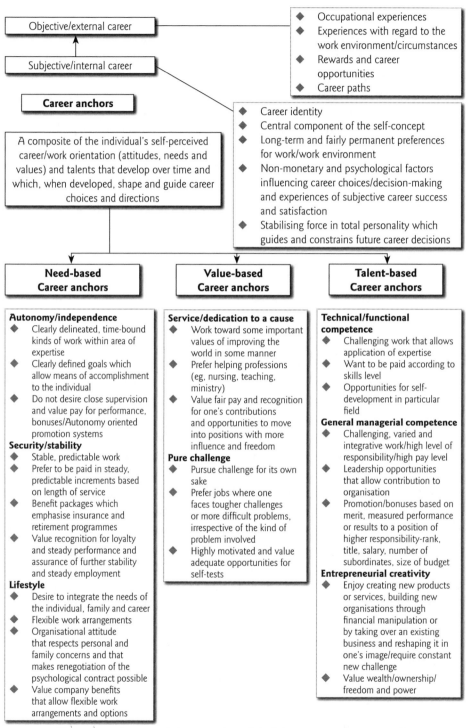

Figure 6.1 *Integrated theoretical model of the construct career anchors (Coetzee and Schreuder, 2008)*

General/managerial competence

Should employees regard *general managerial competence* as a career anchor, they will always try to use any chance to attain a position in a company that enables them to integrate the efforts of others to ensure the maximum output of the company division they run. These employees need to see their contribution to the general success of a company. Even if the performance of an employee is currently in line with that discussed under 'technical/functional competence', employees may consider this as an essential learning experience, enabling them to reach a desirable position in the company.

People who are aware that they truly wish to progress into *managerial positions* also realise that they have to have competence in three basic fields — *analytical competence* (the ability to analyse business problems); *interpersonal competence* (the ability to influence people towards a goal); *emotional competence* (they are stimulated by emotional crises and like to exercise power). In conclusion, people with a dominant career anchor of general managerial competence are strongly motivated to rise to general managerial positions.

These people are motivated by types of work which are characterised by high levels of responsibility, which are challenging and varied, which require leadership skills and which provide opportunities to contribute to the success of the organisation. A high income is greatly valued by these people, as are bonuses for achieving organisational targets. Brousseau (1990) refers to this career preference as the *'linear career pattern'* because, as far as promotion is concerned, these people place great importance on rapid movement 'up the ladder' to positions of increasing responsibility and authority. This is also the most important form of *recognition* for the general-management-competence-anchored individual. As work becomes more technical and is redesigned around projects, the need for general management increases, especially at the level of project and team manager.

Autonomy/independence

Employees who regard *autonomy/independence* as a career anchor always do a job in their own way. These kinds of individuals need a very variable job, which enables them to decide when and how to do it. These employees are not suitable for any position involving control and regulations and, if forced into such a position, may well decide to start a business of their own.

The type of work preferred by these individuals has to be *time-bound,* such as contract or project work, full-time or part-time and without close supervision. With regard to pay and benefits, they prefer cafeteria-style benefits, merit pay for performances, immediate payoffs and bonuses. More *freedom and autonomy* means promotion. These employees will even turn down a rank promotion if their autonomy is to be restricted by it. The type of *recognition* that would be acceptable comprises things like medals, testimonials, prizes and awards.

Schein (1996:83) comments as follows on the autonomy-anchored individual:

Individuals anchored in autonomy find the occupational world an easier place to navigate. The autonomy anchor is aligned, at least for the present, with most organisational policies of promising only employability. The self-reliance that may be needed in the future is already part of the psychological make-up of this group of people. They may well become the role models for future career incumbents.

Security/stability

An employee who regards *security/stability* as a career anchor needs both *job and material security*. These employees are always prepared to carry out work the way their employer wants them to. They aim to achieve a position in a company which allows them to settle down and relax. Moreover, because they possess the right skills, many employees of this kind do in fact achieve their desired aim.

The *type of work* that these people prefer must be characterised by stability and predictability, with no possibility of relocation and little travelling. As far as pay and benefits are concerned, they prefer to be paid in steady, predictable increments based on length of service. This person prefers a formalised promotion system, which stipulates the length of service required before promotion can be expected. The type of *recognition* that this person responds to is to be recognised for loyalty and steady performance. Individuals with security as career anchor are currently the most threatened by the unstable and unpredictable world of work.

As discussed in chapters 2 and 3, employment security is not high on the priority list of most organisations. The most that can be expected from organisations is to provide opportunities for training and development. This group will probably have to find a work environment that still meets their requirements or will have to develop and update their skills to increase their *employability*.

Entrepreneurial creativity

Employees who regard *entrepreneurial creativity* as a career anchor will always consider the possibility of creating their own business. These individuals may work hard in a company, considering this as a way to gain the necessary experience and leave when they feel that they can manage on their own.

Because of these individuals' strong need for *creativity,* they would prefer a type of work that is characterised by *originality of thought* and that continually requires risks and presents new challenges. In terms of payment and benefits, ownership is the most important issue. *Power and freedom* in key roles, where their creativity can be exercised, are important. *Types of recognition* that this individual prefers are sizeable enterprises, building fortunes, high personal visibility and public recognition.

Today's economy favours individuals with an entrepreneurial anchor. As people are encouraged to develop their own business, opportunities for the entrepreneur are increasing. As opportunities in the formal sector are decreasing, training should focus more on entrepreneurial skills and to prepare people for autonomous careers.

Service/dedication to a cause

An employee who regards *service/dedication* to a cause as a career anchor will always be prepared to do something to improve life in general, whether to upgrade the state of the environment, to promote peace, etc. These employees may even change employers in order to carry on doing this kind of job and do not accept any promotions unless the new position meets the requirements of their value system. Service-anchored people clearly want *types of work* that allow them to influence the organisation or social policies according to their values. Regarding *pay and benefits*, these employees want fair pay and portable benefits. They will respond best to a promotion system that recognises their contributions and will prefer to be promoted into positions with more influence. With regard to types of recognition, people with a service orientation feel a need for the recognition and support of their values by colleagues and superiors, wanting them to have a similar value system.

The service-anchored employee expresses the desire, apart from earning an adequate income, to be involved in something meaningful. Community problems can be addressed successfully by these people, especially when the service anchor and the entrepreneurial anchor are combined.

Pure challenge

An employee who regards *pure challenge* as a career anchor always aspires to be in the front line. Employees of this kind get the greatest job satisfaction out of trying to solve seemingly unsolvable problems and coping with the most difficult tasks. These individuals consider the result of any work as either winning or losing and would not be satisfied with even a fairly high managerial position, unless it allows them to continue achieving the impossible. They do not look for easy ways to work and an easy job means a boring job for them.

Although many people seek a *level of challenge*, the person with a dominant anchor of pure challenge regards this as the most important issue. The *type of work*, the pay system, the promotion system and the *types of recognition* are all subordinate to whether or not the job provides constant *opportunities for self-tests*.

This group seems to be growing, probably because today's working environment presents individuals with more challenges.

Lifestyle

Employees who regard *lifestyle* as a career anchor will always want to harmonise personal life with career requirements. These employees are unlikely to aim for any promotion that would involve a geographical move, considering their career as a part of their personal lives and trying to integrate their lives as a whole. These people enjoy *general growth* and see their jobs as part of their personal developmental progress.

As far as *benefits* are concerned, the lifestyle-anchored person wants to work flexible working hours, to travel at times which suit family commitments and regards sabbaticals, paternity and maternity leave and day-care options as important.

There is a noticeable shift towards the *lifestyle* and *pure challenge* career anchors since the original research of the 1960s and 1970s on career anchors was done. A cross-generational and cross-cultural study of graduate management students conducted by Marshall and Bonner (2003) in Australia, the USA, Malaysia, South Africa and the UK indicates that the *lifestyle* career anchor, which is rooted in the overriding need for a balanced home and work life, strongly dominated the results of the study, with the exception of the UK and South Africa, where it was placed second and third respectively in order of importance. *Pure challenge* attracted high scores across the regions, with South Africa placing this career anchor highest in importance. *General managerial competence* achieved low scores across all five regions, as did *security/stability*, with the exception of the Asian region.

Results drawn from 123 honours students in the Industrial and Organisational Psychology Department at Unisa indicated significant differences between the career anchor preferences of males and females and Africans and whites. The sample constituted 20 per cent males and 80 per cent females, 53 per cent Africans and 47 per cent whites. The mean age of the sample was 29 years. 83 per cent of the sample was employed part-time and 17 per cent full-time. The *service/dedication to a cause* and *pure challenge* career anchors reflected the highest scores within both the male and female groups, with females showing a higher preference for the *service/dedication to a cause* career anchor. Females also showed a higher preference for the *lifestyle* career anchor in comparison to *men* who showed a higher preference for the *autonomy* career anchor. In terms of *race*, the *service/dedication to a cause* and *pure challenge* career anchors attracted the highest scores for *Africans*, whilst the *lifestyle* and *technical/functional competence* career anchors attracted the highest scores for *whites*. The *general managerial competence* career anchor attracted the lowest score for the total sample (Coetzee, Schreuder and Tladinyane, 2007). In addition to former results, a comprehensive South African study on career anchors conducted by Coetzee and Schreuder (2009) (sample = 2 978) showed that Schein's career anchor model applies equally to blacks and whites and that black and white people show similar career anchor preferences. Both blacks and whites indicated a significant preference for the lifestyle career anchor.

The possible increasing number of employees who value *lifestyle* will impact significantly on the relationship between organisations and individuals in meeting their respective work and career values. Training and development programmes that promote strategies to identify and maintain balance between personal well-being and work will strengthen that relationship (Marshall and Bonner, 2003). These findings also suggest that there has been a significant shift of values and motivations in the workplace toward *work-life balance*. In today's economy this should be regarded as a positive sign as a different employment relationship is being established in the sense that organisations owe their workers less and less. The work-family relationship increases employees' demands and organisations should retain their best employees by adjusting personnel policies and offering support to employees in the form of childcare, flexi-time and flexible work arrangements and part-time work (Chalofsky, 2010; Marshall and Bonner, 2003; Schein, 1996).

The South African emphasis on the *pure-challenge* career anchor may be an indication that the respondents of the studies are possibly active learners, requiring ongoing training opportunities through on-the-job experience to enable them to take full advantage of change such as evolvement of technology, development of job roles and organisational restructuring. It would also appear that security/stability of the job has indeed reduced in career value for the large majority of respondents in the two studies, across all cultures and both genders. The message that 'employment security' needs to be replaced by *'employability security'* (Coetzee et al, 2007; Marshall and Bonner, 2003; Schein, 1996) is upheld by the findings of this research.

Organisational career management and training and development initiatives would, therefore, better serve employees by supporting the shift from dependence on the organisation to *dependence on oneself* (Marshall and Bonner, 2003).

The subjects who participated in Schein's study in 1961 were primarily motivated to achieve *technical* or *general managerial competence* which requires, by definition, a close association with organisational structure, status and/or professional excellence. These findings are significant in terms of organisations seeking to motivate employees in the 21st century workplace. Employees may be more motivated through the opportunity to pursue *balance in their lifestyle* and *challenge in the work* they are asked to do, rather than through the promise of increased compensation, security and lifelong benefits. Furthermore, these findings may support the contention that employees may now be more oriented towards the *outer,* rather than the inner, core of organisational life (Marshall and Bonner, 2003).

Career anchors and career development

The determination of a career anchor is a process of *self-discovery*. Employees reaching thirty may come to the conclusion that their present career is no longer desirable. This realisation may often result in the experience of the so-called *quarterlife quandary* (Jowell, 2003). Other needs, values and motives may have become more dominant and individuals may want to integrate these in their career. On the basis of previous experience, individuals now have a better idea of their competence, as well as needs and values which they will not give up. Becoming aware of one's career anchor can have a major impact on *career decisions* and personal life. These decisions will be more valid if employees have a clear understanding and awareness of their self-perceived talents, motives and values, that is, their career anchor. If an organisation ignores the primary career anchor of employees, employees will continue to strive to implement it, although this may mean that they have to leave the organisation.

Organisations need people with *divergent career anchors:* they provide a flexible, diverse workforce. Attracting, retaining and motivating good quality employees is accomplished by the employee receiving ongoing development through the provision of advice on which career options to strive for given their skills, interests and perceived potential, all of which may be represented in their career anchors (Marshall and Bonner, 2003).

Organisations should take note that career anchors do not necessarily determine the type of work or occupation an individual chooses as individuals with different career anchors are found within one occupation. This emphasises the importance of individuals to be aware of their career anchor to ensure effective career development. Human resource practitioners or the people responsible for managing careers in the organisations should be aware of the prevalence of the various career anchors in the organisation before implementing human resource policies. Should, for example, a group of people value autonomy as a career anchor it would not be wise to impose strict working hours and methods on them. Similarly, a group of people valuing technical/functional as career anchor would rather be interested in building their identity around the content of their job instead of aspiring to become general managers and moving up the corporate hierarchy. Today's working environment often requires long working hours which might pose a problem for the lifestyle career anchor as balancing work and family may become increasingly difficult (Arnold and Randall, 2010).

Research has revealed a relationship between *career anchors* and *jobs/occupations*. Studies have also shown that, where there is a fit between employees' dominant career anchor and their job perception, such employees experience a higher quality of working life and job satisfaction than in the case where there is no congruence between career anchor and job perception (Ellison and Schreuder, 2000; Schreuder and Flowers, 1991, 1992). A study conducted by Steele and Francis-Smythe (2010) showed that career anchors can be matched to job roles. The findings revealed that an optimal fit between individuals' career anchors and the nature of their job roles increases their job satisfaction and organisational commitment. Career anchors are also relatively good predictors of *job involvement* for most professional people; this is especially true of the career anchor pure *challenge* (Boshoff, Bennett and Kellerman, 1994). Findings of a South African study conducted by Coetzee, Bergh and Schreuder (2010) reported that people's career anchors are significantly related to their life satisfaction, job/career satisfaction, sense of happiness and perceptions of work as a valuable activity.

A clear distinction between the traditional large organisation, perhaps with fewer rungs and various kinds of small organisations (or virtual organisations) is emerging in South Africa. The careerist is faced with the choice of joining a large global organisation, to search for employment in a smaller organisation or to take up contract work that is more temporary in nature. The *technical/functional-anchored* individual is probably better suited to the large organisation where more opportunities exist. Careerists with autonomy, entrepreneurial, service, pure challenge or lifestyle anchors will probably find the smaller organisation more suited to the kind of work they want to do. Probably all the career anchor types will eventually find a place in the different organisational settings (Schein, 1996). Gubler, Arnolds and Coombs (2010) found that career anchors can be used as a tool for career development. The findings of their study showed that the various career anchors tend to prefer different types of career development support activities (see also chapter 8). People with a security career anchor tend to prefer mentoring, informal career discussions and feedback, on-the-job learning programmes, outplacement opportunities, a transparent internal job market and a clear description of their career paths and job levels. People with a preference for the autonomy/independence career anchor tend to prefer informal and formal feedback, online networking/communities and outplacement opportunities. The pure challenge and lifestyle career anchors tend to prefer mentoring programmes.

In a study to determine the career motivations of the self-employed, it was found that individuals who pursued self-employment out of a desire for entrepreneurial creativity experienced higher levels of job satisfaction and psychological well-being as well as an overall life satisfaction. Those who pursued self-employment out of a desire for autonomy reported the highest level of skill utilisation, intent to remain self-employed and life satisfaction. Those who entered self-employment to maximise security had the least successful career outcomes. From the above, it can be derived that career anchors seem to influence the goals that individuals hope to achieve through self-employment, their satisfaction with self-employment, overall life satisfaction, psychological well-being, skill utilisation and their intentions to remain self-employed (Feldman and Bolino, 2000).

Employees should be encouraged to become aware of their established career anchor as its value in *career decision-making* should not be underestimated. By identifying an individual's career anchor, the vacuum that is often left by psychological tests can be filled.

Career patterns

Just as career success and advancement can indicate whether or not an individual's career is oriented around a specific career anchor (Schein, 1993), so too can these factors be indicative of the *career patterns* that individuals follow (Brousseau, 1990). Career success and achievement have *different meanings* for different people — for example: promotion, recognition in a field of expertise, living a life of social contribution or moving frequently from one challenge to another. These differing views are found in all organisations and amongst all employees.

The career pattern model developed by Driver (1979) suggests that individuals have their own *unique views* about the paths their careers should follow. The *values* they hold act as an 'internal gyroscope', defining past *career movements* and guiding future *career decisions*.

The following *four career patterns* describe different types of careers and are ways of describing the ideal career. Each career pattern is based on *underlying motives* (Brousseau, 1990; Brousseau and Driver, 1994).

The linear career pattern

Employees associated with this pattern *prefer* to move up quickly in the hierarchy of the organisation; a tall pyramid and narrow span of control structure relates to this career pattern. They *value* leadership efficiency and logistics management as performance factors and prefer rewards such as promotions, executive bonuses, high salaries, quick recognition and incentives. This pattern is usually found amongst managerial staff.

The linear career pattern faces many *challenges in the contemporary world of work* because of dwindling opportunities to move up the management ladder. Management positions are becoming scarce because of mergers and acquisitions and the flattening of organisational structures which have eliminated many management positions.

The expert career pattern

According to this pattern, individuals choose a career field and remain in it for the duration of their career. The individual identifies strongly with the occupation and typical examples are those of lawyer, doctor and engineer. The expert career pattern relates to a flat organisational structure with strong functional departments. Employees associated with this pattern *value* quality, reliability, stability and technical competence as performance factors and prefer rewards such as fringe benefits, recognition and continual technical training. They usually want to be recognised for their expertise in a specific field.

The *challenge* for the expert career pattern is to be continuously upskilled in his or her field of expertise. Corporate and organisational restructuring programmes are another threat, because they disrupt jobs, lead to retrenchments and generally frustrate the expert-oriented people's needs for stability and security. The challenge is for these people to be willing to experiment with a variety of possible working roles, which would still enable them to express their expertise and variety of talents.

The spiral career pattern

An outstanding characteristic of this career pattern is that these people tend to change fields periodically. These changes are major and entail a change from one field to another, thus allowing the individual to develop new skills and capabilities while using the expertise acquired from previous experience. The spiral career pattern relates to a matrix, self-directed interdisciplinary teams. Individuals associated with this pattern *value* creativity, teamwork and people development as performance factors and prefer rewards such as lateral assignments, cross training and creative latitude.

The spiral career pattern is less threatened by the organisational changes caused by the turbulence of the 21st century economy and technological developments. In fact, people pursuing careers with spiral and transitory career patterns generally benefit from restructuring programmes that reduce hierarchy and bureaucracy because these programmes tend to eliminate barriers to lateral movement. Lateral movement allows one to expand the range of one's knowledge and skills over time.

The transitory career pattern

This career pattern is characterised by many career changes. As a pattern the transitory career has been referred to as a 'consistent pattern of inconsistency'. These people tend to change jobs — or even career fields — every two to four years. The transitory career pattern relates to a loose, amorphous structure and temporary teams. Individuals associated with this pattern *value* speed adaptability and innovation as performance factors and prefer rewards such as immediate cash bonuses, independence and autonomy, special temporary assignments and job rotation.

Traditionally, men saw themselves as following linear careers, whilst women adhered to the transitory and spiral patterns (Woodd, 2000). Generally, men will have to consider changing their expectations of life-long career patterns. Women who trained and qualified in the professions and who would normally fit the linear career pattern, appear to have chosen to leave their jobs or to change direction, taking on or showing preference for a spiral career pattern due to a dissatisfaction with male-dominated organisation environments (Marshall, 1995; Woodd, 2000). However, what is important for both men and women is that the contemporary career is neither linear nor continuous, nor is it always upward. Instead, one's career life is taking more of a zigzag course (Baruch, 2004; Woodd, 2000).

Careers in the 21st century may help to achieve *equality* in careers, as the same options are becoming open to everyone. Both men and women are required to follow a career pattern based on individual needs and desires rather than circumstances. Both gender groups are learning how to deal with an uncertain, turbulent and dynamic changing work environment and how to maximise whichever pattern they find themselves following (Baruch, 2004; Woodd, 2000).

Table 6.1 *Characteristics of the four career patterns*

Career pattern	Frequency of field change	Direction of movement	Career pattern motives
Linear	Infrequent Mobility mostly limited to movements within a field	Upward Individual moves upward rapidly to positions of higher authority	Power Competence Achievement Recognition Self-development
Expert	No change Individual remains within one field for duration of career	Minimal upward movement Individual stays in one position or makes two to three moves upward within a specialty or function	Expertise Security Competence Stability Autonomy Achievement
Spiral	Every five to ten years Individual makes a major change into a new field or occupation	Lateral Individual moves into new type of work that builds on current skills and develops new ones	Personal growth Creativity Developing others Prestige Recognition
Transitory	Every two to four years Individual makes frequent moves into entirely new jobs or fields	Mainly lateral 'Consistently inconsistent' pattern	Variety Independence Creativity Involvement Achievement

Career patterns and career development

As some organisations are still characterised by stability and well-defined structures, there is still room in the current work environment for expert and linear groups to advance their careers. The *traditional organisational culture* favours employees with spiral and transitory careers less. Individuals who are spiral or transitory oriented are more likely to progress in the present business environment, where individuals who are prepared to move and adapt quickly are now required. Employees with linear and expert career patterns are probably less comfortable in the present job situation and may face an unfriendly environment. As organisations have different needs at different times, a *pluralistic* approach to organisational design, which provides opportunities for diverse career experiences, would probably solve the problem best. This approach would help to maintain a mixed workforce to meet a variety of business demands (Driver et al, 1996).

Organisations often have an expert structure and value expert competencies, but emphasise linear rewards (Brousseau et al, 1996). In companies such as these, where the career pattern of an individual is not supported, frustration will occur. To increase career satisfaction organisations should strive for a fit between the *career culture* of the organisation and the *career pattern* of the worker. Organisations can develop career cultures that coincide with all the different career patterns. A career culture can be defined in terms of organisational structure, policies, reward systems, as well as the nature of rewards and training and development activities. After determining the career culture of the organisation by looking at the above factors, the employee's career pattern can be determined. If there is a poor fit between employee and organisation, the employee should be trained in order to adapt or certain organisational policies should be altered.

The Brousseau model can also be used to match individuals' career needs and motives with a career pattern. A *mismatch* between career patterns and individuals' corresponding career motives is often found. A study amongst 188 South African managers showed while 39 per cent of the respondents favoured the linear pattern, only 25 per cent rated linear motives as important and while 45 per cent favoured the spiral career pattern, 30 per cent regarded these motives as important (Schreuder, 1998). Coetzee and Schreuder (2002) found similar results in another South African study and international studies indicate the same trend. The challenge would be to assess individuals' career needs and motives in order to give them advice regarding their true career patterns. This will probably enhance career satisfaction.

Working couples

Firstly, the meaning of the term *working couple* should be clarified. The terms 'dual-career couple' and 'dual-earner couple' have been frequently used in the literature but have not always been clearly distinguished. The literature also refers to two-career relationships and dual-wage relationships as characteristics of the dual-career couple (Gilbert, 2006). *Dual-career couple* refers to the situation where both partners are career-oriented and committed to a career, while at the same time maintaining a family life together (Gilbert and Rachlin, 1987; Rapoport and Rapoport, 1969; Bruce and Reed, 1991). Partners in the dual-career couple are employed in occupations requiring special training and education and a high degree of commitment. The expectations of the dual-career couple is to pursue their careers uninterrupted and be involved in family life (Gilbert, 2006).

The *dual-earner couple* differs from the dual-career couple in the sense that both spouses are involved in the paid labour force, where one may be pursuing a career, while the other views his or her occupational involvement as a job or where both spouses consider themselves to hold jobs (Gilbert and Rachlin, 1987; Gilbert, 2006). There is a lack of psychological attachment to work or upward mobiliy ('Karambayya and Reilly' 1992:586). Today dual-career couples and dual-earner couples are the norm.

Guterman (1991:169) prefers to refer to the *working couple*. He defines a working couple as follows:

> *A working couple consists of any two people in an ongoing, committed relationship, where both partners work, where there may or may not be children and where decisions (family and work) are influenced by the working situation of each partner.*

This definition makes provision for all the different types of working couples represented in our society.

The percentage of women entering the labour force is increasing. In chapter 2 we indicated that the number of females in the labour force will be increasing by a higher percentage than the number of men. The traditional South African household, where the man was the sole earner and the woman took care of the children, has been replaced by *working couple families*. On the negative side, women's careers are often interrupted as a result of family commitments. This negative factor, however, is counterbalanced by positive indications that South African women with tertiary qualifications, once they re-enter the labour market after a career break, pursue their careers with greater determination and desire to achieve excellence at work. The impression is that South African women are also inclined to return to work despite the increase in work and life pressure caused by such a step (Gerber, 2000). The South African worker is becoming predominantly female, in either a two-career relationship or a dual-wage relationship, of child-bearing age, experiencing domestic responsibilities (male and female) in addition to work obligations.

Family factors

The success of the two-career relationship is of paramount importance for the economic viability of organisations and for the welfare of families. A number of *family factors* and factors external to the family have been identified as important to the success of these families. Family factors relate to the behaviour of the partners and include fairness, communication and mutuality between partners and work-family balance. The extent to which partners view their roles as *fair* is an important requirement for combining work and familily life. This would require partners to become involved in activities outside the traditional gender role and to be comfortable with setting norms for themselves. Both partners should view these norms as fair. For the relationship to be successful, *communication* and *spousal support* are important prerequisites. Time should be made available to show interest in each other's professional activities, express appreciation and dicussing problem areas. Communication should centre around aspects such as when to start with a family and how this is going to influence the familily stability and the career of each partner, when to have a second child, the size of the familily, who is going to care for the child/children and who will be resposible for the different household tasks, setting priorities, examining and discussing the different roles and communicating values (what is most important for each one) (Gilbert, 2006).

Another factor for the two career relationship to succeed is to strive for *work-family balance*. Work-family balance can be defined as 'the extent to which an individual is equally engaged in and equally satisfied with, his or her work role and family role' (Greenhaus, Collins and Shaw 2003:513). These authors proposed that work-family balance is a sum of (a) time balance, (b) involvement balance and (c) satisfaction balance (Glendon, Thompson and Myors, 2007). The time spent on work demands and family activities should balance out. Too much time at work is not conducive to family welfare and too little time at work may have an adverse impact on financial security. For many researchers career-family balance represents a vague notion that work and family life are somehow integrated or harmonious (Gilbert, 2006).

Finding a balance between work and family makes the following *demands* on a couple (Singh et al, 2002):

◆ *Quality communication* — spending enough time on intimate discussions about themselves as individuals and their relationships;
◆ *Setting priorities* with regard to time spent on work, managing the home, childcare, leisure and other activities;
◆ *Clarifying values*, for example, work values such as growth, opportunity, security, recognition, power and prestige and life values;
◆ *Concerning hobbies*, leisure, continued learning, religion and being part of society;
◆ *Examining roles* and the relative weight each partner carries, such as provider, nurturer, homemaker and bill payer;
◆ *Managing daily life* by allowing for flexibility in a partners' roles and tasks; and
◆ *Managing stress* by identifying the sources, attempting to tackle the causes, examining one's responses to stress and taking responsibility for managing one's own stress.

It seems that researchers have realised that the work-home interface is a much broader concept that also encompasses a positive side and studies have started to address the prevalence and correlates of positive interaction between work and private life (Frone, 2003; Geurts and Demerouti, 2003). As a result of this new focus, a new definition was developed based on the *Effort-Recovery model* (Meijman and Mulder, 1998) which defines the *work-home interface* as an *interactive process* in which a worker's functioning in one domain (eg, home) is influenced by (negative or positive) load reactions that have built up in the other domain (eg, work) (Geurts et al, 2005). Based on this definition, *work-home interaction* consists of the following four dimensions: (1) *Negative work-home interference* (referring to a situation in which negative load reactions build up at work and hamper functioning at home); (2) *Negative home-work interference* (which refers to negative load reactions that develop at home and impede functioning at work); (3) *Positive work-home interference* (which is positive load reactions that build up at work and facilitate functioning at home); and (4) *Positive home-work interference* (referring to positive load reactions that develop at home and facilitate functioning at work).

Demerouti and Geurts (2004) categorise possible *consequences* of work-home interference into *five major categories,* namely *psychological consequences* (work-related stress, burnout, psychological strain), *physical* (somatic and physical symptoms such as headache, backache, upset stomach and fatigue as well as sleep deprivation), *attitudinal* (job satisfaction, organisational commitment, marital satisfaction), *behavioural* (increased consumption of stimulants like coffee, cigarettes and alcohol) and *organisational consequences* (turnover intentions, job performance). Various studies have shown that work-home interference is associated with these and other consequences, for both the *individual* (including depression, psychosomatic complaints and reduced marital satisfaction) and the *organisation* (eg, reduced job and life satisfaction, low organisational commitment and intentions to quit, stress and burnout, low levels of job performance and the prevalence of accidents) (Allen et al, 2000; Kossek and Ozeki, 1998).

Table 6.2 *Consequences of work-home interference*

Consequences of work-home interference	Description
Psychological consequences	Work-related stress, burnout, psychological strain
Physical consequences	Somatic and physical symptoms such as headache, backache, upset stomach and fatigue as well as sleep deprivation
Attitudinal consequences	Job satisfaction, organisational commitment, marital satisfaction
Behavioural consequences	Increased consumption of stimulants like coffee, cigarettes and alcohol
Organisational consequences	Reduced job and life satisfaction, low organisational commitment and intentions to quit, stress and burnout, low levels of job performance and the prevalence of accidents

In general, various research findings indicate that work negatively influencing home is more prevalent than home negatively influencing work (Bond et al, 1998; Burke and Greenglass, 1999; Eagle, Miles and Icenogle, 1997; Frone et al, 1997; Kinnunen and Mauno, 1998). However, the findings of Grzywacz and Marks (2000) show that positive spillover from family to work is equally prevalent as negative spillover from work to family. This is true for both male and female workers.

Factors outside the family, such as a supportive organisation, are also crucial for the two-career relationship to succeed (Gilbert, 2006). Most employers realise it is to their advantage to assist their employees in balancing their work and family lives. What was once a 'woman issue' has now become an employee issue and a company necessity (Greenhaus et al, 2010). *Work-family issues are* viewed as affecting company competitiveness and are therefore not only a problem for employees but also for organisations (Cascio, 2003; Hankin, 2005). Research indicates that providing family benefits such as day-care facilities, flexible schedules, working from home facilities, job sharing, part-time employment and assistance with childcare, promotes a dedicated, loyal workforce among people who benefit directly from the policies as well as from those who do not.

Research found that employees of a family-supportive organisation enjoy higher levels of career satisfaction and are more committed to organisational success (Gilbert, 2006). Ballout (2008:455) emphasised the responsibility of the organisation as follows:

> As careers become increasingly 'proteans or boundaryless' organisations need to improve equity in rewards and create flexible, accommodated and promised career paths that centre around the practice of helping employees balance work-family relationships and gain specific work skills and experiences that are necessary to their career progress. Otherwise lack of work-family balance may encourage employees to decrease their level of commitment and to leave their organisations for career opportunities that better satisfy their expectations.

Consider the following cases:

Case 1

Michael and Mary have been married for fifteen years and have three children. Mary, a qualified secretary, entered the labour market again after her last child had gone to school. Michael is employed as a financial manager at a well-known financial institution. Their children are happy in their respective schools and represent their schools in different sporting activities.

Michael is offered a promotion which involves relocating. To Michael it is a career challenge and in the interest of his career progress. Mary feels that for her to go and find another job on her own for the same salary in a new area is too much to ask. She feels that Michael's employer must also take her position into consideration.

Case 2

Consider the following conversation between a working couple with two children:

Helen: It's Monday morning, I am still tired and feel that the weekend was not long enough to recover from last week's activities.

Carl: Let's talk about this week's activities.

Helen: Here's my schedule for the week.

Monday: I work until 13:00 and then I must take Brenda to drama classes and after that to hockey practice. Wayne also has to go to cricket practice. The children are writing tests this week and you know that Brenda does not work on her own. On Monday evening I go to gym.

Tuesday and Wednesday: I work full day; I arranged with Paula to take the children to their outside activities. On Tuesday evening I have to attend a work meeting and on Wednesday evening a training session. So, I will arrive home late both nights.

Thursday: Brenda must be taken to drama classes again and after that she has a dentist appointment. As you know, Thursday evenings are gym time again.

Friday: I work until 13:00 and after that I must do the shopping for the weekend and for Brenda's birthday party on Saturday afternoon. You know that we have invited John and Mary for dinner.

Saturday: Wayne and Brenda play cricket and hockey matches and I would like to watch Brenda. Her birthday party is in the afternoon.

Carl: Oh! You know that my schedule is not much better! On Monday and Tuesday I work into the evening and on Wednesday I fly to Cape Town for a meeting. Thursday is work again and I promised Wayne that I would take him with me in the afternoon to buy Brenda a present for her birthday. Friday is work again and in the evening you have invited John and Mary for dinner. A late night again. Saturday morning I will go and watch Wayne play cricket.

Helen: What about unforeseen events? Where am I going to fit those in? I cannot just take time off work.

Carl: Let's hope that nothing unforeseen happens.

The above could apply to any working couple: it is an ongoing conversation taking place in many homes today. Such situations cause stress, anxiety and serious work-family role conflicts. The *challenge* is to find a *balance* between family and work. Organisations can make a major contribution towards solving this issue by adopting a more flexible attitude.

Family patterns

Gilbert (1994) identifies *three general marital patterns* of dual-career families (where both spouses are committed to their careers, while attempting to maintain their family life). These are the *conventional, modern* and *role-sharing patterns.*

The *conventional pattern* means that both partners are *career-oriented,* but that the *woman* bears most of the responsibility for the children and the household. The *modern pattern* means that the parenting role is *equally shared* by the spouses, but that the woman takes responsibility for the household. In this case, the men value a close relationship with their children, but still regard housework as a woman's responsibility. The *role-sharing pattern* is one where *both spouses are actively involved* in the household, in their roles as parents and in their occupational pursuits.

Table 6.3 illustrates the *personal, environmental and relationship factors* that affect the way in which couples combine their career and family roles. These people do not necessarily experience a loss of job satisfaction, but rather a feeling of satisfaction with the way in which they are managing their lives, as long as both partners perceive the division of labour as fair and feel supported by their spouse.

Table 6.3 *Factors that influence how partners combine occupational and family roles*

Factor	Examples
Personal factors	
Personality	How important is a partner's need to dominate, to be emotionally intimate, to be tops in his or her field?
Attitudes and values	What are a partner's views about rearing a child, about women being as successful as men professionally?
Interests and abilities	How committed is a partner to occupational work, to family relations? Are both partners satisfied with their occupations and career plans?
Stages in careers	Is one partner peaking and the other thinking about retirement?
Relationship factors	
Equity and power	How are decisions made? What seems fair? How do partners come to agreements about household work, about parenting, about money?
Partner support	Can partners count on each other for support in most areas?
Shared values	Do partners share the same views of women's and men's expectations and roles? Do partners have similar life goals?
Environmental and societal factors	
Work situation	Are work hours flexible? Is there evidence of sex discrimination or other kinds of gender bias? Are policies prohibiting sexual harassment in place and understood?
Employer's views	Are policies family oriented? What is the general attitude toward employees who involve themselves in family life?
Availability and quality	Is childcare available? Does it meet parents' childcare criteria for high-quality care?

Gilbert, LA (1994:102)

Work-family conflict

A serious *concern* for working couples is the *number of roles* that they have to manage, namely parent, wife or husband, careerist, self and friend. The demands of the one role sometimes make it difficult to comply with the demands of the other. Individuals often experience conflict between the roles they assume that they must fulfil and the roles that they are expected to fulfil. It is therefore inevitable for working couples to experience conflict between their family and working lives. Work-family conflict can be defined as 'a form of *interrole conflict* in which the role pressures from the work and family domains are mutually incompatible in some respect' (Greenhaus and Beutell, 1985:77).

'Interrole conflict is a form of role conflict in which the sets of opposing pressure arise from participation in different roles' (Greenhaus and Beutell, 1985:77). This definition suggests that difficulties in combining work and family roles may either arise from *time-based conflict* (time demands that make it physically impossible to be in two places at the same time), from *strain-based conflict* (the spillover of strain from one domain to the other) and/or from *behaviour-based conflict* (the incompatibility of behaviours requested in each domain). Previous research has demonstrated that especially time– and strain-based conflict are associated with various negative work, family and health-related outcomes (Allen, Herst, Bruck and Sutton, 2000).

Types of work-family conflict

As illustrated, the demands of one role are often incompatible with those of other roles. Literature indicates that work-family conflict arises from *variables in the work and family domains* (Greenhaus and Beutell, 1985; Greenhaus et al, 1989; Higgins and Duxbury, 1992; Izraeli, 1993) and that people who experience high levels of conflict between their roles in both spheres experience less job and life satisfaction (Kossek and Ozeki, 1998).

Greenhaus and Beutell (1985) identify the following *types of work-family conflict:*

Time-based conflict

Work and family roles compete for the working couple's time. Time that is devoted to one role cannot be devoted to the other. In a comparison of the work and family domains as sources of work-family conflicts, it was found that the work domain was not a significantly greater source of conflict for either women or men than the family domain. The family domain was not a greater source of conflict for women than the work domain, nor was the work domain a greater source of conflict for men than the family domain (Izraeli, 1993). The workload of individuals is increasing in terms of hours worked and the intensity of the effort and working couples need to cope with time-based-issues of role overload and the psychological issues of role quality (Wiersma, 1994; Arnold and Randall, 2010).

Role overload is reconcilable with time-based conflict as it is identified as the most consistent predictor of time-based conflict (Greenhaus et al, 1989). 'Role overload arises when an individual has numerous social roles to carry out, at least one of which requires an excessive time commitment' (Falkenberg and Monachello, 1989:18). When the sum of roles is more than the individual can meet, role overload is experienced. A form of time-based conflict would therefore occur when time pressures in one role make it just impossible to satisfy the expectations of the other role (Greenhaus and Beutell, 1985). Research indicates that excessive work time, an inflexible work schedule and work involvement offer less freedom to meet the demands of the family role and can be related to work-family conflict (Greenhaus and Beutell, 1985; Izraeli, 1993; Keith and Schafer, 1980). It appears that employees who are subjected to these conditions generally experience time-based conflict.

It is not only variables from the work domain that produce time pressure but also variables from the family domain. Research indicates that the following are characteristics of families who are likely to experience more work-family conflict: married, young children, number of children, lack of spouse support, stereotypical gender role attitudes (Greenhaus and Beutell, 1985; Izraeli, 1993; Marshall and Barnett, 1993). Research indicates that time pressures specific to the role of parent and partner are important predictors of depression (Roxburgh, 2001). A study conducted on the effect of job stressors on marital satisfaction indicated that job insecurity, time pressures at work, poor leadership relations and work-family conflict affected marital satisfaction through job exhaustion and psychosomatic symptoms. The results were the same for both sexes, indicating that job stressors had the same effect on both males' and females' experience of marital satisfaction (Mauno and Kinnunen, 1999).

Strain-based conflict

Research indicates that work role stressors, like role conflict and role ambiguity, can cause strain symptoms such as tension, anxiety, fatigue, depression, apathy and irritability (Aryee, 1993; Greenhaus and Beutell, 1985). 'Strain-based conflict exists when strain in one role affects performance in another role' (Greenhaus and Beutell, 1985:80). For example, an aged parent who has to be looked after can cause fatigue, which results in the caregiver finding it difficult to perform well at work.

Work stressors which are identified as strain-based are the following: role overload, role conflict and ambiguity (role ambiguity showed a positive correlation with burnout in both male and female partners), lack of career progress, repetitive tasks, changing work environment, long hours (indirectly cause strain), boring tasks, lack of work challenge, a new job or poor job-person fit (Aryee, 1993; Greenhaus and Beutell, 1985; Greenhaus et al, 1989; Marshall and Barnett, 1993). Literature indicates the following research results:

◆ Strain-based conflict can be caused by sources in the family. If conflict is experienced within the family, a lack of career and family support by the spouse can affect an individual's working life. Spouse and social support in non-work and work environments reduce work-family conflict (Matsui et al, 1995; Carlson and Perrewé, 1999).

◆ A significant correlation was found between role conflict and emotional exhaustion, as work-family conflict significantly related to both emotional exhaustion and job satisfaction (Boles et al, 1997).

◆ While the significant contributors to burnout in male partners were only work-related (job ambiguity and lack of career success), burnout in female partners was both work– and non-work-related (role ambiguity, work schedule inflexibility, job/parent conflict, lack of career progress) (Aryee, 1993).

◆ Male partners of employed women experience a lower level of job satisfaction and quality of life than male partners of homemakers (Parasuraman et al, 1989).

◆ Men and women have similar work attitudes except in terms of job involvement, where dual-career females show the lowest level of job involvement (Cleveland et al, 2000).

◆ Women with flexible work schedules report less strain than those with fixed work schedules (Matsui et al, 1995).

◆ When parents were in a bad mood after work, according to their children, children reported a more negative attitude to school and lower levels of constructive behaviour (Kinnunen et al, 2001).

◆ The more warmth and acceptance as well as monitoring and limit-setting were used by parents, the less adolescents were involved in alcohol abuse and the more positive their attitude was towards school and the more constructive their behaviour in general (Kinnunen et al, 2001).

Behaviour-based conflict

Certain patterns of role behaviour may well be in conflict with the expectations of behaviour in other roles. For example, it is expected of male managers to be self-reliant, emotionally stable, somewhat aggressive, but objective. The manager's family, however, may want him to be a warm, caring and emotional person. Conflict could result if he is unable to adjust his behaviour when switching from his role as an employee to that of husband and father or vice versa. There appears to be a lack of empirical research on such behaviour-based conflict.

Work-family enrichment

Literature and research have mainly focused on the difficulty in complying with family and work demands (work-family conflict). Work and family can also be allies ie 'work can strengthen our family lives and family experiences can improve work lives' (Greenhaus et al, 2010:292). Hammer and Hanson (2006:870) define work-family enrichment as the 'process by which experiences in one role improve the quality of life in the other role'. This topic has been discussed in detail in chapter 1.

Organisational actions

In the past, if employees found that their terms of employment did not meet family requirements, they would resign and seek employment elsewhere. Such action is often not to the benefit of either party. Suitable employment is not always readily available and the employer has invested a great deal in employees and needs their skills and expertise. It is usually the female partner who has to seek other employment in order to accommodate family needs. Where single women have traditionally been considered as the ideal female manager, married women can also be regarded as a valuable source. The question is whether an individual can have a fulfilling career as well as a satisfying family life. People who are too career-focused tend to postpone or avoid marriage or having children, spend little time on children's activities, have little psychological involvement in family, seldom adjust their work schedule for family and are unwilling to interrupt their careers to be with children, while people who are too family-focused tend to have low aspirations for promotion, show less psychological involvement in their careers, adjust their work schedule extensively to accommodate family and are willing to interrupt their career to be with children (Friedman and Greenhaus, 2000).

The challenge that faces individuals who fall in both work and family categories and who value the importance of both career and family involvement, is not to limit their involvement with one role but to accommodate the other role and to pursue both roles with determination.

Family-friendly organisations are beneficial to individuals' career and personal lives. Employees who experience employer support are more likely to aspire to senior positions, are more committed to their organisation, are more satisfied with their careers, experience less conflict between work and family, are more likely to be parents and are more satisfied with their personal growth and development (Friedman and Greenhaus, 2000; Greenhaus et al, 2010). Organisations can assist working couples to find the balance between work and family life through the following considerations (Batt and Valcour, 2003; Byars and Rue, 2004; Cascio, 2003; Gilbert, 2006; Glendon et al, 2007; Greenhaus and Foley, 2007; Greenhaus et al, 2010; Hankin, 2005; Theunissen, Van Vuuren and Visser, 2003; Wilkinson, Bacon, Redman and Snell, 2010):

- Include commitment to work and family life balance in mission statement.
- Introduce work-life balance policies that seek to reduce working hours, enhance employees' flexibility over the scheduling of working hours and the place of work and provide financial support for childcare and eldercare.
- Show more organisational sensitivity for home life.
- Provide training workshops on how to manage the work-home interface.
- Emphasise job performance rather than hours spent at work.
- Include spouses in career discussions.
- Introduce flexible benefits to assist employees with family needs, such as childcare and special care for sick children. These services can range from on-site child-care facilities to homecare, when an employee is away on business and a child is sick. In future, frail care will also become more important, as more ageing parents will move in with their children. To assist employees, the company can provide seminars about the care available for ageing family members.
- Be sensitive to the needs of women as they experience more constraints than men and must make more trade-offs.

- Do not create an environment where people are forced to choose between career advancement and devotion to family.
- Revise relocation policies. Offer spouse relocation assistance as an employee benefit. This could make it easier for employees to accept career moves and could include helping the spouse to find a new position, new schools and childcare for the children and providing more comprehensive home-finding services. Relocation issues can be included in career and succession planning.
- Implement family-friendly benefits, such as travel policies, sick leave, parental leave and vacation policies.
- Demonstrate the value of investing in a family-friendly organisation.
- Develop female managerial skills through training and lateral moves when upward mobility is impossible because of home commitments. This would prevent female employees from falling too far behind and would prepare them for higher positions when their family commitments decrease.
- Provide company resources for family recreational and educational use, such as computers that can be used for family and work purposes to improve family-work integration.
- Introduce family days to encourage families to visit the company and become better acquainted with the organisation.
- Introduce alternative career paths. Not all employees want to climb the corporate ladder. Different career paths (horizontal, slower-paced, stationary) can accommodate the different needs and priorities of people.
- Provide greater flexibility by creating more permanent part-time jobs in professional and managerial positions.
- Introduce a newsletter with information on work and family issues.
- Establish support networks at home and at work.
- Invest in employees' extramural activities.
- Conduct a dual-career audit through a company survey to identify the extent of the problem. Areas the audit should address include the number of dual-career employees, the conflicts they face, how effective they perceive present company policies and opportunities to be and how competent they think they are to manage their careers.

Work-family policies (such as dependant care or flexible scheduling) should be complemented by a broad range of human resource practices that, taken together, shape employees' capacity to meet work and family demands in an integrated fashion. The impact of access to flexible scheduling, for example, is not likely to affect excessive work hours and workloads, that is, the gap between the demands on individuals' time and the actual time they have (Cascio, 2003). Table 6.4 lists some organisational strategies and initiatives that help employees reduce work-life conflict.

Table 6.4 *Organisational strategies and initiatives to reduce work-life conflict (based on Robbins and Judge, 2011:607)*

Organisational strategy	Programme/ Policy initiative
Time-based strategies	◆ Flexitime ◆ Job sharing ◆ Maternity and paternity leave ◆ Transportation ◆ Telecommuting ◆ Paid time off for community service
Information-based strategies	◆ Work/life support (eg, mentoring and advice for parents entering the workforce) ◆ Relocation assistance ◆ Elder-care resources (eg, free consultations and personal family needs assessment from elder-care experts) ◆ Counselling services (eg, lifestyle management coaching, worksite wellness, smoking cessation, disease management, HIV/Aids counselling)
Money-based strategies	◆ Insurance subsidies ◆ Flexible benefits ◆ Adoption assistance ◆ Discounts for child-care tuition ◆ Direct financial services (eg, loans for first-time home buyers) ◆ Domestic partner benefits (eg, equal health coverage to same-sex partners of employees) ◆ Scholarship, tuition reimbursement
Direct services	◆ On-site childcare ◆ Fitness centre ◆ School holidays childcare (eg, parents can send children to company's science/tech school programme for free) ◆ On-site conveniences (eg, on-site car wash, dental care, dry cleaners, ATM and hair salon) ◆ Free or discounted company products (eg, free BlackBerry and usage coverage for new employees; canteen services at reduced price)
Culture-change strategies	◆ Establishing work-life balanced culture ◆ Training for managers to help employees deal with work/life conflict ◆ Tie managers' pay to employee satisfaction ◆ Focus on employees' actual performance, not 'face time'

Batt and Valcour (2003) report findings that suggest that the nature of individuals' work and employees' perceptions of their ability to manage work and family demands are strong predictors of work-family conflict. Co-ordination responsibilities, technology use at home (such as the use of faxes, e-mail, home computers, pagers) and long work hours were associated with significant higher work-family conflict due to the disruptive effect they have on family life. Supportive supervisors were associated with lower work-family conflict and a feeling of employees that they were able to manage work and family demands.

Career plateauing

A career plateau refers to a point in the individual career when opportunities for advancement in the organisational hierarchy have ceased (Byars and Rue, 2004; Godshalk, 2006; Greenhaus et al, 2010). Career plateauing happens to just about everyone in the course of a career.

Take the example of a man aged 43 who works for a large organisation and who has discovered that he is no longer being promoted. He has always expected that he would be able to work his way up in the organisation until he reaches the top. Thus far, he has received promotions frequently, has made steady progress up the corporate ladder and has been rewarded for his efforts with money, fringe benefits and job titles. He has always firmly believed that he is destined for the very top. Then one day a promotion he expects to receive is given to one of his colleagues. Surprised and disappointed, he consults his superiors, only to be told that his work performance is perfectly satisfactory. He continues his work as before, but the next time promotions are announced, he is once again not among them. It is then that he realises that there will be no more promotions for him because his career has plateaued.

Career plateauing will remain an important career issue and the evidence is that it is increasing. The reason for this increase is probably that during the period 1960 to 2000 organisations expanded and promotional opportunities were more available, while the last 10 years was characterised by changes in the business environment, restructuring, downsizing and employment equity, which have an adverse impact on promotional opportunities. Career plateauing is also caused by inappropriate abilities and skills, low need for career mobility, baby-boomers who are holding positions longer, mergers and takeovers resulting in lay-offs, competition (the candidate may be seen by his superior as less qualified than other candidates), age (older people might fall in disfavour) organisational needs (the individual might be regarded as too valuable in his or her present position), managers may consciously or subconsciously have identified individuals who are capable and willing to move up the organisational hierarchy and those who are not, the organisational structure becomes narrower to the top, flatter organisational structures, an employee might choose to be plateaued (this could be due to personal, health and family reasons) (Godshalk, 2006; Ongorri and Agolla, 2009).

Types of career plateauing

Bardwick (1986) distinguishes between *structural and content* plateauing and *life-plateauing*. The organisational hierarchy is usually the cause of *structural plateauing* and to individuals this means that they have reached the end of the road with no further chances for promotion. *Content plateauing* refers to when an employee knows the work so well that he or she perceives it as unchallenging, boring and routine. Such content plateauing can be more easily avoided than structural plateauing, as individuals who become structural plateaued do not necessarily experience content plateauing. An individual might be structural and content plateaued, with no opportunities to progress in the hierarchy of the organisation and with no opportunities to grow in his or her current job (Greenhaus et al, 2010). *Life plateauing* refers to when committed individuals begin to feel unsuccessful in their work and this spreads to feeling plateaued and trapped in life (Burke and Mikkelsen, 2006).

Leibowitz et al (1990) identify the following *four kinds of plateaued performer.*

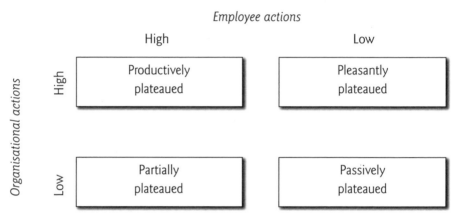

Figure 6.2 *Four kinds of plateaued performer employee actions*

Productively plateaued

Such employees and organisations try hard to encourage stimulation and challenge. The employees feel that they have achieved their ambitions and experience job satisfaction. They are proactive and willing to take risks and are supported in this by their organisations. They are loyal to their organisations and regard themselves as indispensable. Their efforts are recognised by their colleagues and supervisors. They are productive and they perform, but they need to be motivated.

Partially plateaued

These employees feel that the organisation does not do much for them, but they usually have an interest that maintains their involvement in the job. These people are usually experts in their fields, but although they are valued by their organisations, the job seems routine for them. They always appreciate new opportunities to learn, because these maintain the excitement.

Pleasantly plateaued

These employees are not interested in the training courses and opportunities for advancement offered by their organisations. They are happy to be where they are and do not welcome change. They like to have a routine and a well-defined place within the organisation. They usually stay with one organisation for a long time and are not innovators.

Passively plateaued

Such employees often feel that they are in a rut and unable to alter that fact. They have usually been in the same job for more than five years and know it thoroughly, leaving little opportunity for learning. These people are neither curious nor creative and have no interest in the training courses provided by their organisations. They do not initiate change and have a narrow definition of their own jobs.

Outcomes of career plateauing

Career plateauing can be associated with negative and positive outcomes (Eddington, 1998; Godshalk, 2006; Greenhaus et al, 2010). The following are some of the *negative outcomes:*

- low levels of job involvement and work motivation;
- lower individual self-image;
- lower productivity and work performance;
- low levels of job and career satisfaction;
- employees are less committed to the organisation;
- loss of employee morale;
- plateaued employees may view them as deadwood and sidelined by supervisors and co-workers; and
- work-related stress and strain.

The following are some of the *positive outcomes:*

- Due to organisational changes (flatter structures), plateauing may be less embarrassing or stressful as previously. More employees' career progression is affected by fewer career opportunities lately than a decade ago.
- Allow for reflection and time to plan for personal growth and obtain new knowledge. An introspective analysis should be undertaken to identify where they are at, where they would like to be within a realistic time framework and what changes should be made in order to achieve these goals. The individual should investigate ways of moving beyond the career plateau and should see it as an opportunity rather than an obstacle.
- Plateaued workers have the opportunity to invest more in non-work activities such as families and community activities. 'According to compensatory theory, disappointments in one sphere of life tend in some way to be made up for in another sphere' (Godshalk, 2006:137). Employees become more involved in non-work issues.
- Successful career plateauing would be the *challenge* where individuals still perform effectively and experience job satisfaction despite the fact that their chances of promotion are limited.

Organisational actions

Certain steps can be taken by the organisation to address the problem of plateauing. However, there is no one single answer to the problem. The following are possible solutions to career plateauing (Allen et al, 1999; Appelbaum and Finestone, 1994; Brooks, 1994; Burke and Mikkelsen, 2006; Cascio, 2003; Chau, 1998; Ettington, 1998; Feldman, 1988; Greenhaus et al, 2010; Leibowitz et al, 1990; Ongori and Agolla, 2009; Tan and Salomone, 1994):

◆ change the climate through education;
◆ create an equitable personnel policy;
◆ change the structure of the organisation;
◆ encourage plateaued workers to identify their own challenges;
◆ make promotion expectations more realistic;
◆ set up job rotation programmes to create lateral movement and broaden skills;
◆ set up communication channels to ask plateaued employees what would motivate them;
◆ introduce mutual job switches (temporary or permanent);
◆ give candid feedback;
◆ train supervisors about their role in reducing employee perceptions of career plateauing;
◆ redesign jobs to create more flexibility;
◆ provide exposure for all personnel, not just for the stars;
◆ encourage new ways of doing tasks;
◆ be honest to employees about their chances for advancement and encourage employees at all levels to accept that promotion do not go on forever;
◆ reduce the importance of promotion and increase the value of challenge;
◆ reanalyse the selection system;
◆ provide career information systems;
◆ offer job enrichment;
◆ introduce policies facilitating lateral cross-functional moves;
◆ reassess performance appraisal systems;
◆ encourage involvement in decisions and activities;
◆ use managers' experience and knowledge in ways that go beyond their jobs;
◆ shift linear-career-pattern people to other patterns;
◆ establish a career plan and goals;
◆ provide individual career planning opportunities (for example, career planning workshops, self-assessments of skills);
◆ encourage career exploration;
◆ encourage further education;
◆ encourage skill-based (not position-based) career paths;
◆ create more 'project type' jobs; and
◆ arrange temporary moves to be exposed to a new area.

Obsolescence

Obsolescence is another typical career issue. *Obsolescence* is the degree to which an organisation's professionals lack the up-to-date knowledge or skills necessary to maintain effective performance in either their current or future work roles (Kaufman, 2006: 539). Aspects such as a lack of new knowledge or skills, ineffectiveness in their current job and professional roles are dimensions included in this definition. Obsolescence occurs when the worker fails to remain current and lacks new knowledge or skills and when it results in ineffectiveness it becomes a problem for the employee and the organisation. Not all ineffectiveness can be attributed to obsolescence, but only when it is as a result of a lack of current knowledge and skills. When workers lack the skills and become ineffective to perform their current jobs or professional roles, it has been referred to as job obsolescence (Kaufman, 2006).

Obsolescence simply means that an individual's knowledge or skills have become outmoded and outdated. Rapid advances in technology and the unpredictable changes taking place in organisations mean that obsolescence will become even more widespread. In today's changing workplace, multiple skills are becoming essential to prevent obsolescence. Three *personal characteristics* tend to be associated with low obsolescence: high intellectual ability, high self-motivation and personal flexibility. Obsolescence has been found to influence the decision to retire (Cascio, 2003; Paul and Townsend, 1992). The performance appraisal can be used as a valuable instrument to indicate levels of obsolescence in certain areas.

Models of obsolescence

Worker obsolescence is a *continuous process* and there are a number of *factors* related to obsolescence. The worker obsolescence model in figure 6.3 illustrates the continuity of the process of worker obsolescence. There is an ideal *balance* between the worker and the job until it is disrupted by *technological factors* (computers, substitute products, information explosion) and *organisational factors* (organisational structure, corporate culture, performance expectations, performance measures, job itself) or by the *behaviour of the worker* (motivation, values, loyalty, stress, creativity) or any combination of these three. After this disruption, obsolescence is observed through *symptoms* like tension, frustration, depression, hostility, gradual lowering of morale, being resistant to change, etc. *Treatment* follows the observation of these symptoms and is usually in the form of retraining, changes in the organisation, career assessment and counselling, a long-range commitment to the prevention of worker obsolescence and encouraging the pursuit of learning and the updating of skills. This treatment creates a balance between the worker and the job. The cycle is then complete until the balance is again disrupted by a change in technology, the organisation or the worker. Then the cycle begins again (Bracker and Pearson, 1986).

The worker obsolescence model shows the continuity of the process of worker obsolescence, the factors by which it is influenced, the symptoms that arise and the treatment that can be applied.

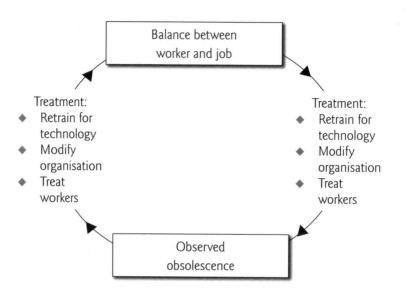

Figure 6.3 *Worker obsolescence model*

By analysing extensive research on obsolescence, Kaufman (1989, 2006; Greenhaus et al, 2010) has identified *four broad components* that could constitute an *open systems model* for explaining how obsolescence comes about (figure 6.4). The components are:

◆ *environmental change*: 'The roots of obsolescence have been traced to the knowledge revolution, the information explosion and the dynamic changes that have occurred in technology organisations, occupations and management methods' (Kaufman, 2006: 540). Changes in technology can force workers to learn the new technology or face obsolescence.

◆ *individual characteristics* (age, cognitive ability, motivation): The general assumption is that obsolescence increases with *age*. More research is needed to determine the relation between age and obsolescence as some results illustrate that the performance and contributions of some workers decline with age, while others maintain their level of contributions and performance or even improves it over time. Cognitive ability can facilitate or inhibit obsolescence. Different types of cognitive abilities appear to be related to obsolescence, depending on the occupation. Workers who enter the labour market with weak cognitive abilities would be more susceptible to obsolescence. Research indicates that workers who suffer a lack of motivation fail to keep current in their field, despite the fact that they may have the ability (Kaufman, 2006).

◆ the *nature of the work*, which involves the extent to which the individual's knowledge, skills and abilities (KSAs) are required in the job. The KSAs that are required can change so rapidly that the worker finds it difficult to keep up.

◆ *organisational climate:* The organisational climate has a direct influence on obsolescence. Aspects such as interaction and communication, leadership style, management policy, rewarding of professional growth and updating of job skills are all relevant to obsolescence.

Each of the above components can contribute directly to the development of obsolescence but, as part of a system, they play a *complex interactive role* that results in obsolescence being a multi-faceted phenomenon. Environmental change as the primary component directly affects not only obsolescence but also each of the other components. Organisational climate has a direct effect on obsolescence, as well as on the nature of the work. The nature of the work is the most significant component of the entire system, in that it not only affects obsolescence directly but it also affects individual characteristics and the consequences that these characteristics have for obsolescence.

Kaufman maintains that in the practical application of the model the main focus could be on organisational climate, the nature of the work and individual characteristics. These components are more amenable to changes that the organisation or the individual can bring about, while environmental changes involve external factors that are relatively beyond their control.

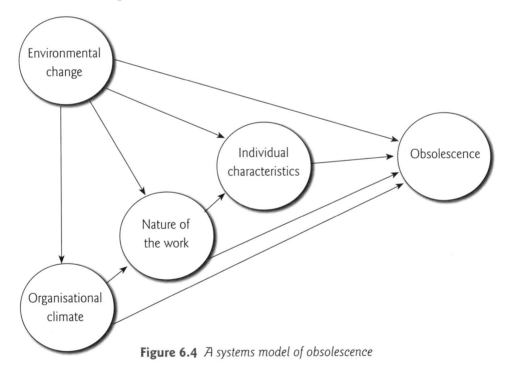

Figure 6.4 *A systems model of obsolescence*

Organisational actions

Certain actions can be taken by the organisation to prevent obsolescence and to reduce feelings of obsolescence. By taking these actions into consideration, management can contribute to the development of policies and practices that keep professionals up to date. These *actions* include the following (Cascio, 2003; Greenhaus et al, 2010):

- ensuring proper training and integration with the demands of job innovation;
- educating the workforce to become adaptable to change;
- implementing a performance management system that will encourage growth and development;
- encouraging continuous learning and the updating of skills by attendance of professional conferences;
- 360 degree performance feedback;
- implementing periodic changes in assignments, projects or jobs;
- ensuring continual job challenge and job rotation;
- creating a work climate that includes communication;
- rewarding employees for performance, lifelong learning and development and success in challenging jobs;
- providing participative leadership; and
- providing challenging initial work.

Job loss and unemployment

Job loss and unemployment could occur at any stage of an individual's career, but if it happens during the later stages it could be more traumatic. *Job loss* can be described as any involuntary withdrawal from the workforce (Leana and Feldman, 1988; McKee-Ryan, 2006). Job loss is a traumatic and stressful event and it does not affect the individual only, but has an adverse impact on the relationship with spouses and children (McKee-Ryan, 2006). 'Job loss is often not only about the loss of a job and the accompanying financial security, but also about losing oneself, one's self-identity and sense of purpose' (http://www.biankalegrand.com/job/2010/01/is).

Many people in South African organisations are affected by job losses due to mergers and acquisitions, restructurings and downsizings, privatisation, recession and the Employment Equity Legislation. *Unemployment* in South Africa is also high due to low educational and skills levels and other economic factors. The recession of 2009 was a major contributing factor to millions of job losses not only in South Africa but worldwide. More than 770 000 employees have lost their jobs from October 2008 until October 2009 and unemployment had increased by 3.5 per cent for the same period. The unemployment rate for blacks was 27.4 per cent in 2008 and 28.8 per cent in 2009. For coloureds it was 19.2 per cent in 2008 and 21.6 per cent in 2009. For Indians it was 11.7 per cent in 2008 and 12.7 per cent in 2009 and for whites it was 4.1 per cent in 2008 and 4.8 per cent in 2009 (Finweek, 2010). The unemployment rate for the first quarter in 2010 was 25.2 per cent (Department of Statistics, 2010).

Unemployment usually has a major effect on the emotional well-being of individuals and their families. Job loss can be even more traumatic if any of the following conditions are present:

- the employee views the present employment as a job for life;
- the employee has few transferable skills;
- the employee has never worked anywhere else; and

◆ the employee (rightly or wrongly) perceives himself or herself to be unemployable (McKnight, 1991).

Ways in which individuals are affected by losing a job

Losing a job affects a person *inter alia* in the following ways (Crossland, 2009; Greenhaus, 2010; Kates et al, 1990; Leana and Feldman, 1991; McKee-Ryan, 2006):

◆ *losses* (loss of social contacts, friendships and support in the workplace, daily structure);
◆ *economic deprivation* (loss of income);
◆ *changes in roles* (roles associated with work change);
◆ *changes in self-esteem* (feel rejected and unwanted, self-blame);
◆ *increased stress* (stress is increased by the need to find a new job, financial hardship);
◆ *changes in social support* (reduction in social activities, withdrawal);
◆ *changes in family relationships* (changes in behaviour of unemployed affect relationships); and
◆ *deficits/illness* (physical or psychological deficits can be exposed by job loss).

Unemployed men and women differ in their focus. Men rely more on problem-focused activities, such as job search, while women rely more on symptom-focused activities, such as seeking social support. On the positive side, job loss can be a growth experience, it can allow the individual to secure a job which provides a better work-life balance or the opportunity to work for oneself, which was perhaps always an ambition. People can be forced to use the career management model and look for new opportunities for personal fulfilment.

Kates et al (1990) suggest an *integrated model* to explain the ways in which losing a job affects an individual (figure 6.5).

The model explains that losing a job may well result in further problems, the so-called *provoking factors*, which render individuals more susceptible to the *negative impact* of job loss. These include stress, poverty and a negative self-image, all of which necessitate adjustment on the part of the individual. *Successful adjustment* will lead to the reinforcement of the so-called *protective factors*, which lessen the adverse effects of job loss. These include support received from individuals' families and from society, as well as skills and financial resources. The protective factors boost individuals' self-confidence and help them to cope with the new situation. However, should individuals not be able to adjust successfully to job loss, their sense of self-worth may well be reduced, resulting in further problems. It is necessary to understand the above-mentioned factors in order to acknowledge the full impact that job loss has on an individual. *Three other factors* must, however, be added. They are:

◆ what the job means to the individual;
◆ the stages through which individuals pass after job loss; and
◆ the personal and environmental factors that can either exacerbate the loss or temper it.

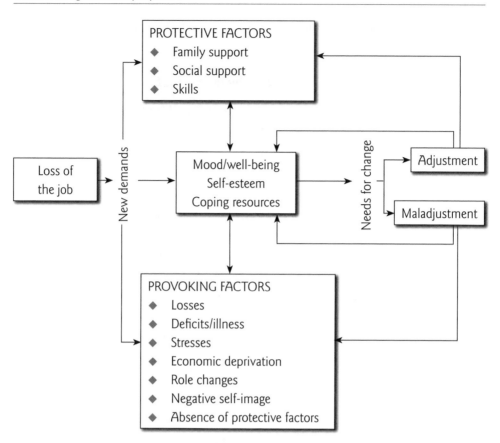

Figure 6.5 *Factors affecting the outcome of losing a job*

Stages of job loss

Regardless of one's emotional state, the literature indicates that the subsequent process of job loss follows various stages. It has identified *four stages* of job loss.

The *first stage* is shock, relief and relaxation. Initially it is a shock, but often employees have been expecting it for a while and, when it happens, they get a feeling of relief and stop worrying. Finally individuals relax and separate themselves from the situation. The *second stage* is referred to as a period of concerted effort. During this stage, the unemployed spend all their time and energy in finding another job. This include a number of activities such as preparing and mailing (e-mailing) up to date curriculum vitaes, working with personnel agencies and following up contacts. During this time, individuals also receive the maximum support from their friends, families and partners. Research also indicates that professionals in mid-career are the most vulnerable to stress during the second stage. Fortunately, a number of people find work during this stage and their coping with job loss ends here.

The *third stage* is characterised by vacillation, self-doubt and anger. Individuals enter this stage after months of unsuccessful job searching. They doubt their ability to find a job and anxiety starts to increase. This stage is also characterised by high levels of frustration and anger that affect relationships. This period lasts for about six weeks. The *fourth stage* is characterised by withdrawal. Psychologically, the withdrawal tends to 'stabilise, being characterised by a loss of motivation as a reaction of not being able to find work' (Kaufman, 1982:104). Individuals experience a loss of drive and start to feel that they have lost control of their lives (Kaufman 1982; Greenhaus et al, 2010; McKee-Ryan, 2006).

It is important for individuals who lose their jobs to seek support, vent their anger and make a positive assessment of the situation. They should be encouraged to express their feelings in writing. Research has revealed that 52.2 per cent of those who expressed their feelings in writing found new employment, while only 13.6 per cent of those who did not express their feelings in writing found employment (Laabs, 1993; Crossland, 2009).

Organisational actions

Various programmes can be considered by organisations to assist employees in coping with job loss (Casio, 2003; Crossland, 2009; Greenhaus et al, 2010; Knowdell, 1994):

◆ introduce training programmes to assist employees in managing the stress and on how to develop new opportunities;
◆ the services of a coach can be important by increasing the self-awareness of the individual through exploring their thoughts and feelings about what is going on;
◆ employee outplacement consultants can help employees through the initial shock of job loss and give advice on career moves; and
◆ group training sessions for the notifying managers will allow these managers to practise appropriate behaviours as well as to prepare for a very difficult management task. Such a group training session may cover the following (Knowdell et al, 1994):
   ■ discuss emotions associated with death and divorce and a job loss model such as the one presented by Kates et al. (1990);
   ■ discuss and practise techniques that will enable managers to be objective and emotionally controlled, while at the same time expressing genuine and appropriate feelings;
   ■ discuss and practise specific sentences that confirm that the termination is final and irrevocable;
   ■ discuss and role-play reactions and responses to the employee who does not accept the fact that the termination is final and irrevocable; and
   ■ brief all parties regarding the items that should be covered with the employee (that is, severance payment, severance policy, insurance options, retirement benefits, unemployment compensation, career/job transition counselling and assistance).

Career assistance to retrenched employees

In the career counselling, career transition and job search business, much emphasis is placed on the differences between these types of service and the professional capabilities of the individuals who provide these services (Knowdell et al, 1994). Career counsellors usually assist individuals or groups with identifying their values and abilities, their interests and their career direction. Companies that are serious about the development of their employees usually appoint career counsellors to assist in the process. The general career counsellor sees a wide range of clients with a wide range of needs. The individual client might be a high school or a university graduate looking for a first-time job, someone wanting to explore different career options, a retiree wanting employment or an employee who has been retrenched.

In contrast with the general career counsellor, the career-transition counsellor focuses specifically on out-of-work candidates who are actively seeking employment. The psychological and financial needs of the unemployed are generally more immediate and demanding than the needs of the general career counsellee (Knowdell et al, 1994). Career-transition counsellors must be able to handle emotional venting, depression and the sense of urgency most employees who suffer job loss feel. While both the job-search counsellor and the more general career counsellor focus on the various phases of personal career development (that is, self-assessment, exploration of options and job search techniques), the emphasis for career-transition counsellors is on the job search strategy, setting up informational interviews and networking for contacts and job interviews.

Managing job/career transition

There are an enormous number of services that an organisation can provide in-house or through outsourcing that will help their ex-employees to find a new job as soon as possible. Knowdell et al (1994) describe four categories of typical career-transition services, namely:

◆ executive career-transition services;
◆ professional and mid-level manager career-transition services;
◆ lower level employee career-transition services; and
◆ special services.

Executive career-transition services are programmes designed for executives, senior managers or highly paid professionals. The services are always provided on a one-on-one basis by an experienced career-transition consultant who knows the business community. In addition, there may be a psychologist on the staff or at least one who is available on a consulting basis. Sometimes, additional counsellors and trainers will be made available for group or individual coaching on specific job-search skills or broad issues such as financial or business planning.

The full range of services a candidate might receive includes:

◆ an initial interview;
◆ an opportunity to vent his or her feelings;
◆ one-on-one counselling;
◆ individual assessment;
◆ individual coaching;

◆ psychological testing;

◆ résumé writing assistance;

◆ financial planning advice;

◆ assistance with goal setting;

◆ a job search strategy;

◆ a support group;

◆ salary negotiation training and advice;

◆ business plan evaluation;

◆ family and spousal counselling;

◆ library use;

◆ computer use;

◆ job postings from executive and senior level search services; and

◆ interview training.

Professional and mid-level manager career-transition services are programmes designed for employees who are mid- to lower-level managers and professionals. Generally, group services and some additional individual services are provided. In-house career centres organise one– to three-day training sessions with groups of ten to fifteen people. At the end of the programme, one-on-one sessions are organised for each individual. Training content might include the following:

◆ group ventilation of feelings associated with job loss;

◆ identification of career values, interests and style;

◆ identification of skills;

◆ training in identifying a network of contacts;

◆ setting new goals;

◆ training in résumé writing and interviewing;

◆ generalised personal financial planning advice; and

◆ training in salary negotiations.

Lower level employee career-transition services are in-house or external programmes conducted for the lower-level employee. A transition centre is sometimes provided that operates on a self-help basis. Group-training programmes are also provided, ranging from half- to three-day sessions that focus on specific topics, such as completing an application form or compiling a résumé or that cover some of the same topics as the programme for middle managers.

Services and equipment provided at the transition centre may include phones, desk space, library or reference books, job listings from local companies, support groups, job clubs, information on how to apply for unemployment or welfare services, help in getting assistance from various community resources, job search counsellors, résumé printing and mailing assistance.

Training is similar to that provided for the mid-level managers and professionals and might include:

◆ group ventilation;
◆ résumé writing;
◆ completing application forms;
◆ developing a contact network;
◆ assessment of values, interests and goals;
◆ interviewing skills;
◆ salary negotiations;
◆ skill identification;
◆ job search skills; and
◆ phone skills, dress and etiquette.

The career-transition centre

Knowdell et al (1994) view the career or resource-transition centre as the hub or home base of the job-seeking candidate. These centres are a source of information and inspiration. The *physical elements* of a transition centre may include:

◆ a library for business magazines and specialised periodicals, newspapers, reference books on organisations and a resource guide;
◆ a notice board with job postings and listings from companies in the surrounding communities near the job site;
◆ a copier to make copies of job postings, résumés and company information;
◆ a fax machine to send and receive information;
◆ a kitchen area for coffee, tea and soft drinks, with a refrigerator and microwave;
◆ a training room and/or conference room;
◆ individual or shared working space; and
◆ private counselling offices.

Activities presented at the centre may include:

◆ counselling sessions;
◆ group training;
◆ phone calls;
◆ scheduling of on-site interviews; and
◆ crisis lines, 24-hour hot lines and similar services to assist those in distress.

The *psychological elements* include

◆ a businesslike atmosphere; and
◆ a convivial environment that encourages individuals but does not allow them to become too comfortable.

Special services are sometimes required for the visually or hearing impaired or for those who are mentally or physically challenged. Often there are resources available in the community that can be used to assist these people. *Employee assistance programmes* should be available on a one-on-one or group basis or through community service agencies for all employees who are affected by job loss. Individuals under stress have a greater propensity for drug and alcohol abuse and for family violence. Assistance programmes usually include services such as grief and individual image counselling to help individuals cope with negative emotions and with self-esteem problems that may hinder them from moving successfully on to a new job.

Conclusion

The career issues discussed in this chapter are the result of a changing environment. Changes are taking place worldwide in the economy and the business environment. The environment is turbulent and unpredictable and organisations and individuals have to be flexible and adaptive to succeed. Career issues such as plateauing, job loss, obsolescence and working couples, as a result of these changes, are increasingly becoming the rule rather than the exception. Individuals should learn how to cope with the challenges of each of them and the organisation should understand its supportive role by promoting effective career management as well as assisting the individual with career transition.

Currently career development within the context of employment equity is a relevant challenge facing South Africa. Different models and programmes are suggested that may be useful for career development and succession planning. Chapter 7 discusses the impact of the changing world of work and careers on individuals' *health and well-being* and chapter 8 provides an overview on organisational choice and key *organisational career support practices* relevant to the contemporary workplace concerns.

Review and discussion questions

1. Explain the three components which comprise individuals' self-concept and together form the individual's career anchor.
2. List the career anchors and explain how career anchors influence individuals' career development.
3. What are the challenges of the linear, expert, spiral and transitory career patterns respectively?
4. How can the notion of career patterns and motives assist individuals in managing their careers in the contemporary workplace? How can the notion of career patterns and motives help organisations in retaining talent?
5. Explain how flexible work arrangements influence working couples.
6. Explain the typical factors that influence the quality of working couples' relationship. What can organisations do to help working couples achieve greater work-life balance?
7. Explain how career plateauing influences individuals' career satisfaction by discussing the sources of career plateauing. Suggest actions that organisations can take to address the issue of career plateauing.

8. Write a paragraph describing the advice that you would offer a friend who has experienced job loss or who is currently unemployed.

Reflection activity

Read through the two case studies below and answer the questions that follow:

Anne (24 years)

As a twenty-four-year old white female South African currently living in London my idea of career success may vary significantly from someone of a different age and life stage. At this point in both my personal and career life, I find that career success is measured by the contribution that I make to another individual's life.

When I arrived in London I had student debts and the fear hanging over my head that if I didn't pay them off within a few years in London I wouldn't be able to pay them off when I returned to South Africa. As a result of this I took a job in the HR department of an international investment bank. The work I did was impersonal and the hours ridiculous. By focusing on the financial rewards of my job I was able to continue going in to a job I didn't particularly enjoy day after day. Finally a few months ago, after living and working in London for two years, my debt was paid off.

Free from financial constraints I quit my job and am now happily employed, offering advice and training on government benefits to people who need to get work experience in order to re-enter the job market. My salary has dropped, but so too have my hours and my energy and happiness levels have soared.

For many people I went to school with my job at the investment bank sounded impressive and the status and financial security appealed to many of them. For me, job success isn't measured by the big office, security passes and salary but rather by being able to smile for eighty percent of my day and to come home feeling relaxed and happy even when I've had a few difficult clients. I would rather enjoy what I do every day and not need a big holiday at the end of it to recover and recharge my batteries. To me, career success is knowing that I am helping people. In some cases these people have been out of work for up to twelve years and I help them develop the self-confidence and experience to enable them to find work and to support not only themselves but also their families.

Sam (35 years)

I am married and have a three-year-old daughter. I live in Secunda. My wife is a full-time student at a local tertiary institution. I grew up in Limpopo and after completing my high school education, I moved to Secunda where I attended an artisan's training programme. After completing the training, I began working as a semi-skilled employee for various contractors in the petrochemical industry, which involved relocating from one area to another. I have recently started working as a superintendent and have just bought a house where I live with my family. I am now in the process of re-evaluating my personal values, aspirations, motives, needs and my vocational and life roles. I am looking for a permanent job so that I do not have to relocate as often as I used to do when I was still single.

I have always dreamt of qualifying as an artisan because I saw many artisans were able to 'live the good life'. I feel proud of my personal career achievements. It is very unusual to become a superintendent at my age — people in this industry manage to become a superintendent in their forties or fifties, yet at the age of 35 I was already appointed in the position of superintendent.

I feel strongly attached to my job and feel that I am lucky to feel that my personal motives and values and interests are congruent with my current job. I have always liked working with machines and I am good at 'fixing things up'. As a contract worker I realise that my job security is not always assured, hence I save most of my earnings while I am employed. This enables me to continue to live 'the good life' with my family which is very important to me. I also try to continuously broaden my skills and experience by sometimes working in the mines as I feel that this will increase my chances of finding a job should I become unemployed. I have a good reputation and am known for my ability to get a job done quickly and efficiently. Passing a trade test has also helped and this has led to me being appointed as a superintendent. My willingness to work overtime and on weekends has also played an important role in creating a good image for me. I find it easy these days to get a job because many people know me in the industry.

Questions

1. Review the motives and needs of the various career anchors. What is Anne's dominant career anchor? What is Sam's dominant career anchor? Give reasons for your answer.
2. How do their career anchors compare with your personal motives and needs? How would you describe your personal career anchor?
3. Study chapter 7 on career well-being. How does a mismatch or match between one's dominant career anchor and the type of job influence one's sense of well-being?
4. Review chapter 2. What does career success mean to Sam? How does his career anchor motives and values relate to his feelings of career success?

5. Sam emphasises lifelong learning and employability attributes as being important to him being a contract worker. Name the employability attributes that Sam describes in the case study. Would you say that the employability attributes that Sam demonstrates are a natural consequence of the motives and values of his dominant career anchor? Give reasons for your answer.

6. Review chapter 3. How would you describe Sam's career competency? Would you say his career competency contributed to his career success? Give reasons for your answer.

7. Review the challenges that married couples face. Being a contract worker and married with a family, what potential work-family conflict may Sam have to deal with in the future?

Career well-being

Introduction

People's experiences of subjective career success have been linked to their sense of well-being at work (see chapter 3). While the notion of *career well-being* has been used by Kidd (2008) to measure people's subjective career experiences as expressed by their positive and negative feelings about their careers, other researchers such as Gottfredson and Duffy (2008) and Coetzee and Bergh (2009) use more general measures of subjective well-being (including happiness and satisfaction) in the careers context. In order to prosper and to survive in a continuously changing environment organisations need employees who are well. Individuals' experiences, be they physical, emotional, social or spiritual in nature, affect their well-being in the workplace. Individuals spend almost one third of their waking time at work. Therefore, work affects the well-being of employees (Hart, 1999; Kelloway and Barling, 1991).

Well-being of employees can be explained from two models, namely the *disease model* and the *positive psychology model* (see figure 7.1).

◆ **Disease model.** Psychologists have long been concerned with the psychopathological underpinnings of suffering, ill-health and deviance. Focusing on these psychopathological aspects culminated in the *disease model* (Peterson and Seligman, 2004). Although the disease model produced accurate means for the classification, identification and treatment of psychopathology, well-being and optimal development have not been studied to the same extent (Seligman and Csikszentimihalyi, 2000).

◆ **Positive psychology model.** Decades of research which focused on the disease model overshadowed efforts to enhance the states which make life worth living. In 2000, Martin Seligman and Mihaly Csikszentmihalyi introduced the paradigm of positive psychology. According to Seligman and Csikszentimihalyi (2000), positive psychology refers to the science of subjective experiences, positive institutions and individual traits which improve the well-being and prevent the onset of psychopathology or shortly the *science of happiness* (Seligman, 2002).

 ☹	*Disease model*: Focuses on ill-health and un-well-being. Almost 96 per cent of articles in scientific journals in psychology focused on negative outcomes (eg, aggression, alcoholism, bullying, burnout, conflict, harassment, job insecurity, occupational stress and work-life interference).
 ☺	*Positive psychology model*: Focuses on well-being and happiness. About 4 per cent of articles in scientific journals focused on positive outcomes (eg, engagement, happiness, hope, job satisfaction, optimism and meaning).

Figure 7.1 *Models of well-being*

Approaches to well-being

Three approaches to well-being are distinguished, namely subjective, psychological and eudaimonic well-being.

Subjective well-being

Subjective well-being researchers assert that people react differently to the same circumstances and that they evaluate conditions based on their unique expectations, values and previous experiences. Subjective well-being refers to subjective judgements of the quality of an individual's life with regard to both the presence and relative frequency of positive and negative moods and emotions over time, one's overall level of life satisfaction and one's satisfaction with specific domains such as work, family, health, leisure, finances, the self and the group (Diener, Kesebir and Lucas, 2008). A person is as well as he or she perceives himself or herself to be (Diener, Suh, Lucas and Smith, 1999).

The components of subjective well-being can be described as follows (Diener et al, 2008):

◆ *Moods and emotions.* Moods and emotions (which together are labelled *affect*) represent people's evaluations of the events that occur in their lives. Pleasant (positive) affect and unpleasant (negative) affect form two independent factors.

◆ *Life satisfaction.* Life satisfaction is defined as the degree to which the experience of an individual's life satisfies his or her wants and needs, both physically and psychologically.

The factors that influence subjective well-being are divided into bottom-up processes and top-down approaches (Diener et al, 1999). *Bottom-up processes* refer to external events, situations and demographics. The bottom-up approach is built on the notion that basic and universal human needs exist and that a person will be well if these needs are fulfilled. The experience of daily pleasurable events is related to pleasant affect and the experience of daily undesirable events is related to unpleasant affect. However, research showed that external, objective variables and demographic factors (eg, income, education age, sex, race and marital status) accounted for a relatively small percentage of variance in subjective well-being. As far as *top-down processes* are concerned, personality is one of the strongest and most consistent predictors of subjective well-being. Various explanations have been given for the strong effect of personality on subjective well-being.

◆ *Genetic factors.* The first explanation is that people have a genetic predisposition to be well or unwell. Tellegen et al (1988) examined monozygotic and dizygotic twins who were reared together and others who were reared apart. Tellegen et al estimated that genetic factors account for about 40 per cent of the variance in positive emotionality and 55 per cent of the variance in negative emotionality, whereas shared family environment accounts for 22 per cent and 2 per cent of the variance in positive emotionality and negative emotionality, respectively. Lykken and Tellegen (1996) reanalysed the findings of Tellegen et al (1988) and found that although 40 per cent to 55 per cent of the variation in current subjective well-being can be explained by genes, 80 per cent of long-term subjective well-being is heritable. Based on these findings it could be said that it is hard to change a person's happiness.

◆ *Personality traits.* Traits that are related to subjective well-being included extraversion and neuroticism. Extraversion influences positive affect, whereas neuroticism influences negative affect.

The subjective well-being approach implies that career experiences could be linked to positive and negative affect, life satisfaction and satisfaction with different life domains. Research on subjective well-being has established a wide range of associated variables indicative of successful functioning, including positive relationships with self-esteem, locus of control, authenticity and effective decision-making styles, as well as negative associations with worry, anxiety and depression (Waterman, 2008). Few existing theories attempt to explain why variables differentially relate to the separate components of subjective well-being. Therefore, the differential relations among most input variables and the components of subjective well-being are poorly understood.

Psychological well-being

Psychological well-being is an objective approach to understanding well-being in terms of the presence of an array of psychological qualities indicative of mental health. Subjective well-being focuses on specific outcomes (eg, positive affect and life satisfaction), while psychological well-being focuses on the contents of one's life and the processes involved in living well (Waterman, 2008). Psychological well-being consists of six dimensions, namely autonomy, environmental mastery, personal growth, positive relations with others, purpose in life and self-acceptance (Ryff and Singer, 1998).

- *Autonomy* refers to self-determination and independence, the ability to resist social pressures to think and act in certain ways to regulate behaviour from within and evaluate the self by using personal standards.
- *Environmental mastery* is defined as the individual's ability to choose or create environments suitable to his or her psychic conditions and is defined as a characteristic of mental health.
- *Personal growth* refers to the continued development of one's potential, seeing the self as growing and expanding, being open to new experiences, having a sense of realising one's potential and seeing improvement in the self and behaviour over time.
- *Positive relations with others* is defined as having warm, satisfying and trusting relationships with others, being concerned about the welfare of others, being capable of strong empathy, affection and intimacy and understanding give and take of human relationships.
- *Purpose in life* refers to having goals and a sense of directedness, feeling that there is meaning to past and present life, holding beliefs that give life purpose and having aims and objectives for living.
- *Self-acceptance* is defined as possessing a positive attitude towards the self, acknowledging and accepting multiple aspects of the self, including good and bad qualities and feeling positive about one's past life.

The psychological well-being approach implies that career experiences which allow autonomy, environmental mastery, personal growth, positive relations with others, purpose in life and self-acceptance will result in employee well-being.

Eudaimonic well-being

Eudaimonic well-being refers to quality of life derived from the development of a person's best potentials and their application in the fulfilment of personally expressive, self-concordant goals (Waterman, 2008). Central to this perspective on eudaimonia is living in a manner consistent with one's daimon (or 'true self'). To live in truth to one's daimon is an expression of personal integrity through identifying one's potential strengths and limitations and choosing those goals that provide personal meaning and purpose in life.

Eudaimonic well-being refers to well-being incorporating both subjective and objective elements. The subjective elements are experiences of feelings of personal expressiveness. The objective elements include behaviours involved in the pursuit of eudaimonic goals such as self-realisation, entailing the identification and development of personal potentials and their utilisation in ways that give purpose and meaning to life. The dimensions of eudaimonic well-being include self-discovery, perceived development of one's best potentials, a sense of purpose and meaning in life, investment of significant effort in pursuit of excellence, intense involvement in activities and enjoyment of activities as personally expressive (Waterman et al, 2010).

- *Self-discovery.* This makes the process of self-discovery central to eudaimonic functioning. It also serves to link eudaimonic well-being to success in the process of identity formation.
- *Perceived development of one's best potentials.* One of the most important elements to learn about oneself concerns those unique potentials that represent the best a person is able to become. It is not only necessary to identify those potentials; one must also actively strive to act upon them so that they can become fully developed.
- *Sense of purpose and meaning in life.* In order to experience eudaimonic well-being, individuals must find ways for putting their skills and talents to use in the pursuit of personally meaningful objectives.
- *Investment of significant effort in pursuit of excellence.* Eudaimonic well-being results because of the full use of one's skills and talents in personally meaningful activities. Therefore, the level of effort invested in such activities will be considerably greater than in other activities in which a person engages.
- *Intense involvement in activities.* When individuals are engaged in personally meaningful activities that make full use of their skills and talents, the intensity of their involvement in these activities should be considerably higher than when engaging in other, more routine activities.
- *Enjoyment of activities as personally expressive.* Persons characterised as high on eudaimonic well-being should report that what they are doing in their lives is personally expressive of who they are and they should do so far more often than those with lower eudaimonic well-being.

The eudaimonic well-being approach implies that career experiences which allow self-discovery, perceived development of one's best potentials, a sense of purpose and meaning in life, investment of significant effort in pursuit of excellence, intense involvement in activities and enjoyment of activities as personally expressive will result in employee well-being.

Authentic happiness

The three approaches to well-being, namely subjective, psychological and eudaimonic well-being, can be integrated. One example of a model that integrates the three approaches is the authentic happiness model (Seligman, 2002). Subjective and eudaimonic well-being focus on specific outcomes (eg, positive affect, life satisfaction and enjoyment of activities), while psychological and eudaimonic well-being focus on the contents of one's life and the processes involved in living well.

Happiness is an important goal and it entails more than the absence of unhappiness. Happiness refers to the experience of a sense of joy, satisfaction and positive well-being, combined with a sense that one's life is good, meaningful and worthwhile. Authentic happiness has three components, namely pleasure (a pleasurable life), meaning (a meaningful life) and engagement (a good life) (Seligman, 2002). Figure 7.2 shows the *authentic happiness formula*.

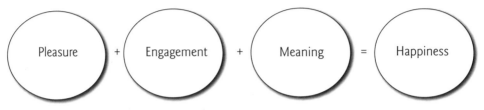

Figure 7.2 *The authentic happiness formula*

The first route to happiness is hedonic and entails the pursuit of *pleasure* through the experience of positive affect. Positive affect is a state of pleasurable engagement and reflects the extent to which a person feels enthusiastic, alert and active (Watson, Clark and Tellegen, 1988). The state of positive affect captures how one feels at given points in time, whereas the trait of positive affect captures stable individual differences in the level of affect generally experienced. The state of positive affect is a separate factor from negative affect (George and Brief, 1992). People in a positive state process information more strategically and people in a negative state process information more systematically. Those in a positive mood are 'smarter' at processing information than those in a negative mood. Positive affect has been shown to be effective in medical contexts, improving decision-making among medical students and creative problem-solving and diagnostic reasoning processes among practising physicians. Within limits, individuals can increase their positive affect about the past (by cultivating gratitude and forgiveness), their positive emotions about the present (by savouring and mindfulness) and positive emotions about the future (by building optimism and hope). Increasing the pleasure component of happiness will not have a lasting influence on happiness for the following reasons:

◆ Positive affect is heritable and therefore people's emotions probably fluctuate within a genetically-determined range. It can therefore be said that people have a genetically determined set-point for pleasure.

◆ People quickly adapt to pleasure (referred to as the hedonic treadmill).

Frederikson's (1998) 'broaden-and-build' theory of positive emotions states that positive emotions, including joy, interest, contentment and happiness, all share the ability to 'broaden' an individual's momentary thought-action repertoires. In addition, these positive emotions assist in building the individual's enduring personal resources. The tendency to experience the positive is considered to be central to one's ability to flourish, to prosper mentally and grow psychologically. Therefore, positive emotions have a potentially adaptive and interactive nature and might moderate the relationship between job satisfaction and job performance.

The second route to happiness is through pursuing gratification, which *engages* one fully in activities. Individuals may find gratification in participating in a great conversation, fixing a bike, reading a good book, teaching a child, playing the guitar or performing a challenging task at work. A person can take shortcuts to pleasures (eg, eating ice cream, having a massage or using drugs), but no shortcuts exist to gratification. He/she must involve him– or herself fully and the pursuit of gratifications requires that he or she applies his/her signature strengths, such as creativity, appreciation of beauty and excellence and perseverance. Although gratifications are activities that may be enjoyable, they are not necessarily accompanied by positive emotions. The pursuit of gratification may also be unpleasant at times (eg, when you are training for an endurance event). Finding gratifications from engagement need not involve anything larger than the self.

The third route to happiness is to use strengths to belong to and in service of something larger than the self (eg, knowledge, goodness, family, community, politics, justice or a higher spiritual power), which give life *meaning*. Meaningfulness is the extent to which one feels that work makes sense emotionally, that problems and demands are worth investing energy in, are worthy of commitment and engagement and are challenges that are welcome.

Peterson, Nansook and Seligman (2005:36) studied the three orientations to happiness and concluded as follows: 'These orientations are distinguishable, are not incompatible and thus able to be pursued simultaneously and that each is associated with life satisfaction' Engagement and meaning as routes to happiness seem more under deliberate control of individuals than pleasure (Seligman, Parks and Steen, 2004). Therefore, interventions which target engagement and meaning seem most fruitful, linked with pleasure flowing from them.

Authentic happiness and work engagement

Definition and dimensions of work engagement

Engagement is defined as a positive, fulfilling, work-related state of mind that is characterised by vigour, dedication and absorption (Schaufeli and Bakker, 2004). Engagement is the willingness and ability to contribute to company success; the extent to which employees put discretionary effort into their work, in the form of extra time, brainpower and energy. Employees are engaged when many different levels of employees are feeling fully involved and enthusiastic about their jobs and their organisations.

Macey and Schneider (2008) distinguished three broad conceptualisations of employee engagement, namely state, trait and behavioural engagement. State engagement overlaps with concepts such as job satisfaction, organisational commitment, job involvement, psychological empowerment and positive affect. Engagement can be directly observable behaviour in the work context, such as putting forth discretionary effort, namely extra time, brainpower and energy, doing something different that extends beyond expected in-role performance. Trait engagement refers to an inclination to experience the world from a particular vantage point, including trait positive affectivity, the autotelic personality (one who engages in an activity for its own sake) and personal initiative. Behavioural engagement of employees is indicated by discretionary effort (namely extra time, brainpower and energy) and doing more and different things than expected.

Building on ethnographic work of Kahn (1990:694), who conceptualised engagement at work as '... the harnessing of organisational members' selves to their work roles', May, Gilson and Harter (2004) introduced a *three-dimensional concept* of engagement consisting of a *physical* component, an *emotional* component and a *cognitive* component (see figure 7.3). The physical component refers to being physically involved in a task (vigour and positive affective state). The cognitive component concerns alertness at work (absorption and involvement). The emotional component refers to being connected to job/others while working (dedication and commitment).

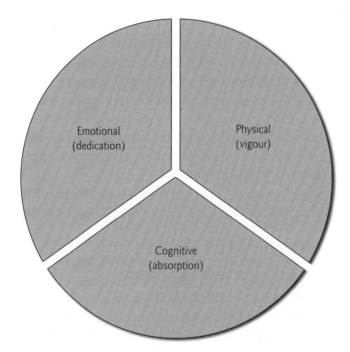

Figure 7.3 *Dimensions of state engagement*

Manifestation of work engagement

According to a recent Gallup study on employee engagement, about 54 per cent of employees in the United States are not engaged and 17 per cent are disengaged. Only 29 per cent are engaged. Research with 10 918 employees in different organisations in South Africa showed that 26 per cent were engaged, while 16 per cent were disengaged. Table 7.1 shows the average levels of work engagement in different occupations and organisations in South Africa (Rothmann, 2005).

Table 7.1 *Engagement in different occupations in South Africa*

Occupation	Sten	Occupation	Sten
Pharmacists	4.56	Employees in the insurance industry	4.88
Support staff at higher education institutions	5.19	Emergency health technicians	5.25
Correctional officers	5.29	Secondary school educators	5.34
Academics in higher education institutions	5.60	Professional nurses	5.60
Call centre operators	5.61	Specialists in the petrochemical industry	5.64
Police officers	5.75	Production supervisors	6.32
Primary school educators	6.47	Non-professional counsellors	6.49
Train drivers	7.72		

Interpretation of sten scores: 1 = low and 10 = high   Average sten = 5.5

Table 7.1 shows that occupations such as pharmacists, employees in the insurance industry, support staff members at higher education institutions, emergency health technicians and secondary school educators obtained the lowest scores on work engagement. Occupations such as train drivers and non-professional counsellors obtained the highest scores on work engagement.

Factors associated with work engagement

People can use varying degrees of their selves, physically, cognitively and emotionally, in the work they perform. It seems that the more people draw on their selves to perform their roles, the more stirring their performances. Engagement is the simultaneous employment and expression of a person's preferred self in task behaviours that promote connections to work and to others. The combination of employing and expressing a person's preferred self yields behaviours that bring alive the relation of self to role (Kahn, 1990).

Three psychological conditions impact on an individual's engagement, namely psychological meaningfulness, psychological safety and psychological availability. Furthermore, various antecedents affect the three psychological conditions, which in turn affect work engagement (see figure 7.4).

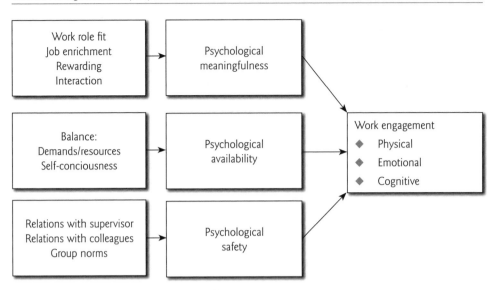

Figure 7.4 *Psychological conditions and antecedents of work engagement*

Psychological meaningfulness

Psychological meaningfulness refers to 'a feeling that one is receiving a return on investment of one's self in a currency of physical, cognitive or emotional energy; (Kahn, 1990:703-704). Psychological meaning refers to the value of a work goal in relation to the ideals of an individual (Hackman and Oldham, 1980). A lack of meaningfulness in work can lead to apathy and detachment from one's work (Thomas and Velthouse, 1990) and disengagement (May et al, 2004). Individuals are usually estranged from their selves under these kinds of conditions and restoration of meaning in work is a method of fostering an individual's motivation and attachment to work (Seeman, 1972).

Two factors in the work context contribute to psychological meaningfulness, namely work-role fit and good co-worker relations (Kahn, 1990). Individuals seek work roles in which they can express their authentic selves fully in creative ways. Fit between an individual's self-concept and his/her work role will lead to a sense of meaning due to the ability of the individual to express his/her values and beliefs (Shamir, 1991). Individuals' engagement will be high when it is possible for them to apply their strengths at work. Participating in activities that are congruent with their strengths contribute to the experience of meaning and engagement in work. Peterson and Seligman (2004) distinguished between six virtues, which are divided into 24 strengths (see table 7.2). *Virtues* are defined as the core characteristics valued by moral philosophers and religious thinkers. *Character strengths* refer to psychological processes or mechanisms that define the virtues.

In research with 198 000 employees in 36 companies by the Gallup Organisation, responses to the following question were analysed: 'At work, do you have the opportunity to do what you do best every day?' When employees answered 'strongly agree' to this question, they were 50 per cent more likely to work in businesses with a low turnover, 38 per cent more likely to work in productive business units and 44 per cent more likely to work in business units with high customer satisfaction scores (Buckingham and Clifton, 2001). Furthermore, it was found that globally, only 20 per cent of employees working in large organisations experienced that their strengths are utilised every day. Also, the longer employees stay with an organisation and the higher they climb the traditional career ladder, the *less likely* they are to strongly agree that they are performing to their strengths. The researchers attributed this finding to the following flawed assumptions about people: (1) each person can learn to be competent in almost anything and (2) each person's greatest room for growth is in his or her areas of greatest weakness.

Table 7.2 *Classification of strengths (Peterson and Seligman, 2004)*

a. Wisdom (Cognitive strengths entailing the acquisition and use of knowledge)
◆ Creativity: thinking of novel and productive ways to do things
◆ Curiosity: taking an interest in ongoing experience; exploring and discovering
◆ Open-mindedness: thinking things through and examining them from all sides; not jumping to conclusions
◆ Love of learning: mastering new skills, topics and bodies of knowledge
◆ Perspective: provide wise counsel to others; having ways of looking at the world which make sense to the self and others
b. Courage (Emotional strengths involving the exercise of will to accomplish goals)
◆ Bravery: do what needs to be done despite of fear
◆ Perseverance: finishing what one has started, keeping on despite obstacles, staying on task
◆ Integrity: the genuine presentation of oneself to others, taking responsibility for one's feelings and actions
◆ Vitality: feeling alive, feeling vigorous and energetic, approach life with energy
c. Love (Interpersonal strengths that involve tending and befriending others)
◆ Intimacy: valuing close relationships with others; being close to people
◆ Kindness/altruism: doing favours and good deeds for others; helping them; taking care of them
◆ Social intelligence: being aware of the motives and feelings of other people and the self; knowing what to do to fit in to social situations
d. Justice (civic strengths that underlie healthy community life)
◆ Citizenship: working well as a member of a group or team; doing one's share
◆ Fairness: treating all people the same; not letting personal feelings bias decisions about others; giving everyone a fair chance
◆ Leadership: encouraging a group of whom one is a member to get things done and at the same time maintaining good relationships within the group

---

e. *Temperance* (Strengths that protect against excess)

◆ Forgiveness: forgiving those who have done wrong; giving people a second chance

◆ Modesty: letting one's accomplishments speak for themselves; not seeking the spotlight

◆ Prudence/caution: being careful about one's choices; not taking undue risks; not saying or doing things that might later be regretted

◆ Self-regulation: regulating what one feels and does; controlling one's appetites and emotions

f. *Transcendence* (Strengths that provide meaning)

◆ Appreciation of beauty and excellence: noticing and appreciating beauty, excellence and skilled performance in all life domains

◆ Gratitude: being aware of and thankful for the good things that happen, taking time to express thanks

◆ Hope/Optimism: expecting the best in the future and work to achieve it

◆ Humour: liking to laugh and tease; bringing smiles to other people

◆ Spirituality: having coherent beliefs about the higher purpose and meaning of the universe; knowing where one fits within the larger scheme

---

Employees should experience more meaning in the work environment when they have rewarding interpersonal interaction with their colleagues (Locke and Taylor, 1990). Individuals will experience a sense of meaning from their interactions when they are treated with respect and dignity and are valued for their contributions. The level of interaction an individual has with his/her co-workers will also foster a stronger sense of social identity, a sense of belonging and greater meaning (Kahn, 1990).

Psychological safety

Psychological safety entails feeling able to show and employ one's self without fear of negative consequences to self-image, status or career (Kahn, 1990). Individuals who are working in a safe environment will understand the boundaries surrounding acceptable behaviours. Psychological safety might lead to engagement, because it reflects one's belief that a person can employ him/herself without fear of negative consequences. The opposite would occur in a work environment which is ambiguous, unpredictable and threatening. Employees in unsafe environments with ambiguous, unpredictable and threatening conditions are likely to disengage from the work and would be more cautious to try new things.

Supervisory and co-worker relations that are supportive, trustworthy as well as flexible with regard to the behavioural norms lead to feelings of psychological safety. Edmondson (2004) indicated that a supportive supervisor who is not controlling at work would have subordinates who experience a sense of safety in the work environment. Supervisor trustworthiness can be linked to five categories of behaviour, namely behavioural consistency, behavioural integrity, sharing and delegation of control, accurate and open communication and a demonstration of concern (May et al, 2004). Managerial reluctance to loosen their control can send a message to their employees that they are not to be trusted, which might cause employees to be afraid of taking any chances or of overstepping their boundaries. This fear will be strengthened when managers behave unpredictably, inconsistently or hypocritically. Trustworthy supervisory behaviours should lead to feelings of psychological safety as well as willingness among employees to invest themselves at work. Interpersonal trust can either have cognitive or affective bases (McAllister, 1995). The reliability and dependability of others are related to cognitive-based trust, where the emotional relationships between individuals impact on affective trust.

Organisations are governed by attitudes, behaviour and the emotional dimensions of work (Hochschild, 1983). As long as individuals stay within the boundaries of appropriate behaviour they will experience psychological safety at work (Kahn, 1990). Group norms refer to the informal rules groups accept to regulate group members' behaviours (Feldman, 1984). Norms are enforced if: (a) they facilitate the survival of a group; (b) make group member behaviour more predictable; (c) assist the group to avoid embarrassing interpersonal problems and (d) express the central values of the group (Kahn, 1990). If employees feel they must follow the group norms, it would lead to feelings of less psychological safety than when they feel they are allowed more flexibility in their behaviour.

Psychological availability

Psychological availability can be defined as the sense of having the physical, emotional or psychological resources to engage at a particular moment. It indicates whether the individual is ready or confident to engage in his/her work role given the fact that people are also engaged in many other life activities. Factors such as the individual's resources or work role insecurities might influence an individual's beliefs, which might have a direct influence on his/her psychological availability.

When engaging themselves at work, individuals depend on their specific physical, emotional and cognitive resources to complete work-related tasks. Different jobs require various and different kinds of physically exertion and challenges, which can result in injuries (May et al, 2004). Less physically challenging jobs, like sitting at a desk, can also put tremendous stress on an individual's back (Hollenbeck, Ilgen and Crampton, 1992). Individuals vary in their stamina, flexibility and strength to successfully meet these physical challenges. Lacking these physical resources can lead to disengagement from one's work role. Emotional demands, especially in the services sector, require emotional labour (Hochschild, 1983; Sutton, 1991).

Morris and Feldman (1996) state that continuous emotional demands could lead to the depletion of emotional resources (ie, exhaustion) and they continue by indicating that the frequency, duration, intensity and variety can decrease these resources. The consequences are that these individuals become overwhelmed by the amounts of information they need to process and as a result their ability to think clearly diminishes. The expectation is that the presence of resources (physical, emotional and cognitive) would lead to greater availability and engagement. Those individuals who experience an overload tend to withdraw or disengage from their work in order to replenish their energy levels (Ganster and Schaubroeck, 1991). When employees receive physical, emotional and cognitive resources from their organisation, they feel obliged to repay the organisation with greater levels of engagement (Saks, 2006).

Self-consciousness has an influence on an employee's feeling of work role security, by distracting them to focus on external rather than internal cues. Employees' psychological availability may suffer when they feel insecure and preoccupied with the impression they leave on others. May et al (2004) found that self-consciousness is a negative predictor of psychological safety.

The Job Demands-Resources (JD-R) model (Demerouti, Bakker, Nachreiner and Schaufeli, 2001) could also be used to explain psychological availability. According to the JD-R model, every occupation has specific work characteristics associated with well-being. It is possible to model these characteristics in two broad categories, namely *job demands* and *job resources.*

Job demands represent aspects of the job that could potentially cause strain in cases where they exceed the employee's adaptive capability. More specifically, job demands refer to physical, social or organisational aspects of a job that require sustained physical and/or psychological effort on the part of the employee and that are therefore associated with certain physiological and/or psychological costs. According to the JD-R model, demanding characteristics of the working environment, work pressure, overload, emotional demands and poor environmental conditions may lead to the impairment of health and ultimately to absenteeism.

Job resources refer to those physical, psychological, social or organisational aspects of the job that: (a) reduce job demands and the associated physiological and psychological costs, (b) are functional in achieving work goals and/or (c) stimulate personal growth, learning and development. Thus, resources are not only necessary to deal with job demands, but also are important in their own right. Resources may be placed at the level of the organisation (eg, salary, career opportunities, job security), at the level of interpersonal and social relations (eg, supervisor and co-worker support, team climate), at the level of the organisation of work (eg, role clarity, participation in decision-making) and at the level of the task (eg, performance feedback, skill variety, task significance, task identity, autonomy).

Work engagement is positively associated with job resources; that is with those aspects of the job that have the capacity to reduce job demands, are functional in achieving work goals and may stimulate personal growth, learning and development. Work engagement is positively related to social support from co-workers and superiors, performance feedback, coaching, job control, task variety and training facilities (Rothmann, Steyn and Mostert, 2005). Hence, the more job resources that are available, the more likely that employees feel engaged. These results on the positive relationship between job resources and work engagement are in line with the Job Characteristics Theory (Hackman and Oldham, 1980). This theory assumes that particular job characteristics such as skill variety, autonomy and feedback contribute to intrinsic motivation (which is close to work engagement).

Job burnout, occupational stress and work engagement

A common conception exists that occupational stress and burnout impede happiness at work. Given that engaging in work is an important component of happiness, a way to increase work engagement would be to reduce stress and burnout levels (Schiffrin and Nelson, 2010).

Definition and dimensions of job burnout

Herbert Freudenberger (1974) introduced the term 'burnout' in the mid-1970s. He used it to describe the symptoms of emotional depletion and a loss of motivation and commitment amongst volunteers with whom he was working in an alternative care setting. The concept of burnout was initially linked to human services where 'people' work of some kind is done (Maslach and Jackson, 1986). However, since the late nineties researchers acknowledged that individuals in any kind of job can develop burnout (Schaufeli, 2003).

Burnout is defined as 'a persistent, negative, work-related state of mind in "normal" individuals that is primarily characterised by exhaustion, which is accompanied by distress, a sense of reduced effectiveness, decreased motivation and the development of dysfunctional attitudes and behaviours at work' (Schaufeli and Enzmann, 1998: 36). *Exhaustion* is a core indicator of burnout and a *sense of reduced effectiveness* as an accompanying symptom, but it has three additional general symptoms, namely distress (affective, cognitive, physical and behavioural), decreased motivation and dysfunctional attitudes and behaviours at work.

According to Schaufeli (2003), burnout consists of three interrelated but conceptually distinct characteristics, namely *exhaustion, mental distance* (cynicism and/or depersonalisation) and *low professional efficacy*:

◆ *Exhaustion* describes a reduction in the emotional resources of an individual. When asked how they feel, burned-out employees typically answer that they feel drained or used up and physically fatigued.
◆ *Mental distance* refers to the interpersonal dimension of burnout and is a negative, callous or detached response to various aspects of the job (cynicism) and/or cynical and insensitive attitudes towards work, colleagues, clients and/ or patients.
◆ *Low professional efficacy* refers to a feeling of being unable to meet clients' needs and to satisfy essential elements of job performance.

Exhaustion and mental distance (cynicism and depersonalisation) constitute the two key aspects of burnout. Exhaustion refers to an incapability to perform because of drained energy, whereas mental distance indicates that the employee is no longer willing to perform because of an increased intolerance of any effort. Mental distancing or psychological withdrawal from the task can be seen as an adaptive mechanism to cope with excessive job demands and resultant feelings of exhaustion. However, when this coping strategy becomes a habitual pattern, as in cynicism or depersonalisation, the person becomes dysfunctional because it disrupts adequate task performance.

Manifestation of burnout

It is estimated that about 4 per cent to 7 per cent of the working population suffers from severe or clinical burnout. Research in the Netherlands showed that 9.7 per cent and 13.9 per cent of the same representative sample of Dutch primary and secondary school teachers suffered from severe burnout in 1996 and in 1997 respectively (Taris, Schaufeli, Schreurs and Caljé, 2000). Two-thirds of the teachers were burned-out at both occasions, whereas only one-third recovered within one year, which illustrates the chronic nature of burnout. Bakker, Schaufeli and Van Dierendonck (2001) summarised the prevalence of burnout in several representative Dutch occupational samples:

◆ Volunteers, who care around the clock for their mentally disturbed relatives, family members or friends — 13.9 per cent
◆ Occupational physicians — 11.3 per cent
◆ General practitioners — 8.2 per cent
◆ Community nurses — 7.8 per cent
◆ Physiotherapists — 5.4 per cent
◆ Dentists — 4.7 per cent
◆ Oncology nurses — 1.7 per cent

Schaufeli and Enzmann (1998) found that physicians and nurses experience about the same level of exhaustion, but physicians have much higher scores on depersonalisation, whereas nurses experience a strongly reduced sense of personal accomplishment. Furthermore, teachers experience high levels of emotional exhaustion, while police officers also experience high levels of depersonalisation.

Table 7.3 shows the burnout levels (expressed as sten scores) in different occupations in South Africa (Rothmann, 2005).

Table 7.3 *Burnout in different occupations in South Africa*

Occupation	Sten	Occupation	Sten
Emergency health technicians	7.46	Secondary school educators	6.92
Call centre operators	6.89	Employees in the insurance industry	6.50
Production supervisors	6.18	Higher education educators	5.93
Pharmacists	5.91	Correctional officers	5.80
Specialists in the petrochemical industry	5.76	Primary school educators	5.68
Insurance workers	5.68	Professional nurses	5.58
Support staff in higher education institutions	5.55	Police officers	5.31
Non-professional counsellors	4.29	Train drivers	4.20

Interpretation of sten scores: 1 = low and 10 = high   Average = 5.5

Table 7.3 shows that the highest scores on burnout were obtained by emergency health technicians, secondary school educators, call centre operators, employees in the insurance industry, production supervisors, higher education educators and pharmacists. The lowest scores on burnout were obtained by non-professional counsellors (volunteers) and train drivers.

Factors associated with job burnout

Job burnout is observed more often among *younger employees* compared with those older than thirty or forty years. Furthermore, burnout is negatively related to work experience. The greater incidence of burnout in younger and less experienced employees is attributed to a reality shock and an identity crisis due to unsuccessful occupational socialisation. Although research has shown that burnout symptoms decline with growing age or work experience, Schaufeli and Enzmann (1998) warn that a selection effect ('survival' bias) might explain the decline of burnout symptoms: 'those who burn out early in their careers are likely to quit their jobs, leaving behind the survivors who exhibit low levels of burnout'.

Women tend to score higher on exhaustion, whereas men score higher on distancing. This can partly be explained by sex role-dependent stereotypes. For example, men hold instrumental attitudes, whereas women are more emotionally responsive and seem to disclose emotions and health problems more easily. Furthermore, due to additional responsibilities at home, working women experience higher workloads compared with men (Schaufeli and Enzmann, 1998).

Unmarried people (especially men) seem to be more prone to burnout compared with those who are married. However, it is possible that age or psychosocial problems may influence this proneness. Individuals with a higher level of education were more prone to burnout than less educated employees. This could be attributed to the higher expectations of the more educated individuals. Another explanation might be that the more highly educated individuals (compared with less educated individuals) more often gain positions with more responsibility (Schaufeli and Enzmann, 1998).

Concerning job-specific factors, burnout can be explained in terms of social exchanges which take place (Schaufeli, 2003). If an individual experiences high demands (eg, emotional load) but lacks resources, burnout could develop. This is especially true if the individual experiences a lack of reciprocity from recipients and/or the organisation. Table 7.4 on the next page shows the job-specific factors which are related to burnout.

Table 7.4 *Job-specific factors and burnout*

Factor	Strength of relationship
Work overload	+++
Time pressure	+++
Number of work hours	+
Direct contact with clients	++
Role conflict	++
Lack of social support	++
Lack of autonomy	+
Lack of participation in decision-making	++
Lack of feedback	+

+ Moderate relationship ++ Strong relationship +++ Very strong relationship

Burnout is not a response to tedious, boring or monotonous work. Chronic exhaustion can lead people to *distance* themselves emotionally and cognitively from their work, so that they are less involved with or responsive to the needs of other people or the demands of the task. A work situation with chronic, overwhelming demands that contribute to exhaustion or cynicism is likely to erode an individual's *sense of accomplishment* or effectiveness. Also, it is difficult to gain a sense of accomplishment when feeling exhausted or when helping people toward whom the individual is hostile. In some situations, the lack of efficacy seems to arise more clearly from a lack of relevant resources, while exhaustion and cynicism appear from the presence of work overload and social conflict.

Occupational stress and burnout

Burnout can be considered as a particular kind of prolonged job stress. An individual experiences job stress when the demands of the workplace exceed his/her adaptive responses. Burnout is seen as the final step in a progression of unsuccessful attempts to cope with a variety of negative stress conditions. *Occupational stress* is considered to be the product of an imbalance between environmental demands and individual capabilities (Lazarus and Folkman, 1984). The term *'stress'* describes either the external stimulus from the environment or the response of the individual or sometimes both meanings simultaneously. *Stressors* refer to characteristics of the *external environment* that cause distress, while *strain* describes any response of the individual to these characteristics (ie, physical and psychological ill-health, job satisfaction and impaired job performance). However, stressors do not inevitably lead to strain — a wide range of individual differences moderate this relationship.

Types of occupational stressors

Cartwright and Cooper (2002) distinguish between *seven occupational stressors,* namely work relationships, work-life imbalance, overload, job insecurity, control, resources and communication, pay and benefits and aspects of the job.

- *Work relationships.* Most jobs demand a great deal of contact with other people at work. Poor or unsupportive relationships with colleagues and/or superiors, isolation (a perceived lack of adequate relationships) and unfair treatment can all be a potential source of stress. Mistrust of colleagues can create role ambiguity, which can lead to psychological strain. Conversely, good relationships can help individuals to cope with stress.
- *Work-life imbalance.* The demands of work have the potential to spill over and interfere with individuals' personal and home lives. This can put a strain on relationships outside work and can impact upon the level of stress.
- *Overload.* When a person is expected to do more than the time available permits him or her to do, such a person is likely to experience strain. It is true that almost everybody experiences role overload from time to time, but for some people role overload is a chronic thing they have to contend with. There are different types of role overload, namely working long hours, meeting deadlines and responding to time pressures, qualitative overload and having many separate, essentially unrelated, tasks to perform.
- *Job insecurity.* Job insecurity is as an overall concern of losing one's job. It is a subjective experience, which might differ from the objective reality. Some employees will feel insecure when there is no objective reason to, while others may feel secure when their jobs are in fact threatened. Furthermore, job insecurity also implies uncertainty about the future. For the person concerned it is uncertain whether he or she will be able to continue working in the organisation. Therefore, job insecurity can be considered a work stressor.
- *Control.* The experience of stress is strongly linked to perceptions of control. Lack of influence in the way in which work is organised and performed can be a potential source of stress. When there is great interdependence between the person's tasks and the tasks of others, the person is likely to experience stress.
- *Resources and communication.* To perform their job effectively, individuals need to feel they have the appropriate training, equipment and resources. They also need to feel that they are adequately informed and that they are valued.
- *Pay and benefits.* The financial rewards that work brings are obviously important because they determine the type of lifestyle that an individual can lead. In addition, they often influence individuals' feelings of self-worth and perception of their value to the organisation.
- *Aspects of the job.* The fundamental nature of the job could cause stress. Factors such as physical working conditions, type of tasks and the amount of satisfaction derived from the job itself are all included.

The results of South African studies regarding these occupational stressors are reported in Table 7.5 (Rothmann, 2005). The scores are compared with an international norm base and are expressed as sten scores.

Table 7.5 *Occupational stressors in South African organisations*

	Correctional officers	Government employees	Insurance staff	Educators in higher education	Educators in primary education	Educators in secondary education
Work relations	7	5	5	5	5	5
Work-life balance	6	5	4	7	5	6
Overload	6	5	5	7	6	7
Job security	6	4	7	5	6	7
Control	7	6	6	6	5	6
Resources	7	6	5	6	5	6
Job aspects	8	5	5	4	6	7
Pay/benefits	5	5	6	6	5	6

Interpretation of sten scores: I = low and I0 = high   Average = 5.5

Table 7.5 shows that the stressors for employees in different occupations in South Africa differ. Job insecurity was the highest stressor for employees in the insurance industry and secondary school educators. For educators in higher education institutions, the highest stressors were work-life balance, overload and pay and benefits. For correctional officers the highest stressors were the nature of the job they are doing, work relations, job control and resources. In secondary schools, the highest stressors were overload, job insecurity and the nature of the job educators are doing.

The *Transactional Process Model* (Lazarus, 1991) and the *Spielberger State-Trait model* of *occupational stress* (Spielberger, Vagg and Wasala, 2003) conceptualise stress as a complex process that consists of three major components, namely (a) sources of stress that are encountered in the work environment, (b) perception and appraisal of a particular stressor by an employee and (c) the stresses that are evoked when a stressor is appraised as threatening. According to Spielberger et al (2003), employees evaluate their work environment in terms of the severity and frequency of occurrence of specific job demands and pressure and the level of support provided by supervisors, co-workers and organisational policies and procedures. Failing to take the frequency of occurrence of a particular stressor into account may contribute to overestimating the effects of highly stressful situations that rarely occur, while underestimating the effects of moderately stressful events that are frequently experienced.

The *stressors* for emergency health technicians, employees in a local government, nurses and police members in South Africa are reported in table 7.6 (Rothmann, 2005).

Table 7.6 *Intensity and frequency of stressors in South African organisations (Note: Higher scores indicate high stress)*

	Call centre staff	City council staff	Technical staff	Pharmacists	Nurses	Emergency health workers	Police officers
Working overtime	16.65	19.43	13.69	**37.01**	19.55	**29.15**	21.62
Lack of advancement	26.76	**29.22**	**32.59**	19.02	13.70	**33.54**	24.59
New or unfamiliar duties	18.43	20.05	19.45	22.11	18.33	**27.08**	18.01
Colleagues not doing their work	**35.88**	26.39	21.32	**40.81**	**31.57**	**39.17**	**34.89**
Lack of supervisor support	24.33	20.51	25.34	23.67	18.75	**31.43**	23.58
Crisis situations	**27.87**	23.18	15.34	**32.91**	27.51	**30.95**	23.41
Lack of recognition	**39.62**	27.09	21.73	26.93	25.64	**35.40**	28.58
Tasks not in job description	**25.64**	27.30	20.4	23.56	22.46	**31.02**	**25.81**
Inadequate equipment	**43.88**	25.88	25.18	23.72	18.43	**36.67**	**33.50**
Increased responsibility	23.31	23.23	21.37	26.77	26.87	27.39	23.32
Periods of inactivity	15.27	11.17	17.18	8.51	10.98	17.99	15.81
Attitudes toward organisation	**30.67**	19.54	11.63	24.61	19.64	**31.23**	23.32
Insufficient staff	28.41	33.19	27.19	**39.42**	**38.36**	**49.12**	30.91
Making critical decisions	21.59	20.76	21.44	28.06	**25.80**	**25.94**	20.28
Insult from customer/colleague	**27.26**	20.60	20.41	17.12	14.33	**26.92**	21.28
Lack of participation	22.36	21.54	19.75	17.42	17.10	**27.45**	20.61
Inadequate salary	**48.64**	31.41	24.94	**40.31**	**42.60**	**41.07**	**34.68**
Competition for advancement	21.16	19.16	27.48	11.57	14.54	23.55	21.41
Poor or inadequate supervision	17.25	16.29	15.40	18.22	15.80	25.73	19.67
Frequent interruptions	27.95	23.42	9.00	**43.90**	27.53	26.57	23.94
Frequent changes	20.81	18.45	16.92	21.98	21.25	25.69	18.98
Excessive paperwork	**33.69**	20.52	23.15	30.91	**41.78**	19.26	29.81
Meeting deadlines	26.28	21.72	**30.06**	26.50	24.88	19.85	22.84
Insufficient personal time	23.12	21.62	16.99	24.01	24.26	26.46	19.56
Covering work for others	24.86	24.85	15.31	**30.24**	23.28	**29.80**	25.88
Poorly motivated co-workers	**35.95**	29.18	25.34	**32.98**	**30.12**	**37.76**	**30.27**

Table 7.6 shows that insufficient staff is the stressor with the highest severity (ie, intensity and frequency) in all four groups that were sampled. Inadequate salary is experienced as a severe stressor by emergency health technicians, employees in a city council and police officers. Another stressor that is experienced as severe is poorly motivated co-workers (or fellow workers not doing their jobs).

Meaning and authentic happiness

Man's main concern is not to gain pleasure or to avoid pain, but rather to see meaning in his life (Viktor Frankl, 1959:115). *Meaning of work* (see also chapter 1) refers to the output of having made sense of something. *Meaningfulness of work* refers to the amount of significance an individual attaches to his/her work (Pratt and Ashforth, 2003).

Chalofsky and Krishna (2009) identified three themes related to the construct of meaningful work, namely sense of self, the work itself and sense of balance. They point out that that these themes represent a deeper level of motivation than traditional intrinsic values such as accomplishment, pride, satisfaction from completing a task and praise of supervisor.

- ◆ *Sense of self.* People need to bring their whole selves to their work. Sometimes they do not bring their whole selves to work because of a fear of rejection, prejudice or misunderstanding. People experience a loss of interconnectedness because they cannot bring their whole selves to work. People need to be assisted to integrate their work and spiritual lives so that the time they spend working is more joyful, balanced, meaningful and spiritually nourishing. Before an individual can bring the whole self to work, he or she must first be aware or his or her own values, beliefs and purpose in life. Sense of self includes constantly striving to reach one's potential and believing in one's ability to reach that potential. One's purpose for work should also be aligned with the purpose in life. One must move from focus on self to focus on and concern for other people. Fulfilment comes from the feeling that you are making a difference for other people. People who move beyond self-actualisation are involved in a calling.
- ◆ *The work itself.* In the past managers made decisions about the structure and process of work activities in the name of efficiency. Organisations now realise that they need to rely more on workers to make decisions about how the work should be accomplished. This requires more worker autonomy, flexibility, empowerment, continuous learning, risk-taking and creativity. An individual wants to carry out his or her life purpose through the work itself. It is not about productivity, it is about working and growing as a never-ending process.
- ◆ *Sense of balance.* The sense of balance concerns choices individuals make between the time spent at paid work, unpaid work and at pleasurable pursuits such that no area of our lives is so dominant that we cease to value the other areas. Too much work and no play is stressful, while too much play and no work is boring. Meaningful work is not just about the meaning of paid work that we perform; it is the alignment of purpose, values, relationships and activities that we pursue in our lives.

Sources of meaning in work include the self, other persons, the work context, as well as God and the spiritual life. The self refers to the totality of a person's thought and feelings about himself/herself. Individuals' values, motivations and beliefs influence their perceptions of meaning of work.

Values are the products of cultural, institutional and personal forces acting upon an individual. Work values are end states people desire and they feel they ought to be able to realise through working. As discussed in chapter 1, individuals may self-select into occupations that align with their personal values and experiences of work may reinforce those values. Internal work *motivation* is linked to meaning of work. Experienced meaningfulness is a critical psychological state necessary to the development of internal work motivation (Hackman and Oldham, 1980).

Experienced meaningfulness also results from expected congruence between one's self-concept and a particular environment or activity which results in intrinsic motivation (Deci and Ryan, 2008). Beliefs about the role or function of work in life can shape the meaning of work; in this regard the work orientation, ie, work as a job, career or calling (Wrzesniewski, McCauley, Rozin and Schwartz, 1997; Wrzesniewski and Tosti, 2005).

- *Job orientation.* Individuals who have a job orientation are only interested in the material benefits from work and do not seek or receive any other type of reward from it. The work is not an end in itself, but instead is a means that allows individuals to acquire the resources needed to enjoy their time away from the job. The major interests and ambitions of job holders are not expressed through their work.
- *Career orientation.* Individuals who have a career orientation have a deeper personal investment in their work and mark their achievements not only through monetary gain, but through advancement within the occupational structure. This advancement brings higher social standing, increased power within the scope of one's occupation and higher self-esteem for the employee.
- *Calling orientation.* Individuals with a calling orientation find that their work is inseparable from their life. They are working for the fulfilment that the work brings. The word 'calling' was initially used in a religious context (called by God to do morally or socially significant work). A calling implies that people see their work as socially valuable, involving activities that may, need not be, pleasurable.

In a South African study, Van Zyl, Deacon and Rothmann (2010) found that the calling orientation to work predicted both psychological meaningfulness and work engagement of industrial psychologists. Work orientation predicted work-role fit, which in turn predicted psychological meaningfulness. Work-role fit partially mediated the relationship between a calling orientation and work engagement.

Mechanisms through which work can become meaningful include authenticity (ie, the alignment between one behaviour and perceptions of the true self), self-efficacy (ie, individuals' beliefs that they have the autonomy, competence and perceived impact to produce intended effect or to make a difference), self-esteem (ie, an individual's assessment of his own self-worth), purpose (ie, a sense of directedness and intentionality in life), belongingness (ie, a pervasive drive to form and maintain at least a minimum quantity of lasting, positive and significant interpersonal relationships) and transcendence (ie, connecting the ego to an entity greater than the self or beyond the material world).

Individual factors and authentic happiness

Individual factors could affect how employees deal with issues during their careers. According to Nelson and Simmons (2003) there is benefit in identifying those *individual differences* that would promote well-being through their role in more positive appraisals of demands. Alternatively, these characteristics could work to arm individuals with the belief that they are equipped to handle a demand. These factors include, amongst others, personality traits, a sense of coherence, self-efficacy, optimism and coping strategies.

Personality traits

Over the past 30 years, research has converged on the existence of five major dimensions of personality, the so-called big five, namely *neuroticism, extraversion, openness to experience, agreeableness* and *conscientiousness* (Costa and McCrae, 1985). Individuals high on *neuroticism* are characterised by a tendency to experience negative emotions such as anxiety, depression or sadness, hostility and self-consciousness, as well as a tendency to be impulsive. Those high on *extraversion* tend to experience positive emotions and to be warm, gregarious, fun-loving and assertive.

People high on *openness to experience* are inclined to be curious, imaginative, empathetic, creative, original, artistic, psychologically-minded, aesthetically responsive and flexible. *Agreeableness* reflects a proclivity to be good-natured, acquiescent, courteous, helpful, flexible, co-operative, tolerant, forgiving, soft-hearted and trusting. Those high on *conscientiousness* have been characterised as having a tendency to be habitually careful, reliable, hard-working, well-organised and purposeful.

In the United States of America, Barrick and Mount (1991) found that conscientiousness is a valid predictor of job performance across occupations and across criteria and that the other personality factors only generalise their validity for some occupations and some criteria. Barrick and Mount found that extraversion is a valid predictor for managers; emotional stability is a valid predictor for police; and agreeableness is a valid predictor for police and managers. Extraversion is a valid predictor of training proficiency, as are emotional stability, agreeableness and openness to experience.

In a meta-analytic study in South Africa, Rothmann, Meiring, Van der Walt and Barrick (2002) found that extraversion, emotional stability and conscientiousness were valid predictors of job performance, although the obtained relationships were moderated by the level of education of employees.

Regarding the relationship between big five personality dimensions and *burnout*, Mills and Huebner (1998) found that exhaustion correlated significantly with neuroticism, extraversion, agreeableness and conscientiousness, mental distance was related to neuroticism and agreeableness, while reduced professional efficacy was related to neuroticism and extraversion. In a study among nurses working in a hospital, Zellars, Perrewe and Hochwarter (2000) found that only neuroticism significantly predicted levels of exhaustion. Nurses higher in extraversion and agreeableness reported lower levels of mental distance. Openness also negatively predicted mental distance, although this relationship was only marginally significant. A meta-analytic study summarising 12 studies on burnout and anxiety showed that this trait correlates most highly with exhaustion (shared variance 23 per cent), followed by depersonalisation (17 per cent shared variance) (Schaufeli and Enzmann, 1998).

Table 7.7 shows the personality traits that were found to predict burnout and work engagement of police officers in South Africa ($N = 1794$).

Table 7.7 *Personality traits predicting burnout and work engagement of police officers*

Personality trait	Exhaustion	Cynicism	Professional efficacy	Work engagement
Conscientiousness		X	X	X
Neuroticism	X	X	X	X
Agreeableness				X
Openness				X

Table 7.7 shows that two personality traits (namely low emotional stability and low conscientiousness) predicted burnout. Conscientiousness, emotional stability, agreeableness and extraversion predicted work engagement (Mostert and Rothmann, 2006). Pienaar, Rothmann and Van de Vijver (2007) showed that suicide ideation is predicted by two personality dimensions (ie, low emotional stability and low conscientiousness).

Sense of coherence

Sense of coherence is defined as

a global orientation that expresses the extent to which one has a pervasive, enduring though dynamic feeling of confidence that (1) the stimuli deriving from one's internal and external environments in the course of living are structured, predictable and explicable, (2) the resources are available to one to meet the demands posed by these stimuli and (3) these demands are challenges, worthy of investment and engagement (Antonovsky, 1991).

The definition of sense of coherence includes *three dimensions* which represent the concept, that is, comprehensibility, manageability and meaningfulness:

◆   *Comprehensibility* refers to the extent to which one perceives stimuli from the internal and external environment as information that is ordered, structured and consistent. The stimuli are perceived as comprehensible and make sense on a cognitive level.

◆ *Manageability* refers to the extent to which individuals experience events in life as situations that are endurable or manageable and can even be seen as new challenges.

◆ *Meaningfulness* refers to the extent to which one feels that life is making sense on an emotional level.

A strong sense of coherence is strongly related to feelings of competence, general well-being, job satisfaction, work engagement and life satisfaction. A weak sense of coherence is strongly related to burnout (Rothmann, 2001; Van der Colff and Rothmann, 2009).

Table 7.8 shows the differences in perceptions of helping and restraining factors at work between employees with a weak and strong sense of coherence (Muller and Rothmann. 2009).

Table 7.8 *Perceptions of helping and restraining factors of employees with strong and weak sense of coherence* (rank 1 = highest frequency; rank 10 = lowest frequency)

	Strong sense of coherence	Weak sense of coherence
Helping Factors	**Rank**	**Rank**
1. Having a challenging job	1	7
2. Being satisfied and passionate about job	2	-
3. Colleagues' support and co-operation	3	10
4. Reaching goals and being performance-driven	4	3
5. Obtaining knowledge — continued training and development	5	6
6. Being able to render support to others and delivering a high-quality service	6	-
7. Managerial style and skills	7	-
8. Relationships among colleagues, management and workers	8	8
9. Monetary reward (monthly salary)	9	1
10. Being self-driven/self-motivated	10	9
11. Gratitude; being thankful for having a job	-	4
12. Good team work among colleagues	-	5
13. Receiving support and motivation from management	-	2
Restraining Factors		
1. Work overload and long working hours	1	2
2. Workforce being unskilled and having no knowledge of product selling	2	9
3. Monetary reward (salary) insufficient	3	1
4. Managerial style being autocratic	4	4
5. Unnecessary administrative tasks and meetings	5	-

	Strong sense of coherence	Weak sense of coherence
Restraining Factors	**Rank**	**Rank**
6. Company bureaucracy/red tape/company culture	6	-
7. No training, exposure or possible career progression	7	7
8. No recognition and appreciation from management, colleagues and clients	8	5
9. Mistrust among colleagues	9	8
10. No assistance and support from management and colleagues	10	-
11. Quality relationship between management and workers and among colleagues	-	3
12. Stress and pressure in the workplace	-	6
13. Experiencing uncertainty regarding the future of the company	-	10

The helping factors most frequently reported by employees with a strong sense of coherence concerned a challenging and satisfying job they are passionate about. It seems that factors intrinsic to the job were most frequently listed by employees with a strong sense of coherence. In contrast, employees with a weak sense of coherence most frequently reported factors extrinsic to the job as helping factors for them, including monetary rewards and the relationship with managers. Employees with a strong sense of coherence might perceive unnecessary administrative tasks, bureaucracy and red tape as withholding them from maintaining coherence. In contrast, employees with a weak sense of coherence report that they are restrained by the relationships in the organisation, stress and pressure and uncertainty with regard to the future of the organisation.

Self-efficacy

Self-efficacy refers to 'beliefs in one's capabilities to mobilise the motivation, cognitive resources and courses of action needed to meet given organisational demands' (Wood and Bandura, 1989:408). Self-efficacy is a belief in the probability that one can successfully execute some future action or task to achieve some result. Self-efficacy can be viewed from both a specific and a general angle. *Task-specific self-efficacy* is a state-based expectation or judgement about the likelihood of successful task performance measured immediately before any effort is expended on the task. It is a powerful motivator of behaviour because efficacy expectations determine the initial decision to perform a task, the effort expended and the level of persistence that emerges in the face of adversity (see also chapter 3).

Self-efficacy can also be viewed as a *general, stable cognition* (trait) that individuals hold and carry with them. It reflects the expectation that they possess the ability to perform tasks successfully in a variety of achievement situations (Judge, Locke, Durham and Kluger, 1998). People with a strongly developed self-efficacy are therefore less susceptible to stress and consequently to burnout (Rothmann and Malan, 2003).

As a dimension of psychological empowerment self-efficacy indicates that individuals believe that they have the skills and abilities necessary to perform their work well (Mishra and Spreitzer, 1998). Feeling competent and confident with respect to valued goals is associated with enhanced intrinsic motivation and work engagement (Stander and Rothmann, 2010).

Optimism

As an individual difference variable, optimism has been associated with good mood, perseverance and health. Nelson and Simmons (2003) distinguish between two conceptualisations of optimism, namely dispositional optimism (Carver and Scheier, 2002) and learned optimism (Seligman, 2002). *Dispositional optimism* is defined as a global expectation that good things will be plentiful in the future and that bad things will be scarce. *Learned optimism* relates to an optimistic explanatory style.

Based on the analyses of various studies by Wrosch and Scheier (2003) the pathway through which optimism could affect the well-being of employees can be described as follows: Optimists use different strategies to manage critical life situations than pessimists do. Individuals who are confident about their future exert continuing effort, even when dealing with adversity, whereas those who are pessimistic about their future try to distance themselves from adversity. Optimists engage actively in the processes of goal attainment and/or reappraise situations in a positive way if an important goal is blocked. Furthermore, optimism/pessimism indirectly affects distress and psychological well-being through its effect on coping strategies. Optimists (in contrast with pessimists) use problem-focused coping strategies and if problem-focused coping is not possible, they use adaptive emotion-focused coping strategies.

There is evidence that optimism and pessimism have opposite effects on well-being. If individuals expect positive outcomes, they will work harder for the goals that they have set, whereas those who expect failures will disengage from the goals that have been set. Higher optimism and lower pessimism were shown to be negatively related to burnout (Riolli and Savicki, 2003) and positively related to work engagement (Xanthopoulou, Bakker, Demerouti and Schaufeli, 2009). However, there is also evidence that optimism can moderate the effects of a stressor on well-being among depressed patients (eg, De Graaf, Hollon and Huibers, 2010). Optimism is a potential moderator of the relationship between job stressors and psychological strain. Atienza, Stephens and Townsend (2002) found that optimism moderated the effects of stress on depressive symptoms and life satisfaction.

Coping

Coping represent the efforts, both behavioural and cognitive, that people invest in order to deal with stressful encounters (Lazarus and Folkman, 1984). Coping has been differentially conceived in several ways (Livneh, Antonak and Gerhardt, 2000): (a) both as personality trait and situational determined response; (b) as a dynamic process and a static construct; (c) as a strategy which is mature, adaptive and flexible, but also as a reaction, which is neurotic, maladaptive and rigid; and (d) as a global, generally dichotomous concept, but also an intricate, hierarchically structured, multilevel concept.

According to Carver, Scheier and Weintraub (1989) stress consists of three processes, namely primary appraisal, secondary appraisal and coping. Primary appraisal is the process of perceiving a threat to the self. Secondary appraisal is bringing to mind a potential response to the threat. Coping is the process of executing the response. Folkman and Lazarus (1980) suggested two general types of coping. The first is problem-focused coping: the person finds a method for resolving stress at its source (ie, tries to stop whatever was posing the harm or threat from occurring). The second is emotion-focused coping: the person feels that the source of the stress must somehow be tolerated and he/she endeavours to manage or lessen the emotional discomfort associated with the situation. Emotion-focused coping places its emphasis on interpretation of the situation or how the individual attend to it.

Literature on coping often makes an additional distinction between active and avoidant coping strategies. Active coping strategies are either behavioural or psychological responses designed to change the nature of the stressor itself or how one thinks about it, whereas avoidant coping strategies lead people into activities (such as alcohol use) or mental states (such as withdrawal) that keep them from directly addressing stressful events. Generally speaking, active coping strategies, whether behavioural or emotional, are regarded as better ways to deal with stressful events and avoidant coping strategies appear to be a psychological risk factor or marker for adverse responses to stressful life events (Holahan and Moos, 1986).

Avoidant coping strategies are sometimes viewed as less adaptive methods of coping. Denial (pretending the stressor is not present or that it is not causing any significant distress), mental disengagement (distracting oneself from thinking about the goal with which the stressor is interfering) and behavioural disengagement (giving up on the goals with which the stressor is interfering) are examples of avoidant coping strategies. Endler and Parker (1990) also refer to avoidance as a third basic strategy that may be used in coping with stress. Avoidance can include either person-oriented or task-oriented strategies. Avoidance differs from problem– and emotion-focused coping in that avoiding a situation actually removes the person from the stressful situation, whereas problem– and emotion-focused coping might help the person manage the stressful situation while he/she remains in it (Kowalski and Crocker, 2001).

Storm and Rothmann (2003) found that *active coping strategies* were associated with Emotional Stability, Extraversion, Openness to Experience and Conscientiousness, while *passive coping strategies* were associated with Neuroticism, low Agreeableness and low Conscientiousness. In turn, these personality traits were associated with lower emotional exhaustion and depersonalisation and higher personal accomplishment. Constructive coping strategies were associated with personal accomplishment. Two approach coping strategies play an important role in engaging at work, namely problem-focused coping and positive reinterpretation and growth.

Table 7.9 *Individual factors associated with career well-being*

Personality variables	Career well-being
Big Five Personality Traits: Neuroticism, Extraversion, Openness to Experience, Agreeableness and Conscientiousness	Predictors of job performance correlates with experiences of job burnout. *Active coping strategies* are associated with emotional stability, *Extraversion, Openness to Experience* and *Conscientiousness*, while passive coping strategies are associated with *Neuroticism, low Agreeableness* and *low Conscientiousness.*
Sense of coherence	Individuals with a strong sense of coherence are able to make cognitive sense of the workplace and experience their work as consisting of experiences that are bearable, with which they can cope and as challenges that they can meet.
Self-efficacy	Inefficacious thoughts could cause distress and depression, leading to reduced levels of satisfaction. High self-efficacy includes repeated success at a specific task, the accumulation of successful experiences leading to positive self-images.
Optimism	Optimists tend to approach challenges with confidence and persistence, while pessimists are doubtful and hesitant. Optimists assume they can handle adversity successfully. They experience less distress than pessimists who typically anticipate disaster.
Coping	*Problem-focused coping* is directed at managing and improving an unpleasant experience or reducing the effects thereof. *Emotion-focused coping* is directed at reducing the effects of stressful feelings caused by an unpleasant experience through relaxation, the use of alcohol and drugs, social activities and/or defence mechanisms.

Outcomes of well-being at work

Employee happiness (defined as frequent experiences of positive emotions) is related to workplace success. According to Boehm and Lyubomirsky (2008), happiness leads to success through the experience of positive affect. Although the exact mechanism is unclear, the following pathway is likely: Positive emotions are associated with *approach-*

oriented behaviour. People in good moods are more likely to enter novel situations, interact with other people and pursue new goals. According to Fredrickson (1998), a safe and comfortable environment allows a person to 'broaden and build' resources, which can be called on in later times of need. Armed with these resources and primed to pursue new goals, people who experience positive affect are well-suited to experience career success.

The following evidence from cross-sectional studies exists that happy people engage in successful behaviours and are accomplished in the workplace (Boehm and Lyubomirsky, 2008; Seligman, 2008):

◆ Employees with high positive affect have jobs characterised by variety, meaningfulness and autonomy. These qualities may be associated with workplace success because they make a job more pleasant and may buffer against burnout.

◆ Happy people are more satisfied with their jobs compared with unhappy people. Positive affect is also a good predictor of job performance. Happy people are also judged to perform better by their supervisors.

◆ Happy employees perform relatively better on objective work-related tasks. Brief raising of positive mood enhances creative thinking and makes positive physicians more accurate and faster to come up with proper liver diagnosis. Furthermore, it has been found that insurance agents with a positive disposition have been found to sell more insurance policies than their less positive counterparts.

◆ The presence of positive affect predicts behaviour that extends beyond a job description, but that benefits other individuals or the organisation itself. Such behaviour has been called organisational citizenship behaviour. Happy people are more likely to help fellow workers and customers than unhappy people.

◆ Happy people (compared with unhappy people) are more sociable and energetic, are more charitable and co-operative, have richer networks of friends and social support, are more flexible and ingenious in their thinking and are more resilient in the face of hardship.

◆ Compared with unhappy people, happy people have stronger immune systems and live longer. It was found that positive emotion could prevent the onset of common cold. Furthermore, among 96 men who had their first heart attack, 15 of the 16 most pessimistic died of cardiovascular disease over the next decade, while only five of the 16 most optimistic died.

◆ Happy people are more involved in their work than unhappy people. Withdrawal behaviour (eg, burnout, absenteeism and turnover) are negatively related to positive affect. Therefore, happy people (compared to unhappy people) show less burnout, less absenteeism and are less likely to quit their jobs. Individuals with high positive affect (compared to those with low positive affect) cope better with organisational change and are also more committed to their organisations.

◆ In business meetings a ratio of greater than 2.9:1 for positive to negative statements predicts economic flourishing.

◆ Managers with a positive mood (compared with those with a less positive mood) at work receive more rewards from their supervisors. A small positive relationship also exists between happiness and income. People who experience positive emotions receive more social support from both colleagues and supervisors compared with those who experience less positive emotions.

Research shows that engagement (a component of happiness) has the following benefits:

◆ Highly engaged employees outperform their disengaged colleagues by 20 per cent to 28 per cent. There are also costs associated with a disengaged workforce. In one 2003 study with low levels of employee engagement it was found that their net profit fell by 1.38 per cent and operating margin fell by 2.01 per cent over a three-year period. Conversely, companies with high levels of engagement found that their operating margins rose by 3.74 per cent over a three-year period.

◆ Engagement predicts positive organisational outcomes (eg, productivity, job satisfaction, motivation, commitment, low turnover intention, customer satisfaction, return on assets, profits and shareholder value). Engaged employees are more productive than disengaged employees. Disengaged employees produced 28 per cent less revenue than their engaged colleagues.

◆ Engagement fuels discretionary efforts and concerns for quality. A 10 per cent improvement in commitment leads to 6 per cent improvement in discretionary effort and 2 per cent improvement in performance.

◆ Engagement affects the mindset of employees (84 per cent of engaged employees believe that they can positively impact the quality of their organisation's products; 72 per cent believe that they can positively affect customer service; 68 per cent believe that they can positively impact costs in their job).

◆ Disengagement may result in turnover: turnover of employees is costly (more than 75 per cent of an employee's annual salary).

◆ The experiencing of high levels of stress may lead to feelings of anger, anxiety, depression, nervousness, irritability, tension and boredom. This may lead to lower job performance, lower self-esteem, resentment of supervision, inability to concentrate and make decisions and job dissatisfaction. Behaviours which are directly related to job stress include the following: under-eating or over-eating, sleeplessness, increased smoking and alcohol and drug abuse. Occupational stress also results in absenteeism and labour turnover.

Table 7.10 shows the effects of occupational stressors on physical ill health, psychological un-well-being and organisational commitment in a sample of 4 737 employees in South African organisations (Rothmann, 2005).

Table 7.10 *Outcomes of occupational stress in South African organisations*

Stressor	Physical ill-health	Psychological well-being	Organisational commitment
Work relations	X	X	X
Work-life balance	X	X	
Overload	X	X	
Job insecurity	X	X	
Control		X	X
Resources			X
Aspects of the job	X	X	X
Pay and benefits			X
Percentage of variance explained	14 per cent	25 per cent	21 per cent

Table 7.10 shows that stress because of work relations, work-life balance, overload, job insecurity and aspects of the job predicted 14 per cent of the variance in physical ill-health. Stress because of work relations, work-life balance, overload, job insecurity, job control and aspects of the job predicted 25 per cent of the variance in psychological (un)well-being. Stress because of work relations, job control, resources, aspects of the job and pay and benefits predicted 21 per cent of the variance in individuals' commitment to their organisation.

Authentic happiness interventions

Authentic happiness (subjective well-being, engagement and meaning) could be addressed through organisational and individual interventions.

Organisational interventions

One way to address the well-being and authentic happiness of employees is to change the situation. The following organisational interventions could be considered (Rothmann and Cilliers, 2007; Schaufeli and Bakker, 2004; Swindall, 2007).

Assessment and evaluation of employees

The ultimate purpose of assessment and evaluation of individuals is to have the right person in the right job. This means that the optimal fit must exist between the values and goals of the employee and those of the organisation. A psychological contract, which reflects an optimal fit between the employee and organisation in terms of mutual expectations should be formed. The psychological contract can be drafted by (a) assessing the employee's values, preferences and personal and professional goals; (b) negotiating and drafting of a written contract that acknowledges these goals and provides the necessary resources to be supplemented by the organisation (eg, training, coaching, equipment and budget); (c) monitoring this written agreement in terms of goal achievement, including the readjustment of goals and the provision of additional resources. A process of goal setting, which might be integrated into existing systems of performance appraisal and evaluation could be used. The focus should be on personal goals (eg, development of skills and competences, promotion, mastery of particular tasks or duties) and the necessary resources to achieve these personal goals.

Coaching programme for newcomers

The first day at an organisation is a key factor in determining the level of employee engagement in the years ahead; what happens as a newcomer is critical. The coach, who is someone in the work group of the new employee, spends time with the new employee on his or her first day and then on a weekly basis over the next several weeks.

Career conversations

A formal career conversation programme ensures that managers sit down with each of their direct reports on an annual basis to discuss their career advancement and career plans. These discussions can focus and inspire employees and managers can also spot employees whose work-role fit is problematic.

Participation in large group meetings

The level of engagement increases when employees representing all parts of an organisation gather together to give input to the organisation, These meetings can be used to review a vision, plan for the future, review progress to date or introduce a new programme such as an employee engagement initiative. This is a good way to reach all employees when there is an important message or a shift in direction. When employees participate in making decisions, they feel more engaged in the organisation. Decision-making needs to be pushed down to the lowest possible level.

Job redesign and work changes

The redesigning of jobs could reduce the exposure to psychosocial risks and could increase employee engagement. A meaningful job helps employees remain dedicated. It has several characteristics. Firstly, it must make a significant impact, eg, in other people's lives. However, the individual must be able to see the significant impact of the job. Secondly, the job should provide intellectual challenge. Thirdly, the job must provide scope to experience change to prevent boredom. Fourthly, the individual should be able to cultivate his or her special interests in the job.

Many *preventive organisational-based strategies* exist to tackle high job demands, such as job redesign, flexible work schedules and goal setting. Increasing job resources (eg, through participative management, increasing social support and team building) on the other hand, would eventually lead to more engagement at the job, but its direct effect on burnout is small. Hence, to prevent burnout, *decreasing job demands* is to be preferred above increasing job resources (Schaufeli and Enzmann, 1998). Burnout and strain could be decreased by reducing the exposure to stressors such as work overload, role problems and conflicts. In addition, lacking job resources such as job control and support from co-workers and supervisors should be supplemented. Engagement could be stimulated by increasing resources to reach the organisational objectives and to stimulate personal growth, learning and development of employees. The Vitamin Model of Warr (1994) lists nine types of job resources ('vitamins') that are related to employee well-being, namely opportunity for control, opportunity for skill use, externally generated goals, variety, environmental clarity, availability of money, physical security, opportunity for interpersonal contact and valued social position.

Empowering leadership

An important task of leaders is to optimise the emotional climate in their team. In order to stimulate a positive socio-emotional climate and thus to enhance engagement leaders should: (a) acknowledge and reward good performance instead of exclusively correcting substandard performance; (b) be fair towards employees because this will strengthen the psychological contract; (c) put problems on the agenda and discuss these in an open, constructive and problem-solving way, both in work meetings and in individual talks; (d) inform employees on a regular basis and as early and completely as possible in face-to-face meetings about important issues; (e) coach employees by helping them with setting goals, planning their work, pointing out pitfalls and giving advice as necessary; and (f) interview employees on a regular basis about their personal functioning, professional development and career development.

Training

In addition to be purely directed at the job content, training programmes that promote employee engagement should also be directed at personal growth and development. For instance, they should include time-management, stress management, personal effectiveness and self-management. Work training is a learning process across the entire life-span that is ultimately related to the employee's job performance. A powerful tool to achieve this is to increase employee's efficacy beliefs.

Effective communication and feedback

Most organisations do well in terms of communication down from management to employees. Mechanisms for employees to communicate up on a regular basis are often missing. Relying on a suggestion box and an annual employee survey are not effective mechanisms. Two helpful ways to ensure the upward flow of feedback are employee meetings and regular online surveys that capture the changing concerns of employees.

Employee empowerment

Employees need to understand how their job fits into the big picture and what they must do more of and do differently to help the business succeed. Employees should be assisted to clarify which competencies they need, the capacities that this particular organisation needs to grow and helping employees upgrade their skills to match the needs of the future. A perceived 'fit' between an individual's self-concept and his/her role will lead to an experienced sense of meaning, due to the ability of the individual to express his/her values and beliefs. People are not just goal-oriented; they can express themselves in a creative way. People have unique self-concepts and they want to express these and therefore seek roles in which they can do so.

Career development

Engagement levels rise when there is a formal career development system that includes components such as formal career tracks, mobility systems to help employees move about in the organisation, training and development programmes and annual career conversations (see chapter 8).

Interaction with co-workers

Individuals will tend to experience a sense of meaningfulness if they are treated with respect, dignity and appreciation for their contributions. Co-worker interactions create a sense of belonging and a stronger sense of social identity. The opposite is also true. A loss of social identity can lead to a sense of meaninglessness. Reliability and dependability of others lead to cognitive-based trust, while emotional relationships between employees impact on affective trust.

Individual interventions

Individual interventions can be implemented to increase the authentic happiness and well-being of employees. Lyubomirsky (2008) provided a framework that can be used to promote individual happiness and well-being. According to Lyubomirsky, the key to happiness lies not in changing individuals' genetic make-up and not in changing our circumstances, but in their daily intentional activities (what they do and think). The approach of Lyubomirsky (2008) is based on research which shows that intentional activities contribute approximately 40 per cent to individuals' happiness. A total of 50 per cent of individuals' happiness will be influenced by genetic factors; while approximately 10 per cent is influenced by situational factors (see figure 7.5).

A summary of the happiness activities distinguished by Lyubomirsky (2008) is given in figure 7.6.

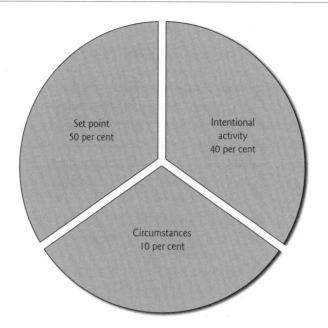

Figure 7.5 *Estimated contribution of different aspects to happiness*

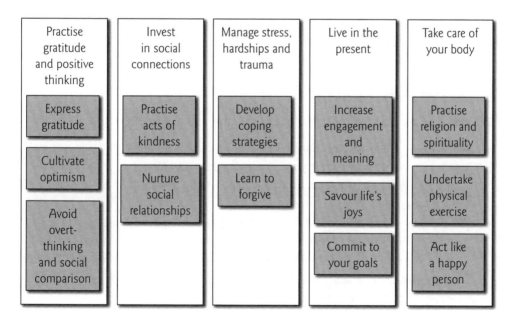

Figure 7.6 *Summary of individual happiness activities*

Practising gratitude and positive thinking

The individual learns to practise gratitude, to cultivate optimism and to avoid overthinking and social comparison.

◆ *Activity 1 — Practise gratitude.* Thanking someone who has played an important role in your life, thanking God, counting your blessings will help you to achieve happiness. Gratitude is more than saying thank you for a gift or benefit: it is a sense of thankfulness and appreciation for life. Examples of gratitude include calling a mentor and thanking him/her for guiding you through life's crossroads, appreciating moments with your child or recalling the good things in your life in the present moment.

◆ *Activity 2 — Cultivate optimism.* Looking at the bright side, noticing what is right (rather than wrong), giving yourself the benefit of the doubt and feeling good about your future are optimism strategies. Making realistic attributions will contribute to optimism. Individuals should also avoid unrealistic beliefs.

◆ *Activity 3 — Avoid overthinking and social comparison.* Overthinking (thinking too much about the meanings, causes and consequences of your character, feelings and problems) worsens sadness and impairs your ability to solve problems. Social comparisons (comparing yourself with others) are harmful as they may lead to feelings of inferiority, distress and loss of self-esteem (resulting because of upward comparisons) and feelings of guilt (resulting because of downward comparisons). Overthinking and social comparisons should be stopped by doing/thinking something else, setting aside a specific time during a day to overthink or by talking to someone. The individual should also act to solve the problems causing the overthinking and social comparison.

Investing in social connections

The individual learns to practise acts of kindness and to invest in social connections.

◆ *Activity 4 — Practise acts of kindness.* Being generous and willing to share will make you happy. Doing more than is your custom is ideal, but timing (eg, once a week) and variety are crucial. Acts of kindness have a ripple effect (ie, it leads to others starting to show kindness).

◆ *Activity 5 — Invest in social connections.* Happy people are exceptionally good at their friendships, families and intimate relationships. Relationships present the opportunity for tangible, emotional and/or informational social support. Therefore, individuals should make time for relationships. They should also express admiration, appreciation and affect in relationships and manage conflict constructively.

Managing stress, hardships and trauma

The individual develops coping strategies and learns the skills of forgiveness.

◆ *Activity 6 — Develop coping strategies.* Coping is what people do to alleviate the hurt, stress or suffering caused by a negative event or situation. Problem-focused coping involves solving problems. Emotion-focused coping involves managing emotional reactions to an event. Finding the value or gain in a negative life event will contribute to happiness. Bereavement and stress have been found to be associated with an elevation in specific hormones; social support can lower these hormones. Finding meaning will help to cope with stress and trauma (eg, a new perspective on life, growth in spirituality).

◆ *Activity 7 — Learn to forgive.* Forgiveness involves suppressing one's motivations for avoidance and revenge and replacing them with positive attitudes, feelings and behaviour. Forgiveness does not necessarily involve the re-establishment of the relationship with the transgressor. Forgiveness is something that you do for yourself and not for the person who has wronged you.

Living in the present

The individual learns to engage in work activities, to savour life's joys and to commit to goals.

◆ *Activity 8 — Engage in work.* The individual should learn to engage in activities at work and to find meaning in life and in work by using their strengths. A calling work orientation (ie, that the individual works for the sake of work itself) provides intrinsic satisfaction and fulfilment.

◆ *Activity 9 — Savour life's joys.* Savouring is any thoughts or behaviours capable of generating, intensifying and prolonging enjoyment. Savouring the past can be done by recalling the good old days, savouring the present by fully enjoying the present moment (such as enjoying food and drinks). Savouring the future can be done by anticipating and fantasising about upcoming positive events.

◆ *Activity 10 — Commit to goals.* A happy person has a project: either in their work, their family or social lives or their spiritual life. Intrinsic goals (ones that are personally involving and rewarding) bring more happiness than goals which are not freely chosen (extrinsic goals). People aim for extrinsic goals as a means to an end, eg, working hard to obtain a reward or avoid punishment. Intrinsic goals satisfy the needs for autonomy, competence and relatedness.

Taking care of your body and soul

The individual learns to take care of his/her body and soul.

◆ *Activity 11 — Practise religion and spirituality.* Spirituality refers to the search for meaning in life through something which is larger than the individual self. Religion involves a spiritual search. Individuals could practise religion by seeking meaning and by praying.

◆ *Activity 12 — Undertake physical exercise and maintain a healthy lifestyle.* Research shows that exercise was just as effective at treating depression as was Zoloft (an anti-depressant) for people suffering from clinical depression. Physical activity reduces anxiety and stress, protects people from dying, reduces the risk of diseases, builds bones and muscles, increases quality of life, improves sleep and protects against cognitive impairments as we age. Individuals should therefore engage in physical exercise that they like and that fits their circumstances. In addition they should maintain a healthy lifestyle, including sleeping 7–8 hours per night, eliminating cigarette smoking, reducing alcohol intake abuse, reduce the intake of excess calories, fat, salt and sugar, eating breakfast regularly, maintaining a near-optimal weight and going for periodic screening for major causes of morbidity and mortality, such as blood pressure and cancer.

◆ *Activity 13 — Act like you are happy.* A happy person acts like he or she is happy.

Conclusion

Employees in organisations face various challenges in the work environment, which could affect their career well-being. In line with the notion that work might have positive as well as negative outcomes, two models were distinguished, namely the *disease model*, which focuses on un-well-being and ill-health and the *positive psychology model*, which focuses on well-being and happiness. Three approaches to well-being were distinguished, namely subjective well-being, psychological well-being and eudaimonic well-being. The *subjective well-being* approach implies that career experiences could be linked to positive and negative affect, life satisfaction and satisfaction with different life domains. The *psychological well-being* approach implies that career experiences which allow autonomy, environmental mastery, personal growth, positive relations with others, purpose in life and self-acceptance will result in employee well-being. The *eudaimonic well-being* approach implies that career experiences which allow self-discovery, perceived development of one's best potentials, a sense of purpose and meaning in life, investment of significant effort in pursuit of excellence, intense involvement in activities and enjoyment of activities as personally expressive will result in employee well-being.

Subjective, psychological and eudaimonic well-being are all aspects of authentic happiness. Authentic happiness is a result of three components, namely *pleasure*, *engagement* and *meaning*. These three components affect people's subjective well-being (consisting of positive and negative affect, life satisfaction, enjoyment and satisfaction with specific life domains). People have a set point for the experience of pleasure, which is genetically determined. Therefore, engagement and meaning should be addressed to promote authentic happiness.

Work engagement is a positive fulfilling state of mind, which consists of three components, namely a physical component (vigour), affective component (dedication) and a cognitive component (absorption). Three psychological conditions contribute to work engagement, namely psychological meaningfulness, psychological safety and psychological availability. These three psychological conditions have various antecedents.

Work-role fit, job enrichment and relationships with colleagues affect the psychological meaningfulness of employees. Utilising individual strengths is an important factor which contributes to work engagement. Relationships with supervisors and colleagues and norms affect the psychological safety of employees. Physical, cognitive and emotional resources affect psychological availability. Stress and burnout could also affect individuals' psychological availability and work engagement and could impact on their authentic happiness. Personality traits, sense of coherence, self-efficacy, optimism and coping might affect the authentic happiness of employees.

Employee happiness is related to workplace success. Employees with high positive affect have jobs characterised by variety, meaningfulness and autonomy. Happy people are more satisfied and perform better than unhappy employees. Happiness predicts behaviour that extends beyond a job description, but that benefits other individuals or the organisation itself. Happy people (compared with unhappy people) are more sociable and energetic, are more charitable and co-operative, have richer networks of friends and social support, are more flexible and ingenious in their thinking, are more resilient in the face of hardship, have stronger immune systems, live longer, are more involved in their work and receive more rewards.

The authentic happiness of employees can be affected by organisational and individual interventions. Organisational interventions include assessment and evaluation of employees, coaching programme for newcomers, career conversations, participation in large group meetings, job redesign and work changes, empowering leadership, training, communication and feedback, employee empowerment, career development and interaction with co-workers. Individual interventions entail intentional activities that contribute approximately 40 per cent to individuals' happiness.

Review and discussion questions

1. Why should organisations consider the well-being and authentic happiness of their employees?
2. How does the concept of career well-being relate to the notion of authentic happiness in the workplace? Review chapter 1 to formulate your answer.
3. What is the major difference between the disease model and the positive psychology model?
4. What are the differences between subjective well-being, psychological well-being and eudaimonic well-being?
5. Distinguish between occupational stress, job burnout and work engagement.
6. Explain how occupational stress, job burnout and work engagement affect the well-being of individuals in the workplace.
7. Describe how personality traits and dispositions influence individuals' career experiences and their coping strategies.
8. Think of a stressful career experience that you recently had to deal with. Describe the stressors in the work environment and how you reacted. Explain the coping strategies you applied to deal with the experience. Did you use problem-focused or emotion-focused coping strategies? How effective were these strategies in dealing with the experience?
9. Review the characteristics of the 21st century world of work and their impact on the nature of careers as discussed in chapter 2. Study Cartwright and Cooper's (2002) seven occupational stressors. Identify which changes in the world of work are related to these seven occupational stressors. Discuss your viewpoints with a colleague. Explain the personality characteristics that will enable individuals to deal with the changing world of work.

10. Identify the factors that contribute to burnout. What can be done to assist employees to recover from burnout?
11. Explain how the characteristics of a job (such as skill variety, autonomy, feedback) and social support can increase individuals' engagement at work? Think about your own job. Which aspects of your job stimulate a sense of greater vigour, dedication and absorption in your work?
12. What can organisations do to increase individuals' work engagement?
13. Which aspects of your personality helped you to deal successfully with your experiences of job stress and job burnout? Identify the personality aspects that enhance your engagement at work.

Reflection activities

Reflection activity 7.1: Happiness workshop

Develop a slideshow (that can be used in a workshop) directed at promoting the authentic happiness of employees. Make use of the authentic happiness model of Seligman (2002) and Lyubomirsky (2008).

Reflection activity 7.2: Stress and burnout

Identify South African studies on stress and burnout by doing a search in the library. Analyse the findings of these studies. Answer the following questions:

1. Which occupational stressors are most prevalent in South Africa?
2. Do the factors that cause burnout and occupational stress differ between occupations?

Reflection activity 7.3: Happiness collage

Gather clippings from old magazines to make a collage. The collage should reflect your happiness in the past, present and future.

Reflection activity 7.4: Crafting a job

Write about a time in your life when you were at your best. Which strengths are evident in this story? Next, complete the VIA Strengths Finder:

- Go to the following website: http://www.authentichappiness.sas.upenn.edu/default.aspx.
- Look under the heading "Engagement Questionnaires".
- Select the VIA signature Strengths Finder.

◆ Register on the site and complete the questionnaire which measures 24 strengths.
◆ Copy the text to a Word file.
◆ Save the report and make a printout.

Answer the following questions:

1. Having completed the VIA Questionnaire think about the extent to which you are able to use your strengths in your daily life.
2. Has it been your experience that on occasions when you have been able to use your signature strengths you have felt most fulfilled?
3. Have you been left with the feeling that something was missing when you have not been able to use your signature strengths?
4. What could you do to change your daily situation so that you had more opportunities to use and deploy your signature strengths?

Reflection activity 7.5: Case study

Read through the case study below and answer the questions that follow.

Mr P Mokgaba has completed an engagement survey in his organisation. Mr Mokgaba has completed a BCom degree. He has been in an administrative position for the last ten years. The last two years his productivity has dropped and this year he received poor performance ratings. It is also known that Mr Mokgaba has over the last few years abused alcohol at organisational functions. His colleagues have heard him complaining about his job often over the last few years.

The engagement survey measured the components of authentic happiness (ie, life satisfaction, pleasure, engagement and meaning) as defined in this chapter. The three psychological conditions which contribute to work engagement (ie, psychological meaningfulness, safety and availability) and the antecedents of work engagement were also included in the survey. Mr Mokgaba obtained the following sten scores:

Life satisfaction	4	Pleasure	8	Engagement	3	Meaning	3
Psychological meaningfulness	3	Psychological safety	6	Psychological availability	2	Work-role fit	3
Job enrichment	4	Relations with supervisor	5	Relations with colleagues	7	Norms	7
Self-consciousness	7	Cognitive resources	3	Emotional resources	3	Physical resources	5

Interpretation of sten scores:

1–3 — Low
4–7 — Average
8–10 — High

Questions

1. How would you interpret the results regarding the authentic happiness and work engagement of Mr Mokgaba?

2. Which factors are impacting on the authentic happiness and work engagement of Mr Mokgaba?

3. Which interventions can be implemented to address the authentic happiness and work engagement of Mr Mokgaba?

8

Organisational choice and career development support

Learning outcomes

After studying this chapter you should be able to:
- explain the concept organisational choice;
- explain the concept organisational entry;
- explain the factors that influence individuals' choice of an organisation by means of different theories;
- explain the importance of organisational career development support by referring to the organisational career development system;
- discuss the different career development support practices; and
- describe ethical principles regarding organisational career development support.

Introduction

This chapter discusses factors that influence individuals' choice of an organisation and organisational career development support practices. *Organisational choice* refers to an individual's choice of a specific organisation for which to work. Although there are many tests and instruments available to assist individuals in making a career choice, there are few available to assist people in choosing an organisation. Career counsellors also devote little attention to advising individuals in organisational choice. Organisational choice refers more to an event, while occupational choice is more of a process. Organisational choice is usually made over a shorter period, it is a more conscious decision and can be more easily reversed than career choice (Wanous, 1977). The choice of an organisation is a matching process, which is a major theme of organisational entry.

Organisational entry is the process whereby individuals move from outside to inside organisations to become more involved in a particular organisation for a period of time (Cascio, 2003; Wanous, 1992). Two processes are involved in organisational entry. One process takes place where individuals evaluate different organisations to determine which one will best meet their career aspirations, needs and values. The other process concerns the organisation's assessment of the candidates' qualities to determine which one will fit best into the organisation with the highest likelihood of success. Organisational entry has therefore an *individual* and an *organisational* perspective. The *individual perspective* concerns the individual's capacity to choose which positions to apply for and which offers to accept, while the *organisational perspective* involves the organisation's capacity to choose from among prospective applicants (Wanous, 1992).

The 'war for talent' and the search for more engaged and committed employees has led to companies realising that following a purely selective approach to hiring based on matching job and person characteristics has become inadequate for finding the 'right' employees. The overall resourcing strategy and in particular the screening and selection process is therefore viewed as an *interactive social process* where the applicant has as much power about whether to engage in the application process as the organisation. This places greater importance on the factors that influence individuals' choice of an organisation (McCormack and Scholarios, 2009).

Theories of organisatonal choice

For the purposes of this book only some theories illustrating how individuals choose an organisation are discussed.

Expectancy theory

Vroom's *expectancy theory* (1964) is the theory most often used in research on organisational choice. According to the expectancy model, the selection of an organisation is based on its *motivational force*, which is the result of the extent to which individuals expect a job offer from the organisation *(expectancy)*, their perception that the organisation will provide certain outcomes *(instrumentality)* and the extent to which each of these outcomes attracts individuals *(valence)* (Osborn, 1990). Vroom defines motivational force as 'a multiplicative function of expectancy and the sum of the products of instrumentalities and the valences of the outcomes'; MF = E[ï = (I x 3 V)] (Osborn, 1990:46). This model is *compensatory* in nature.

Osborn (1990) has questioned whether the decision-making process, when an individual is faced with a job choice, is accurately described by the models of organisational choice based on the expectancy theory. He concurs with other researchers who argue that, when individuals are faced with a real organisational choice, other non-compensatory strategies are followed to simplify the decision-making process. Osborn's research (1990) points to the fact that individuals do not appear to use only a compensatory strategy.

Table 8.1 *Theories of organisational choice*

Expectancy theory	The selection of an organisation based on its *motivational force*, which is the result of the extent to which individuals expect a job offer from the organisation *(expectancy)*, their perception that the organisation will provide certain outcomes *(instrumentality)* and the extent to which each of these outcomes attracts individuals *(valence)*.
Unprogrammed decision-making	A *non-compensatory model*, which suggests that job seekers make use of a *two-phase process* when they choose an organisation. In the *first phase*, they evaluate the various choices according to a few important factors and eliminate those that do not meet their minimum criteria on these factors. Once a job has been found that meets these criteria, applicants will regard it as their 'implicit choice'. During the *second phase*, they will confirm this implicit choice, even going so far as to distort information if this should be necessary.
Theories of position selection	The process by which the individual determines for which organisation to work.
Objective factor theory	A graduate chooses a job by ranking and evaluating a limited number of clearly measurable features of each job offer.
Subjective factor theory	Individuals select a position on the basis of what they perceive their personal and emotional needs to be and the extent to which the image of the organisation meets these perceived needs.
Critical contact theory	Candidates for a job cannot differentiate between the companies that offer them employment. The factors that influence their choices are therefore neither objective nor subjective. Candidates simply lack the experience to evaluate the job offers that they receive and will therefore base the final decision on the experience gained during their contact with the various organisations.
Social comparison theory	Individuals tend to compare themselves to people similar to themselves with regard to sex, age, culture, education and status.
Super's theory	Although largely a theory of *occupational choice*, the theory can also be extended to organisational choice in that the choice of an organisation may also be a means of implementing an individual's self-concept. The relationship between the individual's self-concept (perceptions of the self) and the organisational image (individual's perception of the organisation) could be a determinant of organisational choice.

Unprogrammed decision-making process

The *unprogrammed decision-making process* has been studied by Soelberg (1967), who analysed the organisational choices of master's and doctorate students. He observed that students had a *mental picture* of the type of organisations for which they wanted to work. This *non-compensatory model* suggests that job seekers make use of a *two-phase process* when they choose an organisation. In the *first phase* they evaluate the various choices according to a few important factors and eliminate those that do not meet their minimum criteria on these factors. Once a job has been found that meets these criteria, applicants will regard it as their 'implicit choice'. During the *second phase*, they will confirm this implicit choice, even going so far as to distort information if this should be necessary (Osborn, 1990).

Researchers have found this model to be of *more value* than the compensatory models and overall the use of non-compensatory models has been supported by research (Hill, 1974; Osborn, 1990).

Theories of position selection in organisations

Behling, Labovitz and Gainer (1968) term the process by which the individual determines for which organisation to work as the *'position selection process'*. They outline *three theories* which review the factors on which individuals base their decisions in this regard.

Objective factor theory

The *objective factor theory* states that a graduate chooses a job by ranking and evaluating a limited number of clearly measurable features of each job offer, for example, the salary, type of work and opportunities for further development. Although each individual may rank these factors in a different order, a pattern will emerge which, if detected and used as a basis for structuring the firm's offers of employment, will significantly improve the recruitment effectiveness of the organisation.

Subjective factor theory

According to the *subjective factor theory*, individuals select a position on the basis of what they perceive their personal and emotional needs to be and the extent to which the image of the organisation meets these perceived needs. Such decisions are made on the grounds of personal preferences and emotions.

Critical contact theory

The *critical contact theory* states that typical candidates for a job cannot differentiate between the companies that offer them employment. The factors that influence their choices are therefore neither objective nor subjective. Candidates simply lack the experience to evaluate the job offers that they receive and will therefore base the final decision on the experience gained during their contact with the various organisations, for example the friendliness of the person who conducted the interview, the facilities offered by the company and the speed with which their job application is processed.

Social comparison theory

According to the *social comparison theory,* we tend to compare ourselves to people similar to ourselves with regard to sex, age, culture, education and status (Louw and Edwards, 1997). Kilduff (1990, 1992) uses the social comparison theory as a framework to study the effects of social networks on the organisational choice process. Kilduff's (1990) research supports the predictions derived from the social comparison theory. His research shows that two individuals who are friends or who regard each other as similar tend to make similar organisational choices. This is true even if their academic orientation and job preferences differ considerably.

Super's theory

Super's theory is seen largely as a theory of *occupational choice.* Tom (1971) postulates that Super's theory can also be extended to organisational choice in that the choice of an organisation may also be a means of implementing an individual's self-concept. The relationship between the individual's self-concept (perceptions of the self) and the organisational image (individual's perception of the organisation) could be a determinant of organisational choice. An important career decision would then be to find a fit between the self-concept of the individual and the image of the organisation. Tom (1971) has found support for his hypothesis that the congruence between individuals' perception of themselves and their perception of the organisation which they prefer most will be greater than the congruence between those individuals' perception of themselves and their perception of the organisation which they least prefer. On the basis of these results, Tom comes to the conclusion that Super's theory of vocational choice can also be extended to the issue of organisational choice.

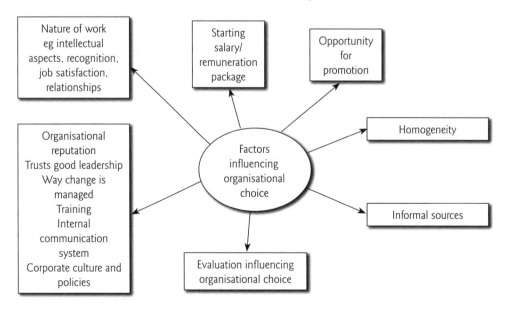

Figure 8.1 *Factors influencing organisational choice*

Other factors influencing organisational choice

Besides these theoretical formulations, earlier researchers have found *factors* that influence organisational choice *per se*. These findings indicate that organisational choice is influenced by *nature of work, progress, starting salary, opportunity for promotion, intellectual aspects* and *recognition* (Dickinson, 1953; Barmeier and Kellar, 1957; Braunstein and Haines, 1968; Dickinson and Newbegin, 1967; Oosthuizen, 1985; Richardson, 1966; Walton, 1960). Furthermore, *homogeneity* also plays a role in organisational choice. People who are attracted to a particular organisation prove to be more homogeneous than the applicant pool in general (Bretz et al, 1989).

Organisational reputation, corporate culture and policies are also found to be an important factor when considering an organisation (Byars and Rue, 2004; Chalofsky, 2010; Hankin, 2005). As far as the obtaining of information which could assist individuals in making organisational choices is concerned, students tend to rely more on *informal sources,* such as other students or people they know in industry. Research indicates that overall *evaluations of site visit, perceptions of the location* and *host likeableness* are related positively to job acceptance decisions. This implies that if organisations make use of a site visit, careful attention should be paid to how the site visit is conducted and to matching the host with the applicants. As location attributes also influence job-offer decisions organisations should emphasise the positive aspects of the area and take applicants on a tour (Aamodt, 2010).

To make a realistic job choice, the individual should assess the organisation carefully. This requires the collection of data from different sources. Types of information that would be helpful are *inter alia* the size and structure of the organisation, the industries in which the organisation does business, financial health of the organisation, the organisation's business plan, availability of training and development opportunities and promotion and advancement policies (Greenhaus et al, 2010).

A South African survey was done among 42 companies, including 1 955 employees, to obtain information on which factors attract, motivate and retain staff. The results indicated that except for *remuneration packages,* which are always important to employees, factors like *relationships, job satisfaction, trust* and *good leadership* are very high on employees' priority lists. The following factors also rated high: the *way in which change is managed, training* and the *internal communication system.* The results indicated that prospective employees had a good understanding of what was happening or not happening in a particular company prior to joining the company. The results also indicated that, as employees started to act more in the interest of their own careers organisations came to realise that their best employees would move on. With a view to recruiting these ex-employees back in future, programmes were implemented to maintain positive relations with them (Dicks et al, 2001).

Organisational career development support practices

Career development in the modern workplace is regarded very differently from the way it was regarded in the past because the business context has changed so much. Employers now have the managerial prerogative to change the content of tasks as the situation demands and the employees can no longer rely on the organisation to provide clarity and direction regarding their career paths. In addition, employees can no longer bargain collectively as effectively as they did before on employment security, incentives and promotional opportunities.

The changes in organisational and individuals' responses to career development directly correspond to environmental changes. In the traditional environment where competition, technology and market characteristics were relatively stable organisations structured their activities in a mechanistic form with a view to attain stability, efficiency, order and control, whereas individuals relied on specialisation, organisational loyalty and steady and predictable career progression under the guidance and supervision of their employers. However, in the contemporary environment — which is characterised by intense and unprecedented global competition, technological breakthroughs at an immense speed and service and quality-driven economies — organisations are turning towards extremely organic structures, knowledge- and technology-based learning systems and the empowerment of people. Individuals are thus taking more responsibility for their careers (Baruch, 1999, 2002; Thite, 2001).

In the traditional career development framework organisations adopted a 'help us to help yourself' approach to career management and took charge of navigating the careers of their employees. In the modern organisation, many organisations have taken nearly the extreme opposite approach by almost abandoning any responsibility for career development.

When there is career support for individual career development, it seems to be linked to the composition of current organisations (Thite, 2001). Mega-mergers and strategic alliances (in banking, in the automobile, petro-chemical, aviation, energy and media industries and in Internet service provision) are creating super organisations and can offer long-term employment to people with a wide range of evolving skill sets. These super organisations are more willing to take an active role in the career development of their core employees. Small organisations, on the other hand, are extremely flexible in hiring and firing and are unlikely to play any active role in the career development process of their small number of employees (Baruch, 1999, 2002; Thite, 2001).

However, as the competitive advantage of the organisation lies in the effective use of its human resources, it is perhaps now, more than ever, to the advantage of the organisation to participate in career development (Arnold, 2001; Thite, 2001). According to Byars and Rue (2004), increased employee mobility and related environmental factors have made career development support increasingly important for today's organisations. Employees need to:

- understand to what extent the organisation supports the development of their careers;
- be given tools and services to help them to formulate career plans;
- know the direction of the company's business and the skills that will be required in future; and
- understand what methods are available to them for keeping their skills up to date (Byars and Rue, 2004; Colby, 1995; Thite, 2001).

While the employee is responsible for career planning, the responsibility of the organisation is to support employees in managing their careers. The initiative, however, must come from the individual. Career development is therefore a joint responsibility, the individual being the initiator and the organisation the supporter.

Research indicates that, when responsibility is shared, employees are likely to have more successful careers, both objectively and in terms of their career experiences (Byars and Rue, 2004; Orpen, 1994; Thite, 2001). Employers who are concerned about career advancement are more successful in attracting and retaining employees (Riggio, 2009).

Organisational career development system

The *organisational career development system* consists of a *set of activities and practices* designed by the organisation to promote employee career ownership and insight, career goal and strategy development and/or appropriate feedback on career progress. The *purpose* of an organisational career development system is to manage its talent and develop and enrich the *organisation's* human resources in the light of both the employees' and the organisation's needs. The activities and practices of an organisational career development system can help *individuals* to improve their personal career management, development and advancement throughout the various stages of their work life (Greenhaus et al, 2010; Harrison, 2009).

From the viewpoint of the organisation, formalised career development support practices and activities can promote the retention of key talent and avoid employee turnover and thus reduce costs. Taking an interest in employees' careers can also improve morale, increase productivity and help the organisation become more efficient. A 13-month study by Maurer, Weiss and Barbeite (2003) followed 800 workers in several different organisations who were involved in career development and learning activities. The researchers concluded that prior participation in career development activities was a good predictor of present and future intentions to undertake more such learning activities. The more supportive organisations are of career development activities, the greater are employee beliefs that their participation will lead to positive personal benefits. The major reason for intending to stay with a company, instead of looking for a job with another organisation, was the opportunity for career growth, development and learning provided by the present employer (Schultz and Schultz, 2010).

From the *organisation's viewpoint*, a formalised career development system has *three major objectives* (Byars and Rue, 2004):

◆ to meet the immediate and future *human resource needs* of the organisation in good time;
◆ to better *inform* the organisation and the individual about *potential career paths* within the organisation; and
◆ to *utilise existing human resource programmes* to the fullest by integrating the activities that select, assign, develop and manage individual careers with the organisation's plans.

A *formalised organisational career development system* can also help create a positive *career development culture* which can help address a range of issues, such as productivity and competitiveness, employment equity, succession planning and workforce forecasting, talent retention, management potential selection and development and upskilling due to technological changes. A career development culture can contribute to the ultimate financial profitability of the organisation and visibly support the workplace skills plan if there are adequate budget and personnel allocations (Baruch, 1999; Conger, 2002). For example, a large South African financial institution stated the following as the principles governing its employees' career development:

◆ Career managemernt is a joint effort between the company and its employees, and employees will take responsibility for their careers;

◆ The company will provide a Career Framework, guidelines and tools to facilitate the process of career management;

◆ The Career Framework supports all human resource (HR) processes to ensure an integrated HR offering;

◆ All line managers will conduct a minimum of one personal development conversation with their staff within the first six months of the year;

◆ Managers will be measured on the completion and actioning of personal development conversations;

◆ The company believes in balancing the potential, performance and aspirations of its staff with the actual business/human resourcing needs;

◆ The company supports the internal mobility of staff across business clusters and depending on the roles, preference for new employment opportunities will be given to employees before considering external applicants;

◆ The company will create an environment for continuous learning by supporting staff development that is aligned to individual and business needs;

◆ Career management enables employee development and growth. However, opportunities are subject to the availability of vacancies in the company and relevant busines constraints; and

◆ Though career management is firmly the responsibility of the individual to manage through their working life, the company's responsibility is to assist its people in managing their carees within the context of the company. The company understands that whilst individuals are contracted to the company, it is the organisation's responsibility to offer the guidance and necessary assistance to enable employees to make informed career decisions and facilitate their progress towards these.

The National Skills Development Strategy of the South African government promotes the establishment of a career development culture in South African organisations through legislation such as the Employment Equity Act and the Skills Development Act. The Employment Equity Act emphasises the accelerated development of designated groups such as black people, women and people with disability, while the Skills Development Act emphasises the development of a competent labour force according to national and international standards.

The following organisational *career development support practices* are deemed as being valid for the contemporary organisation and should form an integral part of the organisational career development system (Arnold and Randall, 2010; Baruch, 1999, 2002; Byars and Rue, 2004; Conger, 2002; Nabi, 2003):

- advertising internal job openings;
- formal education as part of career development;
- performance appraisal as a basis for career planning;
- career counselling, advising and discussions;
- lateral moves to create cross-functional experience;
- succession planning;
- retirement preparation programmes;
- mentoring and executive coaching;
- dual ladder;
- customising career progression and development;
- career booklets and/or pamphlets and career development centres;
- assessment and development centres;
- career self-management training and career planning workshops;
- orientation, induction or socialisation;
- secondments;
- redeployment and outplacement programmes; and
- special programmes for designated groups, dual career couples, expatriates and repatriates, high flyers and people on learnerships.

Table 8.2 provides an overview of these *career development support practices*. These different practices will now be discussed in more detail.

Table 8.2 *Career development support practices in the 2000s*

Career management practice and system	Strategy	Advantage	Example
Advertising internal job openings	Publishing of vacancies within the organisation's boundaries	Indicates a preference for internal promotion and recruitment	Postings on notice boards, newsletters or distribution via e-mail and intranet
Formal education	Selecting people with high potential and of designated groups to attend formal training programmes of study	Fast-track formal development of a competent labour force	Skills Development Act Executive and management development programmes (eg MBA)

Career management practice and system	Strategy	Advantage	Example
Performance appraisal 360-degree performance appraisal system	Establishing a link between performance appraisal and career development Approach to gain feedback from various sources such as peers, subordinates, manager and customers	Gives an indication of people ready for promotion Provides feedback to the employee from different points of view	Performance appraisals Personal development plans 360-degree performance and development solutions
Career counselling/ advising/discussions	Establishing two-way communication between the employee and the employer	Direct manager has good knowledge of the employee's skills, behaviours and attitudes	Line managers are trained in counselling techniques
Lateral moves to create cross-functional experiences	Job transitions on the same hierarchy level to create cross-functional experience	Creating opportunities by moving on a horizontal level	Project teams Rotation in various positions on the same level
Succession planning	A framework to determine the possible replacement of senior employees	Identifies potential of people Provides a long-term planning view	Development panels or review committees
Retirement preparation programmes	Presenting pre-retirement workshops with a targeted population	Eases the transition of older employees, for example in terms of finance, health, leisure and social contact	Retirement workshops with employees and spouses Counselling
Mentoring	Building of relationships between a mentor and junior employee	Provides the junior employee with an advisor, tutor and 'godfather' in the workplace	Formal mentorship programmes Informal advice or role model Career workbooks Career discussions
Dual ladder	Upward mobility and recognition for technical or professional staff, not interested in managerial positions	Rewarding and retaining high performing employees by providing alternatives to management	Technical or specialist career paths
Booklets and/or pamphlets and career development centres	Formal communication to employees regarding career issues	Releases direct manager from sharing career information with new employees	Career centres Career newsletters Career information on the intranet
Assessment and development centres	Evaluation of potential of present and future managers and identification of general development areas in preparation for future roles	Effective selection tool for managerial recruitment or indicator of managerial potential and development requirements	Assessment centre Development centre

Career management practice and system	Strategy	Advantage	Example
Career planning workshops	Short-term workshops focusing on specific career management aspects	General career development programmes, which are offered by organisations themselves or by professionals, to assist individuals in career planning	Career mastery workshop Career planning workshop Career management course
Induction/ socialisation	Introducing new people to organisational aspects such as behaviours, attitudes, norms, culture and systems (also referred to as induction or socialisation)	First contact with career practice in the organisation that the employee experiences	Formal orientation workshops Informal on-the-job socialisation
Secondments	Temporary assignment to another area within the organisation or even another organisation	Acquires a different perspective of the organisation, the industry and even business in world	6, 12 or 18 month secondments
Redeployment and outplacement programmes	Programmes to support individuals during phases of restructuring, downsizing or job losses	Supports the employee in finding new or alternative jobs	Outplacement agencies
Special programmes	Specific programmes to support special populations in the organisation	Attends to the specific needs of employees on special related issues	Diversity training Learnerships Quality of life programmes Expatriates and repatriates programmes

Advertising internal job openings

Advertising internal job openings is a method of informing employees of job vacancies by posting a notice in central locations. Employees are given a specified period to apply for the available jobs. Other methods used in publicising jobs include memos to supervisors and listings in employee publications. Normally, the job notice specifies the job title, rate of pay and necessary qualifications. The usual procedure is for all applications to be sent to the human resource department for an initial review. The next step is an interview by the prospective manager. Then a decision is made, based on qualifications, performance, length of service and other pertinent criteria (Byars and Rue, 2004).

A successful job-posting programme requires the development of specific implementation policies. Some suggestions include the following (Byars and Rue, 2004:139):

- both promotions and transfers should be posted;
- openings should be posted for a specified time period before external recruitment begins;
- eligibility rules for the job-posting system need to be developed and communicated;
- specific standards for selection should be included in the notice;
- job applicants should be required to list their qualifications and reasons for requesting a transfer or promotion; and
- unsuccessful applicants should be notified by the human resource department and advised as to why they were not accepted.

Formal education

Formal education is generally a long-term investment in people. Many organisations are becoming less prepared to invest in long-term formal education due to the short-term period of the modern era employment contracts. However, legislation such as the Employment Equity Act, the Skills Development Act and the Skills Development Levies Act encourages employers to invest in the formal education of their employees as part of the National Skills Development Strategy in developing a competent and productive South African labour force.

The formal education of managerial personnel, as well as professional and non-managerial employees, is an important career development support practice to ensure that an organisation is able to compete against international standards. Formal education generally includes adult graduate or post-graduate studies and vocational qualification courses registered with the South African Qualifications Authority (SAQA) on the National Qualifications Framework (NQF).

Performance appraisal

The importance of combining organisational career development support practices with the *performance appraisal system* is increasingly being emphasised, particularly with regard to *360-degree feedback* practices (Baruch, 2006; Brutus, London and Martineau, 1999; Byars and Rue, 2004). The use of varied sources (eg, employee self, supervisor, peer, subordinate, customer, vendor/supplier) has become known as the '360-degree' evaluation. The concept of 360-degree or *multi-source survey* feedback rests on the assumption that performance information about an individual collected from *different perspectives* and fed back to that same individual will lead to individual development (Landy and Conte, 2004).

Multi-source feedback can help to increase *employee self-awareness* in the career management process. Assessment of one's skills and development areas are important to determine effective career development interventions. A 360-degree survey is generally viewed as an appropriate channel for receiving feedback from peers, direct reports and the employee's supervisor. Performance appraisals and multi-source feedback practices create self-awareness and an appreciation for the need for behaviour change which, in turn, increases the effectiveness of career development interventions (Landy and Conte, 2004; McCarthy and Garavan, 1999).

A 360-degree feedback discussion on development interventions should explore career-enhancing strategies. *Career-enhancing strategies* encompass a range of employee behaviours such as the development of a network of contacts, consultation with mentors and communication of career goals and objectives to peers. Career-enhancing strategies reflect a proactive approach to effective career self-management, employee performance and career success (Nabi, 2003).

Career-enhancing strategies can be considered as career management interventions that have implications for career success by empowering individuals to take ownership of their own careers and to take responsibility for their own career development and performance (Nabi, 2003).

Career counselling, advising and discussion

Career counselling

Career counselling can be defined as a 'process which enables people to recognise and utilise their resources to make career-related decisions and manage career-related issues (Nathan and Hill, 2006:2). Brown (2006:88) defines it as a multifaceted set of activities designed to help people (a) make or remake occupational choices, (b) find jobs or (c) achieve satisfaction and success in the workplace. Career counselling is the term used most frequently to describe how counsellors and psychologists work to help individuals develop self-understanding and articulate a career direction that allows them to achieve their potential and find purpose in their daily activities. The process of career counselling is a verbal process in which a professionally trained counsellor and client are in a dynamic and collaborative relationship, focused on identifying and acting on the client's career goals. It deals with problems concerned with the client's work, career and life roles. Career counselling can be done by a specialist inside or outside the organisation or a line manager who has received training (Arnold and Randall, 2010; Coetzee and Roythorne-Jacobs, 2007; Niles, 2003).

Career counselling appears to be most effective when it contains (a) individualised interpretation and feedback, (b) occupational information, (c) modelling opportunities, (d) building support of choices within the employee's social network and (e) written exercises (Brown and Ryan Krane, 2000).

Cybercounselling and computer-assisted career guidance are new technological developments in relation to career exploration and planning, especially the creation of information systems and networks on the Internet (Hansen, 2003). However, the importance of individual discussions and career workshops should not be underestimated. Career interventions that have a counselling component were found to be more effective than career interventions that do not involve counselling (eg, reading occupational information on the Internet) (Whiston, Brecheisen and Stephens, 2003).

Assessment is integral to career counselling. Counsellors need to be careful when selecting and applying career-assessment instruments because of concerns related to the culture-free properties of the instrument, as well as reliability, validity and ethical issues that need to be considered as required by the Employment Equity Act and the Health Professions Council of South Africa.

Several approaches are followed in career counselling. A common approach is the *person-centred approach*, based on the work of Carl Rogers (Otte and Hutcheson, 1992).

Person-centred approach to career counselling

The *person-centred approach* means that the counsellor is led to understand the root causes of the person's problem and can then help the employee to define and solve the problem and make decisions. The career issue is personalised and the resulting emotions are analysed. This approach can be followed if employees have personal problems that prevent them from attaining their full potential for productivity and development. The actual problem must be identified and gradually eliminated, enhancing employees' understanding of the problem and prompting them to take action. The counsellor remains in the *background* during the discussion, allowing employees to guide the discussion within the broad limits of the questions asked by the counsellor. It is only when employees have defined their own problems that the counsellor will *guide* them through the process of solving them in their own way.

Reflective listening is an important component of the counsellor-employee relationship, allowing employees to identify the actual problem, which may have nothing to do with their career, but which may nevertheless inhibit productivity and job satisfaction.

Employees are made to feel that somebody cares about them and that they are afforded an opportunity to voice their anxieties. It is only at a later stage that definite plans are made to solve problems, implement changes and identify the available options. A choice is then made and the necessary steps to achieve results are identified, target dates are set and an evaluation schedule is drawn up.

Tests may be used as an aid in defining the problem or in planning solutions, but usually the information gained from these tests can also be supplied directly by the employee.

The counsellor must be a *well-trained, sympathetic person* who will gain the confidence of employees sufficiently to make them talk openly about their problems. The counsellor must encourage employees to talk about themselves.

Career advising

Career advising is another method that can be used by organisations to manage employees' careers. An individual does not need to have professional training to be a career advisor, but can fulfil the duties by using career advising models. These models can be general, specifically designed by an advisor to handle a particular case or custom-designed for a specific organisation. The advising function usually involves sharing information about where to find resources for self-assessment and information about careers, listing education possibilities and referring employees for career counselling. Career advisors can be human resource staff and can be trained by career counsellors.

Career discussion

A *career discussion* is one of the most common methods used by superiors to advise subordinates with regard to their careers.

> *A career discussion is a planned discussion between a manager and an employee who are attempting jointly to clarify developmental options in the employee's current job, examine career issues in light of current job performance and goals of the organisation and/or clarify future career options for that employee' (Otte and Hutcheson, 1992:46).*

Jackson, Kidd and Hirsh (2001:1) offer a broad definition as they define a career discussion as 'a discussion [or series of discussions] with another person about aspects of his/her career which was of significant positive value'.

The discussion involves various steps and various skills are required of the manager to follow each step successfully. The *steps are* as follows (Otte and Hutcheson, 1992):

Setting the stage

Managers must create a physical and psychological environment conducive to the discussion of any issue. Privacy and a pleasant atmosphere should be ensured — for example, a room without a desk to separate the participants. Employees should be made to feel important by fixing the date of the meeting well in advance so that they can prepare for it. The manager's attitude during the meeting should be helpful and sympathetic.

Active listening

Managers must establish a relationship of trust by demonstrating their acceptance of employees' opinions and points of view, so that honesty and frankness are engendered during the discussion. Such active listening skills have a threefold aim:

- to find out about employees' concerns;
- to check that employees' concerns have been correctly understood; and
- to establish which issues are recurrent and therefore important to employees.

Responding

At this stage of the interview, managers will express their own points of view and provide the information necessary to give direction to the discussion. This may be done by:

- summarising what the employee has said;
- expressing the manager's view of the employee;
- pointing out inconsistencies in the employee's presentation;
- providing specific information on factors that may influence the employee's career plans; and
- providing the manager's opinion on the extent to which the employee's aspirations may be deemed realistic.

Developing alternatives

Instead of simply suggesting a training programme which the employee may follow, the manager should concentrate on providing information about career opportunities within the company and on solving the employee's problems.

Reaching joint conclusions

This consists of a summary of the main points of the discussion, the identification of steps to be taken and plans for subsequent action. However, it should be up to the employee to take responsibility for these steps.

Although managers sometimes tend to believe that they have the necessary skills to conduct such career discussions, it usually requires some practice before they can use these skills effectively.

Videos or role playing may be used to show managers how to direct career discussions. Such behavioural models establish a knowledge base to be used by managers when practising their newly acquired skills.

To improve the effectiveness of career discussions, the interviewer should adhere to the following principles (Jackson et al, 2001):

- ◆ show a real interest in the interviewee;
- ◆ establish a relationship of trust;
- ◆ give honest feedback on skills and potential;
- ◆ provide constructive challenges and advice;
- ◆ offer a wide view of career opportunities;
- ◆ manage the process effectively;
- ◆ attend to the interviewee's agenda, not his or her own, not deal with important issues at a moment's notice;
- ◆ follow up on promised actions; and
- ◆ not take control away from the interviewee.

Table 8.3 *Conducting a career development discussion*
(Adapted from Coetzee and Stone, 2004)

1. Set the stage	Explain to the employee that the purpose of the discussion is to: – discuss career/development goals and development plans; and – raise any concerns regarding the development programme. Explain the flow of the discussion, for example: – the topics to be addressed; and – the importance of two-way communication and support, for example: `This discussion is intended to benefit you. I am a resource. Ultimately, your learning progress/career is your responsibility and I want to help.'
2. Listen actively and explore career programme goals	Ask the employee to share his/her self-assessment first: – What is important to him/her, ie values? – Likes/dislikes, ie interests? – Abilities, ie competencies and personal qualities? Review the employee's individual development plan; ask questions to get clarification on all points and to ensure full understanding.
3. Develop alternatives and plan of action	A specific plan of action is required for each development goal. Managers can help by: – making a mutual decision about the employee's development needs; and – identifying how the developmental needs will be met, eg through workshops, special assignments or additional coaching; Determine whether growth opportunities are provided. Offer new assignments and special projects that will help the learner develop, for example: – leading a project team; – analysing complicated data; and – making key presentations and getting involved more directly with stakeholders, clients and customers. Agree on the employee's developmental needs and how they will be met. Anticipate barriers to achieving developmental/training/career goals, including organisational constraints. Brainstorm ways to overcome these barriers.
4. Reach joint conclusions	Specify what actions are needed to accomplish each goal and assign each action a deadline. Some actions associated with a career goal are: – discussing a development plan with a spouse or friend; – learning a new technical skill; – completing a special programme; and – talking to a key resource in another part of the business.
5. Finalise the plan	Agree on follow-up details and set a date to review progress.

Lateral moves to create cross-functional experiences

Lateral moves and cross-functional moves will characterise the career path of managers in the contemporary organisation, while job rotations and role changes will be frequent for professional and technical personnel. Lateral moves are on the increase due to the flattening of organisations and upward mobility not always being freely available. The implementation of this should be in such a way that individuals experience their careers as a success rather than a failure (Baruch, 1999, 2002, 2006).

Career pathing is an organisational support practice that can assist individuals in planning developmental activities such as informal and formal education, skills training and job experiences to facilitate their readiness and capability to hold more advanced jobs. Career paths exist on an informal basis in almost all organisations. However, career paths are much more useful when formally defined and documented. Such formalisation results in specific descriptions of sequential work experiences, as well as how the different sequences relate to one another (Byars and Rue, 2004).

The basic steps involved in *career pathing are* as follows:

◆ Determine or reconfirm the abilities and end behaviours of the target job. Because jobs tend to change over time, it is important to determine or confirm the requirements and review them periodically;
◆ Update and confirm employees' records concerning skills, experiences, potential abilities, career interests and objectives;
◆ Undertake a needs analysis comparison that jointly views the individual and the targeted job;
◆ Reconcile employee career desires, developmental needs and targeted job requirements with those of the organisational career management system;
◆ Identify the individual actions (work, education and training experiences) necessary for the individual to progress to the targeted job; and
◆ Create a time-oriented blueprint or chart to guide the individual.

Succession planning

Succession planning involves the recording of potential successors for managerial and other critical positions within the organisation. Succession planning can be valuable when long-term organisational planning occurs. It will be different, but not less important, in a flattened organisation where lateral movements persist. Succession planning in the contemporary organisation may be more complicated, but it is still an important practice to determine who should first be considered when a new vacancy arises or when job rotation is planned (Arnold and Randall, 2010; Baruch, 2006; Byars and Rue, 2004).

Skills inventories are an important element of the succession-planning process. A skills inventory provides certain types of information about an organisation's current management pool, potential managerial talent and employees who possess critical skills without which the organisation may suffer severe losses. Skills inventories often include information such as present position, length of service, retirement date, education and past performance evaluations. A skills inventory can be used to fill vacancies that occur unexpectedly, for example, as a result of resignations or death. Another use is in planning the development needs of individuals and using those plans to pinpoint development activities for the total organisation.

Skills inventories and succession plans are generally kept confidential and can be computerised. They are also maintained by the human resource department for the use of top executives of the organisation (Byars and Rue, 2004).

Retirement preparation programmes

Retirement preparation programmes as an organisational career management practice are directed at employees who are approaching retirement and who are about to leave the organisation. Retirement is defined as 'the departure from a job or career path, taken by individuals after middle age, where the individual displays a limited or nonexistent psychological commitment to work thereafter' (Greenhaus et al, 2010:249). In the modern workplace, many people will leave the organisation at an earlier age than the legal retirement age (which is the age of 65). An investment in this practice of providing retirement programmes manifests a high commitment of the organisation to its employees (Baruch, 1999, 2006).

Early retirement has become more common over the past two decades. Early retirement is generally viewed as the decision to retire prior to the age at which one is eligible for full corporate pension (Greenhaus et al, 2010:250). Some organisations offer incentives or early retirement packages to encourage early retirement. This method of reducing the workforce is often viewed as a humanitarian way to reduce the payroll and reward long-tenured employees. The types of incentive vary, but often include a lump-sum payment plus the extension of other benefits, such as medical insurance (Byars and Rue, 2004; Greenhaus et al, 2010).

Retirement preparation programmes can help individuals to deal constructively with the *transition* between work and retirement. Successful retirement preparation programmes should focus on both the extrinsic and intrinsic aspects of retirement. *Extrinsic elements* include financial security, housing alternatives and legal issues. *Intrinsic factors* include the various psychological issues related to disengagement from work. Programmes should ideally be run in small groups that encourage two-way communication and provide opportunities for counselling to address the social and psychological consequences of retirement. Participation in retirement preparation programmes should begin at least five years prior to anticipated retirement to allow adequate time to address all issues.

Phased retirement programmes should also be considered for older employees. Phased retirement refers to 'arrangements that provide for employees approaching retirement to ease into retirement gradually by reducing their work time and responsibilities' (Collins, 2006:695). This includes short-term projects, part-time jobs, work at home, etc. Companies should also consider *flexible work patterns* for the more competent, adaptable late-career employees, which will enable them to continue working beyond the normal retirement age.

Spouse participation in retirement preparation programmes can be beneficial and should be encouraged (Greenhaus et al, 2010).

The *pre-retirement programme* could also be transformed into a *pre-redundancy programme*. In this kind of programme, the organisation will first prepare the employees for the possibility that they could be affected by forced pre-retirement. Subsequently, the focus will move onto what can be done and how an employee in a plateau-stage career can be trained to look successfully for a new job in declining industrial sectors. In addition to such a pre-redundancy programme, the same organisation will need an after-redundancy programme, to confront the possible survivor syndrome that may affect those who have stayed (Baruch, 1999; Brockner, Tyler and Cooper-Schieder, 1992).

Mentoring and executive coaching

Mentoring is an organisational career development support practice aimed at enhancing the development of people. Clutterbuck (2001:3) defines mentoring as 'offline help by one person to another in making significant transitions in knowledge work or thinking'. This definition emphasises the importance of establishing an *informal partnership relationship* between an experienced and mature person (the mentor) and an inexperienced person (the mentee), which is built upon trust. Mentoring is a process in which the mentor offers ongoing support and development opportunities to the mentee. Addressing issues and blockages identified by the mentee, the mentor offers guidance, counselling and support in the form of pragmatic and objective assistance. The mentor and mentee share a common purpose of developing a strong *two-way learning relationship*.

Mentoring is developmental in nature and therefore a critical career development activity. Mentors can advise on development and on the way to manage a career plan; they can challenge assumptions and, where relevant, they can share their own experience. Mentoring has proved to be very effective in transferring tacit knowledge within an organisation, highlighting how effective people think, take decisions and approach complex issues. Sharing views and ideas builds understanding and trust. The mentor and mentee relationship often evolves into a key friendship, invaluable when difficult decisions arise (Allen, 2006; Clutterbuck, 2001).

A distinction is usually made between *informal* and *formal* mentoring. *Informal mentoring* involves a spontaneous relationship, while *formal mentoring* is arranged and overseen by the employer. It seems that the majority of organisations have some form of structured mentoring (Allen, 2006;).

Organisations can do the following to support mentoring that will foster career success (Allen, 2006; Hill and Bahniuk, 1998; Klasen and Clutterbuck, 2002):

◆   design formal mentoring programmes that correspond with informal mentoring;
◆   encourage an organisational learning and development climate;
◆   ensure that the corporate structure supports mentoring relationships;
◆   introduce sessions for potential mentors by focusing on mentoring functions;
◆   investigate innovative programmes, such as using an 'electronic mentor';

◆ use the existing pool of managers more creatively;
◆ use top performers in the company effectively;
◆ consider group mentoring, where one mentor is assigned to a team of four to six proteges that work together on career advancement; and
◆ consider offering incentives to top managers to encourage the mentoring of diverse groups.

Mentorship relationships should be actively promoted by organisations. The individual's career success can be enhanced and the individual's chances for survival in the organisation are probably also increased.

Executive mentoring and *coaching* is a rapidly expanding area of practice. *Executive mentoring* is done by professional mentors who help top executives get down to their own issues and build their own insights and self-awareness. *Executive coaching* is aimed at building a particular skill set and designed to solve individual problems as they arise. The most frequent use of executive coaching has been a follow-up to poor ratings on 360-degree feedback appraisals (Schultz and Schultz, 2010). *Executive coaching* includes feedback coaching, in-depth development coaching and content coaching (Clutterbuck, 2001; Thach and Heinselman, 1999). Because feedback alone is often not sufficient motivation for a manager to alter his or her behaviour, a coach will be brought in to help interpret the feedback, with the manager to devise strategies for eliciting the desired changes in behaviour (Schultz and Schultz, 2010:146). Research by Smither, London, Flautt, Vargas and Kucine (2003) showed that managers' performance ratings improved significantly after receiving coaching and that managers tend to agree with their coaches' recommendations. They also tend to rate the process as valuable to their career development.

Thach and Heinselman (1999) describe a common executive coaching scenario as follows:

◆ Leader completes 360-degree instrument.
◆ First coaching session: 360-degree data analysis and development planning sessions (one to four hours).
◆ Telephone coaching sessions every two to four weeks to assess progress and roadblocks and to give encouragement (30 to 60 minutes).
◆ Three-month mini assessment on development areas to assess whether progress was made.
◆ Final coaching session: Debrief mini-assessment, update development plan, offer encouragement and decide on continuation of coaching.

Executive mentoring is an important aspect of the executive coaching process. The professional mentor/coach uses current issues to explore patterns of thinking and behaviour, often starting with the executive's values. They ask penetrating questions that stimulate thinking, challenge the executive to take control of issues avoided, help the executive put his or her own learning in context and raise his or her ability to cope with new issues through greater self-understanding and confidence (Clutterbuck, 2001).

Table 8.4 gives an overview of the *key roles of mentors and mentees,* while table 8.5 sets out the *typical responsibilities* that are linked to the roles of mentors and mentees in a career discussion.

Table 8.4 *Roles of mentors and mentees (Coetzee and Stone, 2004)*

Role of the mentor	Role of the mentee
Advisor: gives an opinion about what to do or how to handle a specific situation	*Self-knower*: understands own needs, aspirations, goals, beliefs, values, interests, competencies and skills; is aware of personal style and behaviour and of how these influence the relationship
Counsellor: a person who is close to the learner, who the learner trusts and to whom the learner confides personal issues and concerns on a more confidential level	
Encourager: recommends actions or gives advice	*Owner*: takes ownership of learning, career, choosing a mentor, preparing for discussion and personal development
Subject matter expert: gives courage, hope, or confidence to another; helps and gives support; and celebrates successes	
Friend: supporter or ally; a person at the other end of the journey	*Portfolio builder*: develops a portfolio that includes transferable skills and competencies
Guardian: watches over, protects, cares for and defends	*Action taker*: does concrete action planning and takes action; measures progress towards specific goals
Leader: directs or guides	
Motivator: excites or moves another to action	*Evaluator*: evaluates mentor-learner relationship, personal needs and aspirations, and initiates new relationships
Role model: a person in a specific role to be followed or imitated owing to the excellence or worth of that role	
Knowledge developer: shares knowledge or insight	
An instructor: shows or guides another to do something	

Table 8.5 *Conducting review discussions: Roles of mentor and mentee (Coetzee and Stone, 2004)*

Conducting progress-review discussions		
Mentor's role	**Mentee's role**	**Organisational results**
Listen	*Communicate*	Clear understanding by mentee and mentor of mentee values, interests and skills
Encourage learner to talk about himself/herself	Talk openly about satisfaction/dissatisfaction	
Listen to results of learner's self-assessments and assessors' assessments	Use resources to assess values, interests and skills	
Ask questions to clarify learner's assessments	Communicate results of assessments to mentor	
Give ideas on resources for further exploration	Consider own talents and abilities	

Conducting progress-review discussions		
Mentor's role	**Mentee's role**	**Organisational results**
Clarify Establish clear standards and expectations Give feedback with supporting evidence and rationale Add information overlooked by learner Link learning progress/ performance to potential	*Ask for information* Ask for feedback on realism of self-assessments and on formative assessments by assessor Accept feedback without becoming defensive Ask for clarification and specific examples	Mentee gains a clear understanding of mentor's perceptions of his or her skills and development needs
Look ahead Give views about current problems regarding development programme and about career options and challenges Link learner with others who have relevant information Provide awareness and insights regarding changes in industry, sector organisation, and profession	*Explore* Seek advice on organisational realities, employment realities/options and career implications Follow up on network and alliance building Seek data on changes in industry, sector organisation, and profession	Organisation's strategic direction linked to career opportunities
Give guidance Relate changes/challenges/ options to learner career/ employment/further education goals Express support or reservation related to learner goals Provide ideas and input regarding opportunities	*Develop strategies* Select multiple career/ employment/further education options Use information to make options realistic, relevant and specific Communicate goals to mentor	Clearly defined multiple mentee career/employment/ further education goals that are realistic and relevant to the organisation and the mentee
Review Review development plan Offer suggestions to strengthen plan Refer to resources that can assist with implementation Schedule reviews Debrief development plan assignments	*Plan* Analyse development needs Identify development activities and complete a written plan Submit plan for mentor review Move forward to implement plan	A written plan for mentee development leading to constructive action and follow-through

Dual ladder

The *dual ladder* is a parallel hierarchy, initially created for professional or technical staff, which allows them upward mobility and recognition without occupying a managerial role. In the modern workplace, those with managerial skills and aspiration who have no prospects of promotion in the old sense, as well as those working in crucial roles with a responsibility and remuneration level similar to that of managers, will also become eligible for the dual-ladder initiative (Baruch, 1999). The dual ladder can also be seen as the creation of multiple promotion paths that recognise, encourage and reward employees regardless of the career path they choose (Greenhaus et al, 2010).

Customising career progression and development

Benko and Weisberg (2009) developed a model of career progression and development called *Mass Career Customisation* (MCC) that offers employees options for customising career paths. The MCC model is a framework for career progression and development that is based on the idea of a corporate lattice. A lattice allows one to move in many directions, it is not limited to upward or downwards progress and can be repeated infinitely at any scale. Corporate lattices are living platforms for growth that allow upward momentum along multiple paths, taking into account the changing needs of both the individual and the organisation across various intervals of time. By means of continuous collaboration between employer and employee, a corporate lattice can foster a new kind of loyalty (Chalofsky, 2010).

As shown in figure 8.2, the MCC framework is based on four sets of options or four dimensions of a career: *pace* (options relating to the rate of career progression), *workload* (choices relating to the quantity of work output), *location and schedule* (options for where and when work is performed) and *role* (choices in position and responsibility). The MCC profile is a snapshot of each employee's career at any given point in time and it can be adjusted over time. Like adjusting the sound on a stereo equalizer by moving the sliders up or down, MCC allows employees to dial up or dial down to optimise their career path at varying career stages (Chalofsky, 2010: 116). Employees derive a psychic benefit from knowing that options and an organisational process for managing them are available should they need to deviate from normal, full-time employment status sometime in the future. The MCC framework addresses individuals' needs for achieving work-life balance without compromising their career options.

Initially most employees will have a profile that looks more or less the same as the others. However, over time, every employee's MCC profile will exhibit its own path, recording the series of choices made over the course of the employee's career. For many, this path will look like a wave of sorts (referred to as the *MCC Sine Wave*), with climbing and falling levels of contribution over time. For example, an employee in the early life stage (pre-kids phase of his life) and entry-level stage of his career may experience an accelerated career path with a full workload and being unrestricted in terms of location/schedule. Then, as he gets married and as children and his career progresses, his level of contribution may rise and fall. He may decide to dial down his career (slow down his career pace and restrict his location/schedule) for a period of time to enable him to deal constructively with his work-family life interface. He may also decide to dial up his career pace and location/schedule in part so that his wife can dial down and spend time at home with the kids before they go off to university (Benko and Weisberg, 2009).

Pace	Workload	Location/schedule	Role
Accelerated	Full	Not restricted	Leader
↕	↕	↕	↕
Decelerated	Reduced	Restricted	Individual contributor
Options relating to the rate of career progression	Choices relating to the quantity of work output	Options for where and when work is performed	Choices in position and responsibility

Figure 8.2 *The four dimensions of Mass Career Customisation*

Booklets and/or pamphlets and on-line career development centres

Booklets and/or pamphlets

Booklets, pamphlets or leaflets on career issues are a formal presentation by the organisation of all kinds of career-related information (Baruch, 2006). They introduce what is being offered by the organisation in terms of career opportunities and all available career-management support practices.

Not all employees in an organisation are exposed to the facilities of career centres and workshops. To assist these employees, alternative tools, such as well-designed *career-planning workbooks*, can be used. 'Career workbooks are structured to accomplish the same objective as career planning workshops except that these workbooks are self-paced, self-directed and designed to be completed by individuals themselves' (Singh, 2006:711). A career-planning workbook enables individuals to work on their own through a series of assessment exercises that will assist them in career planning. The advantage of these books is that they are designed so that people can work at their own pace. A counsellor may sometimes give employees a workbook to work through beforehand so that the counsellor can discuss the results with them at a later stage. It often happens that individuals can solve their career problems on their own simply by working through a career-planning workbook.

The contents of a workbook can vary, although many books make use of a model and there are several common elements. A workbook usually covers the following aspects: self-assessment, examining career directions, finding a job that fits, preparing for a career development discussion and preparing a career development action plan.

On-line career development centre

An *online career development centre* can be useful in supporting the practice of making booklets and pamphlets available to employees. Electronic boards and directions where structural changes can be fed into the system will result in an updated version of the electronic booklet. Online services can provide many types of career and employment-related information on demand, such as:

◆ information about employment trends and job opportunities;
◆ details of the competencies and skills required for jobs to which employees aspire;
◆ self-assessment tools such as culture-free personality tests and interest indicators that employees can use to determine which types of job they may best pursue;
◆ links to online employment resources such as job listings and career development information;
◆ employee online employment counselling, including advice on preparing for interviews;
◆ job search guides;
◆ résumé preparation tools; and
◆ career-related articles (Byars and Rue, 2004).

By establishing an on-line career development centre, the organisation effectively communicates to employees at every level to take charge of their own careers (Albrecht, 1996).

Assessment and development centres

Assessment and development centres have been found to be a reliable and valid tool for career development (Baruch, 2006; Howard, 1997; Iles, 1999; Woehr, 2006). Assessment centres focus on multiple attributes relevant to an individual's overall performance and are used for identifying individuals' relative strengths and weaknesses with respect to key performance domains for selection purposes (Woehr, 2006:27–28). Assessment centres are generally used for making decisions regarding employee redeployment such as promoting, evaluating and training individuals with managerial potential by exposing individuals to simulated problems that would be faced in a real-life managerial situation (Byars and Rue, 2004).

Development centres evolved from assessment centres and are directed at the general development and enhancement of managers, preparing them for future roles.

A development centre is most appropriately used to diagnose individual training needs, facilitate self-development and usually forms part of the organisational career development support system (Harrison, 2009). In a development centre, the purpose of identifying individuals' strengths and weaknesses is solely for development purposes and not for the purpose of selection as is the case with an assessment centre (Arnold and Randall, 2010; Baruch, 1999). Development centres bring not only current and potential skills to the surface, but also personal values and motivation, providing a valuable opportunity for individuals to clarify what kind of career path they want and seem equipped to follow (Harrison, 2009).

Trained professionals such as industrial psychologists are frequently used as assessors in assessment and development centres. In addition, successful managers are often used as assessors in the belief that these people would best know the qualities required for success (Byars and Rue, 2004). Following development centre participation each individual should have a personal development plan agreed with their manager, opportuinities to develop and support from colleagues, superiors and internal development staff (Harrison, 2009).

Career self-management training and career planning workshops

Career self-management training

An integrated career development support system should stimulate and support a process of continuous development through which all employees have opportunities to acquire new skills, expand their experience and develop their potential to sustain their employability. At the individual level many employees will need help in making the most of their opportunities (Harrison, 2009). *Career self-management training* is offered by many organisations to help employees assume the responsibility to upgrade their skills and learn new ones to ease the passage through critical career transition points, the three most common being (Harrison, 2009):

◆ *Organisational entry*, the first point at which, when working in an organisation, career development opportunities become accessible. A motivating induction and socialisation process, supported by mentoring and personal development plans, formal further education and core competency training or on-the-job coaching, usually act as the first stage of career development within the organisation. The focus of career self-management training is on helping new employees gain or improve learning strategies and skills that will equip them to take up career development opportunities as and when they arise.

◆ The *plateau* reached when little if any further upward career movement within the organisation is likely. During this stage career self-management training focuses on career counselling, joint planning and job redesign to help boost the commitment levels of employees who feel that they are stagnating and in some cases, to re-orientate them to expanded or different tasks or stimulating external opportunities. Offering employees training to become coaches or mentors is another way of utilising their skills and accumulated experience to the benefit of others and of aiding their access to rewarding new roles.

◆ *Approaching exit* from the organisation. Career self-management training focuses on developing the skills and attitudes that will help ease the passage through the transition before the change takes place.

Career self-management training aims to help individuals address four core questions to which each individual continuously seeks answers during a career (Harrison, 2009):

◆ Who am I (in terms of abilities and potential)?;
◆ How am I viewed by others?;
◆ What are my career options?; and
◆ How can I achieve my career goals?

A typical career self-management training programme consists of three stages presented in the form of career planning workshops on successive days (Schultz and Schultz, 2010):

Workshop 1:   Assessing career attitudes, values, plans and goals.
Workshop 2:   Analysing how these goals have or have not been met by the current job.
Workshop 3:   Discussing career strategies to create opportunities to meet one's plans and goals, whether on or off the job. This stage includes upgrading skills, soliciting feedback from colleagues and supervisors, networking and being mobile in seeking new job opportunities.

Career planning workshops

'Career planning workshops involve a structured group format in which participants interact with one another to formulate, share and discuss personal information that leads to self-analysis and eventual self-awareness' (Singh, 2006:711). Career planning workshops are general career-development programmes which are offered by organisations themselves or by professionals to assist individuals in career planning. In such workshops, people are usually actively involved, obtain self-knowledge, are introduced to the world of work opportunities in the organisation and develop their own career plans. A common pattern for participants is a discussion of strengths and weaknesses, the provision of feedback about each other's behaviour, participating in self-assessment exercises and making plans for future career moves. It offers chances for discussion and feedback from others (Arnold and Randall, 2010; Baruch, 1999).

Advantages of a career workshop (Baruch, 1999, 2006; Haskell, 1993; Shivy, 2006) are the following:

◆ people are helped to manage their own careers;
◆ individuals take personal responsibility for their career paths and learn how to make career decisions;
◆ career options are created;
◆ people are helped to find career planning information;
◆ confidence and self-esteem are engendered;
◆ self-assessment organisational opportunities and career counselling are combined;
◆ career workshops can improve the employability of the participants, enhancing their career resilience; and
◆ career planning workshops are one of the most efficient and cost-effective ways of assisting individuals with their career concerns.

Contents of a career workshop

Although the contents of career workshops differ, in general they have the following components in common (Otte and Hutcheson, 1992):

◆ individual assessment (information about self);
◆ environmental assessment (information about work);
◆ comparison of self-perceptions with those of others (reality testing), establishing long– and short-term goals (goal setting);
◆ choosing among alternatives (decision-making); and
◆ establishing and implementing the plan (action planning).

Self-assessment forms a central part of all programmes; this means obtaining knowledge of the individual's skills, abilities, interests, values, personality, interpersonal orientations, preferences and needs. Among the many ideas on which career workshops can focus are how to increase employability, how to create new satellite companies or joint ventures and the concept and practice of management buy-outs. All these and other ideas would help participants develop new insights into the future of their careers — within the organisation or elsewhere (Baruch, 1999).

Preparing for the career workshop

The person responsible for conducting the workshop should be well prepared. All material should be carefully planned and designed well in advance. The organiser must ensure that there is enough material available for the delegates and that activities are planned according to a time schedule set out in an agenda. It is often difficult to decide whether or not to send information directly to the delegates prior to the workshop. Both approaches have advantages and disadvantages. Very often some of the delegates fail to complete the material and do the required reading in advance, which results in frustration and wasted time for those who have.

An introductory letter should be sent to all delegates as preparation for the workshop. Table 8.6 provides an example of the *agenda* for a career workshop.

Table 8.6 *Example of an agenda for a career workshop*

I	**Introduction**
I.I	Welcome by managing director
I.2	Overview of agenda
I.3	Participants introduce themselves — they explain their current position in the company and their expectations from the programme
I.4	Explanation of the company's philosophy with regard to career management
2.	**Self-assessment**
2.I	Individuals make an analysis of their likes/dislikes, values, life skills, personality, qualities, strengths, needs, weaknesses, career patterns. Information about the following can be obtained: values, career anchors, career patterns, interests, personality, etc
2.2	Reality test: How the group sees you
3.	**Environmental assessment**
3.I	Supplying information about opportunities and alternative future jobs in the organisation
3.2	Supplying information on current jobs
3.3	Identifying what experiences are needed for future assignments
3.4	Obtaining information about family needs and aspirations
4.	**Career goal setting**
4.I	Identifying where you are and where you want to go
4.2	Formulating long-term conceptual goals (ie preferred environment in eight to ten years)
4.3	Formulating short-term conceptual goals, ie in support of the long-term ones
4.4	Translating conceptual goals into long-term and short-term operational goals
5.	**Action plan**
5.I	Making decisions
5.2	Re-evaluating goals in accordance with options
5.3	Developing an action career plan

Conducting the career workshop: Phase I

Opening

The opening of the workshop is of prime importance. The intention should be to create a warm and comfortable atmosphere. The opening could be done by the managing director if it is an in-house programme. The managing director should stress the importance of such a workshop for the individual as well as for the organisation. The delegates should be left with the feeling that they are partners with the organisation in the process.

Introduction of participants

The introduction of the delegates follows the opening. The participants should be given the chance to introduce themselves spontaneously. Usually people are required to name their position, their past positions and their expectations of the programme. It is crucial that the course leader should ensure that the expectations of the delegates are related to the goal and the objectives of the programme. Unrealistic expectations should be dealt with early.

Self-assessment

As explained, self-assessment is a prominent part of the career planning workshop. The data gathered during such a session usually assists individuals in clarifying who they are, what they can do and what they want to do. Many authors emphasise that self-knowledge is a prerequisite and the cornerstone of career planning. Individuals who know themselves well are in a better position to make rational decisions. Individuals' careers are founded on the type of person they are, as well as on the type of life they lead outside the work environment. Self-insight concerns such aspects as abilities, personality, strengths, weaknesses, interests, values, lifestyle, individuality, etc and is therefore crucial. The following are examples of instruments that can be used for self-assessment:

- ◆ *Personality:* 16 Personality Factor Questionnaire (16 PF), Myers-Briggs Type Indicator (MBTI) and Occupational Personality Questionnaire (OPQ);
- ◆ *Interest:* Holland's Self-Directed Search (SDS);
- ◆ *Career anchors:* Schein's (1990) Career Orientation Inventory and structured interview (COI);
- ◆ *Life values:* The Value Scale, published by the HSRC;
- ◆ *Interpersonal orientations:* Firo-B;
- ◆ *Career patterns:* Brousseau and Driver's Career Concept Questionnaire (CCQ).
- ◆ *Career adaptability*: Savickas's Career Adaptability Inventory;
- ◆ *Employability:* Employability Inventories; and
- ◆ *Psychological career resources*: Coetzee's Psychological Career Resources Inventory (PCRI).

Delegates can also complete a questionnaire explaining what they would like to continue doing and what they would prefer to stop doing, based on their strengths and weaknesses and on the frustrations experienced in their present position.

Conducting the career workshop: Phase 2

Environmental assessment

The second phase of a career workshop is to undertake an environmental assessment. Once the individual assessment has been made the information is linked to options available in the world of work. The aim is to strive for a better fit between individuals and their future jobs.

Career counsellors report that people often lack knowledge about the work options available in the labour market. Individuals often feel frustrated by the fact that, having done a thorough self-assessment and having been well trained, they then have to look for work in a depressed economy, which sometimes makes an ideal job fit out of the question. It is important that, although jobs are scarce, individuals should still be encouraged to do career planning and try to find a job that will best suit their abilities, values and skills.

In the case of an in-house programme, the course leader should give the delegates information on developments in the organisation and on future career prospects and opportunities. Employees should be fully aware of the strategy of the organisation and try to envisage how their own careers will be changing and which other careers will become more relevant.

Depending on the level of the workshop, such aspects as study options, relevant educational institutions and the availability of finances should also be covered. Sometimes, course leaders go even further and teach people how to draw up a curriculum vitae and how to cope in an interview.

Reality testing

During this session, the participants are given the opportunity to verify their personal perspectives regarding their skills, abilities and options (Otte and Hutcheson, 1992). Other people's views about an individual's skills and knowledge are obtained. This information can be examined and integrated in career decisions.

Establish life and career goals

As discussed in chapter 2, the setting of life and career goals gives direction to the career planning process. Employees should set long- and short-term goals. Delegates should create a vision of the future and should not leave a career workshop without specific career goals. Goals should be put down on paper and should include the activities that will be necessary to attain them.

Action plan

The objective of career planning is to achieve the career goals that have been set; the development of an action plan is therefore crucial. Due to changes in organisations (flatter structures, downsizing, etc) and the fact that opportunities are limited, the focus of action plans should not always be on upward mobility but rather on training, development of the present position and on acquiring the necessary skills to increase employability.

Evaluation of workshop

One way of measuring the effectiveness of a programme is to obtain the reaction of the participants (see table 8.7).

Table 8.7 *Career management skills workshop feedback*

			Agree				Disagree
Please let us know your reaction to this programme. You do not need to sign this page, but we do ask that you complete it fully and honestly.							
Part I			Agree				Disagree
How much do you agree with the following statements?							
1.1	I now have an action plan for managing my career.		5	4	3	2	1
1.2	I have specific information on my skills, interests, and values to use in ongoing career management.		5	4	3	2	1
1.3	I have information on how to find out about work and job options inside and outside the company.		5	4	3	2	1
1.4	The instructor for this course was knowledgeable about the subject and able to present it effectively.		5	4	3	2	1

			High				Low
Part 2			High				Low
2.1	How would you rate your skills in managing your career before coming to this workshop?		5	4	3	2	1
2.2	How would you rate your skills in managing your career now?		5	4	3	2	1

Part 3

We would also like to know your specific comments.

(Use back if you need more room.)

3.1   What was the most useful part of the workshop for you?

3.2   What part of the workshop was least useful for you?

3.3   Are there parts of the workshop that you would like to see expanded? If so, what?

Would you recommend this programme to other managers? Why or why not?

Hutcheson and Otte (1997), Helping Employees Manage Careers

Orientation, induction or socialisation

Orientation

Orientation can be described as the process whereby newcomers are introduced to the organisation, the job itself, their workplace and the policies and procedures of the organisation. It is a *formal programme* with the primary objective of giving the newcomer *information about the job and the organisation*. New employees always experience anxiety and a well-planned orientation programme can *reduce anxiety* and *accelerate the adjustment* of new employees to their jobs and to the organisation.

Objectives of orientation

The following are regarded as important:

◆ familiarising new employees with the mission and objectives of the organisation, as well as how to strive for them;
◆ familiarising new employees with the work methods and procedures and with their specific departments;
◆ familiarising new employees with the content and procedures of their jobs;
◆ explaining the requirements of their jobs to new employees;
◆ establishing good interpersonal relations between new employees and their colleagues and supervisors; and
◆ indicating the desired behaviour that employees should show in the execution of their duties.

To achieve the above-mentioned objectives, the following *guidelines* usually apply:

◆ a distinctive orientation programme must be compiled for each department in accordance with the approved guidelines;
◆ a mentor must be appointed for each new employee; and
◆ feedback about the progress made during the orientation programme must take place on a three-monthly basis and reports must be submitted for checking.

For orientation programmes to be effective the following guidelines should be followed:

◆ the first day should be well planned and managed. These first impressions will be remembered for many years to come;
◆ the orientation programme should also be managed well in the first two months, as impressions that are formed within this period are often lasting;
◆ teach newcomers about the total organisation so that they can understand how they fit into the organisation; and
◆ do not overload newcomers with information.

Effective orientation can, amongst other factors, lower personnel turnover, motivate employees and develop a positive attitude towards training and development.

Responsibility for orientation

Although the responsibility for orientation is primarily the function of the line manager, different people play an important role. *Newcomers* are central in the orientation process and it is expected of them to be actively involved in the process and to share responsibility for their orientation. The immediate *supervisor* is responsible for planning, organising and controlling the duties of newcomers and for appointing mentors. *Mentors* arranged by the supervisor are responsible for training and supporting new employees. The *human resource department* is responsible for the overall co-ordination of the orientation effort and for the training of supervisors and mentors in orientation practices. The newcomer and the organisation therefore have a *shared responsibility for* orientation.

Induction or socialisation

Induction or socialisation is the process whereby all newcomers are introduced to the organisation and where they learn the behaviours and attitudes necessary for assuming roles in the organisation. It can also be viewed as a process of adaptation and it requires the new employee to learn to understand his new employer (Cascio, 2003). It is a process of learning and development. From an integration perspective, it is a strategy for achieving congruence of organisational and individual goals. Part of it is formal, led by organisational officials, whereas other aspects are learned in an informal manner, not necessarily in line with formal organisational norms and policies (Baruch, 2006; Greenhaus et al, 2010).

One of the main changes in the modern workplace is the much wider age span of newcomers. Whereas, in the past, many people joined organisations at an early age and, in many cases, stayed for their whole working life in the same workplace, people now tend to have multiple career paths and frequent changes of employer are common. The induction process should be adapted to the different needs of experienced professionals or managers and young school-leavers, people on learnerships agreements and new graduates.

Stages of socialisation

The process of organisational socialisation can best be described in terms of a model consisting of various stages.

Feldman's three-stage entry model

Feldman (1976) established a model of socialisation based on previous research, which was supported by research undertaken on 118 hospital employees (nurses, nurses' aides, radiology technologists, tradesmen and accounting clerks). His model consists of *three stages*, namely *anticipatory socialisation, accommodation* and *role management*.

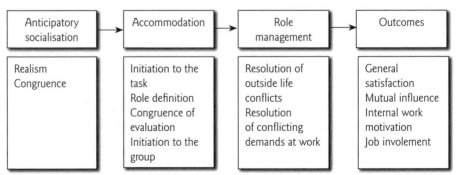

Anticipatory socialisation	Accommodation	Role management	Outcomes
Realism Congruence	Initiation to the task Role definition Congruence of evaluation Initiation to the group	Resolution of outside life conflicts Resolution of conflicting demands at work	General satisfaction Mutual influence Internal work motivation Job involement

Figure 8.3 *Process and outcome variables of socialisation*

Anticipatory socialisation

This *first stage* is the *learning* that takes place *before* the prospective employee joins the organisation. At this stage, the principal activities are the formation of expectations, a process that involves the processing of information gained from prospective employers and decision-making about employment. The progress is measured by:

◆ the accuracy of prospective employees' picture of the organisation (realism); and
◆ the extent to which the organisation is likely to satisfy the prospective employees' needs and use their skills (congruence).

Research indicates that anticipating one's job prior to employment has a strong relationship with socialisation processes and outcomes. Non-anticipatory newcomers were significantly less satisfied with their jobs, less committed to the organisation, not internally motivated to work and less successful psychologically (Holton and Russell, 1997).

Accommodation

The *second stage* is the period of *accommodation,* during which the employee gets to know the organisation and tries to *participate* in its activities.

During this period, employees learn new tasks, enter into interpersonal relationships with their colleagues, clarify their roles and evaluate their progress in the organisation. At this stage, progress is measured by:

◆ the extent to which employees feel proficient at their new tasks and are accepted as competent (initiation to the task);
◆ the extent to which employees feel accepted by their colleagues (initiation to the group);
◆ the extent to which employees have agreed with the work group on the activities they are to carry out (role definition); and
◆ the extent to which employees and their supervisors agree on the progress made by employees and on their strengths and weaknesses (congruence of evaluation).

Role management

The *third stage* is the period of *role management,* during which the employee has *solved the initial problems* that have arisen within the work group and can now *concentrate on relations* with other groups, both in the workplace and outside. An example may be a conflict between the employee's work and home life or a disagreement between the employee's work group and another work group within the organisation. At this stage, progress is measured by:

◆ the extent to which employees have learnt to deal with conflicts between their home life and work life (resolution of outside life conflicts); and
◆ the extent to which employees have learnt to deal with conflicts between the various work groups (resolution of conflicting demands).

Outcomes

According to this model, socialisation results in *different outcomes*. The following variables are identified:

◆ general satisfaction — an overall satisfaction and happiness which are experienced by the employee;

◆ mutual influence — the extent to which employees feel control over the way work is carried out;

◆ internal work motivation — this can be referred to as the degree to which employees are self-motivated; and

◆ job involvement — the degree of personal involvement in their work.

Wanous (1992) combines the older models (Buchanan, 1974; Feldman, 1976; Porter, Lawler and Hackman, 1975; Schein, 1978) into a single integrated view of post-entry organisational socialisation (table 8.8). The first *three stages* refer to the *socialisation process proper* and the *last stage* is an example of the *transition from new member to insider.*

Table 8.8 *Stages in the socialisation process*

Stage 1: Confronting and accepting organisational reality Confirmation/disconfirmation of expectations Conflicts between personal job wants and the organisational climates Discovering which personal aspects are reinforced, which are not reinforced and which are punished by the organisation
Stage 2: Achieving role clarity Being initiated to the tasks in the new job Defining one's interpersonal roles – with respect to peers – with respect to one's boss Learning to cope with resistance to change Congruence between a newcomer's own evaluation of performance and the organisation's evaluation of performance Learning how to work within the given degree of structure and ambiguity
Stage 3: Locating oneself in the organisational context Learning which modes of behaviour are congruent with those of the organisation Resolution of conflicts at work and between outside interests and work Commitment to work and to the organisation stimulated by first-year job challenge The establishment of an altered self-image, new interpersonal relationships and the adoption of new values

> *Stage 4: Detecting signposts of successful socialisation*
> Achievement of organisational dependability and commitment
> High satisfaction in general
> Feelings of mutual acceptance
> Job involvement and internal work motivation
> The sending of 'signals' between newcomers and the organisation to indicate
> mutual acceptance.

Wanous, JP (1992:209)

Rate of socialisation

Reichers (1987) suggests a model with *factors* that influence the rate of interaction between newcomers and insiders. He says that the socialisation rate will increase if both parties pro-act and look out for opportunities to interact with each other. *Pro-action* is characterised by activities such as asking questions, talking to other people, suggesting social opportunities, etc. A group *of factors* (personal and situational) are identified, which can *increase interaction frequency* between insiders and newcomers in the workplace, namely: (1) newcomer characteristics; (2) insider characteristics; (3) situational factors. Further, Reichers (1987) describes *three individual difference variables* which *motivate* insiders and newcomers towards *increased interaction frequency:*

◆ *Field dependence:* This indicates employees' reliance on situational context to interpret the behaviour of others. Field-dependent individuals should concentrate on the interpersonal skills required to approach fellow employees, to understand them within the context of the workplace and to place themselves in this context.

◆ *Tolerance of ambiguity:* New employees may find themselves in a situation which is ambiguous or difficult to interpret. If employees are not able to handle this ambiguity, they may jump to conclusions, thus gaining a distorted view of reality. Intolerance of ambiguity could therefore inhibit the socialisation process. Such employees could rely on the opinions of one or two people whom they regard as significant, instead of taking the entire work group as a reference point.

◆ *The need for affiliation:* New employees with a high need for affiliation will initiate interpersonal interaction in the workplace, such as lunching with colleagues and social chatter.

It could happen, however, that the work situation does not respond to new employees' attempts at establishing interaction. Situational variables are thus important and can *facilitate a proactive approach* on the part of new employees. Some *situational variables are* as follows:

◆ *Other people* in the workplace, such as colleagues, supervisors, subordinates and customers, act as agents of socialisation, teaching the new employees about their work roles. They make a significant contribution to the speed with which new employees will adjust to the organisation. It is therefore not only the new employees' field dependence, tolerance of ambiguity and need for affiliation that are important, but also the same characteristics (insider characteristics) as shown by other people in the workplace, who may or may not initiate interaction with newcomers.

◆ *Interdependent tasks* may serve to bring about interaction between new employees and their colleagues, even if new employees are not proactive.

◆ *Formal orientation programmes, on-the-job training* and *early performance appraisals* bring about interaction between newcomers and insiders.

To sum up, there are thus *three categories of variables* that facilitate interaction in the workplace:

◆ variables that cause *new employees* to follow a proactive approach;
◆ variables that cause their *colleagues (insiders)* to follow a proactive approach; and
◆ variables resulting from *organisational procedures and practices* (Reichers, 1987).

Information sources

Socialisation also means obtaining the necessary *information* to enable newcomers to *understand their new environment* better. During the *first period of employment,* employees' major concerns are to gather information, to acquaint themselves with the job and to get role clarification (Ostroff and Kozlowski, 1992). To obtain this information employees have to rely on sources like supervisors, co-workers, mentors (interpersonal sources) and official organisational literature, experimenting with new behaviours and observation (non-interpersonal sources). Research has shown that newcomers obtain information regarding organisational contextual domains from the following *sources* (Ostroff and Kozlowski, 1992):

◆ *observation of others* is a primary source;
◆ *task and role-related aspects* are the primary focus;
◆ *observation and experimentation* are the most useful sources for obtaining knowledge; and
◆ *supervisors* as an information source and obtaining knowledge about the task and role domains are most important for positive socialisation outcomes.

In conclusion, the following *approaches* to socialisation can be suggested (Ardts and Van der Velde, 2001; Byars and Rue, 2004; Jokisaari and Nurmi, 2009):

◆ provide incentives, training and/or support for initiative shown by newcomers;
◆ train and sensitise insiders regarding the key elements of socialisation; and
◆ make supervisors more aware of the importance of newcomers.

Secondments

Secondment is the temporary assignment to another area within the organisation. At a more advanced level, secondments can be taken outside the organisation. The stimulus for offering people secondments can be derived from the managers of employees, from mentors or from career counselling and performance appraisal systems. Secondments require long-term human resource planning. In addition, there is also the risk of losing successful managers to the company to which they are seconded (Arnold and Randall, 2010; Baruch, 2006).

Redeployment and outplacement programmes

Redeployment and outplacement programmes are ways of terminating employees that can benefit both the employees and the organisation. *Redeployment,* often the result of a business slowdown or a reduced need for certain skills, refers to the transfer of an employee from one position or area to another. Redeployment is usually coupled with training for the transition to new job skills and responsibilities (Cascio, 2003:673). *Outplacement* refers to a benefit provided by an employer to help an employee terminate his or her employment and find new employment opportunities elsewhere (Byars and Rue, 2004:239). The organisation gains by terminating the employees before they become deadwood; employees gain by finding new jobs and, at the same time, preserving their dignity (Byars and Rue, 2004).

Skills assessment, establishment of new career objectives, résumé preparation, interview training and generation of job interviews are services generally offered through an outplacement programme. The outplacement programme is generally supported by the career centre, which includes services such as training for those who notify terminated employees, office support, spouse involvement and individual psychological counselling. Most companies make use of outplacement consultants or a recruitment agency to provide immediate support to the employees concerned (Byars and Rue, 2004).

Special programmes

The prominence of *special programmes* for designated groups (black people, women and people with disabilities) and other unique populations, such as expatriates and repatriates, high-flyers and people on learnerships, will increase in the modern workplace (Baruch, 1999, 2002). Special programmes are meant to support unique populations who have special needs in terms of development support.

Designated groups

Designated groups (black people, women and people with disabilities) have historically been discriminated against by being denied educational and developmental opportunities. Ethnic background, disability, age and religious discrimination can prevent appropriate people from contributing. For example, mass early retirements accepted by or imposed on people in their fifties may deprive organisations of a pool of talented and experienced people (Baruch, 1999, 2002).

Expatriates and repatriates

The *management of expatriates and repatriates* is a crucial task for *multinational* or global enterprises. The most important aspect of this type of management is rigorous preparation for the assignment, with emphasis on *cultural induction,* maintaining communication with the expatriates and paying attention to the repatriation period. The expatriate population is likely to expand in the future as globalisation spreads. Career paths in multinational corporations will include overseas posts as a crucial part of the development process for the managerial workplace (Baruch, 1999, 2002).

Retention of high potential talent

The *retention of high potential talent* such as, for example, *high-flyers* or *high potentials* (people who are earmarked for promotion) and *key talent* (people with business-specific technical knowledge or skills or special know-how) is increasingly receiving attention in the contemporary workplace. As discussed in chapter 2, the specialist knowledge workers who are of particular significance in today's knowledge economy all represent 'key talent' (Harrison, 2009). People with talent and leadership potential are a scarce resource and, because of the demographic reduction in workforce numbers, including the managerial layers, most organisations have introduced talent management practices and activities aimed at retaining their high potential pool of talent.

Talent consists of those individuals who can make a difference to organisational performance, either through their immediate contribution or in the longer term by demonstrating the highest level of potential (Harrison, 2009). *Talent management* entails the *sourcing* (finding talent), *screening* (sorting qualified and unqualified applicants), *selection* (assessment/testing, interviewing, reference/background checking of applicants), *onboarding* (offer generation/acceptance), *retention* (measures to keep the talent that contributes to the success of the organisation), *development* (training, growth, assignments), *deployment* (optimal assignment of staff to projects, lateral opportunities, promotions) and *renewal* of the workforce through continuous strategic analyses and planning activities (Schweyer, 2004:22).

Talented individuals want up-to-date skills that will enable them to move easily out of one form into another in pursuit of attractive career moves. Valued specialist workers want to hang on to their unique knowledge, since it is their negotiating tool and key source of employability. Employers who do not want to lose their talented staff invest heavily in a talent development strategy (Harrison, 2009).

A talent strategy and the human resource practices associated with it aim to attract, retain, motivate and develop the particular kind of talent an organisation needs in ways that build commitment, ensure competence and result in a contribution that the business finds valuable and that the individual regards as personally meaningful (Harrison, 2009:424).

Table 8.9 lists the critical components of a talent development programme.

Table 8.9 *Ten critical components of a talent development programme*
(Knowledge Resources, 2010)

1	Explicitly test candidates in three dimensions: ability, engagement and aspiration.
2	Emphasise future competencies needed (derived from corporate growth plans) more heavily than current performance when choosing employees for development.
3	Manage the quantity and quality of high potentials at the corporate level as a portfolio of scarce growth assets.
4	Forget rote functional or business-unit rotations; place young leaders in intense assignments with precisely described development challenges.
5	Identify the riskiest, most challenging positions across the company and assign them directly to rising stars.
6	Create individual development plans; link personal objectives to the company's plans for growth, rather than to generic competency models.
7	Re-evaluate top talent annually for possible changes in ability, engagement and aspiration levels.
8	Offer significantly differentiated compensation and recognition to star employees.
9	Hold regular, open dialogues between high potentials and programme managers to monitor star employees' development and satisfaction.
10	Replace broadcast communications about the company's strategy with individualised messages for emerging leaders — with an emphasis on how their development fits into the company's plans.

Learnerships

Learnerships are structured learning programmes that combine learning at a training institution with practical, work-based learning. The institutional learning component, delivered by registered and accredited training providers, covers the more theoretical aspects. Work-based learning, on the other hand, involves practical learning experiences in the workplace.

A learnership leads to a nationally recognised qualification that is registered with the South African Qualifications Authority (SAQA). A person who successfully completes a learnership will have a qualification that signals occupational competence and is recognised throughout the country. Learnerships can make a critical contribution to the continuing career development, marketability and employability of individuals (particularly those under the age of 30), as well as to the long-term survival of the organisation. Legislation such as the Skills Development Act and the Skills Development Levies Act requires organisations to establish special learner-support practices for people who have learnership agreements with companies. *Learner-support practices* may include induction/socialisation, mentoring, career discussions, career workshops, career counselling, education and development support and outplacement guidance and counselling (Coetzee and Stone, 2004).

Ethical dilemmas

Organisational support practices require *ethical* or acceptable behaviour from managers, industrial psychologists, human resource practitioners and employees. Managers have a responsibility to employees to establish and maintain a social and psychological contract — as well as to ensure that job obligations are met. Inherent in this psychological contract is the mutual trust that each will respect the other's legal and ethical rights, which must exist between employer and employee. At the heart of the social and psychological contract is the practice of sharing information honestly and, of course, mutual trust and respect between manager and employee (Weiss, 2001).

Often managers, psychologists and practitioners encounter situations that make it difficult to maintain a proper balance between the common good and personal freedom of employees, between the legitimate business needs of an organisation and an employee's feelings of dignity and worth. *Ethical dilemmas* are situations that have the potential to result in a breach of acceptable behaviour. Although it is not possible to prescribe the content of ethical behaviour, processes that incorporate procedural justice can lead to an acceptable (and temporary) consensus among interested parties regarding an ethical course of action. Ethical decisions are rarely easy. The challenge in managing organisational career development support practices lies not in the mechanical application of moral prescriptions but rather in the process of creating and maintaining genuine relationships from which to address dilemmas that cannot be covered by prescription (Cascio, 2003).

Some *ethical principles* that apply to organisational career development support practices are the following (Cascio, 2003):

◆ guarding against invasion of employee *privacy;*
◆ guaranteeing *confidentiality;*
◆ obtaining *informed consent* from employees before assessing them;
◆ respecting employees' *rights to know;*
◆ imposing *time limits* on data (ie, removing information that has not been used for human resource decisions, especially if it has not been updated);
◆ using the most *valid procedures* available;
◆ treating employees with *respect and consideration* (ie, by standardising procedures for all candidates);
◆ *not maintaining secret files* on individuals, rather informing them of what information is stored on them, the purpose for which it was collected, how it will be used and how long it will be kept;
◆ periodically allowing employees the *right to inspect and update information* stored on them; and
◆ *avoiding fraudulent, secretive or unfair means of collecting data;* when possible, collecting data directly from the individual concerned.

Employees can demonstrate ethical behaviour by considering the following practices in their personal conduct at work (Weiss, 2001):

- knowing and following the company's written policies;
- fulfilling contractual and job description responsibilities;
- following organisational and job goals and objectives;
- performing procedural rules;
- offering competence commensurate with the work and job to which one is assigned; and
- performing productively according to required job tasks.

Conclusion

In this chapter the factors that influence individuals' choice of an organisation and the various practices and activities that can be used by organisations to support career development have been discussed. Organisational choice has been described both as a systematic choice (expectancy theory) and as programmed decision-making. Both views have been supported by research. It has also been described by the position selection process, which determines which organisation to work for.

The various career development support practices can be used either in isolation or in combination to assist employees in career development. Apart from assisting employees in performing self-assessment exercises and making career decisions, the organisation has the additional responsibility of establishing an environment for personal growth and of providing training and development opportunities. However, the responsibility for the success of a career development culture requires the active support and involvement of top management, supervisors and employees themselves.

Review and discussion questions

1. What factors played a major role in your choice of an organisation?
2. How do individuals choose an organisation according to expectancy theory?
3. How does unprogrammed decision-making influence individuals' choice of organisations?
4. Explain how the contemporary world of work influences an organisation's approach toward supporting the career development of their employees.
5. Why is it important for employees to take control of their careers and responsibility for their careers?
6. List and explain organisational career development practices that can support employees in managing their careers in the 21st century world of work.
7. How can a formalised organisational career development system help organisations to create a positive career development culture?

8. Write a paragraph describing how formal education, training and development and 360-degree performance appraisal may integrate career planning practices in the organisation.
9. Discuss the importance of outplacement programmes for people on learnerships.
10. Review the employment relationships discussed in chapter 2. Which groups of employees would benefit most from lateral moves and dual ladder support practices?
11. How would you go about establishing a mentoring programme? Assume that you have to deal with a diverse group of employees.
12. What are the ethical aspects that need to be considered in assessment practices?

Reflection activities

Reflection activity 8.1

1. The following is an excerpt from an article on job sculpting. Identify the career development support techniques in Mark's situation.
2. Compile a comprehensive list of actions that you would like to implement in your organisation to ensure optimal career development support.
3. Indicate which of these techniques are already implemented in your organisation and, if you have recommendations for improvement, write them down, indicating why they should be implemented. (If you are not working for an organisation, 'create' an organisation by talking to fellow students or people who are involved in organisations).

Job sculpting

By all accounts, Mark was a star at the large bank where he had worked for three years. He had an MBA from a leading business school and he had distinguished himself as an impressive 'quant jock' and a skilled lending officer. The bank paid Mark well and senior managers had every intention of promoting him. Little did they know he was seriously considering leaving the organisation altogether.

Our research over the past 12 years strongly suggests that many talented professionals leave their organisations because senior managers don't understand the psychology of work satisfaction; they assume that people who excel at their work are necessarily happy in their jobs. The answer is, only if the job matches their deeply embedded life interest, will they stay. These interests are not hobbies — opera and so forth — nor are they enthusiasms, such as the stock market or oceanography. Instead, deeply embedded life interests are long-held, emotionally driven passions, intricately entwined with personality and thus born of an indeterminate mix of nature and nurture. Deeply embedded life interests do not determine what people are good at — they determine what kinds of activities make them happy. At work, that happiness often translates into commitment. It keeps people engaged and it keeps them from quitting.

Job sculpting is the art of matching people to jobs that allow their deeply embedded life interests to be expressed. It is the art of forging a customised career path in order to increase the chance of retaining talented people. Many people have only a dim awareness of their own deeply embedded life interests. They may have spent their lives fulfilling other people's expectations of them or they may have followed the most common career advice: 'Do what you are good at'.

Let's return to Mark, the lending officer at a bank. Mark was raised in a city. His mother and father were doctors who fully expected their son to become a successful professional. In high school, Mark received straight As. He went on to attend university where he majored in economics. Soon after graduation, he began working at a prestigious management-consulting firm, where he showed great skill at his assignments, which included building financial spreadsheets. As expected, Mark left the consulting firm to attend a respected business school and then joined the bank. It was located near his family and, because of its size and growth rate, he thought it would offer him good opportunities for advancement.

Mark, not surprisingly, excelled at every task the bank gave him. He was smart and knew no other way to approach work than to give it his all. But, over time, Mark grew more and more unhappy. He was a person who loved running his mind over and through theoretical and strategic 'what-ifs'. (After university, Mark had seriously considered a career in academia but had been dissuaded by his parents.) Indeed, one of Mark's deeply embedded life interests was theory development and conceptual thinking. He could certainly excel at the nitty-gritty number crunching and the customer service that his lending job entailed, but those activities did nothing for his heart and soul, not to mention for his commitment to the organisation.

Fortunately for both Mark and the bank, he was able to identify what kind of work truly excited him before he quit. Consulting a career counsellor, Mark came to see what kind of work interested him and how that differed from his current job responsibilities. Using this insight, he was able to identify a role in the bank's new market-development area that would bring his daily tasks in line with his deeply embedded interests. Mark's work now consists of competitive analysis and strategy formulation. He is thriving and the bank is reaping the benefit of his redoubled energy — and his loyalty.

(Butter and Waldroop, *Harvard Business Review,* September–October 1999)

Reflection activity 8.2

Ethical questions

Read the following excerpts and answer the questions that follow:

Nakampi always wants to keep his options open. He spends several hours a week talking to headhunters while at work. He claims there is no real loyalty between employers and employees these days. If downsizing were necessary and he were targeted, he would be laid off — no questions asked. Therefore, he argues, he has to protect his own future interests, even on company time. Do you agree? (Source: Weiss, 2001:390)

Your situation

You recently went after and received an advertised job you wanted. You did not represent yourself accurately on your résumé, however. The company is known for its openness and high ethical standing among customers, suppliers and other firms in the industry. Another person in the company, you have discovered, is familiar with your background. If that person found out about the exaggeration on your résumé, you could face some consequences. You are wondering whether you should go to the hiring manager and tell the truth, keep quiet and see what happens or have a confidential talk with your acquaintance. What should you do? Why?
(Weiss, 2001:390)

References

Aamodt, MG (2010) *Industrial/Organisational Psychology: An applied approach 6ed* Belmont, CA: Wadsworth Cengage Learning.

Ackah, C and Heaton, N (2003) The reality of "new" careers for men and women. *Journal of European Industrial Training, 28*(2/3/4), 141–158.

Albrecht, CA (1996) Career centres promote employability. *HR Magazine*, August, 105–108.

Allen, TD, Poteet, ML, Russell, JEA and Dobbins, GH (1999) Learning and development factors on perceptions of job content and hierarchical plateauing. *Journal of Organizational Behaviour, 20*, 1113–1137.

Allen, TD, Herst, DEL, Bruck, CS and Sutton, M (2000) Consequences associated with work-to-family conflict: A review and agenda for future research. *Journal of Occupational Health Psychology, 5*, 278–308.

Allen TD (2006) Mentoring. In JH Greenhaus and GA Callanan (eds) *Encyclopedia of career development, 486–493*, New Dehli: Sage Publication.

Allerton, H (1995) Working life: Work versus family. *Training and Development Journal, 49*(7), 71–72.

American Psychiatric Association (1994) *Diagnostic and Statistical Manual of Mental Disorders (DSM-IV)* 4ed. Washington DC: APA

Amirkhan, JH (1994) Criterion validity of coping measures. *Journal of Personality Assessment, 62*, 242–261.

Anderson, M (1999) Project development: Taking stock. In M Anderson (ed) *The Development of Intelligence*. Hove: Psychology Press.

Arnold, J and Randall, R (2010) *Work psychology: Understanding human behaviour in the workplace*. London: Pearsons Education Limited

Atienza, AA, Stephens, MAP, and Townsend, AL (2002) Dispositional optimism, role-specific stress and well-being of adult-daughter caregivers. *Research on Aging, 24*, 193–118.

Antonovsky, A (1979) *Health, Stress and Coping*. San Francisco: Jossey-Bass.

Antonovsky, A (1984) A call for a new question: Salutogenesis and a proposed answer: The sense of coherence. *Journal of Preventive Psychiatry, 2*, 1–13.

Antonovsky, A (1987) *Unravelling the Mystery of Health: How People Manage Stress and Stay Well*. San Francisco: Jossey-Bass.

Antonovsky, A (1991) The structural sources of salutogenic strengths. In CL Cooper and R Payne (eds) *Personality and stress: Individual differences in the stress process*. New York: Wiley.

Applebaum, H (1992) *The Concept of Work: Ancient, Medieval, Modern*. New York: State University of New York Press.

Appelbaum, SH and Finestone, D (1994) Revisiting career plateauing: Some old problems: Avant-garde solutions. *Journal of Managerial Psychology, 9*(5), 13–21.

Ardts, J, Van der Welde, PJ and Van der Welde, M (2001) The breaking in of new employees: Effectiveness of socialisation tactics and personnel instruments. *Journal of Management Development*, 20(2), 159–167.

Argyle, M (1989) *The Social Psychology of Work* 2ed. London: Penguin.

Armstrong, M (2003) *Human Resource Management Practice*. London: Kogan Page.

Armstrong, PI and Crombie, G (2000) Compromises in adolescents' occupational aspirations and expectations from grades 8 to 10. *Journal of Vocational Behavior*, 56, 82–98.

Arnold, J (2001) The psychology of careers in organisation. In C Cooper and J Robertson (eds) *Organisational Psychology and Development*.

Arnold, J, Cooper, CL and Robertson, IT (1995) *Work Psychology: Understanding Human Behaviour in the Work Place*. London: Pitman.

Arnold, J and Randall, R (2010) *Work psychology: Understanding human behaviour in the workplace* 5ed. Harlow, Essex: Pearson Education.

Arthur, MB, Claman, PH and DeFillipi, RJ (1995) Intelligent enterprise, intelligent careers. *Academy of Management Executive*, 9(4), 7–22.

Arthur, MB, Khapova, SN and Wilderom, CPM (2005) Career success in a boundary-less career world. *Journal of Organisational Behaviour*, 26 (1), 177–202.

Arthur, MB and Kram, KE (1989) Reciprocity at work: The separate, yet inseparable possibilities for individual and organizational development. In MB Arthur, DT Hall and BS Lawrence (eds) *Handbook of Career Theory*. Cambridge: Cambridge University Press.

Arthur, MB and Rousseau, DM (1996) *The Boundaryless Career: A New Employment Principle for a New Organization Era*. New York: Oxford University Press.

Arvey, RD and Faley, RH (1988) *Fairness in Selecting Employees*. Reading, MA: Addison-Wesley.

Aryee, S (1993) Dual-earner couples in Singapore: An examination of work and nonwork sources of their experienced burnout. *Human Relations*, 46(12), 1441–1468.

Ashmos, DP and Duchon, D (2000) Spirituality at work: a conceptualization and measure. *Journal of Management Inquiry*, 9(2), 134–145.

Aspinwall, LG and Taylor, SE (1992) Modeling cognitive adaptation: A longitudinal investigation of the impact of individual differences and coping on college adjustment and performance. *Journal of Personality and Social Psychology*, 61, 755–765.

Avery, G, Baker, E and Kane, G (1984) *Psychology at Work: Fundamentals and Applications*. Sydney: Prentice Hall.

Back, KW and Bourque, LB (1977) Graphs and life events. *Journal of Qerontotogy*, 32(6), 673.

Bakker, AB and Geurts, SAE (2004) Towards a dual-process model of work-home interference. *Work and Occupations*, 31, 345–366.

Bakker, AB, Schaufeli, WB, and Van Dierendonck, D (2000) Burnout: Prevalentie, risicogroepen en risicofactoren (Burnout: Prevalence, high-risk groups and risk factors). In ILD Houtman, WB Schaufeli, and T Taris (eds), *Psychische vermoeidheid en werk* (Mental fatigue and work) 65–82 Alphen aan den Rijn, the Netherlands: Samson/NWO.

Ballantine, M (1993) A new framework for the design of career. *British Journal of Guidance Counselling,* 21(3), 233–245.

Ballout, HI (2008) Work-family conflict and career success: the effects of domain-specific determinants. *Journal of Management Development,* 27(5), 437–466

Ballout, HI (2009) Career commitment and career success: moderating role of self-efficacy. *Career Development International,* 14(7), 655–670.

Baloyi, DK (1996) Career development in high schools: A systematic cross-cultural perspective. Unpublished MA thesis, University of Pretoria.

Bandura, A (1982) Self-efficacy mechanism in human agency. *American Psychologist,* 37(2), 122–147.

Bandura, A (1986) *Social Foundation of Thought and Action: A Social Cognitive Theory.* Englewood Cliffs, NJ: Prentice Hall.

Bandura, A (1989) Human agency in social cognitive theory. *American Psychologist,* 44. 1175–1184.

Bandura, A (2001) Social cognitive theory: An agentic perspective. *Annual Review of Psychology,* 52, 1–26.

Bardsley, CA (1987) Improving employee awareness of opportunity at IBM *Personnel,* 64, 58–63.

Bardwick, JM (1986) *The Plateauing Trap.* Toronto, Canada: Bantam Books.

Barnett, BR and Bradley, L (2007) The impact of organisational support for career development on career satisfaction. *Career Development International,* 12(7), 617–636.

Barrick, MR, and Mount, MK (1991) The big five personality dimensions and job performance: A meta-analysis. *Personnel Psychology, 44,* 1–26.

Barker, F (2003) *The South African labour market.* Pretoria: Van Schaik.

Barker, JA (1997) The Mondragon Model: A new pathway for the twenty-first century. In F Hesselbein, M Goldsmith and R Beckhard (eds) *The Organization of the Future.* San Francisco: Jossey-Bass.

Barkhuizen, N and Rothmann, S (2004, March) Burnout of academic staff in a higher education institution. Paper presented at the 2nd South African Work Wellness Conference, Potchefstroom, South Africa.

Barkhuizen, N (2005) *Work wellness of academic staff in South African higher education institutions.* Unpublished doctoral thesis, North-West University, Potchefstroom.

Barling, J (1999) Changing employment relations: Empirical data, social perspectives and policy options. In DB Knight and A Joseph (eds) *Restructuring Societies: Insights from the Social Sciences.* Ottawa: Carlton University Press.

Barmeier, RE and Kellar, RJ (1957) How college graduates valuate job factors. *Personnel,* 33(5), 490–494.

Barnett, RC (1996) *Toward a Review of Work-Family Literature: Work in Progress.* Boston: Wellesley College Center for Research on Women.

Barnett, RC (1998) Toward a review and reconceptualization of the work/family literature. *Genetic, Social and General Psychology Monographs*, 124, 125–182.

Barrick, MR and Mount, MK (1991) The big five personality dimensions and job performance: A meta-analysis. *Personnel Psychology*, 44, 1–26.

Bartlett, CA and Ghoshal, S (1995) Changing the role of top management: Beyond systems to people. *Harvard Business Review*, May/June, 132–142.

Baruch, Y (1999) Integrated systems for the 2000s. *International Journal of Manpower*, 20(7), 432–457.

Baruch, Y (2002) Career systems in transition: A normative model for organizational career practices. *Personnel Review*, 32(2), 232–251.

Baruch, Y (2004) Transforming careers: From linear to multidirectional career paths: Organisational and individual perspectives. *Career Development International*, 9(1), 58–73.

Baruch, Y (2006) Career development in organizations and beyond: Balancing traditional and contemporary viewpoints. *Human Resource Management Review*, 16, 125–138.

Baruch, Y (2009) To MBA or not to MBA *Career Development International*, 14(4), 388–406.

Baruch, Y and Quick, JC (2007) Understanding second careers: lessons from a study of US Navy Admirals. *Human Resource Management*, 46, 471–491.

Baruch, Y and Rosenstein, E (1992) Career planning and managing in high tech organizations. *International Journal of Human Resource Management*, 3(3), 477–496.

Basson, MJ and Rothmann, S (2002) Sense of coherence, coping and burnout of pharmacists. *South African Journal of Economic and Management Sciences*, 5(1), 35–62.

Batt, R and Valcour, PM (2003) Human resource practices as predictors of work-family outcomes and employee turnover. *Industrial Relations*, 42(2), 189–217.

Beehr, TA, Johnson, LB and Nieva, R (1995) Occupational stress: Coping of police and their spouses. *Journal of Organizational Behavior*, 16, 3–25.

Behling, O (1998) Employee selection: Will intelligence and conscientiousness do the job? *Academy of Management Executive*, 12, 77–86.

Behling, O, Labovitz, G and Gainer, M (1968) College recruiting: A theoretical base. *Personnel Journal*, 47(1), 13–19.

Benko, C and Weisberg, A (2009) Mass career customization: building the corporate lattice. *Deloitte Review*. Available at: http://www.deloitee.com/view/en_US/us/Insights/Browse-by-Content-Type/deloittereview/article/35912eefad33210VgnVCM100000ba42f00aRCRD.htm [Accessed on: 6 March 2009].

Ben-Sira, Z (1985) Potency: A stress-buffering link in the coping-stress-disease relationship. *Social Science and Medicine*, 21, 397–406.

Betz, NE (2003) A proactive approach to midcareer development. *The Counseling Psychologist*, 31(2), 205–211.

Betz, NE (2005) Women's career development. In SD Brown and RW Lent (eds) *Career development and counseling: Putting theory and research to work*, 253–280 Hoboken, NJ: John Wiley and Sons, Inc.

Biswas-Diener, R, Kashdan, TB, and King, LA (2009) Two traditions of happiness research, not two distinct types of happiness. *Journal of Positive Psychology, 4*, 208–211.

Boehm, JK, and Lyubomirsky, S (2008) Does happiness promote career success? *Journal of Career Assessment, 16*(1), 101–116.

Boles, JS, Johnston, MW Hair, JF (1997) Role stress, work-family conflict and emotional exhaustion: Inter-relationships and effects on some work related consequences. *Journal of Personal Selling and Sales Management, XVII*(1), Winter, 17–28.

Bond, JT, Galinsky, E and Swanberg, JE (1998) *The 1997 National Study of the Changing Workforce*. New York: Families and Work Institute.

Booth-Kewley, S and Friedman, HS (1987) Psychological predictors of heart disease: A quantitative review. *Psychological Bulletin*, 101, 343–362.

Booth-Kewley, S and Vickers, RR (1994) Associations between major domains of personality and health behaviour. *Journal of Personality*, 62(3), 282–298.

Bordin, ES (1990) Psychodynamic model of career choice and satisfaction in career choice and development. In D Brown, L Brooks and Associates (eds) *Applying Contemporary Theories to Practice* 2ed. San Francisco: Jossey-Bass.

Bornstein, MH and Lamb, ME (1999) *Developmental Psychology: An Advanced Textbook*. Mahwah, NJ: Earlbaum.

Boshoff, AB, Bennett, HF and Kellerman, AM (1994) Career orientations as predictors of the level of job involvement of professional people. *Journal of Industrial Psychology, 20*(2), 8–13.

Botha, L (2007) *The employees' psychological contract and the values underlying perceptions of breach*. Unpublished Masters dissertation, Department of Industrial and Organisational Psychology, University of South Africa, Pretoria.

Bourbeau, J, Brisson, C and Allaire, S (1996) Prevalence of the sick building syndrome symptoms in office workers before and after being exposed to a building with an improved ventilation system. *Occupational and Environmental Medicine*, 53, 204–210.

Boyatzis, RE and Kolb, DA (2000) Performance, learning and development as modes of growth and adaptation throughout our lives and careers. In MA Peiperl, MB Arthur, R Goffee and T Morris (eds) *Career Frontiers: New Conceptions of Working Lives*. Oxford: Oxford University Press.

Bracker, JS and Pearson, JN (1986) Worker obsolescence: The human resource dilemma of the 80s. *Personnel Administrator*, 31(12), 109–116.

Bradford, LP (1989) Can you survive your retirement? In H Levinson (ed) *Designing and Managing Your Career*. Boston: Harvard Business School Press.

Bratton, J and Cold, J (2003) *Human Resource Management: Theory and Practice*. New York: Palgrave McMillan.

Braunstein, DN and Haines, GH (1968) Preference scaling of careers and organizations. *Journal of Applied Psychology*, 52(5), 380–385.

Breed, M (1997) Bepalende Persoonlikheidstrekke in die Salutogenetiese Paradigma. Unpublished doctoral thesis, University of South Africa (UNISA), Pretoria.

Bretz, RD, Ash, RA and Dreher, GF (1989) Do people make the place? An examination of the attraction-selection-attrition hypothesis. *Personnel Psychology*, 42(3), 561–581.

Bridges, W (1995) *Job Shift: How to Prosper in a Workplace without Jobs*. London: Nicolas Brealey

Brief, AP and Nord, WR (1990) Work and nonwork connections. In AP Brief and WR Nord (eds) Meanings *of Occupational Work*. Massachusetts: Lexington Books.

Brink, B and De la Rey, C (2001) Work-family interaction strain: Coping strategies used by successful women in the public corporate and self-employed sectors of the economy. *South African Journal for Psychology*, 31(4), 55–61.

Briscoe, JP and Hall, DT (2006) The interplay of boundaryless and protean careers: combinations and implications. *Journal of Vocational Behavior, 69*, 4–18.

Brockner, J, Tyler, TR and Cooper-Schieder, R (1992) The influence of prior commitment to institution on reactions to perceived unfairness: The higher they are, the harder they fall. *Administrative Science Quarterly*, 37, 241–261.

Bronfenbrenner, U (1979) *The ecology of human development*. Cambridge, MA: Harvard University Press.

Brookings, JB, Bolton, B, Brown, CE and McEvoy, A (1985) Self-reported job burnout among female human service professionals. *Journal of Occupational Behaviour*, 6, 143–150.

Brooks, SS (1994) Moving up is not the only option. *HR Magazine*, March, 79–82.

Brousseau, KR (1990) Career dynamics in the baby boom and baby bust era. *Journal of Organizational Change Management*, 3(3), 46–58.

Brousseau, KR and Driver, MJ (1994) Enhancing informed choice: A career-concepts approach to career advisement. *The Magazine of the Graduate Management Admission Council*, Spring, 24–31.

Brousseau, KR, Driver MJ, Eneroth, K and Larsson, R (1996) Career pandemonium: Realigning organizations and individuals. *Academy of Management Executive*, 10(4) 52–66.

Brown, C, George-Curran, R and Smith, ML (2003) The role of emotional intelligence in the career commitment and decision-making process. *Journal of Career Assessment*, 11(4), 379–392.

Brown, D (1990) *Career Choice and Development*. San Francisco: Jossey-Bass.

Brown, MT (1995) The career development of African Americans: Theoretical and empirical issues. In FT Leong (ed) *Career Development and Vocational Behavior of Racial and Ethnic Minorities*. Mahwah, NJ: Erlbaum.

Brown, D (1996) Summary, comparison and critique of the major theories. In D Brown, L Brooks and Associates (eds) *Career Choice and Development* 3ed. San Francisco: Jossey-Bass.

Brown, D, Brooks, L and Associates (1996) *Career Choice and Development* 3ed. San Francisco: Jossey-Bass.

Brown, SD and Ryan Krane, BE (2000) Four (or five) sessions and a cloud of dust: Old assumptions and new observations about career counseling. In SD Brown and RW Lent (eds) *Handbook of Counseling Psychology*. 3ed. New York: Wiley.

Brown, SD (2006) Career Counselling. In JH Greenhaus and GA Callanan (eds) *Encyclopedia of career development*, New Dehli: Sage Publications.

Brott, PE (2004) Constructivist assessment in career counselling. *Journal of Career Development, 30*(3), 189–200.

Bruce, WM and Reed, CM (1991) *Dual-Career Couples in the Public Sector.* Westport, CT: Quorum.

Brutus, S, London, M and Martineau, J (1999) The impact of 360–degree feedback on planning for career development. *Journal of Management Development,* 18(8), 676–693.

Buchanan, B (1974) Building organizational commitment: The socialization of managers in work organizations. *Administrative Science Quarterly,* 19, 533–546.

Buchner, M (2007) The protean career attitude, emotional intelligence and career adjustment. Unpublished Doctoral thesis, University of Johannesburg, Johannesburg.

Buckingham, M and Clifton, DO (2001) *Now, Discover Your Strengths.* New York: The Free Press.

Buhler, P (1995) Managing in the 90s. *Supervision,* July, 25–26.

Burke, RJ (1993) Organisational-level interventions to reduce occupational stressors. *Work and Stress,* 7(1), 77–87.

Burke, RJ (2002) Organizational transitions. In RJ Burke CL and Cooper (eds) *The New World of Work: Challenges and Opportunities.* Oxford: Blackwell.

Burke, RJ and Cooper, CL (2002) *The New World of Work: Challenges and Opportunities.* Oxford: Black-well.

Burke, RJ and Greenglass, ER (1999) Work-family conflict, spouse support and nursing staff well-being during organizational restructuring. *Journal of Occupational Health Psychology (Special issue: Relationship between Work and Family Life),* 4, 327–336.

Burke, RJ and Mikkelsen, A (2006) Examining the career plateau among police officers. *An International Journal of Police Strategies and Management,* 29(4), 691–703.

Butts, D (1999) Spirituality at work: An overview. *Journal of Organizational Change Management,* 12(4), 328–331.

Byars, LL and Rue, LW (2004) *Human Resource Management.* New York: McGraw-Hill.

Cabrera, JC and Albrecht, CF (1993) Who is in charge of your career? *Executive Excellence,* 10(1), 14–15.

Cadin, L, Bailly-Bender, A and Saint-Ciniez, V (2000) Exploring boundaryless careers in the French context. In MA Peiperl, MB Arthur, R Coffee and T Morris (eds) *Career Frontiers: New Conceptions of Working Lives.* Oxford: Oxford University Press.

Callan, VJ (1993) Individual and organizational strategies for coping with organizational change. *Work and Stress, 7,* 63–75.

Callanan, GA and Creenhaus, JH (1999) Personal and career development: The best and worst of times. In AJ Kraut and AK Korman (eds) *Evolving Practices in Human Resource Management.* San Francisco: Jossey-Bass.

Campion, MA, Campion, JE and Hudson, JP (1994) Structuring interviewing: A note on incremental validity and alternative question types, *Journal of Applied Psychology, 79,* 998–1002.

Campion, MA, Palmer, DK and Campion, JE (1997) A review of structure in the selection interview. *Personnel Psychology, 50,* 655–702.

Carbery, R and Garavan, TN (2005) Organisational restructuring and downsizing: issues related to learning, training and employability of survivors. *Journal of European Industrial Training, 29*(6), 488–522.

Carlson, DS and Perrewé, PL (1999) The role of social support in the stressor-strain relationship: An examination of work-family conflict. *Journal of Management, 25*(4) 513–540.

Cartwright, S and Cooper, CL (1993) The psychological impact of merger and acquisition on the individual: A study of building society managers. *Human Relations, 46,* 327–347.

Cartwright, S, and Cooper, CL (2002) *ASSET: An Organizational Stress Screening Tool — The management guide.* Manchester, UK: Robertson/Cooper Ltd.

Carver, CS, Scheier, MF and Weintraub, JK (1989) Assessing coping strategies: A theoretically based approach, *Journal of Personality and Social Psychology, 56,* 267–283.

Carver, CS, and Scheier, MF (2002) Optimism. In CR Snyder and SJ Lopez (eds) *Handbook of positive psychology,* 231–243 Oxford, UK: Oxford University Press.

Carver, S and Scheier, MF (2003) Optimism. In CR Snyder and SJ Lopez (eds) *Positive Psychological Assessment: A Handbook of Models and Measures.* Washington, DC: American Psychological Association.

Carver, CS, Scheier, MF, and Weintraub, JK (1989) Assessing coping strategies: A theoretical based approach. *Journal of Personality and Social Psychology, 56,* 267–283.

Cascio, WF (1995a) *Guide to Responsible Restructuring.* Washington: US Department of Labour, Office of the American Workplace.

Cascio, WF (1995b) Whither industrial and organizational psychology in a changing world of work? *American Psychologist, 50*(11), 928–939.

Cascio, WF (1998) *Applied Psychology in Human Resource Management.* Englewood Cliffs, NJ: Prentice Hall.

Cascio, WF (2000) Managing a virtual workplace. *Academy of Management Executive, 14*(3) 81–89.

Cascio, WF (2001) Work, workers and organisations for the new millennium. Paper presented at the Assessment Centre Conference, Stellenbosch.

Cascio, WF (2003) *Managing Human Resources: Productivity, Quality of Work Life Profits.* New York: McGraw-Hill.

Cascio, WF and Aguinis, H (2005) *Applied Psychology in Human Resource Management.* Upper Saddle River, NJ: Pearson/Prentice Hall.

Cash, D (1988) A study of the relationship of demographics, personality and role stress to burnout in intensive care nurses. *Dissertation Abstracts International, 49,* 2585A

Caudron, S (1994) HR revamps career itineraries. *Personnel journal,* Apr, 64B-64M Central Statistical Service (CSS) (1994) *RSA Statistics in Brief.* Pretoria: CSS

Chalofsky, NE (2010) *Meaningful workplaces: reframing how and where we work.* San Francisco, CA: John Wiley and Sons.

Chalofsky, N, and Krishna, V (2009) Meaningfulness, commitment and engagement: The intersection of a deeper level of intrinsic motivation. *Advances in Developing Human Resources, 11(2),* 189–203.

Chao, CT (1990) Exploration of the conceptualization and measurement of career plateau: A comparative analysis. *Journal of Management, 16(1),* 181–193.

Chapman, DS and Webster, J (2003) The use of technologies in the recruiting, screening and selection processes for job candidates. *International journal of Selection and Assessment,* 11 (2/3), 113–120.

Chau, CT (1998) *Internal Auditor,* October, 49–52.

Chen, CP (2001) On exploring meanings: combining humanistic and career psychology theories in counseling. *Counselling Psychology Quarterly, 14(4),* 317–330.

Cherniss, C (1995) *Beyond Burnout: Helping Teachers, Nurses, Therapists and Lawyers Recover from Stress and Disillusionment.* New York: Routledge.

Cilliers, F and Koortzen, P (2000) The dynamics view of organisational behaviour. *The Industrial/Organizational Psychologist, 38(2).*

Clark, FA (1992) *Total Career Management.* Berkshire: McGraw-Hill.

Clark, M and Arnold, J (2008) The nature, prevalence and correlation of generativity among men in middle career. *Journal of Vocational Behavior, 73,* 473–478.

Clawson, JB (1985) Is mentoring necessary? *Training and Development Journal, 39,* 36–39.

Cleveland, JN, Stockdale, M and Murphy, KR (2000) *Women and Men in Organizations: Sex and Gender Issues at Work.* Mahwah, NJ: Erlbaum.

Clutterbuck, D (2001) *Everyone Needs a Mentor: Fostering Talent at Work.* London: Cromwell Press.

Cocchiara, FK, Kwesiga, E, Bell, MP and Baruch, Y (2009) Influences on perceived career success: findings from US graduate business degree alumni. *Career Development International, 15(1),* 39–58.

Coetzee, M (1996) *The relationship between career patterns and personality types.* Unpublished MA thesis. UNISA, Pretoria.

Coetzee, M (2004) Logotherapy. In E Mattheus (ed) *The informed choice: The A-Z Guide to the Natural Treatment of Body, Mind and Spirit.* Rondebosch: Kima Global.

Coetzee, M (2005a) *Career counseling in the 21st century: Practical techniques for facilitating career competency and resilience.* Unpublished manuscript, Department Industrial and Organizational Psychology, UNISA, Pretoria.

Coetzee, M (2007) *Career planning in the 21st century: Strategies for inventing a career in a dejobbed world of work.* Cape Town: Juta.

Coetzee M and Roythorne-Jacobs, H (2007) *Career counselling and guidance in the workplace.* Cape Town: Juta

Coetzee, M (2008) Psychological career resources of working adults: A South African survey. *SA Journal of Industrial Psychology, 34*(2), 32–41.

Coetzee, M and Bergh, Z (2009) Psychological career resources and subjective work experiences of working adults: An exploratory study. *SA Business Review, 13* (2), 1–31.

Coetzee, M, Bergh, ZC and Schreuder, D (2010) *Subjective work experiences, career orientations, psychological career resources and factors of job satisfaction/dissatisfaction.* Unpublished research report, Department of Industrial and Organisational Psychology, University of South Africa.

Coetzee, M and De Villiers, MA (2010) Sources of job stress, work engagement and career orientations of employees in a South African financial institution. *SA Business Review, 14*(1), 27–57.

Coetzee, M and Schreuder, AMG (2002) The relationship between career patterns and personality types. *SA journal of Industrial Psychology, 28*(1), 53–59.

Coetzee, M and Schreuder, AMG (2004) *Students' experiences of the meaning of work.* Unpublished article. Department Industrial and Organisational Psychology, UNISA, Pretoria.

Coetzee, M and Schreuder, AMG (2008) A multi-cultural investigation of students' career anchors at a South African higher education institution. *SA Journal of Labour Relations, 32*(2): 1–21.

Coetzee, M and Schreuder, AMG (2009) Psychological career resources as predictors of working adults' career anchors: An exploratory study. *SA Journal of Industrial Psychology, 35*(1), Article #833, 13 pages. DOI:10.4102/sajip.v35i1.833.

Coetzee, M, Schreuder, AMG and Tladinyane, R (2007) Career anchors and its relation to organisational commitment. *Southern African Business Review, 11*(1), 65–86.

Coetzee, M and Stone, K (2004) *Learner Support: Toward Learning and Development.* Randburg: Knowres.

Coetzee, SE and Rothmann, S (2005) Occupational stress in a higher education institution in South Africa. *South African Journal of Industrial Psychology, 31*(1),47–54.

Coetzer, WJ (2005) Occupational stress of employees in a South African insurance company. Paper presented at the 12th European Congress on Work and Organizational Psychology, 13 May 2005, Istanbul, Turkey.

Cohen, L and El-Sawad, A (2009) Understanding and managing careers in changing contexts. In T Redman and A Wilkinson (eds), *Contemporary human resource management* 317–342 London: Prentice-Hall.

Colby, AG (1995) Making the new career development model work. *HR Magazine,* June, 150–152.

Cole, G (2002) *Personnel and Human Resource Management.* London: Continuum.

Collins, G (2006) Retirement. In JH Greenhaus and GA Callanan (eds) *Encyclopedia of career development 693–695* New Dehli: Sage Publications.

Colombo, J and Frick, J (1999) Recent advances in the study of preverbal intelligence. In M Anderson (ed) *The Development of Intelligence 43–71.* Hove: Psychology Press.

Conger, JA (1994) *Spirit at work: Discovering the Spirituality in Leadership.* San Francisco, LA: Jossey-Bass.

Conger, S (2002) Fostering a career development culture: Reflections on the roles of managers, employees and supervisors. *Career Development International,* 7(6), 371–375.

Cook, EP, Heppner, MJ and O'Brien, KM (2001) Career development of women of color and White women: assumptions, conceptualizations and interventions from an ecological perspective. In NC Gysbers, MJ Heppner and JA Johnston (eds), *Career counseling: process, issues and techniques* 2ed. *41–43* New York: Pearson.

Costa, PT and McCrae, RR (1985) *The NEO Personality Inventory Manual.* Odessa, FL: Psychological Assessment Resources.

Coutinho, MT, Dam, UC and Blustein, DL (2008) The psychology of working and globalisation: a new perspective for a new era. *International Journal of Educational and Vocational Guidance, 8,* 5–18.

Craig, GJ (1996) *Human Development* 7ed, Upper Saddle River, NJ: Prentice Hall.

Crawford, A, Hubbard, SS, Lonis-Shumate, SR and O'Neill M (2009) Workplace spirituality and employee attitudes within the lodging environment. *Journal of Human Resources in Hospitality and Tourism, 8,* 64–81.

Crites, JO (1969) Vocational Psychology: *The Study of Vocational Behavior and Development.* New York: McGraw-Hill.

Cropanzano, R and Greenberg, J (2001) Progress in organizational justice: Tunnel through the maze. In C Cooper and I Robertson (eds) *Organizational Psychology and Development.*

Crossland, M (2009) *Dealing with job loss.* www.coachingacademyblog.com

Csikszentmihalyi, M (1990) *Flow: The Psychology of Optimal Experience.* New York: Harper Perennial.

Custodio, LP (2004) Career anchors of Filipino Academic Executives. School of Commerce Research Paper Series: 00–13, College of Business and Accountancy, Virac.

Danna, K and Griffin, RW (1999) Health and wellbeing in the workplace: A review and synthesis of the literature, *Journal of Management,* 25(3), 357–384.

Davis, DD (1995) Form, function and strategy in boundary-less organizations. In A Howard (ed), *The Changing Nature of Work,* 117–134 San Francisco: Jossey-Bass.

Dawis, RV (1996) The theory of work adjustment and person-environment correspondence counselling. In D Brown, L Brooks, *et al* (eds) *Career choice and development: applying contemporary theories to practice* 3ed. *75–120* San Francisco: Jossey-Bass.

Dawis, RV, England, GW and Lofquist, LH (1964) A theory of work adjustment. *Minnesota Studies in Vocational Rehabilitation, 15,* 1–27.

Dawis, RV and Lofquist, LH (1984) *A Psychological Theory of Work Adjustment: An Individual-differences Model and its Applications.* Minneapolis: University of Minnesota Press.

Dawis, RV and Lofquist, LH (1993) From TWA to PEC *Journal of Vocational Behavior, 43,* 113–121.

Day, R and Allen, T (2004) The relationship between career motivation and self-efficacy with protégé career success. *Journal of Vocational behaviour, 64,* 72–91.

DBM (2001) *Career choices and challenges of younger and older workers.* New York: Drake-Morris.

De Bruin, GP and Nel, ZJ (1996) 'n Geïntegreerde oorsig van empiriese navorsing oor loopbaanvoorligting in Suid-Afrika: 1980–1990. *South African journal of Psychology, 26,* 248–252.

Deci, EL, and Ryan, RM (2008) Hedoinia, eudamonia and well-being: An introduction. *Journal of Happiness Studies, 9,* 1–11.

DeFillilippi, RJ and Arthur, MB (1994) The boundaryless career: A competency based perspective, *journal of Organizational Behaviour, 15,* 307–324.

De Graaf, LE, Hollon, SD, and Huibers, MJH (2010) Predicting outcome in computerized cognitive behavioral therapy for depression in primary care: A randomized trial. *Journal of Consulting and Clinical Psychology, 78,* 184–199.

De La Garca, SA (2004) My spiritual sense making: Career path as responses to interruptions of the spiritual project. *Management Communication Quarterly, 17(4),* 603–610.

De Lange, J (2000) Werkverliese in ekonomie duur voort. *Sake Beeld,* 28 June 2000, 1

De Long, (1982) Reexamining the career anchor model. *Personnel, 59(3)* 60–61

De Long, TJ (1982) The career orientations of MBA Alumni: A multi-dimensional model. In R Katz. (ed) *Career Issues in human resource management, 50–64* Upper Saddle River, NJ: Prentice-Hall.

Dean, RA and Wanous, JP (1984) Effects of realistic job previews on hiring bank tellers, *Journal of Applied Psychology, 69,* 61–68.

Dean, RA, Ferris, KR and Konstans, C (1985) Reality shock: What happens when a new job doesn't match expectations? Paper presented at the 93rd Annual Convention of the American Psychological Association, Los Angeles.

Dean, RA, Ferris, KR and Konstans, C (1988) Occupational reality shock and organizational commitment: Evidence from the accounting profession. *Accounting, Organization and Society, 13(3),* 235–250.

De Beer, J (1997) Dealing with personal and cultural transitions. Paper presented at APTXII, Association for Psychological Type International Conference, Boston, MA

Demerouti E, Bakker, AB, Nachreiner, F, and Schaufeli, WB (2001) The Job Demands — Resources model of burnout. *Journal of Applied Psychology, 86,* 499–512.

Demerouti, E and Geurts, SAE (2004) Towards a typology of work-home interaction. *Community, Work and Family, 7,* 285–309.

Demerouti, E, Geurts, SAE and Kompier, MAJ (2004) Positive and negative work-home interaction: Prevalence and correlates. *Equal Opportunities International,* 23(1), 6–35.

Densten, IL (2008) Leadership: current assessment and future needs. In S Cartwright and CL Cooper (eds) *The Oxford Handbook of Personnel Psychology* 93–120 New York: Oxford University Press.

Department of Higher Education and Training (2010) *Framework for the National Skills Development Strategy 2011/12–2015/16.* Pretoria: DOHET

Department of Labour (2008a) *National Qualifications Framework Act, No. 67.* Pretoria: Government Printer.

Department of Labour. (2008b) *Skills Development Amendment Act, No. 37* Pretoria: Government Printer.

Department of Labour (2009) *Human Resource Development Strategy for South Africa.* Pretoria: DoL

Department of Statistics (2010) *List of countries by unemployment rate.* Available at: http://en.wikipedia.org/wiki [Accessed on: 11 June 2010]

De Pater, IE, Van Vianen, AEM, Bechtoldt, MN and Klehe, U (2009) Employees' challenging job experiences and supervisors' evaluations of promotability. *Personnel Psychology, 62,* 297–325.

De Vos, A, Buyens, D and Schalk, R (2005) Making sense of a new employment relationship: psychological contract-related information seeking and the role of work values and locus of control. *International Journal of Selection and Assessment, 13*(1), 41–52.

Dick, P and Ellis, S (2006) *Introduction to organizational behaviour.* London: McGraw-Hill.

Dickinson, C (1953) The relative importance of job factors to college graduates and to employers, *Journal of College Placement,* 14(1), 25–31.

Dickinson, C and Newbegin, B (1967) Pursuing the engineer. *Journal of College Placement,* 28(1), 97–99.

Dicks, H, Smith, N and Martins, N (2001) SA's best companies to work for survey. *HR Future,* 1(6), 48–52.

Diener, E (1994) Assessing subjective well-being: Progress and opportunities. *Social Indicators Research, 31,* 103–157.

Diener, E, Kesebir, P, and Lucas, R (2008) Benefits of accounts of well-being — For societies and for psychological science. *Applied Psychology: An International Journal, 57,* 37–53.

Diener, E, and Suh, E (1997) Measuring quality of life: Economic, social and subjective indicators. *Indicator Research, 40,* 189–216.

Diener, E, Suh, EM, Lucas, RE, and Smith, HL (1999) Subjective well-being: Three decades of progress. *Psychological Bulletin, 125,* 276–302.

Diener, E, and Seligman, MEP (2004) Beyond money: Toward an economy of well-being. *Psychological Science in the Public Interest, 5*, 1–31.

Dixon, RA and Lerner, RM (1999) History and systems in developmental psychology. In MH Bornstein and ME Lamb (eds) *Developmental Psychology: An Advanced Textbook.* 4ed. Mahwah, NJ: Erlbaum.

Dougherty, TW, Dreher, GF and Whitely, W (1993) The MBA as careerist: An analysis of early-career job change, *Journal of Management,* 19(3), 535–548.

Downes, M and Kroeck, KG (1996) Discrepancies between exiting jobs and individual interests: An empirical application of Holland's model. *Journal of Vocational Behavior,* 48, 107–117.

Driver, MJ (1979) Career concepts and career management in organizations. In CL Cooper (ed) *Behavioral Problems in Organizations* 79–139. Englewood Cliffs, NJ: Prentice Hall.

Drucker, PF (1997) In F Heselbein, M Goldsmith and R Beckhard (eds) *The Organisation of the Future.* San Francisco: Jossey-Bass.

Du Toit, LBH (1983) *Manual for the Jung Personality Questionnaire.* Pretoria: Human Sciences Research Council.

Dubin, R(1992) *Central Life Interests, Creative Individualism in a Complex World.* New Brunswick, NJ: Transaction.

Eagle, BW, Miles, EW and Icenogle, ML (1997) Interrole conflicts and the permeability of work and family domains: Are there gender differences? *Journal of Vocational Behavior,* 50, 168–184.

Eaton, SC and Bailyn, L (2000) Career as life path: Tracing work and life strategies of Biotech professionals. In MA Peiperl, MB Arthur, R Goffee and T Harris (eds) *Career Frontiers: New Conceptions of Working Lives.* Oxford: Blackwell.

Eby, LT, Butts, M, and Lockwood, A (2003) Predictors of success in the era of the boundaryless career. *Journal of Organizational Behavior, 24,* 689–709.

Eden, D and Zuk, Y (1995) Seasickness as a self-fulfilling prophecy: Raising self-efficacy to boost performance at sea. *Journal of Applied Psychology, 80,* 628–635.

Edmondson, A (2004) Psychological safety and learning behaviour in work teams. *Administrative Science Quarterly, 44,* 350–383.

Elliot, MA (1994) Managing a mid–career crisis. *Nursing Management,* 25(9), 76–80.

Ellison, J and Schreuder, AMG (2000) The relationship between career anchors, job perceptions and job satisfaction. *Journal of Industrial Psychology,* 26(2) 1–6.

Endler, NS, and Parker, JDA (1990) *Coping Inventory for Stressful Situations (CISS): Manual.* Toronto: Multi-Health Systems.

Erdogan, B, Kraimer, ML and Liden, RC (2004) Work value congruence and extrinsic career success: the compensatory roles of leader-member exchange and perceived organizational support. *Personnel Psychology, 57,* 305–332.

Erdogmus, N (2003) Career orientations of salaried professionals: The case of Turkey. *Career Development International,* 9(2), 153–157.

Erez, A and Isen, AM (2002) The influence of positive affect on the components of expectancy motivation. *Journal of Applied Psychology,* 87, 1055–1067.

Erikson, EH (1963) *Childhood and Society.* Harmonds-worth: Penguin.

Erikson, EH (1966) The concept of identity in race relations: Notes and queries. *Daedalus,* 95, 145–171.

Erwee, R (1991) Accommodating dual-career couples. *IPM Journal,* 9, 29–34.

Ettington, DR (1998) Successful career plateauing. *Journal of Vocational Behaviour,* 52, 72–88.

Falkenberg, L and Monachello, M (1989) Can organizations respond to the role overload in dual-earner families? *Journal of Management Development,* 8(6), 17–22.

Feldman, DC (1976) A contingency theory of socialization. *Administrative Science Quarterly,* 21, 433–452.

Feldman, D (1984) The development and enforcement of group norms. *Academy of Management Review,* 9, 47–53.

Feldman, DC (1988) *Managing Careers in Organizations.* Glenview, III: Scott, Foresman and Company.

Feldman, DC (1994) The decision to retire early: A review and conceptualization. *Academy of Management Review,* 19(2), 285–311.

Feldman, DC (2002a) Second careers and multiple careers. In CL Cooper and RJ Burke (eds) *The New World of Work: Challenges and Opportunities.* Oxford: Blackwell.

Feldman, DC (2002b) *Work Careers: A Developmental Perspective.* San Francisco: Jossey-Bass.

Feldman, DC (2002c) When you come to a fork in the road, take it: Career indecision and vocational choices of teenagers and adults. In DC Feldman (ed) *Work Careers: A Developmental Perspective.* San Francisco: Jossey-Bass.

Feldman, DC and Bolino, MC (1996) Careers within careers: Reconseptualising the nature of career anchors and their consequences. *Human Resource Management Review,* 6(2) 89–112.

Feldman, DC and Bolino, MC (2000) Career pattern of the self-employed: Career motivations and career outcomes. *Journal of Small Business Management,* 38(3), 53–58.

Feldman, DC and Ng, TWH (2007) Careers: mobility, embeddedness and success. *Journal of Management,* 33(3), 350–377.

Feldman, DC and Weitz, BA (1988) Career plateaus reconsidered, *Journal of Management,* 14(1), 69–80.

Feldt, T (1997) The role of sense of coherence in well-being at work: Analysis of main and moderator effects. *Work and Stress,* 11,134–147.

Ferber, MA, O'Farrell, B and Allen, LR (eds) (1991) *Work and Family: Policies for a Changing Work Force.* Washington, DC: National Academy Press. *Finansies en Tegniek.* Die week se nuus, 13 October 2000.

Ferreira, A (2008) History teacher made for IT *Sunday Times,* 7 September, 11.

Finweek, *SA se ekonomiese knelpunte* 21 January 2010, 14.

Folkman, S, and Lazarus, RS (1980) An analysis of coping in a middle-aged community sample. *Journal of Health and Social Behavior, 21,* 219–239.

Folkman, S and Lazarus, RS (1984) *Stress, Appraisal and Coping.* New York: Springer.

Fourie, C and Van Vuuren, LJ (1998) Defining and measuring career resilience. *Journal of Industrial Psychology,* 24(3), 52–59.

Foxcroft, CD (1997) Psychological testing in South Africa: Perspectives regarding ethical and fair practices. *European Journal of Psychological Assessment,* 13, 229–235.

Frankl, VE (1967) *Psychotherapy and Existentialism.* New York: Washington Square Press.

Frankl, VE (1969) *The Will to Meaning: Foundations and Applications of Logotherapy.* London: Souvenir Press.

Frankl, VE (1986) *The Doctor and the Soul: From Psychotherapy to Logotherapy.* New York: Vintage Books.

Frederickson, B L (1998) What good are positive emotions? *Review of General Psychology, 2,* 300–319.

Frederikson, BL (2001) The role of positive emotions in positive psychology: The broaden and build theory of positive emotions. *American Psychologist,* 56, 218–226.

Frederickson. B L (2004) The broaden-and-build theory of positive emotion. *The Royal Society London, 359,* 1367–1377.

Frenz, AW, Carey, MP and Jorgensen, RS (1993) Psychometric evaluation of Antonovsky's sense of coherence scale. *Psychological Assessment,* 5, 145–153.

Freudenberger, HJ (1974) Staff burnout. *Journal of Social Issues,* 30, 159–165.

Friedman, DS and Greenhaus, JH (2000) *Work and Family: Mies or Enemies.* New York: Oxford University Press.

Frieze, IH, Olson, JE, Murrell, AJ and Selvan, MS (2006) Work values and their effect on work behavior and work outcomes in female and male managers. *Sex Roles,* 54(1/2), 83–93.

Frone, MR (2003) Work-family balance. In JC Quick and LE Tetrick (eds) *The Handbook of Occupational Health Psychology.* Washington, DC: American Psychological Association.

Frone, MR, Russell, M and Cooper, ML (1997) Relation of work-family conflict to health outcomes: A four-year longitudinal study of employed parents. *Journal of Occupational and Organizational Psychology,* 70, 325–335.

Frone, MT, Yardley, JK and Markel, KS (1997) Developing and testing an integrative model of the work-family interface. *Journal of Vocational Behavior,* 50, 145–167.

Fry, PS (1995) Perfectionism, humor and optimism as moderators of health outcomes and determinants of coping styles of women executives. *Genetic, Social and General Psychology Monographs,* 121, 213–246.

Fugate, M, Kinicki, AJ and Ashforth, BE (2004) Employability: A psycho-social construct, its dimensions and applications. *Journal of Vocational Behaviour,* 65, 14–38.

Furnham, A (1984) The Protestant work ethic: A review of the psychological literature. *European Journal of Social Psychology,* 14, 87–109.

Furnham, A (1990) *The Protestant Work Ethic. The Psychology of Work-Related Beliefs and Behaviours.* London: Routledge.

Furnham, A (1992) *Personality at Work: The Role of Individual Differences in the Work Place.* London: Routledge.

Furnham, A (2000) Work in 2020: Prognostications about the world of work 20 years into the millennium. *Journal of Managerial Psychology,* 15(3), 242– 253.

Calinsky, E, Bond, JT and Friedman, DE (1993) *The Changing Workforce: Highlights of the National Study.* New York: Families and Work Institute.

Gallagher, DG (2002) Contingent work contracts: Practice and theory. In: CL Cooper and RJ Burke (eds) *The New World of Work: Challenges and Opportunities.* Oxford: Blackwell.

Gandolfi, F (2007) Downsizing, corporate survivors and employability-related issues: A European case study. *Journal of American Academy of Business, Cambridge,* 12(1), 50–56.

Ganster, DC, and Schaubroeck, J (1991) Work stress and employee health. *Journal of Management, 17,* 235–271.

Gardner, DG and Pierce, JL (1998) Self-esteem and self-efficacy within the organisational context: An empirical examination. *Group and Organisation Management, 23,* 48–70.

George, JM and Brief, AP (1992) Feeling good-doing good: A conceptual analysis of mood at work: Organizational spontaneity relationship. *Psychological Bulletin,* 112, 310–329.

Gerber, HM (2000) Career development of SA professional women who take career breaks. *Journal of Industrial Psychology,* 26(2), 7–13.

Gerdes, LC, Moore, C, Ochse, R and Van Ede, D (1988) *The Developing Adult* 2ed. Durban: Butterworths.

Geurts, SAE and Demerouti, E (2003) Work/non-work interface: A review of theories and findings. In MJ Schabracq, JAM Winnubst and CL Cooper (eds) *The Handbook of Work and Health Psychology.* Chichester: Wiley.

Geurts, SAE, Taris, TW, Kompier, MAJ, Dikkers, JSE, Van Hooff, MLM and Kinnunen, UM (2005) Measuring positive and negative interaction between 'Work' and 'Home': Development and validation of the 'Survey Work-Home Interaction — Nijmegen'. *Work and Stress.*

Gevers, J, Du Toit, R and Harilall, R (1992) *Manual for the Self-Directed Search Questionnaire.* Pretoria: Human Sciences Research Council.

Gibbons, P (2000) *Work and Spirit. Spirituality at Work: Definitions, Measures, Assumptions and Validity Claims.* Tonawanda, Canada: University of Toronto Press.

Gibson, DE (2003) Developing the professional self-concept: Role model constructs in early, middle and late career stages. *Organization Science,* 14(5), 591–610.

Gilbert, LA (1994) Current perspectives on dual-career families. *Current Directions in Psychological Science,* 3(4), 101–103.

Gilbert, LA (2006) Two-career relationship. In JH Greenhaus and GA Callanan (eds) *Encyclopedia of career development* 822–828 New Dehli: Sage Publications.

Gilbert, LA and Rachlin, V (1987) Mental health and psychological functioning of dual-career families. *The Counselling Psychologist,* 15(1), 7–49.

Ginzberg, E (1972) Toward a theory of occupational choice: A restatement. *The Vocational Guidance Quarterly,* 20, 169–176.

Ginzberg, E, Ginsburg, SW, Axelrad, S and Herman, JL (1951) *Occupational Choice: An Approach to a General Theory.* New York: Columbia University Press.

Glass, DC and McKnight, JD (1996) Perceived control, depressive symptomatology and professional burnout: A review of the evidence. *Psychology and Health,* 11, 23–48.

Glendon, AI, Thompson, BM and Myers, B (2007) *Advances in organisational psychology.* Bowen Hills: Australian Academic Press.

Godshalk, VM, (2006) Career plateau. In JH Greenhaus and GA Callanan (eds) *Encyclopedia of career development* 133–138 New Dehli: Sage Publications.

Goleman, D (1995) *Emotional Intelligence.* New York: Bantam Books.

Gordon, JR and Whelan, KS (1998) Successful professional women in midlife: How organizations can more effectively understand and respond to the challenges. *Academy of Management Executive,* 12(1), 8–25.

Gottfredson, LS (1981) Circumscription and compromise: a developmental theory of occupational aspirations. *Journal of Counseling Psychology,* 28, 545–579.

Gottfredson, LS (2005) Applying Gottfredson's theory of circumscrioption and compromise in career guidance and counseling. In SD Brown and RW Lent (eds) *Career development and counseling: Putting theory and research to work* 71–100. Hoboken, NJ: John Wiley and Sons, Inc.

Gottfredson, GD and Duffy, RD (2008) Using a theory of vocational personalities and work environments to explore subjective well-being. *Journal of Career Assessment,* 16(1), 44–59.

Gould, RL (1978) *Transformations: Growth and change in adult life.* New York: Simon and Schuster.

Grabmeier, J (1999) *Inside Sources Can Assist with Recruitment.* The Ohio State University: On Campus Research, 29(10). Available at www.osu.edu/oncampus

Grandey, A and Cropanzano, R (1999) The conservation of resources model applied to work-family conflict and strain, *Journal of Vocational Behavior,* 54, 350–370.

Grantham, C and Ware J (2004) On the reformation of work: A dozen predictions for 2010. Paper presented at the Future of Work Conference, 16 October 2004, Johannesburg.

Greenberg, HM and Sweeney, PJ (1999) Hiring expertise: How to find the right fit. *HR Focus,* 6 October.

Greenhaus, JH and Beutell, NJ (1985) Sources of conflict between work and family roles. *Academy of Management Review,* 10, 76–88.

Greenhaus, JH, Callanan, GA and Godshalk, VM (2010) *Career Management* 4ed. New York: Sage.

Greenhaus, JH, Callanan, GFL and Kaplan, E (1995) The role of goal setting in career management. *The International Journal of Career Management*, 7(5), 3–12.

Greenhaus, JH, Collins, D, and Shaw, J (2003) The relation between work-family balance and quality of life. *Journal of Vocational Behaviour, 63, 510–531.*

Greenhaus, JH and Foley, S (2007) The intersection of work and family lives. In H Gunz and M Peiperl (eds) *Handbook of career studies* 131–152 London: Sage.

Greenhaus, JH, Parasuraman, S, Granrose, CS, Rabinowitz, S and Beutell, NJ (1989) Sources of work-family conflict among two-career couples. *Journal of Vocational Behaviour,* 34(2), 133–153.

Greenhaus, JH and Powell, GN (2006) When work and family are allies: a theory of work-family enrichment. *Academy of Management Review, 31,* 72–92.

Griffin, B and Hesketh, B (2005) Counseling for work adjustment. In SD Brown and RW Lent (eds), *Career development and counseling: Putting theory and research to work* 483–505 New Jersey: Wiley.

Grimm, J (1999) One phone call could make all the difference in the world. *Editor and Publisher,* 132(51), 27–28.

Grobler, PA, Warnich, S, Carrell, MR, Elbert NF, Hatfield, RD (2002) *Human Resource Management in South Africa.* London: Thomson.

Grzywacz, JG and Marks, NF (2000) Reconceptualizing the work-family interface: An ecological perspective on the correlates of positive and negative spillover between work and family. *Journal of Occupational Health Psychology,* 5, 111–126.

Gubler, M, Arnold, J and Coombs, C (2010) *Career anchors as a tool for organizational career management in the IT sector.* Symposium paper presented at the 27th International Congress for Applied Psychology, 16 July, Melbourne, Australia.

Guion, RM and Gibson, WM (1988) Personnel selection and placement. *Annual Review of Psychology,* 39, 349–374.

Gunz, H, Evans, M and Jalland, M (2000) Career boundaries in a 'boundaryless' world. In MA Peiperl, MB Arthur, R Goffee and T Morris (eds) *Careers Frontiers: New Conceptions of Working Lives.* Oxford: Oxford University Press.

Guterman, M (1991) Working couples: Finding a balance between family and career. In JM Kummerow (ed), *New Directions in Career Planning and the Work Place.* Palo Alto, CA: Davies Black.

Gutteridge, TG, Leibowitz, ZB and Shore, JE (1993) When careers flower organizations flourish. *Training and Development,* 47(11), 24–29.

Gysbers, NC, Heppner, MJ and Johnston, JA (2003) *Career counseling: process, issues and techniques.* 2ed. New York: Pearson.

Hacker, SK and Dooien, TL (2003) Strategies for living: Moving from the balance paradigm. *Career Development International,* 8(6), 283–290.

Hackett, G (1996) Career development from a social cognitive perspective. In D Brown, L Brooks and Associates (eds) *Career Choice and Development* 3ed. San Francisco: Jossey-Bass.

Hackett, G and Betz, NE (1981) A self-efficacy approach to the career development of women. *Journal of Vocational Behaviour,* 18, 326–339.

Hackman, JR and Oldham, GR (1980) *Work Redesign.* Reading, MA: Addison-Wesley.

Hage, J (1995) Post-industrial lives: New demands, new prescriptions. In A Howard (ed) *The Changing Nature of Work.* San Francisco: Jossey-Bass.

Halbesleben, JRB and Wheeler, AR (2008) The relative roles of engagement and embeddedness in predicting job performance and intention to leave. *Work and Stress,* 22(3), 242–256.

Hale, N (1980) Freud's reflections on work and love. In NJ Smelser and EH Erikson (eds) *Themes of Work and Love in Adulthood.* London: Grant McIntyre.

Halford, G (1999) The development of intelligence includes the capacity to process relations of greater complexity. In M Anderson (ed) *The Development of Intelligence.* Hove: Psychology Press.

Hall, DT (1976) *Careers in Organizations.*CA: Goodyear.

Hall, DT (1996a) *The Career is Dead — Long live the Career: A Relational Approach to Careers.* San Francisco: Jossey-Bass.

Hall, DT (1996b) Protean careers of the 21st century. *Academy of Management Executive* 10(4) 8–16.

Hall, DT and Chandler, DE (2005) Psychological success: When the career is a calling. *Journal of Organisational Behaviour,* 26, 155–176.

Hall, DT and Mirvis, PH (1995a) Careers as lifelong learning. In A Howard (ed) *The Changing Nature of Work.* San Francisco: Jossey-Bass.

Hall, DT and Mirvis, PH (1995b) The new career contract: Developing the whole person at midlife and beyond. *Journal of Vocational Behaviour,* 47, 269–289.

Hall, DT and Moss, JE (1998) The new protean career contract: Helping organizations and employees adapt. *Organizational Dynamics,* Winter, 23–37.

Hall, DT and Richter, J (1990) Career gridlock: Baby boomers hit the wall. *Academy of Management Executive,* 4(3), 7–22.

Hamilton-Attwell, A (1998) Productivity and work ethic. *Work Study,* 47(3), 79–86.

Hammer, M (1997) The soul of the new organisation. In F Hesselbein, M Goldsmith, R Beckhard (eds) *The Organisation of the Future.* San Francisco: Jossey-Bass.

Hammer, LB andHanson, G (2006) Work-family enrichment. In JH Greenhaus and GA Callanan (eds) *Encyclopedia of career development.* New Dehli: Sage Publication.

Handy, C (1990) The age of unreason: A new renaissance? *Soundview Executive Book Summaries,* 12(1), 1–8.

Handy, C (1995) *Beyond Certainty: The Changing Worlds of Organizations.* London: Hutchinson.

Hankin, H (2005) *The New Workforce: Five Sweeping Trends that Will Shape Your Company's Future.* New York: Amacom.

Hansen, SS (2003) Career counselors as advocates and change agents for equality. *The Career Development Quarterly,* 52, 43–53.

Harpaz, I and Fu, X (2002) The structure of the meaning of work: A relative stability amidst change. *Human Relations,* 55(6), 639–667.

Harpaz, I, Honig, B and Coetsier, P (2002) A cross-cultural longitudinal analysis of the meaning of work and the socialization process of career starters. *Journal of World Business,* 37, 230–244.

Harris, TG (1993) The post-capitalist executive: An interview with Peter F Drucker. *Harvard Business Review,* May/June, 115–122.

Harrison, R (2009) *Learning and Development* 5ed. London: CIPD

Hart, PM (1999) Predicting employee life satisfaction: A coherent model of personality, work and non-work experiences and domain satisfaction. *Journal of Applied Psychology,* 84, 564–584.

Harter, S (1999) *The Construction of Self: Developmental Perspective.* New York: The Guilford Press.

Hartung, PJ (2007) Career construction: principles and practice. In K Maree (ed) *Shaping the story: a guide to facilitating narrative counselling* 103–120 Pretoria: Van Schaik.

Hartung, PJ and Taber, BJ (2008) Career construction and subjective well-being. *Journal of Career Assessment,* 16(1), 75–85.

Haskell, JR (1993) Getting employees to take charge of their careers. *Training and Development,* 47(2), 51–54.

Hattingh, S (2003) *Learnerships: A Tool for Improving Workplace Performance.* Randburg: Knowres.

Haywood, BG (1993) Career planning and development. *Hospital Material Management Quarterly,* 14(4), 42–48.

Herriot, P and Pemberton, C (1997) Facilitating new deals. *Human Resource Management Journal,* 7(1), 45–56.

Higgins, CA and Duxbury, LE (1992) Work-family conflict: A comparison of dual-career and traditional-career men. *Journal of Organizational Behaviour,* 13(4), 389–411.

Hill, RE (1974) An empirical comparison of two models for predicting preference for standard employment offers. *Decision Sciences,* 5, 243–254.

Hill, SK and Bahniuk, MH (1998) Promoting career success through mentoring. *Review of Business,* 19(3), 4–7.

Hillage, J and Pollard, E (1998) *Employability: developing a framework for policy analysis.* Research brief No. 85, Department for Education and Employment, London. Available at www.dfes.gov.uk/research/data/uploadfiles/RB85.doc [Accessed on: 2 February 2007].

Hinrichs, K and Pennington, SKG (1998) *Beyond Legislative Compliance: Implementing Employment Equity Successfully.* Johannesburg: SPA Publications.

Hobfoll, SE and Freedy, J (1993) Conservation of resources: A general stress theory applied to burnout. In WB Schaufeli, C Maslach and T Marek (eds) *Professional Burnout: Recent Developments in Theory and Research* 115–129. Washington, DC: Taylor and Francis.

Hobfoll, SE (1989) Conservation of resources: A new approach at conceptualizing stress. *American Psychologist. AA,* 513–524.

Hobfoll, SE (2001) The influence of culture, community and the nested-self in the stress process: Advancing conservation of resources theory. *Applied Psychology: An International Review, 50,* 337–369.

Hochschild, A (1983) *The managed heart.* Berkeley, CA: University of California Press.

Hofstede, G (1984) The cultural relativity of the quality of life concepts. *Academy of Management Review,* 9(3), 389–398.

Holahan, CJ, and Moos, RH (1986) Personality, coping and family resources in stress resistance: A longitudinal analysis. *Journal of Personality and Social Psychology, 51,* 389–395.

Holbeche, L (2000) Work in progression. *People Management,* 8 June, 44–46.

Holland, JL (1973) *Making Vocational Choices: A Theory of Careers.* Englewood Cliffs, NJ: Prentice Hall.

Holland, JL (1985) *Making Vocational Choices: A Theory of Personalities and Work Environments.* 2ed. Englewood Cliffs, NJ: Prentice Hall.

Holland, JL (1997) *Making vocational choices: a theory of vocational personalities and work environments.* 3ed. Odessa, FL: Psychological Assessment Resources.

Hollenbeck, JR, Ilgen, DR, and Crampton, SM (1992) Lower back disability in occupational settings: A review of the literature from a human resource management view. *Personnel Psychology, 45,* 247–278.

Holton III, EF and Russell, CJ (1997) The relationship of anticipation to newcomer socialization processes and outcomes: A pilot study. *Journal of Occupational and Organizational Psychology,* 70, 163–172.

Horton, T (1990) Second careers and third and ... (memo to members). *Management Review,* 79(9), 1–4.

Howard, A (1995) Rethinking the psychology of work. In A Howard (ed) *The Changing Nature of Work.* San Francisco: Jossey-Bass.

Howard, A (1995) *The Changing Nature of Work.* San Francisco: Jossey-Bass.

Howard, A (1997) A reassessment of assessment centers: Challenges for the 21st century, *Journal of Social Behaviour and Personality,* 12(5), 13–52.

Huffcutt, Al and Woehr, DJ (1999) Further analysis of employment interview validity: A quantitative evaluation of interviewer-related structuring methods. *Journal of Organizational Behavior,* 20, 549–560.

Hulin, C and Glomb, TM (1999) Contingent employees, individual and organizational considerations. In DR Ilgen and ED Pulakos (eds) *The Changing Nature of Performance: Implications for Staffing, Motivation and Development.* San Francisco: Jossey-Bass.

Humer, FB (2005) *Innovation in the pharmaceutical industry: future prospects.* Available at http://www.roche.com/fbh_zvg05_e.pdf [Accessed on 28 June 2010].

Ibarra, H (2003) *Working Identify: Unconventional Strategies for Reinventing your Career.* Boston, MA: Harvard Business School Press.

Iles, P (1999) *Managing Staff Selection and Assessment.* Buckingham: The Open University.

Ilgen, DR and Pulakos, ED (1999) *The Changing Nature of Performance: Implications for Staffing, Motivation and Development.* San Francisco: Jossey-Bass.

Ingram, W (2010) *Career choices: The right career for you.* Available at http://www. skillsportal. co.za [Accessed on: 25 February 2010]

Inkson, K (2008) The boundary-less career. In S Cartwright and CL Cooper (eds) *The Oxford Handbook of Personnel Psychology* 545–563. New York: Oxford University Press.

Inkson, K and Arthur, MB (2001) How to be a successful career capitalist. *Organizational Dynamics, 30*(1), 48–61.

Ivancevich, JM (1998) *Human Resource Management.* Boston, MA: Irwin McGraw-Hill.

Izraeli, DN (1993) Work/family conflict among women and men managers in dual career couples in Israel. *Journal of Social Behaviour and Personality,* 8(3), 371–388.

Jackson, C, Kidd, J and Hirsh, W (2001) Effective career discussions at work. Paper presented at the 10th European Congress on Work and Organizational Psychology, Prague.

Jackson, LTB and Rothmann, S (2005, June) Occupational stress, ill-health and organisational commitment of educators in the North-West Province. Paper presented at the 8th Annual Conference of the Society for Industrial and Organisational Psychology, Pretoria.

Jackson, LTB and Rothmann, S (2005, May) A model of work-related well-being for teachers in a province of South Africa. In M Salanova (Chair), *Work engagement in different work settings.* Symposium conducted at the meeting of the 28th European Work and Organization Psychology Congress, Istanbul, Turkey.

Jackson, SE and Schuier, RS (2003) *Managing Human Resources through Strategic Partnerships.* Mason, Ohio: Thomson/South Western.

Jencks, C (1989) *What is Post-Modemism?* London: Academy Editions.

Jokisaari, M and Nurmi, J (2009) Change in newcomers' supervisor support and socialization outcomes after organizational entry. *Academy of Management Journal, 52*(3), 527–544.

Jones, O (1992) Postgraduate scientists and R and D: The role of reputation in organizational choice. *R and D Management,* 22(4), 349–358.

Jones, C and De Fillippi, RJ (1996) Back to the future in film: Combining industry and self-knowledge to meet career challenges in the 21st century. *Academy of Management Executive,* 10(4), 137–158.

Jowell, J (2003) *Managing the Quarterlife Crisis: Facing Life's Choices in your 20s and 30s.* Cape Town: Struik.

Judge, TA and Kammeyer-Mueller, JD (2007) Personality and career success. In H Gunz and M Peiperl (eds) *Handbook of career studies,* 59–78. London: Sage.

Judge, TA, Locke, EA, Durham, CC and Kluger, AN (1998) Dispositional effects on job and life satisfaction: The role of core evaluations. *Journal of Applied Psychology,* 83, 17–34.

Jung, CG (1971) *Psychological Types: The Collected Works of CG Jung*, Vol 6. London: Routledge. (Originally published in German in 1921, translated.)

Kahn, RL, Wolfe, DM, Quinn, RR, Snoek, JD and Rosenthal, RA (1964) *Organizational stress*. New York: Wiley.

Kahn, WA (1990) Psychological conditions of personal engagement and disengagement at work. *Academy of Management Journal*, 33, 692–724.

Kanter, RM (1997) Restoring people to the heart of the organization of the future. In F Hesselbein, M Goldsmith and R Beckhard (eds) *Organization of the Future*. San Francisco: Jossey-Bass.

Karambayya, R and Reilly, AH (1992) Dual earner couples: Attitudes and actions in restructuring work for family. *Journal of Organizational Behaviour*, 13(6), 585–601.

Karasek, R and Theorell, T (1990) *Healthy Work: Stress, Productivity and the Reconstruction of Working Life*. New York: Basic Books.

Kates, N, Greiff, BS and Hagen, DQ (1990) *The Psychosocial Impact of Job Loss*. Washington: American Psychiatric Press.

Kaufman, HG (1974) *Obsolescence and Professional Career Development*. New York: AMACOM

Kaufman, HG (1982) *Professionals in Search of Work: Coping with the Stress of Job Loss and Underemployment*. New York: Wiley.

Kaufman, HG (1989) Obsolescence of technical professionals: A measure and a model. *International Association of Applied Psychology*, 38(1), 73–85.

Kaufman, HG (2006) Obsolescence of knowledge and skills. In JH Greenhaus and GA Callanan (eds) *Encyclopedia of career development*. New Dehli: Sage Publication.

Keith, PM and Schafer, RB (1980) Role strain and depression in two-job families. *Family Relations*, 29, 483–488.

Kelloway, EK and Barling, J (1991) Job characteristics, role stress and mental health. *Journal of Occupational Psychology*, 64, 291–304.

Kelloway, EK, Gottlieb, BH and Barham, L (1999) The source, nature and direction of work and family conflict: A longitudinal investigation. *Journal of Occupational Health Psychology*, 4, 337–346.

Kerr-Phillips, B and Thomas, A (2009) Macro and micro challenges for talent retention in South Africa. South African *Journal of Human Resource Management*, 7(1), Art. #157, 10 pages. DOI:10.4102/sajhrm.v7i1.157

Kets de Vries, MFR (1999) Organizational sleepwalkers: Emotional distress at midlife. *Human Relations*, 52(11) 1377–1401.

Keyes, CLM (2007) Promoting and protecting mental health as flourishing. A complementary strategy for improving mental health. *American Psychologist*, 62, 95–108.

Keyes, CLM, and Annas, J (2009) Feeling good and functioning well: distinctive concepts in ancient philosophy and contemporary science. *Journal of Positive Psychology*, 4, 197–201.

Keyes, CLM, Wissing, M, Potgieter, JP, Temane, M, Kruger, A, and van Rooyen, S (2008) Evaluation of Mental Health Continuum — Short form (MHC-SF) in Setswana speaking South African's. *Clinical Psychology and Psychopathology, 15,* 181–192.

Khapova, SN, Arthur, MB and Wilderom, CPM (2007) The subjective career in the knowledge economy. In H Gunz and M Peiperl (eds) *Handbook of career studies,* 114–130. London: Sage.

Kidd, JM (2006) *Understanding career counselling: theory, research and practice.* London: Sage.

Kidd, JM (2007) Career counselling. In H Gunz and M Peiperl (eds) *Handbook of career studies,* 97–113. London: Sage.

Kidd, JM (2008) Exploring components of career well-being and the emotions associated with significant career experiences. *Journal of Career Development, 35*(2), 166–186.

Kieffer, M (1991) The reference check: What you need to know. *Health Care Executive, 6*(6), 18–19.

Kilduff, M (1990) The interpersonal structure of decision making: A social comparison approach to organizational choice. *Organizational Behaviour and Human Decision Processes, 47,* 270–288.

Kilduff, M (1992) The friendship network as a decision-making resource: Dispositional moderators of social influences on organizational choice. *Journal of Personality and Social Psychology, 62*(1), 168–180.

Kim, S and Feldman, DC (2000) Working in retirement: The antecedents of bridge employment and its consequences for quality of life in retirement. *Academy of Management Journal, 43,* 1195–1210.

King, S and Nicol, DM (1999) Organizational enhancement through recognition of individual spirituality: Reflections of Jacques and Jung. *Journal of Organizational Change Management, 12*(3), 234–242.

King, Z (2001) Career self-management: A framework for guidance of employed adults. *British Journal of Guidance and Counselling, 29*(1), 65–78.

Kinicki, A and Kreitner, R (2009) *Organizational behaviour: key concepts, skills and best practices* 4ed. New York: McGraw-Hill.

Kinnunen, U and Mauno, S (1998) Antecedents and outcomes of work-family conflict among employed women and men in Finland. *Human Relations, 51,* 157–177.

Kinnunen, (J, Roenkae, A and Sallinen, M (2001) Parents, job experiences and well being in adolescents. Paper presented at The 10th European Congress on Work and Organizational Congress, Prague.

Kirchler, E (1985) Job loss and mood. *Journal of Economic Psychology, 6*(1), 9–25.

Klasen, N and Clutterbuck, D (2002) *Implementing Mentoring Schemes: A Practical Guide to Successful Programmes.* London: Butterworth/Heinemann.

Klein, FJ and Verbeke, W (1999) Autonomie feedback in stressful environments: How do individual differences in autonomie feedback relate to burnout, job performance and job attitudes in salespeople? *Journal of Applied Psychology*, 84(6), 911–924.

Kleinke, CL (1991) *Coping with Life Challenges*. San Francisco: Brooks/Cole.

Knaub, PK (1986) Growing up in a dual-career family: The children's perceptions. *Family Relations*, 35(3), 431–437.

Kniveton, BH (2004) Managerial career anchors in a changing business environment. *Journal of European Industrial Training*, 28(7) 563–573.

Knowledge Resources. (2010) *HR Survey 2010*. Randburg: Knowres.

Knowdell, RL, Branstead, E and Moravec, M (1994) *Downsizing to Recovery: Strategic Transition Options for Organizations and Individuals*. Palo Alto, CA: Consulting Psychologists Press.

Koak SR, Field HS, Giles, WF and Norris, DR (1998) The weighted application block: A cost-effective tool that can reduce employee turnover. *Hotel and Restaurant Administration Quarterly*, 39(2) 18–24.

Kobasa, CS, Maddi, SR and Kahn, S (1982) Hardiness and health: A prospective study. *Journal of Personality and Social Psychology*, 42, 168–177.

Kohlberg, L and Ryncarz, RA (1990) Beyond justice reasoning: moral development and consideration of a seventh stage. In CN Alexander and E J Langer (eds) *Higher Stages of Human Development*. Oxford: Oxford University Press.

Koonce, R (1997) The 4 Ms of career success. *Training and Development*, 51(12), 1–15.

Koortzen, P (1995) Die beroepsoriëntasies van mediese dokters. *Journal of Industrial Psychology*, 21 (2), 23–28.

Korn, L (1988) *Blocked! Across the Board*, Jan, 54–59.

Kossek, EE and Ozeki, C (1998) Work-family conflict, policies and the job-life satisfaction relationship: A review and directions for organizational behaviour. *Journal of Applied Psychology*, 83(2) 139–149.

Kotter, JP (1973) The Psychological Contract: Managing the Joining-up Process. *California Management Review*, 15(3), 91–99.

Kowalski, KC, and Crocker, PRE (2001) Development and validation of the Coping Function Questionnaire for adolescents in sport. *Journal of Sport and Exercise Psychology*, 23, 136–155.

Kram, KE (1985) *Mentoring at Work*. Lanham MD: University Press of America.

Kriek, HJ (1991) Die bruikbaarheid van die takseersentrum: 'n Oorsig van resente literatuur. *Journal of Industrial Psychology*, 17(3), 34–37.

Kriek, HJ, Hurst, DN and Charoux, JAE (1994) The assessment centre: Testing the fairness hypothesis. *Journal of Industrial Psychology*, 20(2), 21–25.

Kriek, HJ and Von der Ohe, H (1996) Managerial assessment methods survey. Unpublished report, Department of Industrial Psychology, UNISA

Krieshok, TS, Hastings, S, Ebberwein, C, Wettersten, K and Owen, A (1999) Telling a good story: Using narratives in vocational rehabilitation with veterans. *Career Development Quarterly,* 47, 202–214.

Krumboltz, JD (1979) A social learning theory of career decision making. In AM Mitchell, GB Jones, JD Krumboltz and RI Cranston (eds) *Social Learning and Career Decision Making.* Carroll Press.

Krumboltz, JD, Mitchell, AM and Jones, GB (1976) A social learning theory of career selection. *The Counselling Psychologist,* 6, 71–81.

Kummerow, JM (1991) *New Directions in Career Planning and the Workplace: Practical Strategies for Counsellors.* Palo Alto, CA: Davies-Black.

Kuijpers, MACT and Scheerens, J (2006) Career competencies for the modern career. *Journal of Career Development,* 32(4), 303–319.

Künzel, R and Schulte, D (1986) 'Burn-out' and reality shock among clinical psychologists. *Zeitschrift for Klinische Psychologie, Forschung und Praxis,* 15, 303–320.

Laabs, JJ (1993) Diary of a job seeker. *Personnel Journal,* 72, 16.

Landy, FJ and Conté, JM (2004) *Work in the 21ˢᵗ century: An Introduction to Industrial and Organizational Psychology.* New York: McGraw-Hill.

Landy, FJ, Shankster-Cawley, L and Moran, SK (1995) Advancing personnel selection and placement methods. In A Howard (ed) *The Changing Nature of Work.* San Francisco: Jossey-Bass.

Langley, R (1999) Super's theory. In GB Stead and MB Watson (eds) *Career Psychology in the South African Context.* Cape Town: Van Schaik.

Lankhard, BB (1996) *Career Resilience.* ERIC Clearinghouse on Adult, Career and Vocational Education.

Lawler, EE and Finegold, D (2000) Past, present and future: Individualizing the organization. *Organizational dynamics,* 29(1), 1–15.

Layton, A (1993) Relocation policies must reflect diversity. *Personnel Journal,* 72(8), 22–23.

Lazarus, RS (1991) *Psychological Stress and the Coping Process.* New York: McGraw-Hill.

Lazarus, RS and Folkman, S (1984) *Stress, Appraisal and Coping.* New York: Springer-Verlag.

Leana, CR and Feldman, DC (1988) Individual responses to job loss: Perceptions, reactions and coping behaviours. *Journal of Management,* 14(3), 375–389.

Leana CR and Feldman DC (1991) Gender differences in responses to unemployment. *Journal of Vocational Behaviour,* 38(1), 65–77.

Lefcourt, H (1982) *Locus of Control: Current Trends in Theory and Research.* New York: Wiley.

Leibowitz, ZB, Kaye, BL and Farren, C (1990) Career gridlock. *Training and Development Journal,* Apr, 28–36.

Leibowitz, ZB and Schlossberg, N (1981) Training managers for their role in a career development system. *Training and Developmental Journal,* 35(7), 72–79.

Lent, RW, Brown, SD and Hackett, G (1996) Career development from a social cognitive perspective. In D Brown, L Brookes and Associates (eds) *Career Choice and Development* 3ed. San Francisco: Jossey-Bass.

Levert, T Lucas, M and Ortlepp, K (2000) Burnout in psychiatric nurses: Contributions of the work environment and a sense of coherence. *South African Journal of Psychology,* 30, 36–43.

Levinson, DJ (1986) A conception of adult development. *American Psychologist,* 41, 3–13.

Levinson, DJ, Darrow, CN, Klein, EB, Levinson, MH and McKee, B (1978) *The Seasons of a Man's Life.* New York: Alfred A Knopf.

Lewis, S and Dyer, J (2002) Towards a culture for work-life integration? In CL Cooper and RJ Burke (eds) *The New World of Work: Challenges and Opportunities.* Oxford: Blackwell.

Liber, HS (1982) Applications of a theory of personality functioning and change to three career identity changes faced by the elderly. In JO Raynor and EE Entin (eds) *Motivation, Career Striving and Ageing.* New York: Hemisphere.

Lips-Wiersma, M (2002) The influence of spiritual "meaning-making" on career behaviour. *Journal of Management Development, 21*(7), 497–520.

Livneh, H, Antonak, RF, and Gerhardt, J (2000) Multidimensional investigation of the structure of coping among people with assumptions. *Psychometrics, 41,* 235–244.

Locke, EA, and Taylor, MS (1990) Stress, coping and the meaning of work. In A Brief and W R Nord (eds) *Meanings of occupational work* 135–170. Lexington, MA: Lexington Books.

London, M (1989) Relationships between career motivation, empowerment and support for career development. *Journal of Occupational and Organizational Psychology,* 66, 55–69.

London, M (1983) Toward a theory of career motivation. *Academy of Management Review,* 8(4), 620–630.

London, M and Mone, EM (1999) Continuous learning. In DR Ilgen and ED Pulakos (eds) *The Changing Nature of Performance: Implications for Staffing, Motivation and Development.* San Francisco: Jossey-Bass.

Lorsch, JW and Takagi, H (1989) Keeping managers off the shelf. In H Levinson (ed), *Designing and Managing Your Career.* Boston: Harvard Business School Press.

Louw, DA and Edwards, DJA (1997) *Psychology: An Introduction for Students in Southern Africa.* Johannesburg: Heineman.

Louw, DA, Van Ede, EM and Louw, AE (1998) *Human Development* 2ed. Pretoria: Kagiso.

Lowman, RL (1993) *Counselling and Psychotherapy of Work Dysfunctions.* Washington, DC: American Psychological Association.

Lykken, D, and Tellegen, A (1996) Happiness is a stochastic phenomenon. *Psychological Science, 7,* 186–189.

Lyons, S, Duxbury, L and Higgins, C (2005) Are gender differences in basic human values a generational phenomenon? *Sex Roles, 53*(9/10), 763–778.

Lyubomirsky, S (2008) *The how of happiness: A scientific approach to getting the life you want.* New York: Penguin Press.

Macey, WH, and Schneider, B (2008) The meaning of employee engagement. *Industrial and Organizational Psychology, 1,* 3–30.

Magnussen, D (1990) Personality development from an interactional perspective. In LA Pervin (ed), *Handbook of Personality: Theory and Research.* New York: Guilford Press.

Makikangas, A and Kinnunen, U (2003) Psychological work stressors and well-being: Self-esteem and optimism as moderators in a one-year longitudinal sample. *Personality and Individual Differences, 35,* 537–557.

Makin, PJ, Cooper, CL and Cox, C (2000) *Organizations and the Psychological Contract.* Leicester, UK: British Psychological Society Books.

Mainiero, LA and Sullivan, SE (2006) *The opt-out revolt: How people are creating kaleidoscope careers outside of companies.* New York: Davies-Black.

Maree, K (2002) Theoretical approaches : An overview. In K Maree and L Ebersohn (eds) *Lifeskills and Career Counselling.* Johannesburg: Heinemann.

Maree, K (2007) *Shaping the story: a guide to facilitating narrative counselling.* Pretoria: Van Schaik.

Marin, E (2000) *The Perspectives for a New and Comprehensive Vision of the Protection of Workers.* Proceedings of the 12th World Congress of the International Industrial Relations Research Association, Tokyo, Japan, 1, 151–9.

Marshall, J (1995) *Women Managers Moving On: Exploring Careers and Life Choices.* London: Routledge.

Marshall, NL and Barnett, RC (1993) Work-family strains and gains among two-earner couples. *Journal of Community Psychology, 21*(1), 64–78.

Marshall, V and Bonner, D (2003) Career anchors and the effects of downsizing: Implictions for generations and cultures at work. A preliminary investigation. *Journal of European Industrial Training, 27*(6), 281–291.

Martin, P (1997) *The Sickening Mind: Brain, Behaviour, Immunity and Disease.* London: Harper Collins.

Maslach, C (1982) *Burnout: The Cost of Caring.* Englewood Cliffs, NJ: Prentice Hall.

Maslach, C (1998) A multidimensional view of burnout. In CL Cooper (ed) *Theories of Organizational Stress.* Oxford: Oxford University Press.

Maslach, C, and Jackson, SE (1986) *Maslach Burnout Inventory: Manual* 2ed. Palo Alto, CA: Consulting Psychologists Press.

Maslach, C, Jackson, SE and Leiter, M (1996) *Maslach Burnout Inventory Manual* 3ed. Palo Alto, CA: Consulting Psychologists Press.

Maslach, C and Leiter, MP (1997) *The Truth about Burnout.* San Francisco: Jossey-Bass.

Maslach, C and Schaufeli, WB (1993) Historical and conceptual development of burnout. In WB Schaufeli, C Maslach and T Marek (eds) *Professional Burnout: Recent Developments in Theory and Research.* Washington, DC: Taylor and Francis.

Maslach, C, Schaufeli, WB and Leiter, MP (2001) Job burnout. *Annual Review of Psychology*, 52, 397–422.

Maslow, AH (1954) *Motivation and Personality*. New York: Harper.

Maslow, AH (1970) *Motivation and Personality* 2ed. New York: Harper and Row.

Matsui, T Ohsawa, T and Onglatco, M (1995) Work-family conflict and the stress-buffering effects on husband support and coping behavior among Japanese married working women. *Journal of Vocational Behaviour*, 47(2), 178–192.

Mauno, S and Kinnunen, U (1999) The effects of job stressors on marital satisfaction in Finnish dual-earner couples. *Journal of Organizational Behaviour*, 20, 879–895.

Maurer, T, Weiss, E and Barbeite, F (2003) A model of involvement in work-related learning and development activity: the effects of individual, situational, motivational and age variables. *Journal of Applied Psychology*, 88, 707–724.

May, DR, Gilson, RL and Harter, LM (2004) The psychological conditions of meaningfulness, safety and availability and the engagement of the human spirit at work. *Journal of Occupational and Organizational Psychology*, 77, 11–37.

Mayer, FS and Sutton, K (1996) *Personality: An Integrative Approach*. Upper Saddle River, NJ: Prentice Hall.

Mayer, JD and Salovey, P (1997) What is emotional intelligence? In Salovey, P and Sluyter, DJ (eds), *Emotional development and emotional intelligence*, 3–31 New York: Basic Books.

McArdle, S, Waters, L, Briscoe, JP and Hall, DT (2007) Employability during unemployment: Adaptability, career identity and human and social capital. *Journal of Vocational Behavior*, 71, 247–264.

McAllister, DJ (1995) Affect- and cognition-based trust as foundations for interpersonal cooperation in organizations. *Academy of Management Journal*, 38, 24–59.

McCarthy, AM and Garavan, TN (1999) Developing self-awareness in the managerial career development process: The value of 360–degree feedback and the MBTI *Journal of European Industrial Training*, 23(9), 437–445.

McCarthy, JF and Hall, DT (2000) Organizational crisis and change: The new career contract at work. In RJ Burke and CL Cooper (eds) *The Organization in Crisis: Downsizing, Restructuring and Privatization*. Oxford: Blackwell.

McCauley, CD, Moxley, RS and Van Velsor, E (1998) *The Center for Creative Leadership Handbook of Leadership Development*. San Francisco: Jossey-Bass.

McCaully, MH and Briggs Myers, I (1985) *Manual: A Guide to the Development and Use of the Myers-Briggs Type Indicator*. Palo Alto, CA: Consulting Psychologists Press.

McCook, LI, Folzer, SM, Charlesworth, D and Scholl, JN (1991) Dueling careers. *Training and Development*, 45(8), 40–44.

McCormack, A and Scholarios, D (2009) Recruitment. In T Redman and A Wilkinson (eds) *Contemporary human resource management*, 64–85 New York: Prentice-Hall.

McCormick, EJ and Ilgen, D (1987) *Industrial and Organizational Psychology*. Englewood Cliffs, NJ: Prentice Hall.

McCrae RR and John OP (1992) An introduction to the five-factor model and its applications. *Journal of Personality.* 60, 175–216.

McEnrue, MP (1988) Length of experience and the performance of managers in the establishment phase of their careers. *Academy of Management Journal,* 31(1), 175–185.

McGregor, I, McAdams, DP and Little, BR (2006) Personal projects, life stories and happiness: On being true to traits. *Journal of Research in Personality, 40,* 551–572.

McKee-Ryan, FM (2006) Job loss. In JH Greenhaus and GA Callanan (eds) *Encyclopedia of career development.* New Dehli: Sage Publication

McKnight, R (1991) Creating the future after job loss. *Training and Development, 45,* 69–72.

McMahon, M (2007) Life story counselling: producing new identities in career counselling. In K Mareer (ed) *Shaping the story: a guide to facilitating narrative counselling* 63–71 Pretoria: Van Schaik.

McNall, LA, Masuda, AD and Nicklin, JM (2010) Flexible work arrangements, job satisfaction and turnover intentions: the mediating role of work-to-family enrichment. *The Journal of Psychology, 144*(1), 61–81.

Meijers, F (1998) The development of a career identity. *International Journal for the Advancement of Counselling, 20,* 191–207.

Meijman, TF and Mulder, G (1998) Psychological aspects of workload. In PJ Drenth, H Thierry and CJ de Wolff (eds) *Handbook of Work and Organizational Psychology* 2ed. Hove, Sussex: Erlbaum.

merSETA (2008) *Sector Skills Plan-Annual Review.* Johannesburg:merSETA

Messmer, M (2000) Moving beyond a career plateau. *National Public Accountant, 45*(7), 20.

Miao, CF, Lund, DJ and Evans, KR (2009) Reexamining the influence of career stages on salesperson motivation: A cognitive and affective perspective. *Journal of Personal Selling and Sales Management, 24*(3), 243–255.

Miceli, MP (1986) Effects of realistic job previews on newcomer affect and behaviour: An operant perspective. *Journal of Organizational Behaviour Management, 8*(1), 73–88.

Miller, D (1997) The future organisation: A chameleon in all its glory. In F Hesselbein, M Goldsmith, R Beckhard (eds) *The Future Organisation.* San Francisco: Jossey-Bass.

Miller-Tiedeman, A and Tiedeman, DV (1990) Career decision making: An individualistic perspective. In D Brown, L Brooks and Associates (eds) *Career Choice and Development: Applying Contemporary Theories to Practice* 2ed. San Francisco: Jossey-Bass.

Miller, MJ and Brown, SD (2005) Counselling for career choice: implications for improving interventions and working with diverse populations. In SD Brown and Lent, RW (eds), *Career development and counselling: Putting theory and research to work* 441–465. Hoboken, NJ: John Wiley and Sons.

Mills, LB, and Huebner, ES (1998) A prospective study of personality characteristics, occupational stressors and burnout among school psychology practitioners. *Journal of School Psychology 36*, 103–120.

Millward, LJ and Brewerton, PM (2001) Psychological Contracts: Employee relations for the twenty-first century. In I Robertson and C Cooper (eds) *Personnel Psychology and HRM.*

Minor, CW (1992) Career development: Theories and models. In DH Montross and CJ Shinkman (eds) *Career Development: Theory and Practice.* Springfield, Illinois: Charles Thomas.

Mirvis, PH and Hall, DT (1994) Psychological success and the boundaryless career. *Journal of Organizational Behaviour,* 15, 365–380.

Mishra, AK, and Spreitzer, GM (1998) Explaining how survivors respond to downsizing: The roles of trust, empowerment, justice and work redesign. *Academy of Management Review,* 22, 567–588.

Mitchell, LK and Krumboltz, JD (1996) Krumboltz's learning theory of career choice and counselling. In D Brow, L Brooks and Associates (eds) *Career Choice and Development.* 3ed. San Francisco: Jossey-Bass.

Mitchell, LK and Krumboltz, JD (1990) Social learning approach to career decision making: Krumboltz's theory. In D Brown, L Brooks and Associates (eds) *Career Choice and Development: Applying Contemporary Theories to Practice* 2ed. San Francisco: Jossey-Bass.

Mitchell, LK, Levin, AS and Krumboltz, JD (1999) Planned happenstance: Constructing unexpected career opportunities. *Journal of Counseling and Development,* 77, 115–124.

Mittelman, W (1991) Maslow's study of self-actualization: A reinterpretation. *Journal of Humanistic Psychology,* 31(1), 114–135.

Mondy, RW and Noe, RM (1996) *Human Resource Management.* Upper Saddle River, NJ: Prentice Hall.

Montgomery, AJ, Peeters, MCW, Schaufeli, WB and Den Ouden, M (2003) Work-home interference among newspaper managers: Its relationship with burnout and engagement. *Anxiety, Stress and Coping,* 16, 195–211.

Moore, JE (2000) Why is this happening? A causal attribution approach to work exhaustion consequences. *Academy of Managment Review,* 25(2), 335–349.

Moore, C, Gunz, H and Hall, DT (2007) Tracing historical roots of career theory in managent and organisation studies. In H Gunz and M Peiperl (eds) *Handbook of career studies,* 13–38. London: Sage.

Moos, RH (1994) Conceptual and empirical advances in stress and coping theory. Paper presented at the 23rd International Congress of Applied Psychology, Madrid, Spain.

Morris, JA, and Feldman, DC (1996) The dimensions, antecedents and consequences of emotional labor. *Academy of Management Review,* 21, 986–1010.

Mostert, K, and Rothmann, S (2006) Work-related well-being in the South African Police Service. *Journal of Criminal Justice,* 34, 479–491.

MOW International Research Team (1987) *The Meaning of Working*. London: Academic Press.

Muchinsky, PM (2000) *Psychology Applied to Work*. Pacific Grove, CA: Brooks/Cole.

Muchinsky, PM, Kriek, HJ and Schreuder, AMG (2005) *Personnel Psychology*. Cape Town: Oxford University Press South Africa.

Muller, Y, and Rothmann, S (2009) Sense of coherence and employees experiences of helping and restraining factors in the work environment. *South African Journal of Industrial Psychology, 35*, 89–98.

Myers, DG (2000) The funds, friends and faith of happy people. *American Psychologist, 55*, 56–67.

Myers, IB and McCaully, MH (1985) Manual: A Guide to the Development and Use of the Myers-Briggs Type Indicator. Palo, Alto, CA: Consulting Psychologists Press.

Myers, IB, McCaulley, MH, Quenk, NL and and AL Hammer, AL (2003) *MBTI Manual: A Guide to the Development and Use of the Myers-Briggs Type Indicator* 3ed. Palo Alto, CA: Consulting Psychologists Press.

Nabi, GR (2003) Situational characteristics and subjective career success : The mediating role of career-enhancing strategies. *International Journal of Manpower, 24*(6), 653–671.

Nathan, R and Hill, L (1992) *Career counselling*. London: Sage.

Nathan, R and Hill, L (2006) *Career counseling*. London: Sage

Naudé, JLP and Rothmann, S (2003) Occupational stress of emergency workers in Gauteng. *South African Journal of Industrial Psychology, 29*(4), 92–100.

Nelson, DL, Quick, JC and Joplin, JR (1991) Psychological contracting and newcomer socialization: An attachment theory foundation. *Journal of Social Behaviour and Personality, 6*(9), 55–72.

Nelson, DL, and Simmons, BL (2003) Health psychology and work stress: A more positive approach. In JC Quick and LE Tetrick (eds) *Handbook of occupational health psychology*, 97–119. Washington, DC: American Psychological Association.

Nevid, JS, Rathus, SA and Greene, B (2000) *Abnormal Psychology in a Changing World*. Upper Saddle River, NJ: Prentice Hall.

Niam, E (1998) Check before you hire, *HR Focus,* 10 December.

Nicholson, N (1996) Career systems in crisis: change and opportunity in the information age. *Academy of Management Fxecutive,* 10(4) 40–51.

Nicholson, N and Arnold, J (1991) From expectation to experience: Graduates entering a large corporation. *Journal of Organizational Behaviour, 12*(5), 413–429.

Niles, SG (2003) Career counselors confront a critical crossroad: A vision of the future. *The Career Development Quarterly, 52*, 70–77.

Niles, SC and Hartung, PJ (2000) Emerging career theories. In DA Luzzo (ed) *Career Counselling of College Students: An Empirical Guide to Strategies that work*. Washington, DC: American Psychological Association.

Nishikawa, M (2000) Diversification in the use of atypical workers at the Japanese establishment. Proceedings of the 12th World Congress of the International Industrial Relations Research Association, Tokyo, Japan, 1, 160–8.

Noe, RA, Hollenbeck, JR, Gerhart, B and Wright, PM (1994) *Human Resource Management: Gaining a Competitive Advantage.* Illinois: Irwin.

Noer, D (2000) Leading organizations through survivor sickness: A framework for the new millennium. In RJ Burke and CC Cooper (eds) *The Organization in Crisis: Downsizing, Restructuring and Privatization.* Oxford: Blackwell.

Nord, WR, Brief, AF, Atieh, JM and Doherty, EM (1990) Studying meanings of work: The case of work values. In AP Brief and WR Nord (eds) *Meanings of Occupational Work: A Collection of Essays.* Massachusetts: Lexington.

Olivier, M and Rothmann, S (2001) The development of an internal locus of control in employees in the manufacturing sector. *South African Journal of Economic and Management Sciences,* 2(3), 476–491.

O'Neil, DA and Bilimoria, D (2005) Women's career development phases: idealism, endurance and reinvention. *Career Development International,* 10, 168–189.

Ongorri, H and Agolla, JE (2009) Paradigm shift in managing career plateau in organisation: The best strategy to minimize employee intention to quit. *African Journal of Business Management,* 3(6), 268–271.

Oosthuizen, CF (1985) *Persoonlike evalueringskriteria by organisasiekeuse in die ingenieursberoep.* Unpublished M Com thesis. Pretoria: University of Pretoria.

Orpen, C (1994) The effects of organizational and individual career management on career success. *International Journal of Manpower,* 15(1), 27–38.

Osborn, DP (1990) A re-examination of the organizational choice process. *Journal of Vocational Behaviour,* 36(1), 45–60.

Ostroff, C and Kozlowski, SWJ (1992) Organizational socialization as a learning process: The role of information acquisition. *Personnel Psychology,* 45(4), 849–874.

Ostroff, C, Shin, Y and Feinberg, B (2002) Skill acquisition and person-environment fit. In DC Feldman (ed) Work *Careers: A Developmental Perspective.* San Francisco: Jossey-Bass.

Otte, FL and Hutcheson, PC (1992) *Helping Employees Manage Careers.* Englewood Cliffs, NJ: Prentice Hall.

Otte, FL and Kahnweiler, WM (1995) Long-range career planning during turbulent times. Business *Horizons,* Jan/Feb, 2–7.

Pahl, RE (1988) Epilogue: On work. In RE Pahl (ed) *On Work: Historical, Comparative and Theoretical Approaches.* Oxford: Blackwell.

Palladino Schultheiss, DE (2005) Qualitative relational assessment: a constructivist paradigm. *Journal of Career Assessment,* 13(4), 381–394.

Parasuraman, S, Greenhaus, JH, Rabinowitz, S, Bedeian, AG and Mossholder, KW (1989) Work and family variables as mediators of the relationship between wives' employment and husbands' well-being. *Academy of Management Journal,* 32(1), 185–201.

Parasuraman, S and Greenhaus, JH (1999) *Integrating Work and Family: Challenges for a Changing World.* Westport, CT: Praeger.

Parasuraman, S, Purohit, YS, Godshalk, VM and Beutell, NJ (1996) Work and family variables, entrepreneurial career success and psychological well-being. *Journal of Vocational Behavior,* 48, 275–300.

Park, N, Peterson, C, and Ruch, W (2009) Orientations to happiness and life satisfaction in twenty-seven nations. *The Journal of Positive Psychology,* 4, 273–279.

Parker, P (2008) Promoting employability in a "flat" world. *Journal of Employment Counseling,* 45, 2–13.

Parsons, F (1909) *Choosing a vocation.* Boston: Houghton Mifflin.

Paul, RJ and Townsend, JB (1992) Some pros and cons of early retirement. *Review of Business,* 14(1), 43–46.

Pazy, A (1990) The threat of professional obsolescence: How do professionals at different career stages experience it and cope with it? *Human Resource Management,* 29(3), 251–269.

Peak, MH (1994) Fathers earn the most when their wives stay home. *Management Review,* 83(2), 6.

Peiperl, M and Arthur, M (2000) Topics for conversation: Career themes old and new. In M Peiperl, AM Goffee and T Morris (eds) *Career Frontiers: New Conceptions of Working Lives.* New York: Oxford University Press.

Peiperl, M and Jonsen, K (2007) Global careers. In H Gunz and M Peiperl (eds) *Handbook of career studies,* 350–372. London: Sage.

Perry, AR and Baldwin, DA (2000) Further evidence of associations of type A personality scores and driving-related attitudes and behaviors. *Perceptual and Motor Skills,* August, 91(1), 147–154.

Peterson, C, Nansook, P, and Seligman, M E P (2005) Orientations to happiness and life satisfaction: The full life versus the empty life. *Journal of Happiness Studies,* 6, 25–41.

Peterson, C, Ruch, W, Beermann, U, Park, N, and Seligman M E P (2007) Strength of character orientations to happiness and life satisfaction. *Journal of Positive Psychology,* 2, 149–156.

Peterson, C, and Seligman, MEP (2004) *Character strengths and virtues: A handbook and classification.* Oxford: Oxford University Press.

Pienaar, J and Rothmann, S (2003a) Job stress in the South African Police Services. Paper presented at the 15th Conference of the South African Institute for Management Scientists, Potchefstroom.

Pienaar, J and Rothmann, S (2003b) Coping strategies in the South African Police Service. *South African Journal of Industrial Psychology,* 29(4), 81–90.

Pienaar, J and Rothmann, S (2005) Suicide ideation in the South African Police Service. *South African Journal of Psychology,* 35(1), 58–72.

Pienaar, J, Rothmann, S, and Van De Vijver, AJR (2007) Occupational stress, personality traits, coping strategies and suicide ideation in the South African Police Services. *Criminal Justice and Behavior, 34*(2), 246–258.

Pitt, B (1984) Psychiatry of the change of life. *International Medicine, I,* 1603–1606.

Plug, C, Louw, DA, Couws, LA and Meyer, WF (1997) *Psigologiewoordeboek.* Johannesburg: McGraw-Hill.

Plumbley, P (1991) *Recruitment and Selection.* Worcester: Billing.

Pool, LD and Sewell, P (2007) The key to employability: Developing a practical model of graduate employability. *Education and Training, 49*(4), 277–289.

Poon, J (2004) Career commitment and career success: moderating role of emotion perception. *Career Development International, 9*(4), 374–390.

Popovich, P and Wanous, JP (1982) The realistic job preview as a persuasive communication. *Academy of Management Review, 7,* 570–578.

Porter, G (2004) Work, work ethic, work excess. *Journal of Organizational Change Management, 17*(5), 424–439.

Porter, LW, Lawler, EE and Hackman, JR (1975) *Behavior in Organizations.* New York: McGraw-Hill.

Powell, WW and Snellman, K (2004) The knowledge economy. *Annual Review of Sociology, 30,* 199–220.

Pratt, MG, and Ashforth, BE (2003) Fostering meaningfulness in working and at work. In KS Cameron, J E Dutton and R E Quinn (eds) *Positive organizational scholarship* 309–327. San Francisco, CA: Berrett Koehler Publishers.

Premack, SL and Wanous, JP (1985) A meta-analysis of realistic job preview experiments. *Journal of Applied Psychology, 70*(4), 706–719.

Pretorius, TB (1994) Using the Maslach Burnout Inventory to assess educators' burnout at a university in South Africa. *Psychological Reports, 75,* 771–777.

Pringle, JK and Dixon, KM (2003) Re-incarnating life in the careers of women. *Career Development International.* 8(6), 291–300.

Psychological Association of South Africa (PsySSA) 1987. *Ethical code for psychologists.* Pretoria: PsySSA

Psychological Association of South Africa (PsySSA) 1992. *Guidetines for the validation and use of personnel selection procedures.* Pretoria: PsySSA

Puah, P and Ananthram, S (2006) Exploring the antecedents and outcomes of career development initiatives: Empirical evidence from Singaporean employees. *Research and Practice in Human Resource Management, 14*(1), 112–142.

Purvis, SEC and Panich, RL (1986) Improving upon the first year retention rate of entry-level professionals. *CPA Journal, 56*(12), 101–103.

Quick, JC, Quick, JD, Nelson, DL and Hurrell, U (1997) *Preventive stress management in organisations.* Washington, DC: American Psychological Association.

Raelin, JA (1999) Internal career development in the age of insecurity. *Business Forum,* Winter, 19–23.

Rahim, MA and Psenicka, C (1996) A structural equation model of stress, locus of control, social support, psychiatric symptoms and propensity to leave a job. *Journal of Social Psychology,* 136, 69–84.

Ramakrishna, HV and Potosky, D (2002) Structural shifts in career anchors of information systems personnel: A preliminary emperical analysis. *Journal of Computer Information Systems,* 42(2), 83–89.

Rapoport, R and Rapoport, RN (1969) The dual career family: A variant pattern and social change. *Human Relations,* 22(1), 3–30.

Raubenheimer, JR (1991) Late adulthood. In DA Louw (ed), *Human Development.* 525–567. Pretoria: Haum.

Reichers, AE (1987) An interactionist perspective on newcomer socialization rates. *Academy of Management Review,* 12(2), 278–287.

Retief, A and Cole, J (1995) The job appreciation system. *CTU Position Paper,* 7.

Richardson, LA (1966) Perceived monetary value of job type, company size and location among college seniors. *Journal of Applied Psychology,* 50(5), 412–416.

Ridley, RJ (1982) Changes in motivation in the elderly person. In JO Raynor and EE Entin (eds) *Motivation, Career Striving and Ageing.* New York: Hemisphere.

Riggio, RE (2009) *Introduction to industrial and organizational psychology.* Upper Saddle River, New Jersey: Pearsons Education Inc.

Riolli, L, and Savicki, V (2003) Optimism and coping as moderators of the relationship between chronic stress and burnout. *Psychological Reports,* 92, 1215–1226.

Riordan, CM, Cowan, MA and Gatewood, RD (1995) Stress, coping and well-being following job loss: A longitudinal examination. Paper presented at the 10th Annual Conference of the Society for Industrial and Organizational Psychology, Orlando.

Riordan, DA and Street, DL (1999) Type A behavior in the workplace. The good, the bad and the angry. *Strategic Finance,* 81(31), 28–32.

Robbins, SP and Judge, TA (2010) *Essentials of Organisational Behavior.* New York: Pearson.

Robbins, PR and Judge, TA (2011) *Organizational behaviour* 14ed. Upper Saddle River, NJ: Pearson.

Robbins, SP, Judge, TA, Millett, B, and Waters-Marsh, T (2008) *Organisational behaviour* 5ed. Frenchs Forest NSW, Australia: Pearson.

Roberson, L (1990) Functions of work meanings in organizations: work meanings and work motivation. In AP Brief and WR Nord (eds) *Meanings of Occupational Work: A Collection of Essays.* Massachusetts: Lexington Books.

Roche, GR (1979) Much ado about mentors. *Harvard Business Review,* Jan/Feb, 15–28.

Rodrigues, R (2010) *Career anchors of professional workers: extending Schein's framework.* Symposium paper presented at the 27th International Congress for Applied Psychology, 16 July, Melbourne, Australia.

Roe, A (1956) *The Psychology of Occupations.* New York: Wiley.

Roe, A (1957) Early determinants of vocational choice. *Journal of Counselling Psychology,* 4, 212–217.

Roe, A and Lunneborg, PW (1990) Personality development and career choice. In D Brown, L Brooks and Associates (eds) *Career Choice and Development: Applying Contemporary Theories to Practice* 2ed. San Francisco: Jossey-Bass.

Rogers, CR (1978) *Carl Rogers on Personal Power.* London: Constable.

Rokeach, M (1979) From individual to institutional values: With special reference to the values of science. In M Rokeach (ed), *Understanding Human Values.* London: Collier and Macmillan.

Rosen, B and Jerdee, TH (1990) Middle and late career problems: Causes, consequences and research needs. *Human Resources Planning,* 13(1), 59–70.

Rosenbaum, M (1990) *Learned Resourcefulness: On Coping Skills, Self-Control and Adaptive Behaviour.* New York: Springer.

Rosenbaum, M and Cohen, E (1999) Equalitarian marriages, spousal support, resourcefulness and psychological distress among Israeli working women. *Journal of Vocational Behaviour,* 54(1), 102–113.

Rosin, HM (1990) Consequences for men of dual career marriages: Implications for organizations. *Journal of Management Psychology,* 5(1), 3–8.

Ross, RR and Altmaier, EM (1994) *Intervention in Occupational Stress: A Handbook of Counselling for Stress at Work.* London: Sage.

Rothnie-Jones, D (1991) The stress of job loss: planning, perspective help people cope. *Marketing,* 30 June, 96.

Rothmann, S (2001) Sense of coherence, locus of control, self-efficacy and job satisfaction. *Journal of Economic and Management Sciences,* 5(1), 41–65.

Rothmann, S (2003) Burnout and engagement: A South African perspective. *South African Journal of Industrial Psychology,* 29(4), 16–25.

Rothmann, S (2004) Burnout, psychological strengths and coping strategies of senior managers in the manufacturing industry. *Management Dynamics,* 13(4), 26–37.

Rothmann, S (2005, September) *Work-related well-being in South African organisations: What do we know?* Paper presented at the 7th Annual Conference of the Employee Assistance Professionals Association of South Africa, Durban.

Rothmann, S (2008) Occupational stress, job satisfaction, burnout and work engagement as components of work-related well-being. *SA Journal of Industrial Psychology,* 34(3), 11–16.

Rothmann, S and Agathagelou, AM (2000) Die verband tussen lokus van beheer en werkstevredenheid by senior polisiepersoneel. *Tydskrif vir Bedryfsielkunde,* 26(2), 20–26.

Rothmann, S, and Cilliers, FvN (2007) Present challenges and critical issues for research in Industrial/Organisational Psychology in South Africa. *South African Journal of Industrial Psychology,* 33(1), 8–17.

Rothmann, S, Jackson, LTB and Kruger, MM (2003) Burnout and job stress in a local government: The moderating effects of sense of coherence. *South African Journal of Industrial Psychology*, 29(4), 52–60.

Rothmann, S, and Malan, H (2003) Koherensiesin, selfdoeltreffendheid, lokus van beheer en uitbranding by maatskaplike werkers. *SA Industrial Psychology*, 29(4), 43–51.

Rothmann, S, Meiring, D, Van der Walt, HS, and Barrick, M (2002, April) *Predicting job performance using personality measures in South Africa*. Paper presented at the 17th Annual Conference of the Society for Industrial and Organisational Psychology, Toronto, Canada.

Rothmann, S, Sieberhagen, G and Cilliers, FVN (1998) Die kwalitatiewe effek van 'n groepfasiliteringskursus. *Tydskrif vir Bedryfsielkunde*, 24(3), 7–13.

Rothmann, S, Steyn, LJ, and Mostert, K (2005) Job stress, sense of coherence and work wellness in an electricity supply organisation. *South African Journal of Business Management*, 36(1), 1–9.

Rothmann, S and Strijdom, C (2002) Suicide ideation in the South African Police Service in the North West Province. *South African Journal of Industrial Psychology*, 28, 44–48.

Rothmann, S and Van Rensburg, P (2002) Psychological strengths, coping and suicide ideation in the South African Police Services in the North West Province. *South African Journal of Industrial Psychology*, 28(3), 39–49.

Rotter, J (1966) Generalized expectations for internal versus external control of reinforcements. *Psychological Monographs: General and Applied*, 80(1), 1–28.

Rounds, JB and Armstrong, PI (2005) Assessment of needs and values. In SD Brown and Lent, RW (eds), *Career development and counselling: Putting theory and research to work* 305–329 Hoboken, NJ: John Wiley and Sons.

Rousseau, DM and Wade-Benzoni, KA (1995) Changing individual-organization attachments: A two-way street. In A Howard (ed), *The Changing Nature of Work*. San Francisco: Jossey-Bass.

Rousseau, DM (1990) New line perceptions of their own and their employer's obligations: A study of psychological contracts, *Journal of Organizational Behaviour*, 11, 389–400.

Roxburgh, S (2001) The impact of time pressures on the depression of American workers. Paper presented at the 10th European Congress on Work and Organizational Psychology, Prague.

Ryan, C (1994) Whites pushed to think small. *Business Times*, 13 February, 12.

Ryan, R M and Frederick, CM (1997) On energy, personality and health: Subjective vitality as a dynamic reflection of well-being. *Journal of Personality*, 65, 529–565.

Ryff, CD and Singer, B (1998) The contours of positive human health. *Psychological Inquiry*, 9, 1–28.

Ryff, CD, and Singer, BH (2008) Know thyself and become what you are: An eudiamonic approach to psychological well-being. *Journal of Happiness Studies*, 9, 13–39.

Sadler, P (1991) Designing *Organizations*. London: Mercury Books.

Sake Beeld (1996) Emigrasie lei tot 'n tekort aan bestuurslede. *Sake Beeld*, 22 January, 51.

Saks, AM (2006) Antecedents and consequences of employee engagement. *Journal of Managerial Psychology, 21*, 600–619.

Salovey, P, Rothman, AJ, Detweiler, JB and Steward, WT (2000) Emotional states and physical health. *American Psychologist, 55*, 110–121.

Salthouse, TA (1989) Age-related change in basic cognitive processes. In M Storandt and GR van den Bos (eds) *The Adult Years: Continuity and Change: The Master Lectures.* Washington DC: American Psychological Association.

Savickas, ML (1993) Career counseling in the postmodern era. *Journal of Cognitive Psychotherapy, 7*(3), 205–215.

Savickas, ML (1994) Convergence prompts theory renovation, research unification and practice coherence. In ML Savickas and RW Lent (eds) *Convergence in career development theories.* Palo Alto, CA: Davies Black.

Savickas, ML (2005) The theory and practice of career construction. In SD Brown and Lent, RW (eds), *Career development and counselling: Putting theory and research to work* 42–70. Hoboken, NJ: John Wiley and Sons.

Savickas, ML (2009) Life designing: a paradigm for career construction in the 21st century. *Journal of Vocational Behavior.* DOI: 10.1016/j.jvb.2009.04.004.

Schabracq, MJ (2003) What an organization can do about its employees' well-being and health: An overview. In MJ Schabracq, JAM Winnubst and CL Cooper (eds) *The Handbook of Work and Health Psychology* 2ed (revised). Chichester, Surrey: Wiley.

Scandura, TA (2002) The establishment years: A dependence perspective. In DC Feldman (ed) *Work Careers: A Developmental Perspective.* San Francisco: Jossey-Bass.

Scarpello, VG and Ledvinka, J (1995) *Human Resource Management: Environment and Functions.* Ohio: South-Western.

Schein, EH (1964) How to break the college graduate. *Harvard Business Review, 42*, 68–76.

Schaufeli, WB (2003) Past performance and future perspectives of burnout research. *South African Journal of Industrial Psychology, 29*(4), 1–15.

Schaufeli, WB and Bakker, AB (2003) *Utrecht Work Engagement Scale: Preliminary Manual.* Occupational Health Psychology Unit: Utrecht University.

Schaufeli, WB, and Bakker, AB (2004) Job demands, job resources and their relationship with burnout and engagement: A multi-sample study. *Journal of Organizational Behavior, 25*, 293–315.

Schaufeli, WB and Enzmann, D (1998) *The Burnout Companion to Study and Practice: A Critical Analysis.* London: Taylor and Francis.

Schaufeli, WB and Salanova, M (in press) Work engagement: An emerging psychological concept and its implications for organizations.

Schaufeli, WB, Salanova, M, Gonzalez-Roma, V and Bakker, AB (2002b) The measurement of engagement and burnout: A confirmative analytic approach. *Journal of Happiness Studies, 3*, 71–92.

Schein, EH (1976) *Career Planning and Development.* Geneva: International Labour Office.

Schein, EH (1978) *Career Dynamics: Matching Individual and Organizational Needs.* Reading, MA: Addison Wesley.

Schein, EH (1988) *Organizational Psychology.* Englewood Cliffs, NJ: Prentice Hall.

Schein, EH (1990a) *Career Anchors: Discovering Your Real Values.* San Diego: University Associates.

Schein, EH (1990b) Career stress in changing times: Some final observations. *Prevention in Human Services,* 8(1), 251–261.

Schein, EH (1993) *Career Survival: Strategic Job and Role Planning.* Pfeiffer.

Schein, EH (1996) Career anchors revisited. Implications for career development in the 21st century. *Academy of Management Executive,* 1, 80–88.

Schein, EH (2006) Career anchors. In JH Greenhaus and GA Callanan (eds) *Encyclopedia of career development,* 63–69, New Dehli: Sage Publication.

Schepers, JM (1995) *Die Lokus van Beheer Vraelys: Konstruksie en Evaluering van 'n Meetinstrument.* Johannesburg: Rand Afrikaans University.

Schiffrin, HH, and Nelson, KS (2010) Stressed and happy? Investigating the relationship between happiness and perceived stress. *Journal of Happiness Studies,* 11, 33–39

Schmidt, FL and Hunter, JE (1998) The validity and utility of selection methods in personnel psychology: Practical and theoretical implications of 85 years of research findings. *Psychological Bulletin,* 124(2), 262–274.

Schmidt, FL and Rader, M (1999) Exploring the boundary condition for interview validity: Meta-analytic validity findings for a new interview type. *Personnel Psychology,* 52, 445–464.

Schneer, JA and Reitman, F (1994) The importance of gender in mid career: A longitudinal study of MBAs. *Journal of Organizational Behaviour,* 15(3), 199–207.

Schwoerer, CE and May, DR (1996) Age and work outcomes: The moderating effects of self-efficacy and tool design effectiveness. *Journal of Organisational Behaviour,* 17, 469–487.

Schreuder, AMG (1998) Die loopbaanpatrone van Suid-Afrikaanse Bestuurders. *Journal of Industrial Psychology,* 24(1), 5–9.

Schereuder, AMG and Coetzee, M (2006) *Careers: An organisational perspective* (3ed) Cape Town: Juta.

Schreuder, AMG and Flowers, J (1991) Die verband tussen enkele dimensies van loopbaanankers, pos-persepsie en gehalte van werklewe. *Journal of Industrial Psychology,* 17(2), 23–28.

Schreuder, AMG and Flowers, J (1992) Die modererende invloed van loopbaanontplooiing op loopbaanpassing en gehalte van werklewe. *Journal of Industrial Psychology,* 18(2), 10–13.

Schultz, DP and Schultz, SE (1986) *Psychology and Industry Today.* New York: MacMillan.

Schultz, D and Schultz, SE (2010) *Psychology and work today* 10ed. New York: Pearson.

Schultz, G and Miller, C (2004) The search for meaning and career development. *Career Development International.* 9(2), 142–152.

Schweyer, A (2004) *Talent management systems.* Canada: John Wiley and Sons.

Sdorow, LM (1995) *Psychology.* Dubuque, Iowa: Wm. C Brown.

Seeman, M (1972) Alienation and engagement. In A Campbell and PE Converce (eds), *The human meaning of social change* 467–527. New York: Russell Sage Foundation.

Sekaran, U and Hall, DT (1989) Asynchronism in dual-career and family linkages. In MB Arthur, DT Hall and BS Lawrence (eds) *Handbook of Career Theory* 159–180. Cambridge: Cambridge University Press.

Seligman, MEP and Csikszentimihalyi, M (2000) Positive psychology: An introduction. *American Psychologist,* 55(1), 5–14.

Seligman, MEP (2002) *Authentic Happiness: Using the New Positive Psychology to Realize your Potential for Lasting Fulfilment.* London: Nicholas Brealey.

Seligman, MEP (2002) *Authentic happiness.* New York. Free Press.

Seligman, MEP (2008) Positive health. *Applied Psychology: An International Journal,* 57, 3–18.

Seligman, MEP, and Csikszentmihalyi, M (2000) Positive psychology: An introduction. *American Psychologist,* 55, 1–5.

Seligman, MEP, Parks, A, and Steen, T (2004) A balanced psychology and a full life. *The Royal Society London, 359,* 1379–1381.

Selye, H (1976) *Stress in Health and Disease.* Boston, MA: Butterworths.

Senge, PM (1990) *The Fifth Principle: The Art and Practice of the Learning Organization.* London: Century Business.

Seria, N and Cohen, M (2009) South Africa's unemployment rate increases to 23,5 per cent (Update 2) Available at: www.bloomberg.com

Shamir, B (1991) Meaning, self and motivation in organizations. *Organization Studies, 12,* 405–424.

Shantall, T, Moore, C and Rapmund, V (2002) *Logotherapy: Meaning-Centred Living, Therapy and Counseling.* Pretoria: University of South Africa.

Sharf, RS (2010) *Applying career development theory to career counselling* 5ed. Belmont, CA: Cengage Learning.

Sheehy, G (1976) *Passages: Predictable Crises of Adult Life.* New York: Bantam Books.

Sheehy, G (1995) *New Passages : Mapping Your Life Across Time.* London: Harper Collins.

Sherer, M, Maddux, JE, Mercadante, B, Prentice-Dunn, S, Jacobs, B and Rogers, RW (1982) The self-efficacy scale: Construction and validation. *Psychological Reports,* 51, 663–671.

Shelley, S (1992) Balancing work and family. *Clinical Engineering,* 99(4), 147–158.

Shivy, VA (2006) Career-planning workshops. In JH Greenhaus and GA Callanan (eds) *Encyclopedia of career development,* 132–133. New Dehli: Sage Publications.

Shoffner, MF (2006) Career counselling: theoretical perspectives. In D Capuzzi and MD Stauffer (eds), *Career counseling: foundations, perspectives and applications,* 40–68. Boston, MA: Pearson.

Simmons, BL and Nelson, DL (2001) Eustress at work: The relationship between hope and health in hospital nurses. *Health Care Management Review,* 26, 7–18.

Sinclair, V (2009) Experiencing career satisfaction and career success over the life span. Available at: http://www.counselling-directory.org.uk/counselloradvice98889.html [Accessed on: 2 February 2010]

Singer, M (1993) *Fairness in Personnel Selection.* Alder-shot: Avebury.

Singh, R (1998) Redefining psychological contracts with the US work force: A critical task for strategic human resource management planners in the 1990s. *Human Resource Management.* Spring, 37(1), 61–69.

Singh, R (2006) Self-awareness. In JH Greenhaus and GA Callanan (eds) *Encyclopedia of career development,* 709–713. New Dehli: Sage Publication.

Slabbert, I (1987) *An Evaluation of the Management Training and the Career Anchors of MBA/MBL Graduates.* Pretoria: Human Sciences Research Council.

Smit, PJ and Cronjé, GJ de J (1997) *Management Principles.* Cape Town: Juta.

Smit, PJ and Cronjé, GJ de J (2002) *Management Principles.* Cape Town: Juta.

Smither, J, London, M, Flautt, R, Vargas, Y and Kucine, I (2003) Can working with an executive coach improve multi-source feedback ratings over time? A quasi-experimental study. *Personnel Psychology, 56,* 23–44.

Smither, RD (1998) *The Psychology of Work and Human Performance.* New York: Longman.

Snyder, CR and Lopez, SJ (2002) *Handbook of Positive Psychology.* Oxford: Oxford University Press.

Society for Industrial and Organisational Psychology (2005) *Guidelines for the Validation and Use of Assessment Procedures for the Workplace.* Garsfontein: SIOPSA

Soelberg, PO (1967) Unprogrammed decision making. *Industrial Management Review, 8,* 19–29.

Sonnenfeld, J (1989) Dealing with the aging work force. In H Levinson (ed) *Designing and Managing Your Career.* Boston: Harvard Business School Press.

Sonnentag, S (2003) Recovery, work engagement and proactive behavior: A new look at the interface between nonwork and work. *Journal of Apptied Psychology, 88,* 518–528.

Speakman, M (1976) Occupational choice and placement. In B Karsara and J Korer (eds) *Occupational Structure and Placement.* Milton Keynes: Open University Press.

Spector, PE (1982) Behavior in organizations as a function of employees' locus of control. *Psychological Bulletin, 91,* 482–497.

Spector, PE (1986) Perceived control by employees: A meta-analysis of studies concerning autonomy and participation at work. *Human Relations, 39,* 1005–1016.

Spencer, JT (1999) Thirty years of gender research: a personal chronicle. In WB Swann, JH Langlouis and LA Gilbert (eds), *Sexism and stereotypes in modern society,* 255–290 Washington, DC: American Psychological Association.

Spielberger, C D, Vagg, P R, and Wasala, C F (2003) Occupational stress: Job pressures and lack of support. In Quick, JC and Tetrick, LE (eds) *Handbook of occupational health psychology,* 185–200. Washington, DC: American Psychological Association.

Stajkovic, AD and Luthans, F (1998) Social cognitive theory and self-efficacy: Going beyond traditional motivational and behavioural approaches. *Organisational Dynamics* 26(4), 62–74.

Stander, MW, and Rothmann, S (2010) Psychological empowerment, job insecurity and employee engagement. *SA Journal of Industrial Psychology, 36*(1), 1–8. DOI:10.4102/sajip.v36i1.849.

Staudinger, UM and Bluck, S (2001) A view on midlife development from life-span theory. In ME Lachman (ed) *Handbook of Midlife Development.* New York: Wiley.

Stead, GB and Watson, MB (1999) *Career psychology in the South African context.* Pretoria: Van Schaik.

Steele, C and Francis-Smythe, J (2010) *Investigating the role of career anchor congruence.* Symposium paper presented at the 27th International Congress for Applied Psychology, 16 July, Melbourne, Australia.

Steger, MF, Frazier, P, Oishi, S, and Kaler, M (2006) The Meaning in Life Questionnaire: Assessing the presence of and search for meaning in life. *Journal of Counseling Psychology, 53,* 80–93.

Stephens, GK (1994) Crossing internal career boundaries: The state of research on subjective career transitions. *Journal of Management, 20*(2), 479–501.

Sternberg, RJ (2003) Implications of the theory of successful intelligence for career choice and development. *Journal of Career Assessment, 11*(2), 136–152.

Stewart, TA (1995) Planning a career in a world without managers. *Fortune,* 131 (5) 72–80.

Still, L and Timms, W (1998) Career barriers and the older woman manager. *Women and Management Review.* 13(4), 143–155.

Stone, RJ (2005) *Human Resource Management.* Milton Keynes: Wiley.

Storm, K and Rothmann, S (2003a) A psychometric analysis of the Maslach Burnout Inventory — General Survey in the South African Police Service. *South African Journal of Psychology,* 33, 219–226.

Storm, K and Rothmann, S (2003b) The validation of the Utrecht Work Engagement Scale in the South African Police Services. *South African Journal of Industrial Psychology,* 29(4), 62–70.

Storm, K and Rothmann, S (2003c) The relationship between burnout, personality traits and coping strategies in a corporate pharmaceutical group. *South African Journal of Industrial Psychology,* 29(4), 35–42.

Strah, LK, Bett, JM and Reilly, AH (1994) A decade of change: Managers' attachment to their organisations and their jobs. *Human Resource Management,* 33, 531–548.

Strauser, DR, Lustig, DC and Çiftçi,A (2008) Psychological well-being: Its relation to work personality, vocational identity and career thoughts. *The Journal of Psychology, 142*(1), 21–35.

Strümpfer, DJW (1990) Salutogenesis: A new paradigm. *South African Journal of Psychology,* 20(4), 265–276.

Strümpfer, DJW (1995) The origins of health and strength: From 'salutogenesis' to 'fortigenesis'. *South African Journal of Psychology*, 25(2), 81–89.

Strümpfer, DJW (2003) *Psychofortology: Review of a new paradigm marching on.* Unpublished report. Johannesburg: RAU

Strümpfer, DJW, Danana, N, Gouws, JF and Viviers, M (1998) Personality dispositions and job satisfaction. *South African Journal of Psychology*, 28, 92–99.

Sturges, J (2008) All in a day's work? Career self-management and the management of the boundary between work and non-work. *Human Resource Management Journal, 18(2)*, 118–134.

Sullivan, SE and Arthur, MB (2006) The evolution of the boundary-less career concept: examining physical and psychological mobility. *Journal of Vocational Behavior, 69*, 19–29.

Sullivan, SE and Crocitto, M (2007) The developmental theories: a critical examination of their continuing impact on careers research. In HGunz and M Peiperl (eds), *The Handbook of Career Studies*, 283–309. London: Sage.

Sunday Times, 16/05/1999.

Sunday Times, 07/01/2001.

Super, DE (1957) *The Psychology of Careers.* New York: Harper and Row.

Super, DE (1988) *Career development: Who can contribute?* Unpublished handouts for seminar on Career Development. Pretoria: Human Sciences Research Council.

Super, DE (1990) A life-span, life-space approach to career development. In D Brown, L Brooks and Associates (eds) *Career Choice and Development: Applying Contemporary Theories to Practice* 2ed. San Francisco: Jossey-Bass.

Super, DE (1992) Toward a comprehensive theory of career development. In DH Montross and CJ Shinkman (eds) *Career Development: Theory and Practice.* 35–64. Illinois: Charles C Thomas.

Super, DE and Bohn, MJ (1971) *Occupational Psychology.* London: Tavistock.

Super, DE, Savickas, ML and Super, CM (1996) The life-space approach to careers. In D Brown, L Brooks and Associates (eds) *Career Choice and Development* 3ed. San Francisco: Jossey-Bass.

Sutton, RI (1991) Maintaining norms about expressed emotions: The case of the bill collectors. *Administrative Science Quarterly*, 36, 245–268.

Swindall, C (2007) *Engaged leadership: Building a culture to overcome employee disengagement.* Hoboken, NJ: John Wiley and Sons.

Tallman, RRJ and Bruning, NS (2008) Relating employees' psychological contracts to their personality. *Journal of Managerial Psychology*, 23(6), 688–712.

Tams, S and Arthur, MB (2006) Boundary-less careers. In JH Greenhaus and GA Callanan (eds), *Encyclopeadia of Career Development, vol. 1*, 44–49. Thousand Oaks, CA: Sage.

Tan, CS and Salomone, PR (1994) Understanding career plateauing: Implications for counselling. *The Career Development Quarterly*, 42, 291–301.

Tappan, MB (1999) Moral development in a postmodern world. In RL Mosher, DJ Youngman and JM Day (eds) *Human Development Across the Life Span*. Westport Connecticut: Praeger.

Taris, T, Schaufeli, W B, Schreurs, P J G, and Calje, D G (2000) Opgebrand in het onderwijs: Stress, psychische vermoeidheid en ziekteverzuim onder leraren (Burnt-out in education: Stress, mental fatigue and absence through illness among teachers) In ILD Houtman, WB Schaufeli, and T Taris (eds), *Psychische vermoeidheid en werk* (Mental fatigue and work) 97–106 Alphen aan den Rijn, the Netherlands: Samson/NWO

Tellegen, A, Lykken, D T, Bouchard, T J, Wilcox, K J, Segal, N L, and Rich, S (1988) Personality similarity in twins reared apart and together. *Journal of Personality and Social Psychology, 54*, 1031–1039.

Thach, L and Heinselman, T (1999) Executive coaching defined. *Training and Development,* March, 35–39.

Theunissen, B, Van Vuuren, L and Visser, D (2003) Communication of job-related information and work-family conflict in dual career couples. *South African Journal of Industrial Psychology,* 29 (1), 18–25.

Thite, M (2001) Help us but help yourself: The paradox of contemporary career management. *Career Development International,* 6(6), 312–317.

Thomas, KW, and Velthouse, BA (1990) Cognitive elements of empowerment: An "interpretive" model of intrinsic task motivation. *Academy of Management Review, 15,* 666–681.

Thornburg, L (1998) Computer-assisted interviewing shortens hiring cycle. *HR Magazine,* 43, 73–79.

Tiedeman, DV and O'Hara, RP (1963) *Career Development: Choice and Adjustment.* New York: College Entrance Examination Board.

Tilgher, A (1931) *Work: What it has Meant to Men through the Ages.* London: Harrap.

Tilgher, A (1962) Work through the ages. In S Nosow and WH Form (eds) *Man, Work and Society.* New York: Basic Books.

Tom, VT (1971) The role of personality and organizational images in the recruiting process. *Organizational Behaviour and Human Performance,* 6(5), 573–592.

Topa, CG, Palaci, DF and Alonso, AE (2001) The psychological contract during organizational socialization: Application of a new measure in a longitudinal study. Paper presented at 10th European Congress on Work and Organizational Psychology, Prague.

Torf, B and Gardiner, H (1999) Theories of intellectual development. In M Anderson (ed), *The Development of Intelligence.* Hove, Suffolk: Psychology Press.

Tosi, HL, Rizzo, JR and Carrol, J (1994) *Managing Organizational Behavior.* Cambridge, Massachusetts: Blackwell.

Turban, DB, Campion, JE and Eyring, AR (1995) Factors related to job acceptance decisions of college recruits. *Journal of Vocational Behavior,* 47(2), 193–213.

Turner, N, Barling, J and Zacharatos, A (2002) Positive psychology at work. In CR Snyder and SJ Lopez (eds) *Handbook of Positive Psychology*. Oxford: Oxford University Press.

Twenge, JM (2010) A review of the empirical evidence on generational differences in work attitudes. *Journal of Business and Psychology, 25*(2), 201–220.

Tyler, K (1999) Spinning wheels. *HR Magazine, 44*(9), 34–40.

Vaida, G (2003) Managing your own success. *Sunday Times — Business Times*, 28 September, 1.

Valach, L and Young, RA (2002) Contextual action theory in career counseling: Some misunderstood issues. *Canadian Journal of Counseling, 36*(2), 97–112.

Valach, L and Young, R (2004) Some cornerstones in the development of a contextual action theory of career counseling. *International Journal for Educational and Vocational Guidance, 4*, 61–81.

Valcour, M, Bailyn, L and Quijada, MA (2007) Customized careers. In H Gunz and M Peiperl (eds), *Handbook of career studies*, 188–210. London: Sage.

Valsinger, J (2000) *Culture and Human Development: An Introduction*. London: Sage.

Van Aardt, C (1999) *The Impact of New Demographic Trends on the Labour Market*. Centre for Population Studies, University of Pretoria.

Van der Colff, JJ and Rothmann, S (in press) *Occupational stress of professional nurses in South Africa*. Manuscript submitted for publication.

Van der Colff, JJ, and Rothmann, S (2009) Occupational stress, sense of coherence, coping, burnout and work engagement of registered nurses in South Africa. *SA Journal of Industrial Psychology, 35*(1), 423–433.

Van der Heijde, CM and Van der Heijden, BIJM (2006) A competence-based and multidimensional operationalisation of employability. *Human Resource Management, 45*(3), 449–476.

Van der Sluis, LEC and Poell, RF (2002) Learning opportunities and learning behaviour: A study among MBAs in their early career stage. *Management Learning, 33*(3), 291–311.

Van Vuuren, T (1990) *Met Ontslag Bedreigd: Werknemers in Onzekerheid over hun Arbeidsplaats bij Veranderingen in de Organisatie*. Amsterdam: Uitgeverij.

Van Zyl, L, Deacon, E, and Rothmann, S (2010) Towards happiness: Work-role fit, meaningfulness and engagement of industrial/organisational psychologists in South Africa. *SA Journal of Industrial Psychology, 36*.

Viviers, AM (1999) Die persoonlikheidsoriëntasieprofiel van die salutogeniesfunksionerende mens. *Journal of Industrial Psychology, 25*(1), 27–32.

Viviers, AM and Cilliers F (1999) The relationship between salutogenesis and work orientation. *Journal of Industrial Psychology, 25*(1), 27–32.

Von Cranach, M and Valach, L (1983) The social dimension of goal-directed action. In H Tajfel (ed), *The social dimension of social psychology*, 285–299. Cambridge, England: Cambridge University Press.

Von Glinow, MA, Driver, MJ, Brousseau, KR and Prince, JB (1983) The design of a career oriented human resource system. *Academy of Management Review,* 8(1), 23–32.

Vroom, VH and Pahl, B (1971) Relationship between age and risk-taking among managers. *Journal of Applied Psychology,* 12, 399–405.

Vroom, VH (1964) *Work and Motivation.* New York: Wiley.

Wah, L (1998) The new workplace paradox. *Management Review,* 87(1), 7–14.

Walton, E (1960) What makes engineers move and remain? *Personnel Administration,* 23(3), 22–26.

Wan, HL (2007) Human capital development policies: enhancing employees' satisfaction. *Journal of European Industrial Training,* 31(4), 297–322.

Wanous, JP (1975) Tell it like it is at realistic job previews. *Personnel,* 52(4), 50–60.

Wanous, JP (1977) Organizational entry: Newcomers moving from outside to inside. *Psychological Bulletin,* 84(4), 601–619.

Wanous, JP (1989) Installing a realistic job preview: Ten tough choices. *Personnel Psychology,* 42, 117–134.

Wanous, JP (1992) *Organizational Entry: Recruitment, Selection, Orientation and Socialization of Newcomers.* Reading, MA: Addison-Wesley.

Warr, P (1983) Work, jobs and unemployment. *Bulletin of the British Psychological Society,* 36, 305–311.

Warr, PB (1987) *Work. Unemployment and Mental Health.* Oxford: Clarendon Press.

Waterman, AS (2008) Reconsidering happiness: A eudaimonst's perspective. *Journal of Positive Psychology,* 3, 234–252.

Waterman, AS, Schwartz S J, and Conti, R (2008) The implications of two conceptions of happiness (hedonic enjoyment and eudaimonia) for the understanding of intrinsic motivation. *Journal of Happiness.* 9, 41–79.

Waterman, AS, Schwartz, S J, Zambonga, B L, Ravert, R D, Williams, M K, Agocka, V B, Kim, S Y, and Donellan, M B (2010) The questionnaire of eudaimonic well-being: psychometric properties, demographic comparisons and evidence of validity. *Journal of Positive Psychology,* 5, 41–61.

Waterman, RH, Waterman, JA and Collard, BA (1994) Toward a career-resilient workforce. *Harvard Business Review,* July/August, 87–95.

Watkins, ML (1995) The meaning of working in black and white managerial samples with specific reference to sense of entitlement, *journal of Industrial Psychology,* 21(1), 1–5.

Watkins, ML and Mauer, KF (1994) The performance of white and black managers in South Africa. *South African journal of Psychology,* 24(2), 78–85.

Watson, D, Clark, LA and Tellegen, A (1998) Development and validation of brief measures of positive and negative affect: The PANAS scale. *Journal of Personality and Social Psychology,* 54, 1063–1070.

Watson, MB, Foxcroft, CD and Eaton, MC (2001) *The Career Decision-Making Self-Efficacy of South African High School Students: Implications for Career Education.* Port Elizabeth: Education Association of South Africa.

Watts, AG and Kidd, JM (2000) Guidance in the United Kingdom: past, present and future. *British Journal of Guidance and Counseling, 28,* 485–502.

Webber, RA (1976) Career problems of young managers. *California Management Review,* 18, 11–33.

Weick, KE and Berlinger, LR (1989) Career improvisation in self-designing organizations. In MB Arthur, DT Hall and BS Lawrence (eds) *Handbook of Career Theory.* Cambridge: Cambridge University Press.

Weiss, JW (2001) *Organizational Behavior and Change: Managing Diversity, Cross-Cultural Dynamics and Ethics.* London: Thomson Learning.

Whiston, SC, Brecheisen, BK and Stephens, J (2003) Does treatment modality affect career counseling effectiveness? *Journal of Vocational Behaviour,* 62, 370–410.

White, B, Cox, C and Cooper, C (1992) *Women's Career Development: A Study of High Flyers.* Cambridge: Blackwell.

White, RW (1959) Motivation reconsidered: The concept of competence. *Psychological Review,* 66, 297–323.

Whiteley, WT and Coetsier, P (1993) The relationship of career mentoring to early career outcomes. *Organization Studies.* 14(3), 419–441.

Wiersma, UJ (1994) A taxonomy of behavioural strategies for coping with work-home role conflict. *Human Relations,* 47(2), 211–221.

Wilkinson, A Bacon, N, Redman, T and Snell S (2010) *The sage handbook of human resource management.* London: Sage Publicatiions

Wilpert, B (1993) *Vergeht den Deutschen die Arbeid-lust?* Contribution to the Römerberg Gesprachens, Frankfurt/Main.

Wilpert, B (1995) The two-pronged challenge to psychology in the 21 st century. Contribution to the symposium. Goals, Challenges and Trends of Scientific and Professional Psychology in the 21st Century, IV European Congress of Psychology, Athens.

Wilpert, P and Maimer, H (1993) Culture or society? A research report on work-related values in the two Germanies. *Social Science Information,* 32(2), 259–278.

Woehr, DJ (2006) Career centres. In JH Greenhaus and GA Callanan (eds) *Encyclopeadia of career development,* 27–31. New Dehli: Sage Publications.

Woodd, M (2000) The move towards a different career pattern: Are women better prepared than men for a modern career? *Career Development International,* 5(2), 99–105.

Wood, RE, and Bandura, A (1989) Impact of conceptions of ability on self-regulatory mechanisms and complex decision-making. *Journal of Personality and Social Psychology,* 56, 407–415.

Wood, RE, Bandura, A and Bailey, T (1990) Mechanisms governing organizational performances in complex decision making environments. *Organizational Behavior and Human Decision Processes, 46,* 181–201.

Woollacott, J (1976) Deviant and dirty work. In B Karsara and J Korer (eds) *Occupational Categories and Culture.* Milton Keynes: The Open University.

Wright, TA (2003) Positive organizational behavior: An idea whose time has truly come. *Journal of Organizational Behavior, 24,* 437–442.

Wright, TA and Cropanzano, R (2000) The role of organizational behaviour in occupational health psychology: A view as we approach the millennium. *Journal of Occupational Health Psychology, 5,* 5–10.

Wrobel, K (2003) *Career stages.* Available at: http://wfnetwork.bc.edu/encyclopedia_entry.php?id=222 [Accessed on 28 May 2010]

Wrosch, C, and Scheier, M F (2003) Personality and quality of life: The importance of optimism and goal adjustment. *Quality of Life Research, 12,* 59–72.

Wrzesniewski, A, Dutton, JE and Debebe, G (2003) Interpersonal sensemaking and the meaning of work. *Research in Organizational Behavior, 25,* 93–135.

Wrzesniewski, A, McCauley, C, Rozin, P, and Schwartz, B (1997) Jobs, careers and callings: People's relations to their work. *Journal of Research in Personality, 31,* 21–33.

Wrzesniewski, A, and Tosti, J (2005) Career as a calling. In J H Greenhaus and G A Callanan (eds), *Encyclopaedia of career development.* Thousand Oaks, CA: Sage Publications.

Xanthopoulou, D, Bakker, AB, Demerouti, E, and Schaufeli, W B (2009) Reciprocal relationships between job resources, personal resources and work engagement. *Journal of Vocational Behavior, 74,* 235–244.

Young, RA and Valach, L (2004) The construction of career through goal-directed action. *Journal of Vocational Behavior, 64,* 499–514.

Young, RA, Valach, L and Domene, JF (2005) The action-project method in counseling psychology. *Journal of Counseling Psychology, 52*(2), 215–223.

Zellars, KL, Perrewe, PL and Hochwarter, WA (2000) Burnout in health care: The role of the five factors of personality. *Journal of Applied Social Psychology, 30,* 1570–1598.

Zheng, Y and Kleiner, BH (2001) Developments concerning career development and transition. *Management Research News, 24*(3/4), 33–39.

Zietsmann, G (1996) The validation of the MBTI on a South African sample: A summary of the results. Paper presented at International Type Users Conference, South Africa.

Zunker, VG (1981) *Career Counselling: Applied Concepts of Life Planning.* San Francisco: Brooks/Cole.

Zunker, VG (2006) *Career counseling: a holistic approach* 7ed. Belmont, CA: Thomson Higher Education.

Glossary of terms

A

Affirmative action: Action intended to overcome the effects of past or present discriminatory policies or practices or other barriers to employment equity. Focuses on achieving equality of opportunity in an organisation.

Afrocentric career success: Psychological feelings of career success that are based on a preference for quality of life. Often related to the values of a 'feminine' culture that emphasises nurturance, a concern for relationships and a concern for the living environment.

Anticipatory socialisation: The process of processing information gained from prospective employers and making decisions about employment before joining an organisation, followed by a period of accommodation, active participation and role management once the organisation has been entered.

Assessment and development centre: Formal method aimed at (1) evaluating an individual's potential as a manager by exposing individuals to simulated problems that would be faced in real-life managerial situations and (2) developing and preparing managers for future roles.

Attitudes: Internal states that focus on particular aspects of or objects in, the environment.

Awareness: A relatively complete and accurate perception of one's own qualities and the characteristics of one's relevant environment.

B

Boundaryless career: Career characterised by flexibility, mobility and movement between different global organisational contexts.

C

Career: Significant learnings and experiences that identify an individual's professional life, direction, competencies and accomplishments through positions, jobs, roles and assignments.

Career achievement: The period during which individuals display a desire for promotion and advancement within the organisation.

Career adaptability: Individuals' *readiness* to cope with changing work and working conditions. Adaptive individuals are those who become *concerned* about their future as a worker and then take *action* to increase their *personal control* over their vocational future. Adaptive individuals are *proactive* by displaying *curiosity* and exploring possible selves and future scenarios. They also seek to strengthen their *confidence* (or self-efficacy) to pursue their aspirations.

Career age: Individuals' repertoire of professional work challenges, experiences and relationships across the life-span.

Career anchors: Individuals' (1) self-perceived talents and abilities which originate from actual successes in a variety of work settings, (2) self-perceived motives and needs which originate from opportunities for self-testing and self-diagnoses of their strengths and feedback from others and (3) self-perceived attitudes and values which originate from actual encounters between self and the norms and values of the organisation.

Career appraisal: The process by which people acquire and use career-related feedback.

Career choice: Subjective decisions based on one's preferences, aspirations orientations, images, intentions and objective information regarding economic conditions, employment opportunities and sociological factors such as family and education.

Career coaching: A career service focused on assisting individuals who encounter problems in adjusting to occupational positions to learn better adaptive skills and to become more career resilient.

Career commitment: The passion individuals have for their chosen work roles or personal career goals, including the strength of their motivation to work in a chosen career role.

Career competency: The competencies and qualities which enable individuals to pursue meaningful careers. These consist of individuals' 'know-why' (values, attitudes, internal needs, identity and lifestyle), 'know-how' (expertise, capabilities; tacit and explicit knowledge), 'know-whom' (networking relationships; how to find the right people), 'know-what' (opportunities, threats and job requirements), 'know-where' (entering a workplace, training and advancing) and 'know-when' (timing of choices and activities).

Career counselling: A career service focused on facilitating self-reflection and cognitive restructuring in clients who need to develop career competency, career maturity and career self-efficacy.

Career development: The ongoing process by which individuals progress through a series of stages, each of which is characterised by a fresh set of issues, themes or tasks.

Career discussion: A planned discussion between a manager and an employee who are attempting jointly to clarify developmental options in the employee's current job, to examine career issues in the light of current job performance and goals of the organisation and/or to clarify career options for that employee.

Career education: A career service focused on assisting individuals who encounter difficulties in enacting their subjective career intentions and goals through their objective vocational behaviour.

Career empowerment: Organisational strategy that gives workers more responsibility for owning and managing their careers by providing relevant supportive human resource practices.

Career establishment: The process of assisting new employees in fitting into their jobs.

Career exploration: The collection and analysis of information regarding career-related issues, including self-exploration and environmental exploration.

Career goal: A desired career-related outcome that a person intends to attain by setting specific goals.

Career guidance: A career service focused on helping individuals who are undecided to articulate their behavioural repertoire and then translate it into vocational choices.

Career identity: The way that individuals consciously link their own motivation, values, drives, interests and competencies with acceptable career roles.

Career insight: The extent to which a person has realistic perceptions of himself or herself, the organisation or workplace environment and the way in which he or she relates these perceptions to personal career goals.

Career invention: The process of deep self-reflection, clarification of possible work roles, career goals and intentions, life purpose and experimentation with new career possibilities through realistic career planning.

Career management: The ongoing process whereby the employee obtains (1) self-knowledge and (2) knowledge of employment opportunities, (3) develops career goals, (4) develops a strategy, (5) implements and experiments and (6) obtains feedback on the effectiveness of the strategy and the relevance of the goals.

Career management system: The set of activities and practices designed by the organisation to promote employee career ownership and insight, career goal and strategy development and/or appropriate feedback on career progress.

Career maturity: The ability to make career decisions that reflect decisiveness, self-reliance, independence and a willingness to compromise between one's personal needs and the requirements of one's career situation.

Career model: A picture or representation of the way in which individuals plan and manage their careers.

Career motivation: The persistence and enthusiasm with which individuals pursue their careers, even in the face of adversity, based on their career identity, career insight and career resilience.

Career pathing: Sequence of developmental activities involving informal and formal education, training and job experiences that help make an individual capable of holding a more advanced job in the future.

Career paths: Objective descriptions of sequential work experiences, as opposed to subjective, personal feelings about career progress, personal development or satisfaction.

Career patterns: The personal views individuals have about the paths their careers should follow.

Career placement: A career service focused on assisting individuals who have chosen an occupational field to secure a position in that occupation.

Career planning: An initiative where an individual exerts personal control and agency (initiative) over their career and engage in informed choices as to his or her occupation, organisation, job assignment and self-development by conducting self-assessment, formulating goals and developing plans for reaching those goals.

Career planning workshop: A general career development programme offered by the organisation, aimed at assisting individuals in career planning.

Career plateauing: The point in a person's career at which there is no longer any opportunity to progress in the organisational hierarchy.

Career progress: Individuals' experiences of career growth, which may include moving upward, increasing competence and expertise and gaining broader experience across multi-directional career movements.

Career resilience: The ability to adapt to changing circumstances by welcoming job and organisational changes, looking forward to working with new and different people, having self-confidence and being willing to take risks.

Career self: Individuals' subjective or psychological sense of their careers, including their vocational identity and self-concept.

Career self-efficacy: The degree of difficulty of career tasks, which individuals believe they are to attempt and how well they believe they can execute the courses of actions required to deal with those tasks and the degree to which their beliefs will persist, despite obstacles.

Career self-management: The ability to keep pace with the speed at which change occurs within the organisation and the industry and the ability to sustain one's employability through continuous learning and career planning and management efforts.

Career stage: The typical psychological needs, life tasks and challenges influenced by social factors that are related to a particular life stage and that are significant in the work life of an individual. (See also **Life stage**.)

Career strategy: A sequence of activities designed to help an individual attain a career goal.

Career success: The objective and subjective (psychological) sense of achievement individuals' experience regarding their careers. The real or perceived achievements individuals have accumulated as a result of their work experiences. (See also **Eurocentric career success** and **Afrocentric career success**.)

Career therapy: A career service focused on assisting individuals who have trouble developing a clear and stable vocational identity. The therapy helps them examine what they need to feel secure with in themselves.

Career transition: Moving from one form of employment to another, which may include periods of unemployment or 'being-between-jobs'.

Career-enhancing strategies: Career management interventions that help bring about career success.

Career well-being: People's positive and negative feelings about their careers.

Careerist: Someone to whom making a career within a certain industry takes precedence over a career within a certain company.

Central life interest: The degree of importance that working has in the life of an individual at any given point in time.

Competencies: Sets of behaviours that are instrumental in the delivery of desired organisational results or outcomes.

Competency: Individuals' skills, knowledge and attitudinal values, which enhance their employability and ability to adapt to change and which contribute to satisfying job and organisational requirements.

Composite career: Having more than one working role or holding more than one form of employment.

Contemporary workplace: The 21st century globalised multi-cultural world of work, characterised by turbulence, uncertainty, rapid technological change, competitiveness, knowledge and information technology, driven learning and boundaryless organisations, small components of core employees and multi-directional career movements.

Content theories: Career theories that explain or predict career choice in terms of specific psychological phenomena or individual characteristics by emphasising a structural approach toward matching individual traits with job requirements.

Contingent work: A situation in which workers do not have explicit or implicit contracts for long-term employment and in which the minimum hours can vary in a non-systematic manner.

Continuous change: Ongoing, evolving and cumulative organisational change characterised by small continuous adjustments, created simultaneously across units, that add up to substantial change.

Continuous learning: Process by which individuals acquire knowledge, skills and abilities throughout their careers in reaction to and in anticipation of, changing performance criteria.

Coping: The efforts individuals make to manage situations they have appraised as potentially harmful or stressful. Coping also refers to perceptual, cognitive or behavioural responses that are used to manage, avoid or control situations that could be regarded as difficult. (See also **Problem-focused coping** and **Emotion-focused coping**.)

Core employees: Group of employees permanently employed by the organisation whose critical skills and expertise help to focus the activities of the organisation and give it a competitive advantage.

Critical contact theory: A theory of organisational choice, based on the experience gained during individuals' contact with the various organisations.

Culture: A system in which individuals share meanings and common ways of viewing events and objects. In organisations, it refers to the shared beliefs and values among employees that are created and communicated by the managers and leaders of the organisation.

D

Dispositional optimism: A global expectation that good things will be plentiful in the future and that bad things will be scarce.

Distress: Type of stress resulting from chronically demanding situations that produce negative health outcomes.

Diverse needs: The different meanings that individuals attach to career success.

Diversity: Traditionally, this refers to differences in demographic characteristics, but it also includes differences in values, abilities, interests and experiences.

Dual ladder: A parallel hierarchy for professional or technical staff, which allows them upward mobility and recognition without occupying a managerial role.

Dual-career couple: Any two people in an ongoing, committed relationship, where both partners are career-oriented and committed to a career, while at the same time maintaining a family life together.

Dual-earner couple: Any two people in an ongoing, committed relationship, where both spouses are involved in the paid labour force and where one may be pursuing a career while the other views his or her occupational involvement as a job or where both spouses consider themselves to be holding jobs.

E

Early-life/early-career stage: The typical physical, cognitive, psychosocial development and psychological needs, life tasks and challenges particular to an individual in the 25–45 age group.

Emotion-focused coping: Coping strategy directed at reducing the effects of stressful feelings caused by an unpleasant experience through relaxation, the use of alcohol and drugs, social activities and/or defence mechanisms.

Employability: A person's value in terms of future employment opportunities, which is determined by the accumulation of knowledge, skills, experience and reputation, which can be invested in new employment opportunities as they arise. Also, individual's capacity and willingness to become and remain attractive in the labour market (ie, firm internal and firm external employability). Individual's capability to be successful in a wide range of jobs (job match employability).

Employability security: Psychological feeling of safety, based on a sense of self-efficacy acquired by the accumulation of knowledge, skills, experience and reputation. Also, a sense of inner knowing and belief that one's knowledge, skills, experience and reputation can be invested in new employment opportunities as they arise. (See also **Employability**.)

Emotional intelligence: A kind of intelligence that is focused on our awareness of our own and others' emotions. Also, the ability to manage oneself and interact with others in mature and constructive ways.

Empowerment: An organisational strategy that gives workers more responsibility for decision-making and more involvement in controlling work processes.

Entitlement: Beliefs about the rights of working, for example, that a job should be provided to every individual who wishes to work.

Entrepreneurial career: Choosing self-employment as a career option. Establishing and managing one's own business.

Ethical dilemma: A difficult decision in which any choice is morally problematic. An ethical dilemma has the potential to result in a breach of acceptable behaviour.

Ethics: The study of moral issues and choices.

Eurocentric career success: Psychological feelings of career success that are based on a striving for material success. Often related to the values of a 'masculine' culture that is characterised by assertiveness, being ambitious and being competitive.

Eustress: Type of stress that provides challenges that motivate individuals to work hard and meet their goals.

Executive coaching: Formal help provided by professional mentors or coaches to top executives aimed at building a particular skill set.

Executive mentoring: Formal help provided by professional mentors to top executives aimed at building personal insights and self-awareness.

Exhaustion: A stage of the **General Adaptation Syndrome** in which overall resistance drops and in which adverse consequences (eg, burnout, severe illness and even death) can result unless stress is reduced.

Existential career counselling: A post-modern approach that includes existential guidance (based on the principles of Frankls' Logotherapy) to help individuals recognise the role of the human spirit in finding meaning in life.

Expectancy theory: The selection of an organisation based on its motivational force, which is the result of the extent to which individuals expect a job offer from the organisation, their perception that the organisation will provide certain outcomes and the extent to which each of these outcomes attracts individuals.

Experience: Direct participation in or observation of, events and activities that serves as a basis for knowledge.

Expert career pattern: Remaining in a chosen career field for the duration of one's career.

F

Family-friendly organisations: Organisations with policies such as on-site child care and flexible work schedules, that take into account the families of employees.

Feedback: Evaluative or corrective information transmitted to employees about their attempts to improve their job performance or career progress.

Formal education: The long-term investment in individuals aimed at increasing their formal qualification levels.

G

General Adaptation Syndrome (GAS): A nearly identical response sequence to almost any disease or trauma (eg, poisoning, injury, psychological stress), identified by Hans Selye.

Goal-setting: Motivational approach in which specific goals direct attention and improve performance in training and on the job. (See also **Career goals**.)

I

Independent contractor: A self-employed individual who has been contracted for a specific project for a period of time specified by the business.

Individual differences: The dissimilarities between or among two people.

Individualism: The loyalty individuals have to their profession, their own abilities and reputation.

Industrial and Organisational Psychology: The application of psychological principles, theory and research to the work setting.

J

Job and career embeddedness: The collection of forces that keep people in their current employment situations (eg, the links within the organisation, fit with the job, occupation or career and the perceived sacrifices associated with leaving the job, occupation or career).

Job burnout: Extreme state of psychological strain resulting from a prolonged response to chronic job stressors that exceed an individual's resources to cope with them.

Job loss: Involuntary withdrawal from the workforce.

Juggler: Someone to whom a career is not the most important part of his or her life.

K

Knowledge economy: production and services based on knowledge-intensive activities that contribute to an accelerated pace of technological and scientific advance as well as rapid obsolescence.

Knowledge workers: Highly skilled and talented workers.

L

Late-life/late-career stage: The typical physical, cognitive, psychosocial development and psychological needs, life tasks and challenges particular to an individual of 65 years or older.

Lateral movements: Cross-functional career movements such as job rotations, role changes and secondments.

Learned optimism: An optimistic explanatory style of an individual.

Learnerships: Structured learning programmes that combine learning at a training institution with practical, work-based learning.

Leisure: Activities that fall outside the context of work and which are not necessarily instrumental in sustaining income, but can constitute ways in which work is connected to non-work.

Locus of control: Perception by the individual of his or her ability to exercise control over the environment. Those characterised by an internal locus of control believe they have control over their environment and their personal successes, whereas those with an external locus of control view their lives as controlled by external factors such as chance or powerful others.

Life stage: The typical physical, cognitive and psychosocial chronological development of an individual that is characteristic of a particular age. (See also **Career stage**.)

Linear career pattern: A preference to move up quickly in the hierarchy of the organisation.

M

Meaning of work: The significance that work or working has in people's lives.

Mentoring: Offline help by one person to another in making significant transitions in knowledge, work or thinking.

Mid-life crisis: A period between the ages of 45 and 65 of intense and deep self-reflection involving the integration of psychological polarities such as young/old, destination/creation, masculine/feminine and attachment/separateness. This should enable the person to attain greater individuation, self-confidence and independence in modifying the structure of his or her life.

Mid-life/mid-career stage: The typical physical, cognitive, psychosocial development and psychological needs, life tasks and challenges particular to an individual in the 45–65 age group.

O

Objective career success: Individuals' sense of achievement regarding measures such as pay, personal reputation or position in the organisation.

Objective factor theory: The ranking and evaluation of a limited number of clearly measurable features of each job offer.

Obligation: Beliefs about the duties of work, for example, that workers should be expected to value their jobs and think of better ways of doing their jobs.

Obsolescence: The degree to which an organisation's professionals lack the up-to-date knowledge or skills necessary to maintain effective performance in either their current or future work roles.

Occupational health and well-being: The actual physical health of workers, as defined by physical symptomatology and epidemiological rates of physical illnesses and diseases, as well as the mental, psychological or emotional health of workers as indicated by emotional states and epidemiological rates of mental illnesses and diseases. Occupational health and well-being also includes societal aspects such as alcoholism and drug abuse rates and their consequences. The term health, when applied to organisational settings, is used when specific physiological or psychological aspects are of concern. On the other hand, the term well-being refers to individuals' life experiences such as life satisfaction and happiness and job-related experiences such as job satisfaction, job attachment and satisfaction with pay or with co-workers.

Occupational stress: Non-specific responses of the human body to any demand made on it. Stress is typically the result of an imbalance between environmental demands and individual capabilities.

Optimism: A good mood, also associated with perseverance and health. (See also **Learned optimism** and **Dispositional optimism**.)

Organisational choice: Individuals' choice of a specific organisation for which to work.

Organisational entry: The process whereby individuals move from outside to inside organisations.

Organisational loyalty: The expressed loyalty and commitment by individuals to give priority to the organisation's goals and objectives in their life orientation.

Organisational support: The career management activities and practices provided by the organisation aimed at helping individuals to improve their personal career management, development and advancement throughout the various stages of the work life.

Organisational transitions: Organisational structural changes due to mergers and acquisitions, restructuring and downsizing and privatisation.

Orientation: The process whereby newcomers are introduced to the organisation, the job itself, their workplace and the policies and procedures of the organisation.

Outplacement programmes: Programmes arranged by an organisation to help an employee leave the organisation and get a job somewhere else.

P

Personality: An individual's behavioural and emotional characteristics, generally found to be stable over time and in a variety of circumstances; the individual's habitual way of responding.

Plan-and-implement career model: Views career management as a linear process in which dissatisfaction with the status quo leads to setting a goal, from which flows an implementation plan.

Pooled worker: Someone who prefers to work shorter hours because of personal commitments.

Post-modern approach: A career-choice approach that focuses on individuals' subjective experience of their career development and that views individuals as the agents who construe their careers.

Power structure: Dominant groups in society and organisations that transmit values and goals to the workplace by virtue of their positions of power and control over economic activity.

Problem-focused coping: Coping strategy directed at managing and improving an unpleasant experience or reducing its effects.

Process theories: Career theories that emphasise career choice as a dynamic process that evolves over stages of development.

Protean career: A career shaped and managed by the individual. It consists of all the person's varied experiences in education, training, work in several organisations and changes in occupational field and is characterised by a high degree of mobility, self-reliance and internal career thinking.

Psychological career resources: Refers to skills such as career planning and management skills and self-management and interpersonal skills. Includes also inner-value capital attributes such as behavioural adaptability, self-esteem, sense of purpose, emotional and social literacy. People's psychological career resources enable them to be self-directed learners and proactive agents in the management of their careers.

Psychological career success: Individuals' feelings of pride, happiness, inner peace, self-regard, self-worth and sense of achievement regarding the achievement of their personal career goals. (See also **Subjective career success**.)

Psychological contract: An employee's beliefs and attitudes about the mutual obligations between the employee and the organisation. The unwritten agreement between an employee and the organisation that holds the organisation together and binds the individual to the organisation.

Q

Quarter-life quandary: The career transition crisis experienced by young adults between the ages of 20 and 35 due to the dynamic nature of the contemporary career.

R

Realistic recruitment: The objective presentation of information about the organisation in the recruitment process.

Recruitment: The process of seeking and attracting a pool of people from which qualified candidates for job vacancies can be chosen.

Resilience: A pattern of psychological activity which consists of a motive to be strong in the face of inordinate demands; the goal-directed behaviour of coping and rebounding and of the accompanying emotions and cognitions.

Retirement-preparation programme: An organisational career management practice directed at preparing individuals who are approaching retirement and are about to leave the organisation.

S

Secondment: A temporary assignment to another area within the organisation.

Selection: Process of choosing, from those available, the individuals who are most likely to perform successfully in a job.

Self-actualisation: A process of inner-directedness through which the individual gives expression to his or her intrinsic nature. It involves the tendency to enrich oneself by psychological growth and by seeing meaning in being.

Self-efficacy: Beliefs of individuals in their capabilities to mobilise the motivation, cognitive resources and courses of action needed to meet given organisational demands. Also, beliefs of individuals in their capabilities to affect the environment and the way in which they control their actions to produce the desired outcomes. Self-efficacy is a belief in the probability that one can successfully execute some future action or task to achieve some result.

Self-concept: Individuals' own views of their personal characteristics and abilities which change over time with changes in social, economic and cultural factors, occupations and technology.

Self-employment: Establishing and managing one's own business. Also referred to as the entrepreneurial career.

Sense of belonging in society: The feeling of being useful in society through one's work by supplying ideas, services or products that are useful to society.

Sense of coherence: A global orientation that expresses the extent to which the individual has a pervasive, enduring and dynamic feeling of confidence that (1) the stimuli deriving from his or her internal and external environments in the course of living are structured, predictable and explicable, (2) the resources are available to meet the demands posed by these stimuli and (3) these demands are challenges, worthy of investment and engagement.

Skills inventory: Consolidated list of biographical and other information on all employees in the organisation.

Social comparison theory: Individuals tend to compare themselves to people similar to themselves with regard to sex, age, culture, education and status.

Socialisation: The process by which individuals are transformed from total outsiders of companies to participating and effective members of them.

Spiral career pattern: The tendency to change career fields periodically.

Spirituality at work: The search for spiritual wholeness within the context of the workplace. It involves seeking to discover one's true self, higher life purpose and meaning through one's work activities and roles.

Status: Social and material achievement that determines an individual's place in the status hierarchy of the community.

Strains: Reaction or response to stressors.

Stressors: Physical or psychological demands to which an individual responds.

Subjective career success: Individuals' inner experiences of career satisfaction and achievement. (See also **Psychological career success**.)

Subjective factor theory: The selection of a position on the basis of what individuals perceive their personal and emotional needs to be and the extent to which the image of the organisation meets these perceived needs.

Succession planning: Technique that identifies specific people to fill future openings in key positions throughout the organisation.

Super's theory of organisational choice: The choice of an organisation is a means of implementing an individual's self-concept.

T

Talent: Those individuals who can make a difference to organisational performance, either through their immediate contribution or in the longer term by demonstrating the highest level of potential.

Talent management: The *sourcing* (finding talent), *screening* (sorting qualified and unqualified applicants), *selection* (assessment/testing, interviewing, reference/background checking of applicants), *onboarding* (offer generation/acceptance), *retention* (measures to keep the talent that contributes to the success of the organisation), *development* (training, growth, assignments), *deployment* (optimal assignment of staff to projects, lateral opportunities, promotions) and *renewal* of the workforce through continuous strategic analyses and planning activities.

Temporary workers: People working for employment agencies who are subcontracted out to businesses at an hourly rate for a period of time specified by the business.

Test-and-learn career model: Views career planning and management as a developmental process in which iterative rounds of action and reflection lead to updating personal career goals and possibilities.

Traditional workplace: Workplace characterised by stable environment and protected markets, production-driven services and products, hierarchical multiple management levels, uni-dimensional career movements and high level of job security.

Transitory career pattern: The tendency to make frequent and many career changes.

U

Unemployment: Being out of work and having the desire to work and to take up employment.

Unprogrammed decision-making: A two-phased process in choosing an organisation which involves (1) the evaluation of various choices according to a few important factors and (2) the elimination of those organisations that do not meet the minimum criteria on these factors.

V

Values: Beliefs that represent broad motivational goals or desirable end states of behaviours that apply across context and time. Values guide the selection or evaluation of behaviours and events, remain stable over time and are generally ordered in terms of relative importance by different people.

Vocational self: Individuals' attitudes and behavioural responses related to their vocational tasks and situations.

W

Work: Means of making a living, being occupied, fulfilling a vocation, developing and utilising skills, fulfilling needs, contributing to an all-embracing lifestyle or fulfilling a life purpose.

Work engagement: A positive, fulfilling, work-related state of mind that is characterised by vigour, dedication and absorption. Rather than a momentary and specific state, engagement refers to a more persistent and pervasive affective-cognitive state that is not focused on any particular object, event, individual or behaviour.

Work-family balance: Area of research that investigates whether the satisfaction that one experiences at work is in part affected by the satisfaction that one experiences in non-work and vice versa.

Work-family conflict: A form of inter-role conflict in which the role pressures from the work and family domains are mutually incompatible in some respect.

Work-family enrichment: The extent to which experiences in one role improve the quality of life in the other role, where quality of life includes high performance and positive affect.

Work-home interface: An interactive process in which a worker's functioning in one domain (eg, home) is influenced by (negative or positive) load reactions that have built up in the other domain (eg, work).

Working couples: Any two people in an ongoing, committed relationship where both partners work, where there may or may not be children and where decisions (about family and work) are influenced by the working situation of each partner.

Work-life balance: Area of research that investigates whether the satisfaction that the individual experiences at work is in part affected by the satisfaction that he or she experiences in non-work and vice versa, particularly to the extent that one environment has demands that conflict with the other.

Index